THE CASE-ST
IN PSYCHO
RELATED L

THE CASE-STUDY METHOD IN PSYCHOLOGY AND RELATED DISCIPLINES

D. B. Bromley

Department of Psychology
The University of Liverpool

JOHN WILEY & SONS

Chichester · New York · Brisbane · Toronto · Singapore

Library of Congress Cataloging-in-Publication Data:

Bromley, D. B. (Dennis Basil), 1924–
   The case-study method in psychology and related disciplines.

   Bibliography: p.
   Includes indexes.
   1. Single subject research.   2. Psychology—Research. I. Title.
BF76.6.S56B76   1986   150'.722   85-12335

ISBN 0 471 90853 3 (U.S.)

British Library Cataloguing in Publication Data:

Bromley, D. B.
   The case-study method in psychology and related disciplines.
   1. Psychology—Case studies
   I. Title
   150'.722   BF121

ISBN 0 471 90853 3

Printed and Bound in Great Britain

Contents

Preface

The individual case-study or situation-analysis is the bedrock of scientific investigation. This may sound like an extravagant claim. I hope to justify it by reference to the pervasiveness of the case-study method in scientific and professional work in many different areas including the natural sciences. Case-studies can be found in areas as disparate as: administration, anatomy, anthropology, artificial intelligence, biochemistry, business studies, clinical medicine, counselling, criminology, education, gerontology, history, industrial relations, jurisprudence, management, military studies, personality, politics, psychiatry, social work, and sociology. A basic logic or methodology underlies case-studies in these diverse areas. A particular set of events and relationships is identified. This 'case' is then described, analysed, interpreted, and evaluated within a framework of ideas and procedures appropriate to cases of that sort. Our main concern is with the framework of ideas and procedures appropriate to case-studies in psychology, but reference to the use of case-method in related disciplines is helpful in elucidating its scientific character and its role in professional work.

The term 'case-study' means different things to different people. To the psychologist it means the study of an individual person, usually in a problematic situation, over a relatively short period of time. A psychological case-study is a segment of a life-history. To the social worker it means the study of a unique social situation involving one or more people—a delinquent boy, a family in distress, a marital breakdown. To the anthropologist it can mean the study of an individual person or the study of a group of people or the analysis of a social situation or process. To the psychiatrist it usually means the clinical study of a person with a mental illness. In business and industrial studies it can mean the investigation of a particular firm, an industrial dispute, a major accident. In these and other areas generally— politics, military science, espionage, criminal investigation—it means the study of a major incident or event which is interesting in its own right. The event may be interesting because examination reveals useful information or because it can be used as a 'model' example for teaching or research purposes. Model cases are prototypical instances of the class of phenomena— elections, battles, propaganda, crimes, accidents, strikes, or whatever—to which they belong.

It is obvious, therefore, that the term 'case-study' refers to a class of investigations far wider than the *psychological* study of individual cases. In certain areas—business studies for example—there are fairly well-worked-out procedures for carrying out case-studies and making decisions. In other areas, for example clinical medicine, there are standard procedures for diagnosis and treatment. In other areas, however, such as psychology, social work, sociology, and anthropology, there is considerable variation in purpose and procedure.

Across all the areas mentioned it is possible to discern a common logic—the logic of scientific method. It is the purpose of this book to demonstrate the logic of the individual case-study with special reference to the psychological study of individual persons. The book is amply illustrated with case-materials. These have been selected not because they represent rare or particularly interesting cases but because they can be understood without formal training in the special concepts, methods, and procedures of the human sciences—psychology, psychiatry, sociology, and so on.

One aim of the book is to ease the transition from lay to professional levels of competence in understanding and dealing with people who need help. A related aim is to improve the reader's ability to understand and deal with people in daily life, even if that means, as it sometimes does, recognizing that one's understanding of, and capacity to influence, a particular person is sometimes embarrassingly poor.

I hope that people in business and industrial studies will recognize how the concepts and methods that they are familiar with have been applied to the psychological study of individual persons. At the same time, I hope they will appreciate the relevance to business and industrial studies of other concepts and methods with which they may be much less familiar. There is, of course, a *direct* relationship between the psychological study of individual persons and the wide spectrum of case-studies referred to above. This relationship arises from the fact that in most of these 'extended case-studies' or 'situation analyses' it is essential to understand the behaviour of the persons involved in the case. The psychological study of individual cases is the study of persons in situations.

The preoccupation of academic psychologists with experimental and psychometric approaches to the study of personality and adjustment has meant that the case-study approach has been seriously neglected. The neglect has been aggravated by the identification of the case-method with psychodynamic psychology and with social work, where there appears to have been no success in developing a *scientifically* acceptable framework for understanding and dealing with individual cases. In many areas of sociology, too, the case-method has been virtually abandoned in favour of quantitative survey methods.

There are two further reasons why case-methods are not prominent in scientific work. One is that they deal with private matters and can usually be reported only with the permission of the person(s) concerned or if suitably modified to avoid identification. The other is that there is no general agreement on the content or organization of a case-study or on the procedure to be employed in carrying it out. I shall describe a general-purpose procedure for studying 'persons in situations'. It has all the essential features of a *scientific* procedure. It provides a descriptive account of the relevant facts; it provides a way of organizing this information in a meaningful way; it shows how a particular case-study investigation can be pursued constructively and creatively; it also shows how a case-study can be evaluated critically and in detail. The proposed general-purpose procedure explores possibilities for predicting outcomes, and for forecasting the behaviour of individuals for the purposes of intervention and evaluation. The aim of the book, therefore, is to provide professional workers and intelligent lay people with scientific concepts and methods that will help them to understand individuals who need their advice and help.

Teachers in the social and behavioural sciences, and in professional areas such as management, health, education, and welfare, should find the book useful in relation to case-studies in their particular areas of interest. Classroom case-studies and real-life case-studies can be used in professional training and in academic education. They can become the focus for reports, discussions, simulations, films, and other sorts of presentation.

Case-material has too often been used simply to illustrate or to add 'human interest' to an otherwise rather dry account of a social policy, housing problem, psychological treatment, or medical condition. It is my belief, however, that the study of individual cases and situations poses a methodological problem of special, maybe even basic, importance in the social and behavioural sciences. It has been said, with regard to the natural sciences, that 'Science is not concerned with the individual case'. This is because the natural sciences deal with phenomena which are susceptible to close control and quantitative analysis, and can be conceptualized by means of highly abstract and general laws. Under these laws, individual instances occur in regular predictable ways. The social and behavioural sciences, on the other hand, deal with phenomena of more complex sorts, much less susceptible to control, quantification, and formal logical analysis. The applied sciences—engineering, agriculture, and so on—work within an abstract, general framework of natural science and mathematics but must be concerned with individual projects—particular bridges, aeroplanes, crops, and pesticides. Similarly, the social and behavioural sciences, as yet lacking satisfactory large-scale abstract and general concepts, must be concerned with the individual human beings and social organizations that constitute their ultimate subject-matter.

Where human nature is concerned, the separation of basic and applied science may be self-defeating in the sense that the most important and interesting aspects of human nature are so context-dependent that abstraction and generalization are severely limited. The value of the case-study approach is that it deals directly with the individual case in its actual context. At the same time, it carries implications about the extent to which the resulting analysis is applicable to other similar cases. Thus, rather than working from the top down, as it were, from abstract theory to individual instance or particular rule, the case-method in psychology works from the bottom up, from the analysis of particular cases—persons in situations—to 'types' of case (cases of greater generality) through the development of 'case-law'. Developing case-law can be every bit as demanding and as rigorous as developing scientific law, even if it is not quantitative or experimental. This important philosophical issue is dealt with in more detail in Chapter 11. It is raised here briefly so that readers may be aware that case-studies and situation-analyses are fundamental to scientific progress. Learning how to carry out and how to evaluate case-studies should help to develop a student's appreciation of scientific method. Studying cases and analysing situations gives practice in solving problems and making decisions or recommendations.

In psychology, the term methodology generally refers to experimental design and statistical analysis. In sociology it refers to survey technique, participant observation, archival analysis, and so on. It seems to me that the quasi-judicial case-study constitutes a crucial but seriously neglected method of inquiry in the social sciences. This book is an attempt to demonstrate its fundamental importance in philosophy of science terms and to provide a practical guide to those who wish to study individual cases in a professional and scientific way.

In a classroom setting, of course, cases and situations can be contrived to fulfil educational objectives. Even a real-life case or situation can be put to educational use, provided this does not interfere with the health and welfare of the person(s) involved. The book has been written with both teachers and students in mind. The cases and situations I have used to illustrate and explain the method necessarily provide only a small and selective set. They are relatively simple, although diverse in character. This should enable students to see how the method applies to the sorts of cases and situations they encounter or hear about in training or in daily life. Teachers usually have access to case-materials of a more complex or technical sort; but there are aspects of even these cases that students can deal with in terms of everyday experience. The approach adopted is systematic and fairly detailed. Its full scope will be appreciated only if each and every chapter is worked through.

With the benefit of hindsight, this book can be regarded as the third part of a trilogy. The first was entitled *Person Perception in Childhood and Adolescence*, a co-authored work by Livesley and Bromley (1973). It dealt with the development of self-understanding and understanding others during the school-age years. The second was entitled *Personality Description in Ordinary Language* (Bromley, 1977). This book revised and condensed the developmental aspects described in the first volume and looked in detail at the forms of language used by ordinary adults when they described themselves and other people. That book tried to show what sorts of information are contained in self-descriptions and descriptions of other people, how this information is organized, and how it might be used in personal adjustment and in our dealings with other people. Its main emphases were on common-sense or 'lay' forms of understanding and ordinary language. The present volume, however, deals with the higher levels of professional competence and scientific understanding in the psychological study of individual cases.

In Chapter 1 I have restated some of the ideas contained in the chapter on the psychological case-study in Bromley (1977). There is a great deal of other material in that book, however, which some readers may find relevant and useful—particularly material on content analysis, personal adjustment, and characterization in fiction. Chapter 1 thus provides a convenient platform from which to launch a more substantial account of the case-study method in psychology and related disciplines.

In concentrating on the scientific methodology and the higher professional purposes of psychological case-studies, we must not neglect the fact that case-studies are sometimes carried out in a sloppy, perfunctory, and incompetent manner and sometimes even in a corrupt, dishonest way. Case-studies provide opportunities for people to defend and further their own interests regardless of the truth and fair play. Higher standards of scientific understanding and professional practice in case-studies of all kinds and at all levels should contribute to higher standards of moral conduct—through example and critical, intelligent, informed appraisal.

A grasp of the developmental processes in self-understanding and understanding others in the juvenile period is desirable but not essential to appreciating the complexities of adult social cognition, and the further complexities of scientific and professional levels of understanding human behaviour. The transition to scientific and professional work with individual cases cannot be achieved without specialized training which includes, as part of its specialism, an appreciation of the need to work rationally and empirically, i.e. scientifically, and to be constantly trying to evaluate and improve one's theories, methods, and practices against the best possible evidence of their effectiveness and desirability.

Acknowledgements

I wish to express my thanks to the people who, directly or indirectly, made it possible for me to write this book. Among these are the authors whose works I have found interesting and informative, many of whom are listed in the bibliography. The librarians at the University of Liverpool have been particularly helpful in response to numerous inquiries. Mrs Dorothy Foulds and Mrs Anne Halliwell have, as usual, provided invaluable secretarial assistance. Dr A. D. Lovie and Mr A. Potter gave me the benefit of their advice in respect of topics related to their special interests. Responsibility for the material in this book, however, lies entirely with the author. I also wish to express appreciation of my research subjects for their cooperation. Finally, my thanks are due to my wife Roma who may get a day out without asking, once the page proofs are finished.

CHAPTER ONE

Psychological Case-Studies and the Quasi-Judicial Method

WHAT IS A PSYCHOLOGICAL CASE-STUDY?

A psychological case-study is an account of a person in a situation. Of course, there is usually something interesting or problematical about the person, the situation, or the relationship between them. The account can take many different forms. It can take the form of a summary statement in ordinary language, a detailed technical report containing scientific and professional concepts and data, a judicial or quasi-judicial report, a computerized catalogue of information, a documentary film, and so on. We are concerned with the sorts of case-studies that fall into one or the other of the first three forms. A case-study need not necessarily be concerned with a deviant or difficult person or with an unusual situation. For training purposes it might be better to begin by studying cases involving ordinary people in relatively normal circumstances—coping with their job or their family, organizing their finances or leisure time, moving house, or whatever.

A case-study usually deals with a relatively short, self-contained episode or segment of a person's life. The episode is usually important in that it is formative, critical, or culminant—the sort of episode one would regard as a life-event worth mentioning in a life-history. A case-study can be regarded as a close view of one important life-event. A life-history, by contrast, is more like a series of such episodes viewed less closely but in relation to each

1

other—see Runyan (1982a). Both case-studies and life-histories usually incorporate not only a narrative account of the person's actions, experiences, personal qualities, and circumstances but also a causal analysis which attempts to explain the facts and events described. This chapter describes how a 'quasi-judicial' non-experimental method can be used to investigate individual cases.

The usual purpose of a case-study is to find a solution to the person's problem. This often means making an analysis without having all the information one would like, and arranging for some course of action to be taken, the outcome of which is uncertain. Ideally, the course of action taken should be followed up to evaluate its effectiveness. Case-studies may have other purposes. They can be used to demonstrate 'typical' or 'representative' states of affairs or to illustrate a range of phenomena. For example, case-studies can be used to demonstrate a psychological condition such as anxiety or to illustrate different sorts of reaction to stress.

Case-studies can be carried out at various levels of complexity—from a single, brief, trivial episode to a lengthy major life-event with multiple strands. The term 'case-study' is used to refer not only to the psychological study of individual persons (our main focus of interest) but also to business-study cases of commercial, industrial, and other organizations faced with problems in marketing, manufacturing, or industrial relations—see Easton (1982). Yin (1984) has reviewed the case-study method as a research strategy in public administration and the social sciences generally.

The term 'case-study' can also refer very generally to any singular case or example or incident, the description and analysis of which is thought to contribute to our understanding of an area of inquiry—an accident or near-accident in transport studies, a patient in medical and nursing studies, an organization in management studies, a cultural event or artifact in anthropological studies, a battle in military studies, the production of a textbook in commercial publishing, and so on. The essential and common feature of all these different sorts of case is that they are singular, naturally occurring events in the real world. They are not experimentally contrived events or simulations. It is important to realize, however, that even individual experiments, simulations, and surveys are themselves 'cases' in this general sense provided they are studied as real-world events in their wider context; see Miller *et al.* (1980), for example.

As we shall see, case-studies can be described and explained by reference to appropriate sorts of evidence and reasoning. Moreover, such cases do not exist in isolation. Within a given field of inquiry there may be family resemblances between different cases. By comparing and contrasting cases, a kind of 'case-law' can be developed. Case-law provides rules, generalizations, and categories which gradually systematize the knowledge (facts and theories) gained from the intensive study of individual cases.

Case-law (theory, in effect) emerges through a process of conceptual refinement as successive cases are considered in relation to each other. There comes a time when the developing conceptual framework seems to impose a satisfactory pattern of meaning, such that consideration of subsequent cases adds little or nothing to the analysis. The cases within a category are exemplified by 'prototypical instances' although the category may contain less good examples (analogous, perhaps, to outliers in a statistical distribution). The main point, however, is that the case-laws (conceptual frameworks) arrived at are in no way dependent upon prior considerations regarding representative sampling from a demographically defined population. That is a different approach to a different problem. The proper comparison is with the emergence of case-law in jurisprudence.

There also emerges a kind of procedural framework which prescribes norms and standards for conducting case-studies of a given sort. The value of a case-study depends on the extent to which it reveals facts and relationships which make that particular case explicable, and at the same time adds to the 'case-law' in that general area of interest. Consider, for example, the cases, the procedural frameworks, and the 'case-law' associated with marital counselling, tax evasion, or communicable disease.

A psychological case-study is essentially a reconstruction and interpretation of a major episode in a person's life—see Bromley (1977). It is a reconstruction to the extent that the facts have to be established through what is in part an exercise in historical research, although it may not be recognized as such. It is an interpretation in the quasi-judicial sense of having to arrive at a verdict (a conclusion, solution, decision, or recommendation) on the basis of a rational argument about the relevant evidence. Clearly, it is possible for the facts to be badly reconstructed and/or for this evidence to be misinterpreted.

A case-study is not exhaustive in its description and analysis of the person and situation; it is selective in the sense that it addresses itself to some issues and ignores others. Thus some facts about the person and the situation are relevant to those issues (and so constitute evidence), whereas others are not.

There is no standard way of conducting psychological case-studies since they vary so much in so many ways. This does not exclude a measure of standardization, however, as regards content, organization, procedure, presentation, and so on, within any well-defined field of inquiry, such as parole board cases, management selection, rehousing, neuropsychological assessment, accident investigation, or adoption.

A psychological case-study is an account of how and why a person behaved as he or she did in a given situation. It is usual for case-studies to include a certain amount of life-history information which is remote (distal) from the situation or event in question. Care should be taken, however, not to let life-history information bias one's assessment of the immediate (proximate) causes of the Subject's behaviour. Similar care is taken to avoid bias arising from 'similar facts' in a judicial inquiry.

Case-studies are often carried out so that a desirable course of action can be implemented, whether in the interests of the Subject, or the Investigator(s), or the wider community, e.g. putting someone on probation, seeking divorce, recommending surgery. In order to arrive at a decision about the best course of action to take, one needs to estimate the likelihood of achieving a desired outcome, and the costs and benefits of implementing the associated course of action. This can be effective only if the problems which gave rise to the case have been adequately defined, and the requisite solutions formulated. These topics are taken up in detail in later chapters.

Case-studies are always carried out in a context, and the context helps to determine the procedure and the end-result. Case-studies carried out by students as class exercises are different from case-studies carried out routinely in an organization for the purpose of promotion or performance appraisal, and these are different again from case-studies of one-man businesses carried out by an academic researcher, or 'human interest' stories produced by a journalist—see Wilby (1980), and Jennings (1981).

A psychological case-study calls for a set of observations on one person, together with some kind of commentary on the significance of those observations. Consider, for example, a series of reports of a child's behaviour which are interpreted in terms of the child's developing understanding of other people and interaction with them—see Wolf (1982). In case-studies of this kind the focus of the inquiry is narrow—rather like many medical case-studies—and the study may be systematic because of the existence of a clear conceptual framework within which the data can be organized and interpreted. Consider, in this connection, Piagetian and Freudian case-studies.

Shore (1984) presents a 'case-study' of a former transsexual. It covers several years of the person's life apart from brief consideration of his life-history background. The case is interesting in so far as it illustrates the complexities that arise from numerous contextual factors, shifts in the focal problem, and multiple explanations of the events, described in a mainly narrative account.

The boundaries of a case-study are arbitrary in the sense that it is up to the Investigator(s) to define the issues and terms of reference. A case-study which, for one Investigator, concerns the rehabilitation of a particular drug addict, for another concerns a particular neighbourhood where narcotics are available.

Clark and Penycate (1976) provide a semi-popular account of the case of Patrick Mackay—a psychopath convicted for several murders and other offences. This 'case', however, is really a 'life-history' and starts, in fact, with a brief life-story of Patrick Mackay's father as it overlapped with the story of his childhood. As with many cases which make newspaper headlines and find their way into popular publication, the case of Patrick Mackay emphasizes the unsatisfactory circumstances and errors of judgment that contributed to what, with the benefit of hindsight (see Chapter 10), looked like preventable crimes. The case of Patrick Mackay is mostly narrative history interspersed with brief comments on the associated persons and events. No claim is made to explain Mackay's behaviour except briefly in terms of inherited disposition and unsatisfactory upbringing.

All the indications are that persons classified as behaviour-disordered, including psychopathic personalities, are best studied in terms of a detailed life-history. The quasi-judicial method provides a way of studying the critical, formative, and culminative incidents in the life-history of such persons. These accounts then provide the data-base for the construction of a life-history which may be able to formulate and test interpretations which would not be possible given only one or two sketchy incidents—see De Waele and Harré (1976, 1979) and Runyan (1982a).

Paranjpe (1975) studied the problem of personal identity during adolescence, using an Eriksonian conceptual framework and a variety of non-quantitative self-report methods including diaries. Investigations restricted to information provided by the Subject of a case-study obviously have their limitations. The fact that studies like this extend over a period of several years does not rule them out as 'case-studies' unless they are also set in the context of life-history development and contain a relatively large amount of life-history data. The essential feature of a case-study, as contrasted with a case-history or life-history, is its emphasis on a particular pattern of behaviour in a particular set of circumstances over a limited period of time. Paranjpe's 'cases' are of an intermediate sort since they focus on a theme—identity formation in adolescence—and use a common, preselected set of data-gathering techniques.

As we have seen, most cases are studied retrospectively using whatever evidence is available. Prospective case-studies are infrequent, although Honess and Edwards (1984a–c) have shown how case-studies can be combined prospectively with representative sampling and standardized assessment procedures in the general area of vocational guidance and employment.

In his book *Life Histories and Psychobiography*, Runyan (1982a) deals with the psychological study of individual lives by exploring a variety of approaches to this topic. His main concern is with the analysis of biographical accounts of famous people: Jesus, Shakespeare, Lincoln, van Gogh, for example, where historical research shows that it is not always possible to ascertain the facts. In addition, he discusses (a) the problem of conceptualizing the course of individual lives, (b) a number of specific 'cases' including George III, Dr Schreber, Little Hans, Daniel Ellsberg and Stephen Biko, and (c) the methods used in studying individuality—see also Runyan (1983). The scope of his inquiry is very wide in that it deals with trans-historical and cross-cultural issues in the explanation of human behaviour. Runyan's text (together with his very useful notes and bibliography) provides an interesting contrast with the present volume, although the two overlap somewhat in their approach to the 'psychological case-study' narrowly defined, and, of course, in their historical sources.

Runyan (1978), reviewing Bromley (1977), says that not enough consideration is given to the 'persuasiveness', 'cost', and 'utility' of case-studies carried out according to the methods advocated by different authors. It is virtually impossible to compare the various methods on these criteria because they are concerned with rather different sorts of problem. The question is what sort of method is most appropriate to the investigation of a particular problem. Within the quasi-judicial case-method the persuasiveness, cost, and utility will vary from case to case depending on the ingenuity of the Investigators and the resources available.

Conrad and Maul (1981) give a traditional account of the case-study method from the point of view of experimental psychology, referring in passing to several interesting studies. But the experimental method itself, together with its traditional statistical and psychometric procedures, has not been free of criticism—see Bakan (1967), Hilgard (1951), Meehl (1972, 1978), Pencil (1976), and Wiggins (1981).

The study of individual cases is the idiographic aspect of personality study. It can be contrasted with the study of individual differences—the nomothetic aspect of personality study. It is sometimes supposed that the idiographic approach is concerned exclusively with particular, unique individuals. This is incorrect. Individual cases can be described and interpreted only in terms of a general conceptual framework within which other cases can also be described and interpreted. The scientific character of the idiographic approach is derived from the abstract concepts which enable us to 'make sense' of individual cases. This becomes particularly clear when we need to make comparisons and contrasts between individual cases.

The nomothetic approach attempts to identify and quantify individual differences on basic common psychobiological characteristics, and to demonstrate the origins and development of these characteristics under given conditions together with their interrelationships and their effects on behaviour and psychological processes.

The two approaches have a common aim—the advancement of scientific knowledge about human nature. The difference between the two approaches is one of strategy or method. The idiographic approach is via the intensive study of individual cases in the expectation that detailed description and analysis will gradually lead to deeper understanding and to practical applications in more and more areas of interest. The nomethetic approach is via the extensive psychometric study of samples of subjects in the expectation that individual variations can be averaged out to reveal basic factors common to all or to certain major classes of people; these basic factors can then be investigated experimentally with a view to discovering their origins and mode of operation.

GLOSSARY

Although the terminology is not particularly technical, readers may find the following glossary useful as an introduction to, and as a reminder of, the meaning to be attached to various words and phrases in the context of the psychological case-study and the quasi-judicial method throughout the book. Some of the items are related only to the background literature and are not essential to the text.

Accounts: a technical term used in social psychology to refer to statements made by a Subject which redescribe, explain, justify, excuse, or otherwise clarify the meaning of an action or situation. Accounts are usually 'negotiated' between Subject and interviewer. That is to say, they are not superficial or initial responses to questions, but statements about the Subject's beliefs revealed after discussion with a trusted Investigator.

Assisted autobiography: a person's life-story produced by the combined cooperative efforts of the Subject of the autobiography and the Investigator(s). The account is nevertheless presented as a personal report (using the first-person singular and purporting to be true). The assistance is concerned not so much with collecting the data as with writing and editing the narrative.

Autobiography: the story of a person's life (told in the first-person singular and purporting to be true) written or told by himself or herself. An autobiography is necessarily selective and biased because of its partly subjective perspective, even though the author may refer to objective facts and use objective records.

Biography: an account of a person's life-history written by someone other than the Subject of the biography. It may or may not involve the cooperation of the person studied. It may or may not be scientifically comprehensive or accurate. A biography may depend on a variety of sources and types of information.

Case: the term 'case' itself is from the latin *casus–cadere*, to fall, meaning simply that which happens, an event, state or condition, something that comes about.

Case-law: rules and interpretations that emerge from comparisons and contrasts between successive cases. Provided the similarities and differences between cases have been stated explicitly, and justified by means of cogent argument and empirical evidence, the resulting 'patterns of meaning' provide convenient conceptual routines for handling subsequent cases of the same type.

Case-material(s): any information usually, but not necessarily, in permanent or semi-permanent form which is or seems to be relevant to a case-study or life-history. Broadly speaking, the information in a case. See also *Case-record(s)*, *Life-record(s)*.

Case-record(s): any permanent or semi-permanent store of information pertaining to a case-study or life-history. Case record(s) take the form of written documents, audio- and video-recordings, test results, medical reports, photographs, institutional files, correspondence, diaries and other personal documents, and so on. See also *Case-material(s)*, *Life-record(s)*.

Case-report: a spoken or written account of a case-study. It may or may not be a full or accurate account.

Case-study: a general term widely used, especially in the social and behavioural sciences, to refer to the description and analysis of a particular entity (object, person, group, event, state, condition, process, or whatever). Such singular entities are usually natural occurrences with definable boundaries, although they exist and function within a context of surrounding circumstances. Such entities also exist over a short period of time relative to that context. See also *Psychological case-study*.

Case-vignette: a very brief case-report often used to illustrate the type of case being referred to.

Characterization: an account of a person, object, or event in terms of its identifying features, i.e. its distinguishing characteristics. A characterization need not refer to a unique (single) entity, but may refer to a class of equivalent or similar entities.

Episode: a definable event in or segment of the life-history of a person (or group, or organization); an interesting incident or life-event. Episodes are of interest in so far as they are formative, critical, or culminative. They occupy a short span of time relative to the life-history and can provide the focus for a detailed case-study.

Epistemology: the study of how we acquire and justify our forms of knowledge. Case-studies and life-histories claim to have knowledge of particular persons; so the question is 'How is such knowledge gained and shown to be valid?'

Extended case-study: a set of interconnected case-studies or life-histories in which the description and analysis of one or more cases depends for its meaning on the description and analysis of other cases in the set, as in a study of a family, tribe, team, or other social organization.

Informal logic: a method of constructing or analysing arguments which takes account of meanings and real-world knowledge expressed in natural language. It does not ignore the requirements of formal logic but is mainly concerned with the substance (rather than the 'form') of an argument—hence also 'substantive logic'. See Chapter 8 for further details.

Investigator(s):   the person or persons who carry out a case-study or life-history (initial capital I throughout for clarity). The term is used for convenience regardless of whether the Investigator is operating in a scientific or professional manner, and so includes lay and semi-professional people.

Life-history: a scientific reconstruction and interpretation, based on the best evidence available, of the major formative, critical, and culminative episodes in a person's life. A life-history is based on both subjective data (life-story evidence) and objective data (observation, independent factual records, the testimony of informants and so on). See also *Case-history, Case-study*.

Life-record(s):   any permanent or semi-permanent store of information pertaining to a life-history. See also *Case-record(s)*.

Life-story: an oral or written account by a person of the events, circumstances, and relationships in his or her life. Its essential feature is its subjective aspect, i.e. the personal thoughts, feelings, and motives it expresses. Life-stories usually have to be elicited by one or more Investigators using one or more methods of inquiry. Also, life-stories are usually systematically revised and edited by the Subject, the Investigator(s) or both. See also *Assisted autobiography, Life-history*.

Memoirs: written records prepared for the purposes of historical record or biography; also records of the observations, inferences, and comments of someone having first-hand experience of the topic being written about. They usually express subjective reactions (personal thoughts, feelings, and wishes) as well as objective knowledge.

Narrative: an orderly account of a series of events. It may take the form of a story or of a log. The emphasis is on description rather than explanation, as in a 'behaviour narrative'. By contrast, in the analysis of stories, the term 'plot' refers to the causal sequences that connect the events in, i.e. provide a 'structure' for, the narrative.

Object: the term used when a case-study is concerned not with an individual person as such but with some other kind of entity—an event for example, such as an accident, business failure, or epidemic.

Personal documents: any information in permanent or semi-permanent form belonging to or produced by the Subject of a case-study or life-history that has a bearing on (is relevant to) describing and understanding the person. Personal documents include letters, diaries, notebooks, photographs, financial accounts, and so on. Nowadays, the term can be used to cover tape-recordings.

Prototype: a basic or central pattern of attributes describing good examples of a category whose members are loosely defined by 'family resemblances' rather than sharply defined by possession of a fixed set of characteristics.

Psychobehavioural: a term used to emphasize the interconnectedness of covert psychological and overt behavioural processes. The 'meaning' of an action depends in part on the intentions of the Subject, which in turn depend on feelings, beliefs, expectations, and the like.

Psychobiography: biographical studies in which psychological concepts, methods, and findings play a major role. The term is used mostly in the context of historical (or rather psychohistorical) research and commentary.

Psychological case-study: a scientific reconstruction and interpretation, based on the best evidence available, of an episode (or set of related episodes) in the life of a person. See also *Case-study, Life-history*.

Quasi-judicial method: a scientific approach to the investigation of singular events or instances. It combines features of judicial procedure and scientific method. It is a way of solving scientific and professional problems raised by the occurrence of actions and circumstances. It attempts to apply rigorous reasoning in the interpretation of empirical evidence systematically collected. See text for further details and examples.

Single-case experiment: a prospective study of one or more aspects of the behaviour of one Subject under closely controlled conditions. The quantitative data obtained through systematic variations of the experimental conditions are analysed statistically to test specific hypotheses derived from prior theory.

Stereotype: a term used in social psychology to refer to a relatively fixed, over-simplified image that certain people have of a person or a social group. It can be expressed as a small set of attributes consistent with an underlying attitude towards that person or group.

Subject: the person investigated by means of a case-study or life-history (initial capital S throughout for clarity).

Triangulation: a metaphor derived from surveying and navigation. The survey metaphor suggests that particular facts, e.g. about persons, incidents, or institutional arrangements, can be placed systematically in relation to other facts. The navigational metaphor suggests that if several independent sources of evidence point to a common conclusion, then one's confidence in that conclusion is strengthened.

BRIEF HISTORICAL BACKGROUND

It is difficult to write a history of the case-study method. Firstly because, as a method of inquiry, it antedates scientific method proper. Secondly because different scientific disciplines have adapted the method to suit their different interests. As a method of practical inquiry and report the case-study method can even be presumed to antedate the rise of philosophy, history, and natural observation in classical times. One might speculate that its origins lie in the activities of investigators (advisors, agents) charged with inquiring into and reporting upon military actions, government projects, social disputes, trading relationships, and so on, in man's early social history. These reports would provide the information (intelligence) needed for planning and decision-making, although naturally they would be influenced by prevailing supernatural beliefs and practices.

Life-stories were widely used in the 1920s and 1930s by the Chicago School of sociologists, especially in relation to the study of deviance—see Shaw (1930 and 1966) for example. The Thomas and Znaniecki (1918–20) studies of Polish immigrants to the USA constitute an important historical marker. The life-story, however, has its drawbacks and limitations as a scientific method of investigation even though it can be useful in exploring some of the personal subjective factors in human conduct. The rise of psychometrics, questionnaire methods, survey design, and statistical analysis, with their obvious 'objective' merits, was accompanied by a decline in the case-study method. The decline was rapid and the method had virtually disappeared from research in sociology by the 1950s but has since recovered somewhat—see Bertaux (1981), Bertaux and Kohli (1984), Mitchell (1983), Becker (1966, 1968), Denzin (1970b) and Runyan (1982a,b, 1983).

By contrast, case-study methods have been widely used in social anthropology and continue to be used, although usually supplemented by so-called objective methods. Extended case-studies in anthropology are used to demonstrate, at the level of human action, more abstract and general notions such as social structures, classes, and processes, see Langness (1965), van Velsen (1979), and Peel (1983).

In Chapter 3 there is a diagram to clarify the relationship between the case-study and the life-history. A psychological case-study is a person's life-history in the making. When this notion is transferred to sociological study we can regard extended case-studies as descriptions of the relationship between social dynamics and historical change. Case-studies show where the action is (or was).

The history of the case-study method in medicine is the history of the clinical method, i.e. the systematic diagnosis and treatment of the individual patient. At first this consisted in recording the signs and symptoms of the patient's disorder, and following his or her progress under treatment. Later, as medical science and technology improved, various objective tests could be made for diagnostic purposes and for monitoring the patient's progress. The clinical method in medicine is essentially a method of solving problems associated with injury and disease—see Beck (1981), Cane and Shapiro (1985), Elstein *et al.* (1978), Slater and Roth (1977), Trethowan and Sims (1983). A medical case-report typically provides a brief statement of the patient's medical history and current circumstances as an introduction to a clinical description of the disorder.

The concepts, methods, and findings of medicine are now so extensive, elaborate, and detailed that many problems can be dealt with in a routine way. There are also computerized expert-systems that help physicians to improve their problem-solving capacities in areas which might otherwise prove too complex.

The emergence of psychiatry as a specialized, hybrid form of medicine led eventually to a greater emphasis on objective, quantitative approaches to psychological assessment—see Woody (1980) and Kleinmuntz (1984). In the early history of psychiatry, however, the psychoanalytic approach to mental disorder put great emphasis on the patient's life-story—an account negotiated between patient and analyst—see Dewald (1972) and Greenwald (1959). The case-study method in neuropsychology is discussed in Shallice (1979).

From the dawn of history to the present day, procedures have evolved for settling social disputes. As societies moved towards more open, democratic, rational systems of organization, judicial procedures were developed as ways of settling disputes (solving social problems). They came to rely more and more on principles such as equity, justice, good evidence, and cogent argument. The word 'case' has a long history of usage in law, where it is used to refer to an account of a legal or authoritative judgment about an issue.

Gradually, through the accumulation of records and decisions about particular cases (disputes), bodies of case-law were established. In some areas, laws were codified. These laws, together with an agreed system of judicial procedures, enabled some disputes to be dealt with in a fairly routine way. More difficult cases would sometimes lead to improvements as laws and procedures had to be modified to deal with them. Notice that is is possible, in law as well as in medicine, to separate the diagnostic or fact-finding aspects of the case from the prescriptive judgment, i.e. the action to be taken as a consequence of the findings. It is usual to give an account of the treatment prescribed in a medical case, together with its effects, although the sceptic might argue that only successful cases tend to get reported! Readers interested in those aspects of jurisprudence which have a close bearing on the quasi-judicial method used to conduct psychological case-studies may care to consult the following references: Cohen (1980), Eggleston (1978), Murphy (1980), Murphy and Beaumont (1982), Nokes (1957), Stone (1984), Trankell (1972), Twining (1980, 1983), Twining and Miers (1976), and Williams (1979, 1980). See also Allen (1964) and Lloyd (1981) for a general introduction to law.

In the early part of the twentieth century social work and psychology began to use case-study methods modelled on medical methods of inquiry. Holbrook (1983) provides some historical background to the case-study method used in social work. The professionalization of social casework and its close association with the law and with medicine, especially psychiatry, led to the adoption of what was in effect a quasi-judicial method of investigation and decision-making in which 'social facts' are collected and interpreted as a 'social diagnosis'—see Richmond (1917). The 'social facts' are taken to be well-authenticated conclusions derived from the case-records. The terms 'diagnosis', 'prognosis', 'treatment', and so on were used in non-medical contexts. It became fashionable to speak of 'social pathology' and 'psychological illness'. At the same time, in social work at least, some of the merits of judicial procedures were recognized and incorporated into the case-work method. By contrast, clinical psychology tended to adopt a more thorough-going 'medical model' of psychological disorders. Psychologists came to rely more and more on clinical assessment and on so-called objective diagnostic psychological tests.

Psychoanalysis had a tremendous impact on both social work and psychology in the early part of the twentieth century. After the Second World War, however, its influence on scientific and professional work in the social and the behavioural sciences declined in favour of more behaviourist, psychometric, and experimental approaches.

Although the case-study method did not disappear entirely from psychology (it struggled to survive in personality study and in clinical psychology), it did not make substantial contributions to scientific progress or to the achievement of important practical applications. Two developments could be regarded as exceptions to this conclusion. First, Kelly's personal construct theory and repertory grid method have proved useful in exploring the individual's psychological states—see Adams-Webber (1979). Second, a variety of experimental and quasi-experimental procedures have made it possible to conduct controlled investigations on single cases—see Chassan (1979), Cook and Campbell (1979), Davidson and Costello (1969), Edington (1984), Hersen and Barlow (1976), Kazdin (1982) and Kratochwill (1978). From the point of view of the case-study method, however, these techniques, although very useful in their place, are not substitutes for the natural case-study method. They are rather specialized techniques that can be incorporated into a more comprehensive scientific—quasi-judicial—approach to individual cases.

Dailey (1971) proposed a humanistic alternative, derived from the approaches developed by Murray, Maslow, and White, to the mainstream behaviourist approach to persons. Rather than relying on objective assessment based on credentials or hard psychometric data, he proposed a form of assessment based on an intuitive clinical appraisal of the Subject's life-history to which the Subject made an active contribution. Dailey rejected objective assessment in personnel work, education, and clinical psychology, on the grounds that it was discriminatory, conservative, unjust, and undemocratic. It placed too much power into the hands of bureaucratic gatekeepers. He proposed that greater reliance be placed on feelings and less on reason. Key episodes in the Subject's life-history would be examined, with particular reference to the Subject's point of view (life-story). Negotiations between Investigator and Subject would be open and direct, not based on case-records. Dailey also proposed that assessment should be synoptic, i.e. global, configural, or holistic, but there is no evidence that such assessment is better than assessment based on the linear statistical model.

Dailey's suggestion that the actual outcomes of cases provide criteria for effective assessment is too demanding because of the complexity and intrinsic indeterminancy of the life-course. However, using 'programmed cases', cases presented in instalments, he claimed to have trained experimental subjects to improve their predictions, although the reason for their improvement is not clear.

Dailey drew attention to the possibility of using novel methods of analysing data, such as applying directed-graph analysis to Freud's (1947) case of Leonardo da Vinci. The effect is to show clusters of related items of information, such as statements in a case-report.

The corresponding developments in social work have been the move towards a more behaviourist (contingency management) approach to the individual case, and the move toward community and institutional arrangements as a means of preventing, containing, or otherwise dealing with individual problem cases—see Breakwell and Rowett (1982), Feldman and Orford (1980) and Smith (1970), Jehu *et al.* (1972), and Tharp and Wetzel (1969).

The traditional view of the case-study method in the social sciences can be assessed by reference to an authoritative contribution by Becker (1968). Becker says that the origins of the method lie in medicine and psychology. I have suggested, however, that the method goes back much further in human history. Early historical accounts, legends, and stories illustrate the way in which fact and fiction could be confused prior to the emergence of systematic rational and empirical methods of inquiry. Administrative reports, military and technical reports, and particularly judicial inquiries, were probably among the earliest branches of knowledge to employ case-studies—there being no more basic rational and empirical method of investigation and report available.

Becker says that, psychology apart, case-studies are typically not about individuals but about communities and organizations, at least in the recent history of the social sciences. Life-histories are rare. Nevertheless, the case-study method has been regarded as having a number of advantages. It seems to offer a more global or comprehensive form of understanding than do other methods of inquiry and can be used to reveal social structures and processes. It reveals important contextual considerations not revealed by more closely controlled investigations. It is useful as an exploratory method even where it is not the definitive method; but in order to be useful it has to be restricted in scope and sharply focused. Although they can provide important negative instances (disproofs or falsifications of general propositions), case-studies are not traditionally used to demonstrate general propositions. In any event, even falsifications can prove to be mistaken.

The tendency in the social sciences has been to use the case-study method in association with other methods: participant observation, life-stories, documentary records, questionnaires, and especially methods which provide quantifiable data. If evidence from several independent sources or several independent methods points to the same conclusion, then this adds to the confidence one feels about its correctness. The term 'triangulation', derived from surveying and navigation, is sometimes used to refer to the way in which data from independent sources help to confirm particular findings—see Becker (1968), Brewer and Collins (1981), and Denzin (1970b). Multiple methods and diverse sources are commonly associated with what are called 'extended cases'. Extended cases deal with large social units—villages, organizations, for example—over lengthy periods of time. In such studies, idiosyncratic and accidental features are less likely to obscure the underlying social structures and processes which are the main objects of the Investigators' theoretical interest.

George (1979) points out that different lessons can be drawn from a single historical case. The same rule applies to psychological cases. The reason is that individual cases exist in a context of surrounding circumstances and have a time dimension. Thus by drawing attention to different contextual and temporal factors one can interpret a case in different ways.

A theory is a system of abstract and general ideas, a conceptual structure, which enables us to account for or explain the similarities and differences between cases. In the *final* analysis, of course, each case is unique; but if a case is to be explained, or if two or more cases are to be compared, then abstract and general terms are needed.

It is for the research worker to decide whether the problem under investigation is best approached by the intensive study of a small number of cases, or by a much less intensive study of a large number of cases, or some combination of these approaches. In some instances the detailed analysis of a particular case may be crucial in confirming or falsifying a theory.

Results derived from effective case-methods of inquiry are, by definition, valid and reliable, and capable of being replicated or otherwise confirmed. The notion that a case-study, even an extended case-study, can only be exploratory, whereas a social experiment or survey can provide definitive results, is incorrect. All scientific methods of inquiry can be exploratory and none can be definitive in the sense of giving results which are incorrigible, i.e. beyond refutation or correction. Case-studies, like experiments and surveys, can generate data relevant to the Investigator's theory about, or 'model' of, the phenomenon under investigation, e.g. stress reactions in disasters, investors' reactions to elections or political news, and so on. What a theory or model tries to do is to account for the natural history of the phenomenon under investigation by means of relatively abstract and general principles (coupled if necessary with certain exceptions and reservations). In other words, the Investigator may be concerned not so much with the unique features of a particular case as with the generic properties of the class of cases under consideration, even if these generic properties are not fully worked out.

The traditional social science approach to case-studies incorporates some reservations about the method. First, that case-studies do little more than help define the problem—like a military reconnaissance. Second, that case-studies suffer from 'Investigator effects' because the matter under investigation is altered by becoming the Subject (or Object) of a case-study, and altered in specific ways because of the characteristics of specific Investigators. Thirdly, informants in case-studies tend to provide subjectively biased and selective accounts. As we shall see, these reservations are too restrictive and by no means confined to the case-study method. In contrast to this over-cautious and somewhat pessimistic evaluation of the case-study method, the traditional social science approach emphasizes two advantages. First, in relation to practical applications, it can provide 'insiders' in the case-study with an objective 'outsiders' view of themselves. Second, in relation to the problem of explanation, it can provide a 'proximal' causal account of events. For example, case-studies can fill in the causal details of marital breakdown or acts of vandalism—they provide an account of the process, the behaviour, not just an analysis in terms of broad structural or demographic variables.

A life-history can be regarded as a series of case-studies about one person. It seeks to portray the connectedness of the individual's life-events and seeks to put them into their appropriate social, cultural, and historical context.

Becker (1966), in his introduction to Shaw (1930 and 1966) summarized the role of the life-history method in the social sciences. He distinguished life-history reports from conventional data of the survey or demographic sort, from conventional autobiography and from fiction—see also Bromley (1977). The main advantage of the life-history lies in its relatively objective control (through negotiated accounts) of important subjective data (feelings, thoughts, desires)—data which help the Investigator(s) to make sense of individual behaviour and social relationships. In trying to understand individual conduct it helps to know what the person wants and does not want; how the person construes his or her past, present, and future circumstances; and what courses of action seem possible. As we shall see in Chapter 10, these and other forms of experience as reported by the individual are not to be accepted at face value.

The skilled Investigator or counsellor can often interpret the Subject's mistaken ideas and feelings in the light of scientific and professional knowledge and in the light of what else he knows about the case. The Investigator, in other words, may understand the Subject better than the Subject understands himself or herself. Thus, even the Subject's ignorance and misunderstandings can be turned to advantage in helping to explain behaviour and make sense of the case.

Becker (1966) reviews some of the more important landmarks in the history of sociology based on life-history data with particular reference to the Chicago School. His main point is that life-histories should be considered in relation to each other and in relation to their social, cultural, and historical context. He uses the metaphor of the mosaic—each piece adds a little to the overall pattern, perhaps in its own particular way—but the overall pattern need not depend critically on any particular piece. Metaphors of this sort are helpful in understanding the way in which the conceptual frameworks of science are built up. These conceptual frameworks are abstract and general systems of ideas which organize and interpret a wide variety of individual studies.

One point not so far mentioned in favour of the life-history and case-study methods is their value as a means of communicating scientific knowledge, especially to those outside the particular branch of science and professional work concerned. Consider, for example, the transmission of knowledge about crime, business success and failure, political and military leadership, poverty, retirement, disability, and child-rearing. Case-studies and life-histories can be used to portray typical patterns and the range of variation in behaviour in these various areas, as well as revealing processes and connections not visible in the results and write-up of experiments and surveys.

It is a serious criticism of personality study in psychology that it has not yet built up satisfactory bodies of psychological 'case-law'. Some case-studies have been published in the literature of psychoanalysis, but these are surprisingly fewer, briefer, and less adequate than one would have supposed—see Sherwood (1969). Social case-studies are often used either singly or multiply in order to illustrate aspects of sociology, including the sociology of language, deviance, family life, and social provision for the elderly or for unmarried mothers. The case-study method in clinical psychology, as in psychoanalysis, has been based largely on the concepts and procedures of clinical medicine. Here, the emphasis is on the signs, symptoms, and history of psychological disorder, which—when properly diagnosed—may, like a physical illness, respond to a specific treatment.

Recently there has been some emphasis on behaviour modification in the natural environment, whereby the behaviour of the patient or client is studied in relation to the available patterns of reinforcement. The terms of reference of this sort of 'functional analysis' are obviously different from those of a psychodynamic approach, but the quasi-judicial method of studying individual cases is capable of assimilating the concepts, methods, and findings of both of these approaches.

Most case-studies in the literature of clinical psychology and social work are brief reports or case-vignettes; they are short on 'content' as regards personality description, and are concerned mainly with focal or critical causal connections and social relationships. Also, many case-studies—more so in the literature of social work than in that of clinical psychology—describe what is essentially a 'human predicament', i.e. a problem of adjustment which would have arisen anyway, almost regardless of the personal qualities of the individual concerned. In some instances the relevant aspects of personality and adjustment are common to most people, or to large numbers of people, and the case-study becomes simply an account of how the situation arose and how it might be dealt with. In other instances the case-study is more concerned with the problem created by the personal qualities of the individual concerned, and with how these personal qualities are to be modified or managed. In yet other instances it is difficult to assess the relative importance of personal qualities and situational factors in creating the problem. An Investigator might attribute a personal quality, e.g. jealousy or aggressiveness, to the Subject because it helps him to understand the Subject's behaviour. Alternatively, he may prefer to explain it by reference to special circumstances, e.g. parental favouritism. Swann (1984) shows how interpersonal perceptions are negotiated. Further consideration of this topic would lead us into the complex area of attribution theory.

By contrasting 'personal' and 'situational' factors in the explanation of human adjustment, we see that clinical psychology and social case-work occupy rather different, although overlapping, parts of the same conceptual and methodological continuum. In works of fiction we find corresponding differences between stories about 'characters' and stories about 'situations', although we take it for granted that character and situation are mutually dependent—see Bromley (1977).

The 'quasi-judicial' nature of the case-study in social work was recognized over sixty years ago—see Richmond (1917), but the scientific merits of this method seem not to have been fully explored. It was seen as a procedure for defining, and finding solutions for, problems created when people are not able to deal effectively with their particular social situation. Alternatively, it was seen in 'quasi-medical' terms as a procedure for diagnosing and prescribing treatments for localized social ailments. The concepts, methods, and values of social case-work have been described by Timms (1964, 1968, 1972, 1984), Hollis and Woods (1981), and Haines (1975). The concept of personality has long been of interest to sociologists: see Burgess (1929) and Spitzer (1969), for example. Breakwell and Rowett (1982) describe a modern social psychological approach to social work, and include short case-studies in disability, child battering, community work, and mental illness.

The application of a quasi-judicial method to the study of persons in situations is by no means new. In a sense it has been the preferred method of social case-work since its inception. However, social case-work has experienced changes of fashion with regard to the social and psychological concepts and skills it has espoused—see Roberts and Nee (1970), and Hollis (1970). Moreover social case-workers seem to be more concerned with practical action, with compassion and advocacy, whereas we are more immediately concerned with establishing the *scientific* status of its basic method. This method is basic not only to social case-work but also so scientific work generally.

Studies like those of Traxler (1949) and Allport (1942) show that the case-study method has a long and distinguished history. According to Strang (1949b), the earliest recorded educational case-study dates from about 4000 BC.

In the latter half of the nineteenth century the Harvard Law School used case-studies to train students, and case-studies in medicine were widespread. The case-study method in education developed together with the interest in individual differences, subnormality, and guidance, early in the twentieth century. Thus by the time psychology came into existence as an applied science and professional specialty, the case-study method was well-established. Psychology, of course, contributed to the further development of the method. In particular it provided more objective and reliable methods of assessment. It vastly extended our understanding of the Subject's psychological processes (motives, feelings, abilities, beliefs, and so on). It made us much more aware of the extent to which the Investigator's methods and preconceptions affected the conduct and outcome of the case-study.

Wigmore (1913) proposed a science of judicial proof—a system of rules and procedures for using evidence to establish facts in particular cases—an idiographic method. The full title of Wigmore's book is *The Principles of Judicial Proof as Given by Logic, Psychology and General Experience and Illustrated in Judicial Trials*. Wigmore's contribution is particularly interesting from an historical point of view, because he not only provides perhaps the first systematic attempt to introduce psychology into the process of judicial proof, but he also proposes a system of substantive logical analysis using symbols and diagrams to represent a network of argument taking account of such things as the weight of positive and negative evidence, doubt, belief, corroboration, and net probative value. There seems to be no indication that his ideas were followed up—see Wigmore (1931). A modern approach to the analysis of substantive arguments is described and illustrated in Chapter 9.

Surprisingly, it appears that the question of how facts are proved in judicial inquiries has not been dealt with in the legal literature in spite of an abundance of material on evidence. Stone (1984) provides a particularly interesting answer to the question because of his detailed consideration of psychological issues in criminal trials; see also Penrod and Borgida (1983).

Early references and later sources

Readers interested in the history of case-study/life-history methods in psychology and related disciplines may care to consult the following early references, later sources or commentaries: Allport (1942), Andrews (1953), Baldwin (1942), Block (1971), Bolgar (1965), Brewer *et al.* (1926), Bristol (1936), Campbell (1975), Carr (1948), Darley (1949), Denzin (1970), Dollard (1935), Fox (1983), Foreman (1948), Garbett (1970), Garraty (1957), Germain (1970), Gottschalk *et al.* (1945), Hawkes (1937), Herbst (1970), Jones (1924), Langness (1965), Langness and Frank (1981), Lazarus and Davison (1971), Lindesmith (1947), McCullough (1984), Polansky (1941), Reavis (1926), Richmond (1917), Runyan (1982a), Sarbin (1940 and 1949), Shapiro (1961, 1966), Shaw (1927, 1930 and 1966), Smithies (1933), Strang (1949a), Tagiuri *et al.* (1968), Thomas and Znaniecki (1918–20 and 1923), Traxler (1949), Watson (1949), Williamson (1939), Williamson and Darley (1937), Young and Ashton (1963).

The above list does no more than indicate some of the paths leading back into the literature of psychology, sociology, and anthropology concerned with case-studies and life-histories. No attempt has been made to cover the massive literature on biography, autobiography, and social history.

A classified selection of case-studies and life-histories

The following classified selection of cases is intended to illustrate the very wide range of the relevant literature. Readers are warned that citation does not necessarily imply approval. Some of the references could be placed in more than one category. The list is by no means exhaustive but several of the references cited include a bibliography. No attempt has been made to cover the massive literature on biography, autobiography, memoirs, or social history.

Many other case-studies are referred to in the text and listed in the References at the end of this book.

Early publications: Brewer *et al.* (1926), Evans (1954), Murray and Associates (1938), Page (1950), Strachey (1933), White (1938).

General: Runyan (1982a), White (1963, 1975), White *et al.* (1976), Yin (1984).

Methods and treatments: Allport (1965), Anderson (1981), Berstein (1984), Bistline and Frieden (1984), Eysenck (1976), Hanley and Lusty (1984), Holt (1969), Ullman and Krasner (1965), Wedding and Corsini (1979).

Abnormal: Burton and Harris (1966), Leon (1984), Meyer and Hardaway-Osborne (1982), Neale *et al.* (1982), Vander May and Neff (1984), Weinberg and Hire (1962), White and Watt (1983), Zax and Stricker (1963).

Neuropsychological: Ellis *et al.* (1983), Shallice (1979).

Personality disorder: Clark and Penycate (1976), Cleckley (1964), Confer (1984), Schreiber (1984), Shore (1984).

Crime: Becker (1963), Klockars (1975), Rettig *et al.* (1977), Samuel (1981), Shaw (1930 and 1966), Snodgrass (1982).

Medical: Cane and Shapiro (1985), Cooper (1973), Heston and Heston (1979), Knight (1984), Locker (1983), Luria (1975), Macalpine and Hunter (1969), Rose and Corn (1984), Spalton *et al.* (1982).

Psychoanalytic: Dewald (1972), Eysenck (1965), Freud (1947, 1953, 1977, 1979), Greenwald (1959), Niederland (1974).

Sociological: Bradley (1984), Festinger *et al.* (1956), Greil and Rudy (1984), Jamil (1985), Lewis (1961), Lewis *et al.* (1977a,b), Peel (1983).

Political: Doig (1984), Keil (1984), Wolfsfeld (1984).

Industrial: Easton (1982), Parker (1982).

Military and Historical: Fuller (1970), Winks (1968).

Arts and sciences: Lubin (1972), Roe (1953), Watson (1968).

Children: Moskowitz (1979), Rutter (1975), Wolff (1973).

Family: Rudestam and Frankel (1983).

Death: Strauss and Glaser (1977), Spencer *et al.* (1984), Young *et al.* (1984), Weisman and Kastenbaum (1968).

Second-order cases: Department of Health and Social Security (1974), Devlin (1976).

Journals publishing case-studies and clinical reports

Although there are relatively few detailed case-studies to be found in the journals of the social and behavioural sciences, there are many brief cases and fragments of cases. The following journals publish brief clinical reports and case-studies of individual persons:

American Journal of Psychiatry
Australian and New Zealand Journal of Psychiatry
Behaviour Research and Therapy

British Journal of Psychiatry
Canadian Journal of Psychiatry
Cognitive Therapy and Research
Hospital and Community Psychiatry
Individual Psychology
Journal of Adolescent Health Care
Journal of the American Academy of Child Psychiatry
Journal of the American Geriatrics Society
Journal of Behavior Therapy and Experimental Psychiatry
Journal of Clinical Psychiatry
Journal of Geriatric Psychiatry
Journal of Nervous and Mental Diseases
The Psychoanalytic Quarterly
Psychosomatics

A NOTE ON THE CASE-STUDY METHOD IN EDUCATION

A particular sort of case-study approach in education developed from about the mid-1960s. Case-studies in education are typically concerned with the evaluation of enterprises such as curriculum development, cross-cultural comparisons (including studies of education in specific cultural groups), mixed ability teaching, language learning, multicultural education, and educational innovation. Detailed case-studies of individual pupils or teachers in various educational circumstances seem not to be prominent in the educational literature. The materials that form the basis of educational case-studies can be of various sorts—attainment scores, teaching aids, observers' notes, video- and audio-records, participant observation, question-naire returns, and so on, as for any other kind of intensive case-study. Similarly, educational case-studies can be presented in all kinds of different ways—as talks, films, workshops, and the like. Indeed, it has been suggested that, in view of the importance of communicating results effectively, educa-tional case-studies should be presented as 'documentaries' rather than as traditional research reports—see MacDonald and Walker (1977).

An educational case-study, like any other case-study, must be limited in scope. There must be conceptual boundaries and empirical limits to it, otherwise the investigation would go on for ever. However, these boundaries and limits are arbitrary in the sense that the Investigators can choose to terminate the study when their scientific curiosity has been satisfied, or when they are confident that they have done all they can do in their professional capacity, or when they run out of resources. This arbitrary termination does not preclude reopening of the case if that seems desirable on scientific or professional grounds. A case-study, in other words, is carried out in a context of existing knowledge and circumstances. The Subject or Object of the case is situated within the enveloping world. It is not surprising that educational case-studies encounter difficulties connected with ethical considerations, professional and institutional considerations, and with the reactions of participants.

In education, as in some other disciplines, the case-study method has not been clearly defined. It has been bracketed, somewhat vaguely, with participant observation, qualitative studies, ethnography, and field-studies. The emergence of the case-study method can be seen as a reaction to the traditional experimental and survey methods of investigation which are thought to represent a different 'positivist' approach to education, to society, and to human behaviour generally—see Hamilton (1980) and Stake (1980). I have tried to make clear that the case-study method is a basic, perhaps *the* basic, method of scientific inquiry, but little or nothing is to be gained by supposing that it somehow excludes other methods designed to deal with particular sorts of problem. The epistemological status of the case-study presents some problems. Some of these problems are discussed in Chapter 11, within the general philosophy of science framework developed throughout this book.

Writing in the context of comparative education, Crossley and Vulliamy (1984) distinguish three rather separate traditions in case-study methodology. First, the anthropological study of a single community or culture. Second, the sociological study of social processes and institutions emphasizing subjective processes (meanings, relationships, feelings), and using direct observation in natural settings (participation, in-depth interviewing, accounting). Third, the educational study of the curriculum and programme evaluation, in which case-studies are able to reveal important contextual factors, unintended consequences and side-effects unnoticed by more formal methods of inquiry. The aim of the case-study method in education is to investigate and illuminate a complex system, e.g. a school, in terms of all the structures and functions that contribute to its operation and performance. Case-study approaches are important in enabling us to represent the day-to-day realities of educational processes and institutional structures.

As with other methods of scientific inquiry, the fundamental source of data in a case-study is descriptive evidence, i.e. systematic empirical observation and report. It is the way these data are collected and interpreted that distinguishes one scientific method from another (ignoring, for the moment, the fact that these different methods have different aims and so use somewhat different means to pursue them).

The case-study is sometimes said to provide insight into, rather than confirmation or refutation of, a law or principle (derived from a theory). This misconception comes about because a case-study is usually reported in such a way that the theoretical background, although extensive, remains largely implicit and taken for granted, whereas in an experiment or survey a much narrower set of theoretical expectations is normally stated explicitly, with the wider context being ignored. Any insight generated by a case-study is a function of the Investigator's sudden formulation of a convincing theory that accounts for the facts of the case, or the realization that one particular interpretation must be correct. This is likely to happen because a rigorous and systematically detailed case-study will often refute any obvious, simple-minded theory and will itself stimulate the sort of original, creative thinking that leads to solutions to difficult problems. An experiment or social survey, by contrast, is deliberately constrained so that evidence and reasoning are brought to bear only on specific issues within the framework of pre-existing theory. Of course, serendipity plays a part in all investigations, and good Investigators, like good generals, need to be lucky as well as clever.

A single case-study can be convincing, even probative; hence its scientific value. But the case-study method is not suitable for all scientific occasions. It is up to competent Investigators to decide what kinds of methods and levels of proof are needed to decide the particular issues with which they are concerned. In this connection we must remember that scientific experiments and surveys can themselves become the Object of a case-study. When an experiment or survey is brought under critical review—from an historical or a methodological point of view—its significance (the interpretation placed upon it) is seen to depend on a variety of contextual factors as well as on certain factors intrinsic to the study. It is out of a continuous process of review and reappraisal that we eventually learn to discriminate between good scientific work and bad. History has the last word.

Cast-studies, by definition, get as close to the subject of interest as they possibly can, partly by means of direct observation in natural settings, partly by their access to subjective factors (thoughts, feelings, and desires), whereas experiments and surveys often use convenient derivative data, e.g. test results, official records. Also, case-studies tend to spread the net for evidence widely, whereas experiments and surveys usually have a narrow focus. The sensible thing to do is to choose the methods most appropriate for the particular investigation.

Failure to carry out detailed case-studies may result in failure to realize what is really happening (to persons in a school, prison, factory, or home). Consequently, investigations may be designed and carried out on the basis of false assumptions, with the result that the evidence collected is not the best evidence, and the conclusions which are drawn are not 'ecologically valid'. Crossley and Vulliamy (1984) refer to the misleading effects of official policy statements and rhetoric on responses to questionnaires, and to the unrealities of experimental investigations into normal schooling.

Published educational case-studies usually deal not with an individual person as such, but with an educational enterprise, e.g. a school, a school subject, a curriculum development exercise. Such case-studies typically employ a variety of techniques of investigation—participant observation, structured and unstructured interviews, direct observation, routine records, incident reports, background and contextual inquiries, and historical re-search— in an attempt to get the full 'inside story' as well as the 'public' and 'outsider's' account. Spectators sometimes see more of the game.

The following references are a small selection from the recent literature:

Adelman *et al.* (1976), Crossley and Vulliamy (1984), Davies (1983), Kenny and Grotelueschen (1984), MacDonald and Walker (1977), Parsons *et al.* (1983), Simons (1980a,b), Stenhouse (1979), Walker (1983).

Readers interested in the history of the case-study method in education may note the following early articles: Brewer *et al.* (1926), Hawkes (1937), McCallister (1936), Morrison (1931), Reavis (1926), Smithies (1933), Strang (1949a,b), Traxler (1949).

One has the impression that whereas the recent literature on the educational case-study is mainly about institutional arrangements, the earlier literature is mainly about individual psychological cases.

BASIC RULES FOR PSYCHOLOGICAL CASE-STUDIES

There are six basic rules for the preparation of a psychological case-study.

Rule One.   The first and most important rule is that the Investigator must report truthfully on the person, his life and circumstances, and must be accurate in matters of detail. The relevance and importance of any particular fact must be established by rational argument and not by resort to rhetoric or special pleading.

Rule Two.   The aims and objectives of the case-study should be stated explicitly and unambiguously. Case-studies vary in content and organization depending upon the purposes they are designed to fulfil; a psychological case-study is usually carried out in order to understand and influence a person's reactions to a predicament.

Rule Three.   The case-study should contain an assessment of the extent to which the stated aims and objectives have been achieved. The point of this rule is that, for practical or other reasons, it may not be possible to investigate all the psychological and environmental factors that seem relevant, or it may not be possible to conceptualize the person satisfactorily, i.e. to make sense of his or her behaviour. For example, information about some of the precipitating and predisposing factors in a case of suicide may be unobtainable, so that it is impossible to choose between several different explanations of the act. The factors which prevent the attainment of the objectives must be described.

Rule Four.   If, as is often the case, the inquiry deals with episodes of deep emotional significance to the person, then it can be carried out properly only by someone trained and equipped to establish and manage a close, fairly long, and possibly difficult personal relationship. The reason for this is that the disclosure of very private thoughts, feelings, and desires requires trust which can usually be built up only over a long period of time. Furthermore, psychologically significant episodes usually have considerable ramifications— in the sense that they are associated with events earlier in the person's life and influence many aspects of current behaviour and circumstance. Considerable time is required to explore these ramifications and influences, to collect the evidence needed to corroborate the person's testimony, and to cross-check its internal consistency. Systematic, friendly interrogation decreases the likelihood of accidental errors and omissions and of deliberate misrepresentation on the part of the Subject.

Rule Five.   The person must be seen in an 'ecological context'; that is to say, a full account must be given of the objects, persons, and events in his or her physical, social, and symbolic environment. The proper focus of a case-study is not so much a 'person' as a 'person in a situation'. This rule reminds us that, in case-studies of normal people in the ordinary circumstances of everyday life, the focus of the inquiry often shifts from short-term 'adjustment' to long-term 'adaptation' or life-style. A case-study, however, is usually undertaken either because the personal qualities of the individual are unusual or because the surrounding circumstances are unusual, or both. Among the psychological and situational factors commonly found in human maladjustment are those associated with interpersonal relationships. The individual person belongs to a number of small, primary, social groups whose memberships overlap and whose functions interlock. It is within these informal, human groups that the person's main satisfactions and dissatisfactions are to be found. His or her problems of adjustment are generally associated with basic emotional relationships with another person or, at most, a few other people. The family is perhaps the most influential of these groups because it provides the formative experiences and acts as the main agent for the transmission of culture from one generation to the next. The 'ecological context' referred to in this fifth rule, therefore, is a context not only in a primary or biological sense, but also in a secondary or cultural sense. The cultural context includes all the man-made systems in which we live: the built environment, the social organization, the communication system, the economic and political system, the value-attitude system, and so on.

Rule Six.   The case-report should be written in good plain English in a direct, objective way without, however, losing its human interest as a story. The writer should present the individual's point of view rather like a barrister presents his client's case in a court of law. This can be done with sympathy and imagination and with due regard for high standards of evidence and argument.

The length of the report depends upon the purpose of the investigation, the complexity of the problem, and the resources available to the Investigator, as well as on the Investigator's abilities and other personal qualities. Case-studies can be done well or badly. They should be evaluated by the scientific and professional standards incorporated in what we are calling the 'quasi-judicial' method.

PROCEDURAL STEPS IN THE QUASI-JUDICIAL METHOD

There are ten procedural steps. They show the complexity and rigour of a method concerned with both 'individual cases' and 'general laws'.

Step One.   The initial problems and issues should be stated as clearly as possible.

Step Two.   Background information should be collected to provide a context in terms of which the problems and issues are to be understood.

Step Three.   On the basis of information available at the time when the problems and issues are raised, *prima facie* explanations and solutions (about the individual's personality and predicament) can usually be put forward immediately. It is these obvious and simple *prima facie* answers that should be examined first of all, otherwise one may needlessly complicate the investigation. Sometimes, of course, the obvious and simple answers are incorrect.

Step Four.   Examination of these more obvious explanations guides the Investigator's search for additional evidence. If they do not fit the available evidence, then alternative explanations (conjectures) have to be worked out. The various possible answers, both initial and subsequent, have implications as regards what should or should not be the case, i.e. they may be compatible with some of the evidence but not with it all.

Step Five.   The next step is to search for and admit for consideration sufficient evidence to eliminate as many of the suggested explanations as possible, in the hope that one of them will be so close to the truth as to account for all the evidence and be contradicted by none of it. The evidence may be direct or indirect; but it must be admissible, relevant, and obtained from competent and credible sources.

Step Six.   The sources of evidence, as well as the evidence itself, must be closely examined. In the case of personal testimony this is analogous to cross-examination in a court of law; otherwise it amounts to checking the consistency and accuracy of all items of evidence.

Step Seven.   There must be a critical inquiry into the internal coherence, logic, and external validity of the whole network of argument claiming to settle the issues and solve the problems.

Step Eight.   It is likely that some lines of argument will be obviously inadequate, whereas others will be possible or even convincing. As mentioned in step five, the 'most likely' interpretation is selected, provided it is compatible with the evidence.

Step Nine.   The formulation of an acceptable explanation for the person's behaviour usually carries implications for treatment or other action, and these have to be worked out.

Step Ten.   An account is prepared in the form of a scientific or professional case-report. It should contribute to psychological 'case-law' in virtue of the abstract and general principles employed in explaining the Subject's tactical adjustments or strategic adaptation to his or her situation. The same abstract and general principles can be applied to comparable cases, perhaps with minor qualifications.

All these issues are taken up in more detail in subsequent chapters.

THE CONTENTS AND ORGANIZATION OF A CASE-STUDY

The basic rules and procedural steps above describe how a case-study should be conducted but do not specify the sorts of information to be included. The treatment of this issue in this book is rather different from that described in Bromley (1977, pp. 173–202), to which readers who are particularly interested in the content analysis of case-studies are referred.

The question of what information is to be included in (or excluded from) a case-report should be answered within the case-report itself. At the heart of the case-report should be a description and analysis of the central problem(s) that the case-study was set up to deal with, together with any recommendations based on the analysis. These central issues, however, are embedded in a wider context of relevant information and procedural considerations.

It will be helpful to review the many sorts of information that commonly find their way into case-reports and personality descriptions. These range from obvious routine statements of fact, through an assortment of common-sense particulars about the case, to technical matters of a scientific and professional nature. Consider the following list of categories based on a content analysis of personality descriptions.

  (i) The identity of the Subject of the case-study: his or her name, age, address, physical appearance.
 (ii) The life-history, present circumstances, and future prospects of the Subject, including his or her routine activities, material possessions, physical health, and any pertinent incidents or life-events.
(iii) The psychological attributes of the Subject, including his or her characteristic reactions, motivations, attitudes, expressive behaviour, abilities, morality, self-image, and 'life-story'.
 (iv) The Subject's social life: his or her social position, role and status, social relationships, family and kin, friendships, and loyalties.
  (v) The relationships between the Subject and the Investigator(s) carrying out the case-study.
 (vi) The value judgments of the Subject's morals in terms of the ethical standards governing the case-study.

In view of the fact that we are pursuing a technical (scientific and professional) approach to the psychological study of individual cases, it might seem out of place to recommend a moral judgment as an element in a case-report. The reasons for including it are as follows. First, moral attitudes and judgments are virtually unavoidable when assessing people; so one may as well recognize the fact and state one's attitude explicitly (otherwise it might affect the way one handles a case without one's being aware of the fact).

Second, moral judgments can be justified by rational argument and reference to empirical data—see Toulmin *et al.* (1979, pp. 309–337), and Chapters 9 and 11 of the present book. One can determine the extent to which a person's conduct matches up to an agreed moral code, i.e. the collective moral code of the community of interest represented by the person(s) carrying out the case-study. Third, in many instances it is the Subject's failure to match up to the moral code of the community to which he or she belongs that gives rise to the need for the case-study; hence it is essential that the ethical issues involved be made clear. Fourth, the moral attitude of the community to which the Subject belongs is an important factor governing the social environment to which the Subject has to adjust; therefore it must be taken into account in the analysis and in any recommendations about the course of action to be taken in the interests of all concerned.

In addition to the sorts of categories of information listed above, a case-report should contain the following items.

(vii) A statement of the central problem(s) under investigation giving the purpose(s) and terms of reference of the case-study together with its authorship and authority.

(viii) A detailed account of the evidence and arguments describing and analysing the issues in the case, bearing in mind its purpose(s) and terms of reference.

 (ix) Where appropriate, a detailed technical (scientific and professional) account of any central issues in the case which fall outside the normal range of commonsense and ordinary language (or can be dealt with more effectively in technical terms).

  (x) A statement of the findings in the case, i.e. conclusions or solutions, justifying the associated decisions and recommendations.

If the case-report is lengthy, it is advisable to incorporate reminders, reviews, and summaries, as follows:

 (xi) A review of the evidence and arguments dealing with the central issues in the case in relation to the conclusions reached and recommendations made.

(xii) A summary of the methods used in carrying out the case-study; a reminder about the context of the case (the circumstances surrounding it, the conditions which gave rise to it, the factors affecting its future); any reservations, implications, or comments deemed appropriate in reporting and publicising the case.

A psychological case-study carried out in a scientific and professional way can be presented as a technical report—see Cooper (1964) and Tallent (1983). Such a report contains three further items.

(xiii) A title and an abstract; the abstract should give simply a brief statement of what the case-study is about.

(xiv) Summary and conclusions: a brief statement of the problem, the methods used to investigate the problem, the main findings, conclusions, recommendations, and forecasts.

(xv) References, sources, acknowledgements.

I emphasize that there is no standard format for psychological case-studies. They vary in length, content, purpose, and organization. Consequently, the information need not cover all of the first ten categories listed above. If the case-report is brief, or if some aspects of the case-report are brief, then the relevant information is simply assimilated to the most convenient category. The aim is to prepare a concise, well-organized account of the case which represents the facts well and is as comprehensible and as useful as possible.

FINAL CHECKS

Before we conclude this section on the quasi-judicial method, we need to list the final checks that an Investigator should make in order to be confident that the case-study is satisfactory. These checks are as follows: that the report fulfils its aims and purposes; that it satisfies its terms of reference, contains no serious omissions, and makes good psychological sense; that subjective factors have been reduced to a minimum, preferably by the incorporation of several independent opinions; that matters of detail are correct and each part is given its due weight; that the sources of evidence and methods of investigation are clearly stated and properly evaluated; that evidence and inference are not confused; that arguments are made explicit and as cogent as possible; that reasons are given for whatever conclusions are reached and for whatever action is recommended; that the evidence and its sources are properly catalogued, so that in the event of another Investigator taking over the case, the original data can be re-examined.

If the investigation is limited to fact-finding, as it might be if called for in connection with a judicial inquiry proper, particular care should be taken that no inadvertent selection and interpretation has been imposed on the empirical evidence, i.e. that the issues have not been 'pre-judged', and that matters of opinion are separated from matters of fact.

In subsequent chapters a number of case-studies, or rather partial case-studies, will be presented. They are intended to illustrate some aspects of the description and analysis of cases and some aspects of the quasi-judicial method. It should be obvious that psychological case-studies carried out according to the full requirements of the quasi-judicial method are major exercises usually undertaken in the interests of some important scientific or professional enterprise. It is not appropriate to include detailed or specialized case-studies in a book of this kind, and readers are referred to the bibliography for sources of case-material or to the journals previously listed which regularly report brief case-studies and clinical reports.

FURTHER POINTS OF GENERAL INTEREST

There are a number of further considerations, originally set out in Bromley (1977), but worth rehearsing here as preliminaries to the more detailed matters to be dealt with in the Chapters that follow.

(i) The first concerns the reasons for carrying out a case-study in the first place. What were its origins? What is its present purpose? What are its terms of reference? Whose initiative and responsibility are involved?

There are many different practical reasons for preparing a case-study: reports on individual people may be needed by a court of law, by a medical or welfare agency, by a selection committee, employer, vocational advisor, or marriage counsellor, by a newspaper or magazine, radio or television broadcasting company, by a business organization, intelligence agency, a school or university, and so on. Naturally, the type of information wanted and the nature of the report vary from one agency to another—a political profile in a newspaper looks rather different from an obituary or psychiatrist's case-report, in spite of the fact that they belong to the same general class of 'personality descriptions' or 'case-reports'. The terms of reference common to these accounts are to report on a particular person in relation to a given situation. A political profile in a newspaper obviously describes the individual's personality in relation to political circumstances; an obituary attempts to sum up the main landmarks and achievements as represented in the individual's reputation; a psychiatrist's report describes the individual's psychopathology, its symptoms, aetiology, and prognosis.

In practice, the terms of reference of a case-study may not be stated very clearly. Usually, the nature of the problem and the relevance of the information made available become clearer as the investigation gets under way. Indeed, the nature of the problem and the scope of the inquiry may not become settled until the report of the case-study is complete. In this respect the quasi-judicial method, as employed in the preparation of a psychological case-study, differs from the British judicial method, as employed in criminal or civil cases, where the 'issues' are clearly stated at the outset and govern the admissibility of evidence and thus the subsequent scope of the inquiry. This comes about partly because, in law, much of the preliminary work is done before a case comes to trial, and the trial itself is a kind of formal test of the relative merits of two well-rehearsed, fully documented, arguments presented according to the rules of a clear and accepted procedure. A quasi-judicial case-study, by contrast, is more an exercise in problem-solving. The aim is to understand scientifically what is going on and to manage the affair in a professional and businesslike manner. It is perhaps more akin to the French 'inquisitorial' system of judicial inquiry.

One of the limitations of the case-study method as traditionally practised in psychology and social work is that it tends to present a one-sided account of the person in a situation, i.e. it fails to consider alternative accounts and so fails to show that one account is more acceptable than another when judged in terms of a common standard of evidence and argument. This limitation is more likely in case-studies carried out by one Investigator than in case-studies carried out by a team, where discussions at case conferences often bring out different points of view.

(ii) The second point of general interest is a reminder about record-keeping. If the case-report is a technical document it should conform to certain standard requirements as already indicated and referenced. In addition, it should show its origins (author, date, place, and so on), have a title, and if necessary a reference number. For the purposes of research and teaching, the real identity of the Subject should be kept confidential. As I show later on, case-studies are robust in the sense that a variety of changes can be introduced into a report to disguise its origins and the identity of the Subject without significantly affecting the validity of the analysis. Naturally, case-reports of this sort should be accompanied by a note to the effect that information has been altered, omitted, or added in the interests of confidentiality or for instructional purposes.

(iii) The third point of general interest, and one that is often forgotten in case-studies, is that the Subject's view of himself (or herself) and the world is a major determinant of that person's behaviour. It follows therefore that no case-study is complete without some account of the Subject's view of his (her) circumstances, personal attributes and actions. In some instances the effort to collect this information can be expected to have beneficial effects in improving the Investigator's understanding and management of the case and in improving the Subject's understanding and management of himself (herself) and his (her) affairs. In other instances, of course, Subjects may not have the ability or the insight needed to give a personal account of themselves and their circumstances, and may not benefit much from counselling directed towards increased self-understanding and self-management.

There is nothing about the quasi-judicial case-study method that precludes the direct involvement of the Subject in the description and analysis of the case. Whether such involvement is feasible or desirable is for the Investigator(s) to decide.

(iv) The fourth point concerns the distinction between lay explanations of human behaviour and technical (professional and scientific) explanations—see Antaki (1981), Secord (1982), and Sherwood (1969). This issue is taken up in detail in later chapters. Briefly, it concerns the fact that many commonsense explanations of human behaviour are found in technical case-reports, and many of the technical explanations can be translated without too much difficulty into lay terms. The commonsense concepts have to do with motivation, disposition, ability, habit, expectation, social role, force of circumstance, and such-like. The technical concepts have to do with conflict, defensive reactions, stress, reinforcement, alienation, family dynamics, biomedical factors, social and cultural factors, and so on. As will become clearer in later chapters, the validity of one's account of a case (assuming it goes beyond mere narrative or description) hinges on the explanatory concepts used, implicitly or explicitly, to make sense of the Subject's behaviour. Such explanatory concepts—lay and technical—can be regarded as conceptual routines, comparable with the schemata, frames, and scripts described in Schank and Abelson (1977) and Minsky (1975), for making sense of and dealing with certain *classes* of problematical behaviour, such as neuroses, accidents, interpersonal conflicts. They constitute the basis of psychological case-law—see Chapter 11.

(v) The fifth general point is a fairly lengthy one. It concerns the fact that one of the commonest ways of summing people up is to specify their salient personality traits, e.g. steady, reliable, humorous. But representing the person in this way is oversimplified and misleading. It is oversimplified because there is much more to being a person than having a few characteristic ways of behaving—see Bromley (1977). It is misleading because it neglects the situational determinants of conduct. A case-study is concerned with the person in a situation, and it must state whatever is important and relevant to understanding the person in that situation. Nevertheless, a person's actions often *seem* more comprehensible if we can attribute them to an underlying trait.

It is a matter of linguistic convenience to define a personality trait in general terms, so as to indicate broadly the range of meanings available for it. A trait name does not have a fixed meaning; it has a variety of meanings depending upon the situational and linguistic context in which it is used. Personality traits can be operationally defined by means of standardized psychometric tests. But the meaning of a trait is not restricted to its operational definition, its 'meaning in use' is field-dependent.

Trait names or dispositional terms can be used to refer to many kinds of behavioural consistencies, temperamental qualities, abilities, beliefs, and moral qualities. Knowing that a person has such and such an attribute leads us to have expectations about his or her behaviour; these expectations are of a general sort, but if we also know the kind of situation that person will be in (and what kind of behaviour that situation usually elicits from people of that sort), then the person's actual behaviour becomes more predictable.

Statements in a personality description can be constructed to fit an endless variety of individual characteristics ranging from the most abstract and general sort of attribute to the most concrete and particular fact. Specific personality traits are referred to by words and statements at an intermediate level of abstraction and generality; they describe more than, say, a mannerism or a routine performance, but less than a broad disposition. In other words they convey information about how the person is likely to behave in response to a *type* of situation (not only in a particular or actual situation). Consider the difference, for example, between 'Careless' and 'Careless of his appearance' or 'Careless with money'. Statements about specific personality traits are not unlike statements about *general* personality traits which have been qualified and organized to make their meaning narrower and more precise, i.e. less general, less abstract.

Many of the items in questionnaire measures of personality refer to specific personality traits. In so far as respondents answer sets of questions consistently and correctly they seem to reveal their underlying *general* traits. In a quasi-judicial investigation, similarly, statements about specific personality traits and actual incidents are closely tied to the empirical evidence; they convey information in their own right apart from providing a basis for the attribution of *general* personality traits.

It is all too easy in carrying out a 'psychological' case-study to overemphasize the psychological aspects of the case whilst neglecting the biomedical and environmental aspects. This raises the whole question of attribution—the psychological process by means of which we identify the causes of and responsibilities for actions. The process is more complicated than one might suppose—see Heider (1958), Shaver (1975), Jones *et al.* (1972) and Jaspars *et al.* (1983). The outcries and debates about rape provide a dramatic illustration of the importance and difficulty of identifying the reasons and causes that lie behind human behaviour, and of assigning moral responsibility. There are, in addition, a number of faults and weaknesses in commonsense reasoning— currently studied under the general rubric of 'social judgment'—which make it difficult to arrive at valid interpretations of people's reports of their actions—see Chapter 10.

The main point, however, is that human behaviour is a function of the interaction between personal characteristics (dispositional factors as well as momentary states of mind) and situational factors (constraints as well as opportunities). As we have said, a case-report is an account of a person in a situation.

Note that some situations *induce* dispositions; some dispositions *induce*, i.e. lead to, select, provoke, situations. The term interaction is therefore more complicated than appears at first glance.

By contrast with the traditional type of psychological case-study, a functional analysis of a case emphasizes the way reinforcement contingencies in a person's environment shape his or her behaviour. We shall examine cases from two perspectives: a psychological perspective which looks at what is going on 'inside' the Subject, and a behavioural perspective which looks at what is going on 'around' the Subject. In this way a more substantial image or representation of the person can be achieved.

(vi) The sixth point is that the main aim of a case-report is to provide some general conclusions about the person, rather than to present a catalogue of particular facts. For this reason, information about actual incidents may be sparse. Although the quasi-judicial method makes it necessary to use actual incidents, i.e. behavioural episodes, as evidence, the incidents themselves are not likely to figure in the general conclusion or assessment. They form part of the 'infrastructure' of the appraisal (rather as the particular responses to a questionnaire, intelligence test, or projective test provide the basis for a psychometric assessment). It is one of the merits of the quasi-judicial method that it obliges the Investigator to take an interrogative attitude towards his informants (including the person who is the focus of the case-study), and towards the evidence they provide. He cannot accept general statements at their face value, but must inquire into the observational evidence for them. Thus, for example, before the general statement 'He is cruel' can even be considered meaningful, there must be reliable testimony, or other good evidence, from a credible source, describing actual incidents involving the person. The Investigator is simply seeking to translate terms which refer to a covert (psychological) process or to a social (evaluative) judgment into terms which refer to an overt (behavioural) process. Whether the person's actions are then still regarded as 'cruel' is another matter. In a similar way, general statements about environmental conditions, e.g. 'He is under stress' or 'Her friends gave her lots of help' must be translated into empirical statements about actual events and circumstances.

(vii) The seventh point concerns the technical question of whether there are any important facts about the person's physical or mental condition that need to be taken into account. It is well known that there are many anatomical and physiological factors in personality and adjustment, e.g. endocrine functions, brain damage, disease, and disability. Such knowledge is derived, in the main, from cases in which these factors have been abnormal to a marked degree. Within the normal range of health, the precise effects of variations within and differences between individuals in these factors may be difficult or impossible to ascertain.

In many cases evidence about a person's general physical and mental health may not be particularly relevant—simply because that person is normal and there is nothing about his health that makes any difference to the pattern of meaning we impose on the behavioural evidence. Moreover, the person is presumed to be physically and mentally normal unless evidence to the contrary is produced. But this presumption need not prevent the Investigator from inquiring briefly and routinely into the individual's health.

An Investigator would need to show the relevance of any *systematic* inquiry into the person's physical and mental health. But, of course, such an inquiry is highly relevant in a variety of cases, e.g. attempted suicide, psychiatric disorder, sexual problems. In such cases the ideal procedure would be for the person to have a medical and psychiatric examination and for a medical history (or such parts of it as seem relevant) to be made available as evidence. Even in cases where there is fairly obvious physical or mental abnormality, it is not always possible to demonstrate a causal connection between that abnormality and the actions of the individual. The Investigator may just 'presume' that the health factor was a contributory cause of the individual's behaviour, e.g. physical illness in suicide, psychiatric illness in crime, physical disability in occupational maladjustment. Where the facts of physical and mental health are known at a commonsense level of understanding, they enter into an observer's implicit theory of human behaviour to help generate expectations about people.

The selection and interpretation of facts about a person's physical and mental condition is thus not as simple or as straightforward as one might suppose. For example, wrinkles and loss of teeth may have little direct medical significance, and may be quite normal; nevertheless they may have a considerable psychological importance for particular people. Similarly, poor colour vision may be unimportant for some aspects of adjustment but be critically important for others; again some symptoms of ill-health, such as skin disorders or insomnia, may have no demonstrable organic cause and yet be relevant to the individual's maladjustment.

The medical relevance of conditions such as drug addiction, including alcoholism, is obvious. In cases of this sort it might seem that the quasi-judicial method is overelaborate, and that all that is required is a valid diagnosis and suitable medical treatment. There are two points to be made here. First, a medical diagnosis is itself a type of 'quasi-judicial' inquiry (the clinical method generates a kind of medical 'case-law'), and it might be that the case could be dealt with adequately within this medical framework. Second, a medical condition exists in a psychological and social context, and may be understood properly only when these contextual factors—attitudes, beliefs, circumstances, and family relationships for example—are taken into account. The applicability and importance of a rigorous quasi-judicial method in psychiatry and some other branches of medicine should be obvious.

The routine appraisal of a person's physical and mental health naturally includes consideration of any special physical assets and disabilities such as might be relevant to a particular occupation; e.g. those relating to vision, hearing, and balance, and to conditions such as asthma or epilepsy.

The individual's attitude towards his own physical and mental condition must not be neglected in a case-study. The person's 'body-image' may be a major component in the self-concept and may be associated with feelings of inferiority, low levels of achievement and aspiration (both physically and socially), and with psychosomatic or compensatory reactions. The person's attitude towards physical health and appearance, bodily functions, medical condition, medical history, and prospects, may be very relevant to understanding his or her behaviour.

(viii) The eighth point concerns the problem of making comparative judgments in case-studies. The relevance and importance of evidence relating to questions of this kind is easy to see. We have few absolute objective measures of psychological characteristics, and the need for at least relative and standardized measures is amply demonstrated in the immense amount of effort that has been devoted to the development of psychometric tests of personality, intelligence, motivation, attitudes, and other psychological and performance characteristics.

The issue of whether the available psychometric measures can provide the evidence needed in psychological case-studies is not one that we need to pursue further. The issue continues to be debated in the technical literature of personality and psychometrics. It is the responsibility of a particular Investigator to decide what use to make of psychometric measures in the study of a particular case. The evidence derived from standardized assessment procedures may or may not be helpful. In any event, such evidence is only one sort of evidence among the many diverse kinds normally available to the diligent Investigator. Among the more obvious cases in which standardized psychometric evidence would usually be appropriate are those associated with scholastic and vocational adjustment and those with definite psychiatric symptomatology.

In many psychological case-studies, however, formal psychometric assessment is not possible—for want of sufficient resources or a suitable assessment method—or not necessary because sufficient relevant evidence of another, more pertinent, kind is available. The psychological case-study focuses on the person in a situation, i.e. it uses a 'behavioural ecology' framework for the study of personal adjustment. This framework requires an Investigator to cast the net for evidence very widely, far beyond the scope of psychometric and laboratory measurement, and to study the situational context of personal adjustment as closely as the personality itself.

Statements about similarities and differences between the Subject of a case-study and other people, when valid, show how the person is placed relative to other people with whom he or she can reasonably be compared: in respect of, say, academic performance, cooperativeness, social isolation, and so on. Such standards of comparison are commonly used in personality descriptions, and are often explicitly called for in requests for testimonials (referees' reports). Standards of comparison with others are implicit in the very words and phrases we use to make statements about people. Indeed, it is obvious that a common language of personality description implies a socially shared frame of reference which must take account of the similarities and differences between individuals (as well as the similarities and differences in behaviour between different occasions for one and the same person). The logic of comparative judgments is that if we know something about the average and range of behaviour of people of a certain kind, the reference group, and if variations in their behaviour are associated with certain other facts or outcomes—e.g. marriage, occupational failure, or whatever—then knowing how a person's actions or personal characteristics compare with those of the reference group enables us to make a more confident prediction about these associated facts. Social comparisons may be more, or less, objective, and more, or less, evaluative; but the ease and confidence with which we make statements comparing one person with another does not necessarily reflect the validity and reliability of such statements. Much of the time, social standards of comparison are vague rather than precise, and normative rather than empirical. In addition, they are subject to the weaknesses and limitations of commonsense judgment—see Chapter 10.

(ix) The ninth and last point of general interest concerns the logical analysis of the case-material—the structure of inference imposed on the available evidence. The basic aim of a quasi-judicial case-study is to formulate a cogent argument, i.e. a rational and empirical argument, which explains the behaviour of the person under investigation. Such an argument is, in effect, a *theory* or *explanation* about that person's adjustment, and is therefore open to question and subject to continual revision in the light of fresh evidence and new ideas. Ideally, the case-study eventually reaches a stage at which it makes good sense: it is internally coherent; it corresponds with the empirical evidence; it successfully predicts how the individual will behave; and it is accepted by competent Investigators working independently of one another. We can then say that we 'understand' the stimulus person (or at least that aspect of his personality which is under scrutiny). In general, to understand the *logic* of human conduct (as expressed in correct explanations) is to understand the *psychology* of human conduct.

An adequate explanation for a person's behaviour in a given situation is one which contains enough empirical evidence, marshalled by a sufficiently cogent and comprehensive argument, to convince competent Investigators that they understand something that previously puzzled them. The issues of logic and argumentation can be dealt with in an 'informal' but systematic way, as described in Chapter 9 and elsewhere. A psychological case-study carried out by means of a quasi-judicial procedure presents a problem—one that calls for understanding and practical action. On the basis of preliminary inquiries the issues are stated and the inquiry gets under way by verifying the basic facts and collecting evidence relevant to the main issues. Gradually, various lines of evidence and argument are followed up, leading eventually, by recognized procedures, and with varying degrees of confidence, to reasonable conclusions and recommendations. Scientific and professional case-work, using a quasi-judicial procedure, assesses the extent to which psychological theory can be tested against the available evidence. A theory, as we shall see, is simply a way of organizing a network of substantial (informal) arguments so that sensible conjectures imposed on good evidence lead convincingly to conclusions which can be held with some confidence.

In one sense an explanation supplies the information which dispels the puzzlement felt by the person seeking an explanation. A simple fact or relationship may be all that is needed to dispel the puzzlement. In general, when we seek an explanation for a person's behaviour we are looking for the evidence we lack, or we are looking for some sort of interpretation or relationship which has so far eluded us. To find an explanation is to be able to impose a pattern of meaning on the information we have available. Metaphorically speaking it means getting those additional pieces of the jigsaw puzzle which enable us to put the whole picture together. Sometimes, however, we do not have all the pieces of the puzzle, and the pieces we do have can be put together in different ways, so that we cannot be sure which is the correct way.

The aim of a case-study, like that of any scientific investigation, is not to find the 'correct' or 'true' interpretation of the facts, but rather to eliminate erroneous conclusions so that one is left with the best possible, the most compelling, interpretation. The conjectures we make, as Investigators, about why the person behaves as he or she does can be regarded as 'proto-theories': simple arguments about facts and relationships. The problem is to propose explanations for the Subject's behaviour and to attempt to refute them by reference to the evidence. Thus, in the end, when the ramifications of the argument have been worked out, we have a complex web of evidence and inference which is compatible with some explanations but incompatible with others.

The requirements for carrying out and writing up a quasi-judicial case-study may seem formidable—especially the requirement that the logic of one's arguments be spelled out in detail. As we shall wee this is not as difficult as one might suppose, although it is laborious—see Chapter 9 especially.

I hope the account that follows will do something to demystify the processes of scientific investigation and explanation. In particular I hope that the frequent substitution of the term 'reasonable argument' for 'theory' and the avoidance of social science jargon, will help those who study individual cases to appreciate the relationship between professional practice and academic theory.

With reference to the problem of identifying the 'causes' of an individual's actions in a situation, it is important to remember that the boundaries of a case-study are arbitrary. They depend on the ingenuity and resources of the Investigator(s) and on the nature of the case. It follows that any causal analysis is at best an approximation to what is in fact the case. Moreover most causal analyses involve unspoken assumptions, reservations, background knowledge, and tacit understanding of what need not be stated. Causal analyses focus on what might be called the critical features of a case; namely, those that are in dispute, those that enable us to prefer one explanation to another.

SUMMARY AND CONCLUSIONS

The question 'What is a psychological case-study?' is answered by drawing attention to the way we describe and analyse a person's behaviour and psychological characteristics in relation to a set of circumstances. The case-study method is basic to scientific investigation, and case-studies are by no means restricted to the social and behavioural sciences. Psychological case-studies are normally carried out for practical purposes associated with the particular case; but case-studies have a theoretical aspect in so far as they give rise to case-law or depend, as they must, on a basic conceptual and methodological framework.

The term 'case-study' is contrasted with the term 'life-history', and a variety of related terms are provided in the form of a glossary.

It is argued that the case-study method has remote origins in human social history, especially in matters calling for practical action. Its more recent history, however, is to be found in judicial inquiries, with contributions later from medicine and the social sciences. The *psychological* case-study is of relatively recent origin and had its sources in psychiatry and social work (via psychoanalysis). The scientific character of the case-study method seems never to have been adequately explored. It received grudging acceptance and scant treatment in most psychology textbooks until the emergence of single-case experimental methods, which are really specialized techniques.

References to earlier and later sources of information on case-study and life-history methods are listed, together with a wide range of references to actual case-studies and life-histories. A number of journals regularly publish brief case-reports.

There appears to have been a recent revival of interest in the case-study method in education. This is partly a reaction to the inadequacies of the so-called 'positivist' approach, and partly a contribution to the growing concern with evaluation research, which has revealed the need for more detailed examination of the ways in which educational and other social processes operate.

Six basic rules for the preparation of psychological case-studies are listed together with ten procedural steps for the conduct of a quasi-judicial inquiry.

There is no standard format for writing up psychological case-studies, but a comprehensive ideal framework is provided which can be adapted according to purpose and circumstances.

Some further points of general interest concern the following: the way case-studies arise, record-keeping, the Subject's point of view, the relationship between commonsense and scientific approaches to cases, personality appraisal, abstraction and generalization, technicalities in physical and mental health, comparative judgments, and logical analysis. These topics are taken up in more detail in subsequent chapters.

The quasi-judicial case-study provides a paradigm for the study of personality and adjustment in clinical psychology, social case-work, and other areas of scientific and professional work with individuals. It is not difficult to state the rules that govern the relevance and admissibility of evidence, the credibility of witnesses, the significance of personal disclosures, the significance of personal involvement in the case on the part of informants or the Investigator(s), the significance of documentary and psychometric evidence, experimental evidence, and so on. Such rules of evidence and procedure are modelled on those of judicial inquiries and include those relating to corroboration, circumstantial evidence, and the like—see the references cited earlier.

Ideally, individual case-work should have principles based on a body of 'case-law' accumulated through the rigorous use of the quasi-judicial method applied selectively but systematically and making psychologically significant comparisons and contrasts between individual cases. In reality, all we appear to have is a few detailed case-studies, together with an assortment of brief descriptions or illustrative fragments of cases. We are aware, of course, that the proposal to rely on 'case-law' as the foundation for a 'science' of personality is so radical that its philosophical and methodological implications are difficult to appreciate. The issue is taken up in Chapter 11.

CHAPTER TWO

An Educational Framework for the Study of Individual Cases

INTRODUCTION

Case-study methods are used extensively not only in clinical psychology, social work, and lay counselling but also in business studies and social administration—see Armistead (1984), Campbell (1984), Chilver (1984), Corey (1982), Honey (1980), Lee (1983), and Leenders and Erskine (1973). Much of the published literature is concerned with specific techniques—contingency management, social skills, decision-making, psychotherapy, leadership, administrative and organizational techniques. My argument, however, is that the case-study method is a basic form of scientific inquiry that underpins effective professional practice especially in relation to human problems. It is this basic theory or approach that concerns us throughout this book.

Case-studies are carried out for a number of reasons. Probably the commonest reason is that a particular issue has arisen which presents a practical problem and requires remedial action, e.g. a child refuses school, a girl is raped, a politician behaves in a 'scandalous' way, a business is not making enough profit or faces a damaging strike. Given enough incidents (cases) of broadly the same type, Investigators classify and generalize. They begin to see that circumstances and actions fall into certain kinds of patterns. Classification and generalization make for routine management in business, medicine, administration, and other areas. Such conceptualization, a sort of routinization of thinking, is quite natural and spontaneous. Indeed, one has to be careful not to classify and generalize too readily.

Another common reason for carrying out case-studies is to illustrate, demonstrate, or test a theory. Many psychoanalytic case-studies fulfil the first or the second of these three functions. Many of the brief case-studies found in the technical literature are similar in this respect. The third function, that of testing a theory, is exhibited in case-studies which are argued from different points of view (theoretical perspectives). In a sense every case-study should fulfil this third function by ruling out those theories which fail to account for the available evidence. Unfortunately, the term 'theory' is rather vague, since theories can vary widely in level of abstractness and scope of subject-matter. Moreover, abstract and general theories in psychology are usually insufficiently detailed to permit falsification on the basis of an individual case, and contribute little to the task of analysing and interpreting the case-materials.

Ideally, a case-study attempts to integrate theory and practice by applying general concepts and knowledge to a particular situation in the real world. Case-studies used in education and training have a number of potential benefits. They encourage students to practise what has been preached to them. They provide a safe environment for asking questions and exercising judgment. They increase the scope of students' relevant experience. They provide a realistic and detailed representation of the real world of human problems that students are likely to encounter in professional practice. They demonstrate the limitations of textbook generalizations and procedures when applied to an individual case in a context of special circumstances—where issues are not clearly delineated, where information is incomplete and of uneven quality, where time is short, where options are limited and opinions divided.

Many psychological and social case-studies are, initially at least, confused and incomplete. They contain assertions of doubtful validity, statements from informants of uncertain credibility, unspoken assumptions, and irrelevant matters. A considerable amount of time and effort is required even to clarify what the case is about and to organize a coherent account of the problem and how it came into existence. Education and training are needed to discourage students from making superficial appraisals and hasty judgments based on insufficient evidence and inadequate reasoning. Psychological case-studies are basically exercises in solving human problems. Education and training can improve students' ability to solve such problems, bearing in mind that practical measures are needed to implement solutions (understanding is not sufficient in itself). In some instances, quantitative data are available of the sort that enable a formal decision procedure to be followed in arriving at recommendations for action. In other instances, however, quantitative data are not available and decisions have to be arrived at by informal methods of rational argument based, for example, on the Investigators' preferences among the various 'scenarios' they can envisage.

A major aim of this book is to bridge the gap between (a) normal adult levels of understanding and dealing with others and (b) scientific and professional levels. As a consequence we shall be dealing mainly with a normal range of individuals in a normal range of situations. These 'normal' ranges, however, are surprisingly wide.

When the case or situation under investigation falls outside the normal range of experience it is necessary to rely on expert knowledge and skill. Thus, for example, psychosis, physical illness, and psychopathy fall some way outside the normal range of understanding and management. To understand and manage them well, expert knowledge and technical methods are obviously required.

The problem is to describe, analyse, and explain the facts of the case as fully as one needs to in order to arrive at objective conclusions. These conclusions may take the form of inferences, decisions, recommendations, or predictions. Conclusions are objective to the extent that other competent observers accept the available evidence and impose the same pattern of meaning, i.e. they put the same construction on the evidence.

The events we are interested in take place in the 'real world' as opposed to the artificial world of experimentation or simulation. They deal with this particular person behaving in relation to this particular situation. Although professional workers have to deal with cases as they occur, with all the real constraints of time, circumstances, and limitations of resources, the student learning case-method or the teacher using cases for instructional purposes can often deal with cases which are documented and static. That is to say, the evidence is written into the case-report, and the information has been fixed and finalized. It is possible of course to compose fictional or semi-fictional accounts of cases falling within a given area of interest—divorce, bereavement, or truanting, for example, which fulfil an educational function.

A teacher may choose to present a case by instalments, or to present one facet of a case at a time. This simplifies the material and makes it more manageable for the purposes of exposition or discussion. It also enables the teacher to demonstrate the complexity and uncertainty of events in the case as they unfold in time, and spread their effects in the surrounding circumstances.

A case-study or situation-analysis can consist of a short description of a person with certain attributes acting in a given set of circumstances which have arisen as a consequence of certain prior events. This general description implies a human problem which calls for a solution, or a set of possible outcomes which need to be taken into account before taking action. Consider the following case.

CASE A

A has been demoted and moved to a post in a firm where he can no longer be a major cause of discontent to the people he used to work with. Economic recession has provided management with a convenient opportunity to make A redundant, but only on terms which will lead to a substantial drop in living standards for A. A has never accepted the blame for the discontent which led to his redeployment and tends to blame others, and to feel that the management have misunderstood him. A is unmarried, has no close friends, and no longer maintains contact with his family. He is anxious about his future and cannot find an acceptable way of coping with this circumstances.

The most obvious objection to such a short description is that it does not contain enough information to justify any inferences or recommendations. Nevertheless, given that the information it contains is correct, it does enable the student, with the help of the teacher, to consider what further information would be helpful. For example, 'Does A have a history of poor interpersonal relationships?' 'What is the state of his physical and mental health?' 'How old is he?' 'What education, experience, and training has he had?' 'What financial and personal assets does he have?' These questions and many others come to mind immediately, and this illustrates the fact that common sense and ordinary language provide us with shared frames of reference for dealing with issues like this which fall within the normal range of adult experience. Such questions also illustrate that information about persons and situations tends to be organized. As the system of ideas grows, it forms internal links and groupings and stimulates the Investigator to seek further information to fill gaps, explore possibilities, eliminate inconsistencies, and reach secure conclusions and confident decisions.

At the other extreme a case-study or situation-analysis could fill a book. Consider, for example, any full-length account of a battle, a scientific discovery, a disaster, each involving a central character. Even such apparently exhaustive accounts provoke some readers to ask pertinent questions not satisfactorily answered by the information given. The implication is that accounts of cases are very rarely complete. To the extent that they are incomplete, it will not be possible to draw firm conclusions about them. Attached to any inference about a case, therefore, there is a degree of confidence (or, rather, diffidence!) which cannot be quantified in an objective, statistical sense, but can be quantified in the sense of assigning to it a subjective probability. This issue is taken up in detail at a later stage—see Chapter 8.

A full-length case-report normally contains a narrative account of the events of interest, as well as a commentary on those events which puts them into context and interprets them. In addition, a full-length case-report may contain documents (or copies of documents) relevant to the issues raised, transcripts of testimony from the Subject of the study (the main character) and by witnesses (observers or participants) of various sorts. In fact it may contain any sort of material, including pictures and diagrams and appendices, which contributes to the evidence used to support the inferences, decisions, and recommendations arrived at by the Investigator(s).

Brief case-studies can be used as classroom exercises. For example, the studies might investigate the role relationships of teacher and student, perhaps in two or more different settings. The problem of role-relationships is important in many case-studies, since any misunderstanding about who is doing what, and why, is likely to lead to confusion and loss of information.

It is also possible to 'role-play' aspects of a case-study given that the characters involved—the 'Subject', the 'informants', the other players—are provided with a broad outline of the situation. Within this broad outline, students can then play their own parts in their own way, making up a story as they go along. The Investigator's role is to make sense of the material thus presented and to exercise skills in handling human problems.

The role-play sessions need to be tape-recorded, otherwise it is difficult to check for accuracy of recall.

Brief case-studies can be found in political profiles, school files, and business records. Full-length case-studies can be found in biographies, histories, and judicial inquiries. Case-studies of intermediate length can be found mainly in the records of people working in a professional or applied capacity in one or another area of human behaviour—social work, clinical psychology, psychiatry, anthropology, criminology, politics, business, education, industrial and domestic accidents, community relationships, and so on.

Our approach deals with the description and analysis of cases and situations of short to medium length, mainly because these sorts of cases lend themselves to the instructional aims of this book. Readers, however, are encouraged to read other sorts of case report; guidance for further reading is given throughout this book.

Teachers and students will find it instructive to make a précis of a full-length report to see the extent to which they agree (or disagree!) on the key features of the case. In fact, this sort of structural analysis is one of the keys to case-method. Another instructive exercise is to serialize a full-length case; at the end of each instalment, students must arrive at provisional interpretations and make the appropriate recommendations and predictions. In this way students gain insight into the complexities and uncertainties associated with individual lives, and learn something about the factors governing the way they, as Investigators, think about people in situations. They become more aware of their assumptions, biases, and implicit rules of inference.

It follows from what I have been saying that case-materials can be found in diverse areas of interest. It is to be expected therefore that each area of interest will have its own expectations and standards as to what constitutes a satisfactory case-study. It is almost inevitable that case-studies will not be completely exhaustive, truthful, or valid. They will be, at best, approximations to knowledge. But this in no way detracts from their scientific value, since any empirical investigation in science is bound to be limited in scope and subject to the errors associated with current theory and the limitations of current technology. Nevertheless, even though a case-study is an approximation to knowledge, it should, by scientific standards of evaluation, contain sufficient relevant evidence, adequately corroborated, to support the inferences and recommendations made in the case-report. In other words, it should be internally logical and coherent and correctly represent the real facts in so far as they can be ascertained.

In addition to scientifically conducted case-studies there are fictional case-studies. These constitute an art form—novels, short stories, films, plays, and so on. They are to be judged mainly on aesthetic, and possibly moral, grounds, rather than on the grounds of scientific validity. However, fictional case-material can be used for instructional purposes; or fictional material may be introduced into a real-life case-study, provided the teacher is careful to separate out the two sorts of data. This can be done using prefatory remarks such as 'What might happen if. . .' or 'Let us suppose that. . .'. The instructional objective here is to help students to think constructively about cases rather than be constrained by their assumptions and the available evidence.

Between the studiously factual case-study and the deliberate fictional account there lies a wide grey area of erroneous and incomplete case-studies in which fiction masquerades as fact, and where the Investigator cannot distinguish between the two.

There are certain kinds of fictional elements which are entirely unobjectionable—those relating to names, places, and other facts in published reports, which would identify the persons concerned and possibly cause embarrassment. All the case-material contained in this book has been *depersonalized*. That is to say, all the evidence which would enable the actual people and circumstances to be identified has been changed in ways that do not affect the analysis of the case for instructional purposes, but do maintain anonymity. This is standard practice in published reports of psychological case-studies and in case-reports and situation-analyses in other areas where privacy must be respected. As we shall see, however, there are disadvantages to this procedure.

The kinds of fictional elements which must be guarded against in case-studies are those which arise from incompetence or deliberate faking designed to mislead or to make up for lack of evidence. This book is mainly concerned with the methods by means of which case-reports can be compiled so as to minimize error and achieve as close an approximation as possible to the real facts of the case (within the acknowledged limitations set by the aims of the study and the resources made available).

Certain kinds of case-study include, as part of their contents, a variety of materials—the results of tests or routine interviews, log-books, balance sheets, school reports. These sorts of data may require technical expertise in their collection and interpretation—interpreting neurological data for example, or responses to a personality inventory. Although occasional reference will be made to technical concepts and methods relevant to a case-study, all the cases used to illustrate the case-study method in this book will refer only to information within the normal range of adult experience. Teachers who are interested in technical methods of assessment and investigation can follow up references to the technical literature or use their own case-materials to enlarge upon the technical features of cases.

LEARNING AND TEACHING FROM CASE-STUDIES

Case-materials can be approached in different ways, depending upon educational objectives. One typical approach is to identify a real person (with certain attributes) in a real situation (with particular circumstances); then a number of people (students or professionals) explore the case from different perspectives, thus revealing its many different facets. Thus, for example, a case of marital disharmony can be examined from several points of view—legal, psychological, financial, social, moral, medical, sociological. These multiple perspectives lead to a much deeper understanding of the complexities, interconnections, and ramifications of individual cases, and provide firmer support for inferences and recommendations.

Another typical approach, already referred to, is to present a complete case by instalments. At the close of each instalment, students make predictions about the next instalment. Their predictions have to be justified by reference to their assumptions, expectations, and inferences, formed on the basis of the available evidence. The subsequent instalment may then refute some or all of their predictions. Students must then work out why their predictions have not been borne out, and learn from their mistakes. The advantage of this approach to training is that the students' decisions and recommendations do not affect the actual individual. Of course, knowledge of this fact may detract somewhat from the realism of the case-study approach to training, in that students fail to take account of the real risks and conditions that affect decision-making in real-life situations. Cases dealt with by instalments can be used to demonstrate overconfidence, as in Oskamp (1982).

This point is worth emphasizing. Simulation techniques in training are intended to help students learn the right lessons at less risk and less expense and in less time than would be the case if real-life training situations were used. However, simulated conditions, by definition, can never match the real situation. Hence there is some risk that students may learn the wrong lessons, e.g. regarding professional standards of conduct.

A third approach could be called 'discovery learning'. Students are given a small amount of information about a complete case. They then ask a question about the case, giving their reasons for asking that question rather than another. The answer to that question adds to the information already available. Students then ask another question. They can take turns, or they can discuss between themselves what question they want answered, and why.

This approach makes clear the students' implicit assumptions, beliefs, values, expectations, and modes of reasoning. It illustrates the important point that case-studies and situation-analyses are to a large extent social constructions of reality and can be looked at from different perspectives. This can be emphasized by the teacher by explaining why this particular case rather than another has been selected for analysis, why these particular issues rather than others are being dealt with, and why they are being dealt with in a particular way. The point is that the case-report is a 'representation' of reality like a map is a representation of territory. Case-reports, like maps, can take various forms; they can be more, or less, accurate, and more, or less, useful as guides to action. Case-reports, like maps, are drawn up for a purpose, and that purpose should be reflected in the content and organization of the report, like a map is designed for showing bus routes or finding streets.

Students, as we have seen, can be taught from a fixed body of case-materials. They can take on real-life case-studies themselves as course-work exercises. They can be given the benefit of multiple perspectives on the same case. Different teachers prefer different classroom and field techniques, e.g. individual or group work, standardized or non-standardized procedures, written or oral presentations, real-life or simulated cases.

Real-life case-studies carried out as course-work by students working as individuals or in small groups make certain demands on students' intelligence, experience, and social skills. For example, they need to be able to approach suitable candidates, explain the nature of the exercise, and persuade someone to volunteer to serve as a Subject. They then need to ask relevant questions, to listen, and to interpret what they are told. They must be able to engage, if necessary, in mutually satisfying disclosures, and to manage any emotional reactions that the case-relationship engenders. They need to disengage from the relationship on completion of the exercise without adversely affecting the Subject.

Alternatively, students may be formally assigned to a case as part of their placement at a professional or voluntary agency. These formally assigned cases need to be more fully supervised by the instructor. In particular, those aspects of the case concerned with reaching decisions and making recommendations need to be formally approved.

Students' case-reports can be assessed for examination purposes, with marks awarded according to how well the report measures up to the standards required. Previously unseen case-material presented for the purposes of written or oral examination must usually be fairly brief because of the time required to read and digest the information and to write an adequate commentary. Examination questions on case methodology can be set in the usual ways.

Teachers should not neglect that aspect of training in case-study method that has to do with presenting cases to an audience, as in a case-conference or before a tribunal, court, committee, or board of directors. It is said that teaching is a very effective form of learning. Hence class presentations of students' case-studies are useful if time-consuming learning experiences, apart from their value as training exercises in communication.

It is important to bear in mind the distinction between real cases and classroom or demonstration cases. Real cases have to be dealt with in real time and in relation to real resources and real outcomes; hence there are limits to the use of real cases for educational purposes.

The two most obvious possibilities are as follows. First, to use volunteer Subjects with real but relatively simple problems of adjustment, so that no unacceptable damage occurs if a student fails to handle the case adequately. Even here, however, access to a supervisor is desirable, and students should have substantial prior guidance on methodology, and preferably some training in social skills and counselling. The second possibility is to use a team approach, i.e. a small group of students under the supervision of an instructor. Here the instructor encourages and guides the students in the investigation of a real and important case but prevents errors of omission and commission by intervening whenever necessary.

A NOTE ON CURRICULUM DEVELOPMENT

The contents and organization of courses in case-study method will naturally vary from one area of professional or scientific interest to another. For our present purpose, all we need consider is the broad outline of the curriculum, stated in terms of its contents and organization. The contents of the curriculum fall into four broad categories: concepts, methods, findings, and applications. The organization of the curriculum comprises four main phases: (i) introduction and outline of the course (i.e. the syllabus, aims, and objectives); (ii) a sequence of instructional activities (lectures, audiovisual presentations, discussions, reading, practical work, report-writing, assessment) dealing with various aspects of the case-study; (iii) supervised field exercises with real cases, either normal volunteers or people referred to the agency where students have formal placement; (iv) final assessment.

The basic concepts in case-studies and situation-analyses are to be found in the terms commonly used to describe and explain the phenomena of interest. The most obvious basic concept is that of personal identity—a notion which includes, among other things, a person's name, location, and physical appearance. The next most obvious concept is that of situation—this usually comprises statements about the circumstances surrounding the individual and the problem(s) that he or she faces. The concept of life-history is familiar, the concept of 'future life prospects' less so. The notions used to describe the person and his or her relationships with the environment can be divided conveniently into three areas: first, those having to do with the internal aspects of personality—traits, abilities, values, and so on; second, those having to do with the external aspects of personality—health, routine activities, material circumstances, and the like; third, those having to do with social and other aspects of personality—social role, family and friendships, social relationships, and moral status.

Even this brief listing of some of the more important and familiar concepts used in the description and analysis of individual cases is sufficient to indicate the complex and wide-ranging character of the phenomena under consideration.

When we consider the role of methods in the curriculum we see that there are three sorts: those needed to collect the data (evidence); those needed to interpret the evidence; and those needed to use these results in practical ways.

Training in methods of collecting data means learning what to look for, how to observe, how to ask questions, how to listen, how to distinguish between observation and inference. Where the data are derived from other people (informants), skills in establishing and maintaining good relationships are needed. General knowledge, as well as technical knowledge of the problem under investigation, will help an Investigator to obtain information from various sources, e.g. libraries, case-records, colleagues.

Training in interpreting data means learning to impose a reasonable pattern of meaning on the available evidence; in other words, formulating a cogent argument that reaches an objective conclusion on the basis of the information collected. Inferential methods in the study of individual cases are quite complex and rather different from those used in reasoning about statistical and experimental data. This issue is dealt with at length in Chapter 9.

Turning to the issue of what sorts of findings should be included in the curriculum for a course on case-study methods, it seems there should be two sorts of material: first, the actual case-materials used for illustration and for practical exercises; second, reports of research using case-methods. There is a surprising shortage of published case-studies—partly because of the private and confidential nature of the information, partly because of the absence of an agreed framework for the description and analysis of cases. Most cases are published as single items fulfilling an illustrative or demonstrative function in the context of a survey, a theoretical exposition, an experimental inquiry or a treatment demonstration. We rarely if ever see classes of cases compared and contrasted in an attempt to develop 'case-law' in a given area of interest, such as adjustment to ageing, sexual deviance, or divorce.

The third methodological component in the curriculum has to do with implementing recommendations and testing predictions. This means exercising skills such as advocacy, arbitration, persuasion, behaviour modification, environmental and resource management, counselling, evaluation, and the like, in the various areas of application.

It should be obvious that one cannot deal with all the concepts, methods, findings, and applications of case-methods in a short course of instruction. The most one can do is to introduce them as and when necessary, and to cover a wide range of issues to help students to generalize what they have learned to the new cases they encounter—see Gingerich (1984).

An educational curriculum often contains or rests upon implicit beliefs and values. It is therefore the responsibility of teachers and students to become aware of what might be called the 'hidden' or 'latent' curriculum. Among the more obvious implicit belief/value systems that we shall encounter are those associated with moral judgments, sex roles, professional roles, social and political attitudes. However, the main aim of the curriculum is to cultivate a scientific attitude towards the study of persons in situations. This itself will be regarded as debatable by some teachers and students who may suppose that a scientific attitude necessarily requires a detached, rational view incompatible with sympathetically understanding and managing human problems.

A successful instructional programme should enable students to behave more competently in their attempts to study individual cases. Their performance is the ultimate measure of the success of the programme. Such success will be reflected, in part, in the improved health and well-being of the cases they have dealt with; but such are the complexities and uncertainties of life that the outcome for the client (case) is not a completely valid index of the adequacy of the Investigator's performance.

The behavioural objectives of a course in case-study methods encompass such skills as identifying and clarifying human problems, collecting relevant data, excluding irrelevant and misleading data, engaging in rewarding and productive social relationships with the Subject of the case-study and with the other people involved, understanding the theory and practice of case-studies and situation-analyses, keeping adequate records as the case progresses, thinking constructively (creatively) as well as critically about how the case is to be conceptualized, avoiding premature judgments, formulating an objective conclusion derived from a cogent argument using the best available evidence, communicating the results effectively, predicting outcomes and evaluating one's recommendations, analysing one's own beliefs, values, and working practices.

One of the drawbacks of case-studies is that there is usually no unique solution or interpretation. Individual cases, remember, have a past, a present, and a future, and are nested in interconnected sets of circumstances. Consequently, it is not possible to be absolutely sure of 'what went before', 'what is', or 'what will happen'. Nor is it possible to work out all the consequences of implementing a recommendation. These drawbacks can be turned to advantage if students can be made aware of them, because they are then fore-armed, as it were, against the dangers of oversimplification and hasty judgment.

A case-study is essentially an exercise in problem-solving, where the problem is to enable a person in a difficult situation to cope with it in the most effective way. By definition, almost, a case-study deals with a human problem which is not susceptible to routine solution. The student therefore must learn to deal with the uncertainty inherent in case-studies.

SOLVING THE CASE-STUDY PROBLEM: A PLAY IN SIX ACTS
(including Case B)

An investigation into a psychological case is usually an attempt to understand and deal with a human problem. As in many other areas of scientific endeavour, problems do not present themselves ready-made. Instead they have to be identified, clarified, and properly formulated by an interested and competent Investigator.

Although human problems vary enormously, it is possible to develop general-purpose procedures or guidelines which are helpful in finding solutions. There is, in fact, a considerable psychological literature on problem-solving. It deals, for example, with cognitive processes, artificial intelligence, decision-making, heuristics and biases, creativity, logic, imagery, reasoning, memory, and so on. It is not necessary to deal directly or in detail with any of these areas. We shall make occasional reference to them because they provide the academic background of our approach to understanding and dealing with human problems.

The stages in solving a human problem by means of a case-study can be thought of as a play with six acts, as follows:

Act One: what is the problem?

The problem has to be located and identified. This is not as obvious as it seems, because the real problem is sometimes misconceived or missed altogether. Sometimes, too, there are barriers to close inquiry because of vested interests on the part of the people concerned. Hence the moral obligation to 'declare an interest' in any public enterprise from which one may benefit or stand to lose. Problems may be presented so as to deflect interest from the real issues.

In some respects, the way the case-problem is formulated is the most important step in the whole exercise because it tends to determine the subsequent course of events. Thus an important skill in conducting a case-study is that of finding out what the 'real' issues are—that is, of asking the 'right' questions. Unfortunately, this step cannot be taken without some preliminary examination of the problem as initially presented: What 'seems' to be the problem? Whose problem is it? When and how did it arise? And in what context? Questions like these help to inhibit the natural tendency to formulate a problem too quickly and uncritically, and so possibly misdirect the subsequent investigation.

Act Two: what are the issues?

No substantial progress can be made until a problem (or a set of related problems) has been formulated. Hence, the information generated by the preliminary examination must be collected, checked and cross-checked, 'weighed', and interpreted. Because of the paucity and unreliability of the evidence at this stage, the Investigator must be prepared at any subsequent stage of the case-study to recognize that he or she is on the wrong track or has raised the wrong issues.

Before continuing, we need to clarify two important concepts: 'question' and 'issue'. A question is simply an interrogative expression used in an examination or inquiry and designed to elicit answers or relevant information. An issue, in jurisprudence, is a matter that is in dispute—a point that one is trying to settle one way or another, or a point on which the answer to a question depends. Thus, one of the questions we thought of immediately after reading the case of A, 'Does he have a history of poor social relationships?', is an interrogative expression which, instrumentally, leads us to search for certain kinds of information. The 'issue' or 'point' to be settled is whether case A did or did not have a history of poor social relationships. The advantage of spelling out the points at issue is that they help us to arrive at decisions about a case. In other words, the question directs us towards relevant evidence which (if we can find it!) helps settle the point at issue. Notice that it may be necessary to rephrase the question to define the real point at issue, e.g. 'Did he have poor relationships with people in his previous job?' The point at issue being whether there is any *independent* evidence that A had a relevant history of poor social relationships.

The second step, therefore, is to reconsider the nature of the problem, to define its 'terms of reference' as it were, bearing in mind that this may be a recursive process because it may not be immediately obvious what the 'real' problem is. Superficial problems may be no more than minor symptoms of a deeper malaise. Treating the symptoms may not affect the underlying problem; treating an underlying problem will not necessarily relieve particular symptoms.

Act Three: human problems are socially constructed, not 'given'

There are advantages in defining a human problem as a discrepancy between an actual state of affairs and a desired state of affairs, between 'What is' and 'What ought to be', or between performance and aspiration. Frequently, but by no means always, a 'problem' is an unpleasant frustrating situation of more than brief duration. It has 'demand characteristics' that lead the individual to react in ways intended to relieve the unpleasantness and end the frustration. In such circumstances the individual's preoccupation is with eliminating the negative features of the situation. For example, one may seek a solution to a marital problem through separation or divorce, leave home to avoid family discord, resort to prostitutes to relieve sexual tension. Such preoccupation with the negative aspects of an undesired state of affairs may lead the individual to neglect its positive aspects, and to neglect the negative aspects of the proposed solution.

There are advantages in defining 'human problems' broadly, as we have indicated, so as to refer to the discrepancy between an undesired and contrasting desired state of affairs. Using this definition it is easier to identify different facets of the problem and to propose appropriate solutions. It is also easier to re-examine and perhaps reformulate the problem, and to put the particular problem into a wider perspective. Another advantage of defining 'human problems' broadly is that it opens up a wider range of cases for students to investigate—their own problems for example in classroom discussions, other people's problems in simple case-study exercises.

The third act in the sequence leading to a solution to a human problem, therefore, is to analyse the nature of the discrepancy between the situation as it is and its more desirable counterpart. This more desirable counterpart is the situation that would result from finding a solution, i.e. resolving the discrepancy. For example, the discrepancy may present itself to an Investigator or to the Subject, B, as follows.

Case B   Case B has spent a year working for a qualification. He finds that he is no longer greatly interested in studying or working in this area. He would like to do something different.

The first thing to notice is that the 'problem' is only partly 'out there' in the environment 'presenting itself' to the Subject (and to the Investigator). It is also partly a product of the Subject's own thoughts, feelings, and desires. Technically speaking, the 'problem' is socially constructed by the people involved, not presented independently to them by an external reality. It is a product of how the Investigator and Case B himself construes the situation. Given this insight, it is easy to see that human problems can be redefined, even solved or 'dissolved', by dealing not with external circumstances but with the Subject's psychological state.

This third act, then, is essentially exploratory. It is important not to define or finalize the problem until a thorough examination of it has been carried out. In Case B, above, the examination would inquire into the motives and circumstances which led the individual to spend a year working for a qualification. The inquiry would not only look into the sources of dissatisfaction with the course, but also look into the benefits that would be lost if it were discontinued. The individual's beliefs, values, aspirations, and self-concept may have changed as a consequence of his educational and social experiences during the year. There may have been changes in his physical health, his social relationships, or his financial circumstances. Next, the inquiry would look into the positively evaluated future prospect(s) which Subject B uses to contrast with his present negatively evaluated situation. He may think that he would enjoy a different course of study, and prefer a different educational environment. He may want a course that is less difficult or less academic or simply more interesting. He may feel that he has little in common with the people studying and working in that area, and want to be with people who share his interests and outlook. If these contrasting circumstances can be described—they take the form of aspirations, expectations, wishes, fantasies, and so on—then the discrepancies between the negative (undesired) state of affairs and the positive (desired) state of affairs can be identified and made explicit. What normally follows is action designed to get rid of these discrepancies and so solve the problem. See Duckworth (1983) for a training programme in this area.

Act Four: creative versus standard solutions to problems

The fourth act in carrying out a case-study, having identified the 'problem' in the sense of describing and analysing the discrepancies between the negative (undesired) situation and the corresponding positive (desired) situation, is to explore possibilities for reducing these discrepancies. This stage of the inquiry demands as much experience and originality as the Investigator can provide. Experience enters in because the case under investigation may present a familiar problem which can be dealt with in a fairly routine way. For example, a college counsellor dealing with Case B, above, may see a familiar pattern of educational and vocational misdirection, and find an adequate solution by transferring the student to a different course within the college. Experience, however, has its dangers in that it may incline an Investigator to resort to habitual ways of thinking and acting, and prevent him or her from exploring a new or better solution for a particular case.

Another aspect of this issue is that in certain areas of professional work with people—social work, for example, or educational guidance—there may be only a limited number of solutions and courses of action open to the Investigator. In such circumstances the Investigator might feel that it is worthless to carry out a detailed case-study when a decision can be reached on the basis of just a few key items of information, e.g. physical and mental health, age, type of offence.

The alternative to such routine or standard forms of treatment for cases is to compare the standard solution with a range of alternative or partial solutions, even if such solutions are presently outside the normal range of actions or require resources or conditions not presently available. Such a move is essential if progress towards a solution is to be made or if there are to be improvements in the sorts of services provided.

The process of exploring the nature of a problem and of generating possible solutions is called 'creative thinking'. In recent years creative thinking has been studied in its own right as a psychological process. All we need to know at this point is that ideas tend to emerge in order of originality, i.e. the obvious solutions are thought of early, whereas the more ingenious solutions tend to come later, and that there are ways of increasing the output of creative ideas.

The creative process in solving human problems is best kept separate from the process of critically evaluating the utility of the ideas generated. But when no more original ideas are forthcoming it is necessary to sort them out according to their likelihood of success—success in terms of moving closer to a solution or of reducing or eliminating the discrepancies between the way things are and the way we would like them to be.

When the problem is being identified and clarified, ingenuity and experience are needed in order to diagnose what is wrong, for the simple reason that things are not always what they seem, and difficult problems, by definition, have non-obvious solutions.

Act Five: taking the consequences

The fifth act in the case-study play, having arranged the proposed remedial actions in order of likelihood of success, is to work out in more detail the consequences of these courses of action. Consequences will be of two sorts: shorter-term and longer-term. If many possible courses of action are possible, it may be necessary to work with a short list of the more promising ones. However, it is only after the likely consequences of action have been worked out that a more considered judgment can be made about the relative desirability of the proposed courses of action. Recommendations which did not look particularly promising in the initial stages of the investigation may have to be reconsidered; recommendations which looked obvious may have to be abandoned.

Problem-solving is to some extent a recursive process, in the sense that the investigation proceeds on the basis of an initial assessment of the available information; but subsequent findings and speculations may bring the investigation back to a new starting point. This process may be repeated several times. Also, it would not be unusual to find a 'solution' to a case proved wrong long after the event. This is unlike the situation in a British court of law where the issues are fixed at the outset (admittedly after prolonged pre-court inquiries) and cannot be changed.

Predicting outcomes for particular courses of action can be difficult and uncertain. To begin with, events have 'knock-on' effects which move forward in time and spread out well beyond the immediate problem area. It is impossible in principle to forecast all the possible consequences of a particular course of action. In relation to case-studies, as in law, one should be held responsible only for the foreseeable consequences of one's actions. The aim of the exercise, however, is to look ahead as far as one possibly can. For example, even a simple action like taking a holiday has possible negative consequences—accidents whilst travelling, loss of luggage, break-in of the unattended home, delay in communication over urgent business or family matters, less money available for alternative use, and so on. Most people take such hazards in their stride and make arrangements to minimize the risks, which are thought to be more than outweighed by the positive consequences—relief from family and work pressures, enjoyment of leisure and cultural interests, enriched experience, and so on.

The predicted outcomes and 'knock-on' effects of actions taken to deal with an individual case are not all equally likely (consider the costs of insuring against different contingencies). Nor are they equally beneficial or detrimental if they occur. The problem of deciding whether or not to take a given course of action therefore is that of weighing the probability of one outcome with its attendant advantages and disadvantages against that of another outcome.

Act Six: making the best decision

The sixth act, therefore, is to deal with these possibilities systematically. Each possible course of action will seem to have certain advantages and disadvantages, depending upon circumstances, as indicated by the anticipated consequences. These foreseeable consequences have positive ($+$) or negative ($-$) values of a certain magnitude (although the magnitudes may be difficult or impossible to quantify). Also, each possible outcome (or circumstance) has a greater or lesser likelihood of occurrence (although, again, it may be difficult or impossible to quantify the degree of likelihood). In the simplest case an Investigator lists the pros ($+$) and cons ($-$) of each possible course of action (including taking no action) and decides whether an outcome is or is not likely to occur. There is obviously little point in choosing a course of action if the given outcome is unlikely (no matter how advantageous the associated consequences); so one must find a rational way of combining the risks and the pay-offs and choosing the 'best bet', for example, by spreading the risks or by minimizing the risk of serious disadvantage.

In more complicated cases, the Investigator needs to work out and compare several possible sequences of outcomes, because the final outcome depends on which of many possible sequences of events happens to occur. Out of such comparisons between different possible outcome sequences, an Investigator usually opts for the one which best combines probability of occurrence with highest benefits and least cost or disadvantage—see Chapter 8 for further details.

COMMUNICATING AND TEACHING

The business of people communicating with people starts from the moment the case is first raised and is completed only when there is no longer any need to talk or write about it. In the simplest kind of case-study, excluding self-studies, there is one Investigator and one informant—the Subject of the study. These two people need to communicate with each other in various ways—by asking questions, giving answers, by persuading, instructing, explaining, promising, and so on. In more complex case-studies there may be several Investigators and possibly more than one Subject, apart from various informants, advisors, service providers, and other interested parties. These people need to share a common pool of information and a common understanding of why and how the case-study is being carried out. For research purposes? For the Education Authority or Social Services? By a voluntary agency following the Subject's request for help? Using a simple standard interview procedure? Using periodic case-conferences only?

Whatever form the communication takes—formal or informal, written or spoken—there are all sorts of guides to improve its effectiveness. This is not the place to describe how to communicate effectively, since there are many references to this topic—see Ley and Spelman (1967). The form and content of a communication is determined by a number of considerations, such as who is involved, what information is being passed, how it is being transmitted and interpreted, its purpose, and the context in which it occurs.

A great deal of 'information' is exchanged informally by non-verbal means, especially information about affective and motivational states. Such information can profoundly influence the course of a case-study, especially in matters concerned with establishing trust, and counselling. The topic of non-verbal communication, however, is far too large and too well-known to be dealt with here—see Argyle (1975).

Stopping to ask what one is trying to achieve is sensible in moments of quiet reflection but a severe handicap in the actual process of communication. So one needs to have a clear idea of what one is doing and where one is going at any particular stage in the case-study in order to communicate effectively (communication is a two-way process). For example, one might explain a possible course of action to a colleague and to the Subject, but use communications very different in style and content. One might present a case to a class of beginning students or to a class of professionals, but use very different ways of organizing and presenting the material. One might use a case to illustrate a technique of counselling or type of emotional reaction or the value of a service—selecting different aspects of the case and adopting different styles of presentation to suit the particular audience.

Cases used as teaching aids, especially in teaching case-study methods, can be presented in all sorts of different ways depending upon what the instructor wants to achieve, what the students need to practise, the teaching resources, and time available. As we have seen, cases can be presented in instalments, or one facet at a time; fictional elements can be introduced to raise technical problems or to stimulate controversy. Teaching case-study methods to children appears to be an unexplored area of primary and secondary education. I have drawn attention only to those aspects of teaching and learning which are particularly relevant to the psychological study of individual cases.

The greatest difficulty is likely to be in persuading people to devote the necessary time and effort to mastering the details of the case. As in many other areas of life, we are often too ready to accept oversimplified accounts. In complex cases it is virtually impossible to work effectively without the aid of text and diagrams, files and indexes, lists and tables.

A case-study can be reviewed and written up in different ways by different people at different times for different reasons. A useful reference for writing the sort of technical report needed on completion of a case-study is Cooper (1964), see also Tallent (1983) on writing psychological reports and Easton (1982, pp. 184–192) on business case-studies.

Case-studies prepared as training exercises have a few special features. The Subject—the person to be investigated—should be reasonably well-adjusted, unrelated to the Investigator, and able to understand the nature of the exercise in which he or she is taking part. The nature of and the reasons for the exercise should be explained to the Subject, who must freely agree to take part (although some friendly persuasion and reassurance may be necessary). The investigation should be entirely confidential, to the point of altering or eliminating data on personal identity when writing up the report. The Investigator should not become emotionally involved with the Subject but should maintain a neutral scientific (rational, objective) attitude. There need be no 'invasion of privacy' since a volunteer Subject will be prepared to disclose enough personal information to satisfy a practice exercise. Since everyone has problems of adjustment of one sort or another, there should be no difficulty in finding a suitable focus (or main issue) for the investigation. The investigation can, of course, deal with the Subject's life-style, i.e. his or her strategic adaptation to a fairly stable environment, whether congenial or not. There may be some benefit to the Subject from the opportunity to talk with someone who is prepared to listen, to ask relevant questions, and to discuss problems in an informed, dispassionate way.

FURTHER ISSUES OF INTEREST IN EDUCATION AND TRAINING

As we have seen, psychological case-studies can be used to explore a wide range of topics of scientific and professional interest.

Some idea of the 'normal range' of issues in the psychology of personal adjustment that can be investigated by means of the quasi-judicial case-study method, in the context of an academic course, can be obtained by considering the following examples drawn by the author from just one collection of studies: occupational stress and maladjustment; lack of drive and direction; relationships with members of the opposite sex; drug abuse; shyness; educational maladjustment and lack of progress; discontent; life-transitions (to independence, work, new people, university, low income, marriage, parenthood); problems of personal identity and social relationships in late adolescence and early adult life; marital disharmony and divorce; chronic minor deviance; homosexuality; family relationships; social anxiety; mild depression; general insecurity and inadequacy; attention-seeking and dependency; chronic mild pain; aggressiveness; religious conversion; social eccentricity; underachievement; racial and religious prejudice; adjustment to nursing training; multiple losses and stresses; ambivalence.

Case-studies carried out as class exercises are handled differently from case-studies carried out in professional practice. Furthermore, it may be impossible or inappropriate for students to deal with certain kinds of case even with volunteer Subjects.

One of their important advantages is that they enable the teacher to demonstrate the many heuristics and biases in social judgment—see Kahneman *et al.* (1982), Nisbett and Ross (1980), and Chapter 10. Consider, for example, the phenomenon of hindsight. The occurrence of a later event—a scientific achievement, a suicide, a road accident—sometimes makes us feel that *it could have been predicted* on the basis of information available earlier—the scientist's abilities and progress, the deceased individual's state of mind, the driver's habits. Hence, when we are presented with a complete case, as in a class exercise, it usually gives the impression of being coherent— the actions and circumstancs seem consistent and the events in the story seem to follow one another in a logical way. Part of the reason for this is that individual differences in behaviour are wide. We learn to accept that stories about people can take many forms and that outcomes may differ widely even for relatively similar initial conditions. Given normal ability and experience in making sense of human behaviour, therefore, we can usually accept the feasibility of a reasonable account. Our experience with fiction and journalism, as well as our scientific education and professional training, enriches our understanding of human nature to the point where few cases that we come across in ordinary life fall outside our range of understanding. The cases that do so are likely to be rather unusual—involving rare forms of psychopathology, social eccentricity, criminal behaviour, or behaviour associated with a very different culture. Such cases may be comprehensible only to a technical expert in the particular field, or may defy understanding altogether.

A useful class exercise can be carried out in which a later event, or the outcome of a case, is not disclosed. Students are asked to anticipate the later stages of the inquiry. For example, in Case D—see Chapter 4—students could be asked to anticipate what happens when Joyce Kingsley's husband loses interest in religion. They then compare their forecasts with the actual outcome as disclosed by White (1975). This should bring home the wide range of outcomes compatible with 'the story so far', and hence the risks of having firm expectations about outcomes. Statistical studies, using multiple regression and causal analysis, can easily demonstrate that the predictability of an outcome, based on information which is only partially and indirectly connected with that outcome, is often poor. There may be many unknown factors at work and many mediating variables. In Figure 2.1 the arrows indicate causal connections, the circles indicate conditions, events or circumstances, the letters indicate different sorts of conditions and their relative temporal position. One is not surprised that the outcome G cannot be predicted accurately from knowledge of A, B, C, and D.

The superiority of statistical over clinical prediction is now well-established. This brings us to a central issue in case-methodology. An individual case-study makes its predictions, if at all, by means of a psychological argument, not by means of a statistical calculation. The cogency of this argument justifies the prediction. The question of what cogency means in the context of arguments in case-studies is taken up in several chapters, and especially in Chapter 9, where a number of case-arguments are dissected for illustration. Chapter 8 deals with decision analysis.

Case-study predictions are not intended to fulfil the same function as predictions made on a statistical basis. Statistical prediction is based on the assumption that, in a given population, each of a certain number of

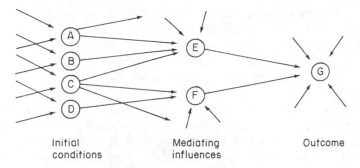

Figure 2.1 The relationships between determinants and outcome in a typical case, shown schematically

characteristics is associated with the likelihood or not of another characteristic (the outcome). Thus, satisfaction with life in old age is associated with, and can be predicted from, such characteristics as marital state, health, housing, and socioeconomic state. These characteristics, incidentally, are no different from the characteristics which would be dealt with routinely in an individual case-study. The statistical procedure is based on a technique which minimizes the errors of prediction (provided new cases are comparable with the cases on which the equations are established). Where it is possible to introduce theoretical considerations into the procedure, for example by giving greater weight to certain factors or by taking account of known causal connections, the predictions can usually be improved. By comparison with case-material, statistical prediction looks crude, oversimplified. Why, then, should it be more effective in prediction? One answer is that the clinical (single-case) Investigator either does not know or cannot carry in his head the main background variables which affect all cases and give rise to what are called 'base-rates', i.e. the extent to which outcomes on average tend to fall into a regular pattern in relation to basic variables, such as age, sex, socioeconomic class, and so on. Instead, he or she may be too much impressed by the singularity and salience of data—the unusual event or circumstance, the striking characteristic, the one-off feature, and so on. These salient factors tend to distract the Investigator from the more mundane common factors previously mentioned. The whole question of heuristics and biases in social judgment as they affect case-studies is taken up in detail in Chapter 10.

Forecasts about outcomes in case-studies are subject to another sort of limitation—the fact that circumstances as well as persons change in essentially unpredictable ways. The attempt to forecast whether a child will be successfully fostered, or whether a period of Army discipline will improve a young man's character, is hindered by the unpredictable multitude of specific factors associated with the particular outcome. These unpredictable factors include: interpersonal relationships, financial circumstances, physical health, and accidents of all kinds. Hence the aim in a case-study is not to predict an actual outcome in all its specific detail, but rather to predict a 'type' of outcome, i.e. a general class of outcomes into which one or another actual outcome will fall. So, for example, one might forecast that a fostered child will, unless there are serious unforeseen circumstances, settle down, get on reasonably well with the foster parents, make satisfactory progress at school, make friends his own age, and so on, through all the criteria of a 'satisfactory' outcome. He would not normally be fostered until this sort of forecast could be officially accepted. Notice that the forecast is couched in general abstract terms—compatible with a wide range of specific outcomes, which an exercise in research evaluation would have to identify more particularly.

We have seen that hindsight is misleading if it leads us to suppose that we could have predicted the observed outcome on the basis of the limited evidence available some time before the event. Hindsight may well lead us to re-examine the evidence and arguments available to us at the time, but it does not, of itself, prove the inadequacy of the earlier assessment. Similarly, we can see that foresight is to some extent attributable to luck, and to our tendency to remember our successes and forget our failures. Foresight is claimed when our forecasts turn out to be correct; when our forecasts are incorrect we explain them away in terms of insufficient data, the complexity of the case, or unexpected circumstances.

Practice in carrying out case-studies and in analysing them systematically and thoroughly is essential if students are to acquire a proper appreciation of the complexities of individual cases and of the rigour of the quasi-judicial method. The greatest dangers in case-studies are superficiality and impatience—an inability or an unwillingness to carry out the work of data-collection, data-analysis, and data-interpretation necessary for an adequate understanding of the case.

The reasons for superficiality and impatience are not hard to find. Apart from sheer professional inadequacy (unsuitability, poor training, and lack of interest), there are factors such as shortage of time and resources. Because there are too many cases chasing too few resources, cases tend to be judged simply in terms of whether one or another of a limited number of 'treatments' is available, e.g. admission to hospital or an old people's home, transfer to a remedial class, making redundant. In such cases, decisions can be arrived at fairly quickly and simply. If a person fails to meet the appropriate criteria the 'treatment' is withheld. Assessment in this case is analogous to medical screening, where a relatively simple test or set of tests is administered to see whether or not a person should receive an available service—tests such as vaginal smear, chest X-ray, and so on. However, a medical screening test is quite different from a full medical examination (although it may form part of such an examination). Similarly, the results of a psychological or social screening test, such as a measure of cognitive dysfunction or an assessment of mobility, may constitute the criterion which determines whether a treatment or a service can be given. But such results form only a small part of a comprehensive case-study, and the significance of such results may well depend upon the context provided by the case-study as a whole.

The tendency, therefore, is to simplify and shorten the assessment, to rely on the routine administration of brief procedures thought to be critical in diagnosis and disposal. Competence in carrying out case-studies should help the student to be more aware of the value, or otherwise, of brief assessment.

In training and in professional practice it is preferable to concentrate initially on organizing the available case-materials. Those items of information that seem to have a bearing on the case should be arranged in a way conducive to closer examination and elaboration. When this has been done the relevance, admissibility, and importance of the materials can be more easily gauged. The credibility of sources too can be tested. The omissions become more obvious, as do the logical implications and the lines of inquiry that need to be followed up.

The methods of organizing and elaborating case-material are listed for convenience in Chapters 3 to 7, and described and discussed in detail under their respective sub-headings. Students should practise applying these methods to the case-materials made available to them. The methods vary in their applicability, depending upon the nature of the case under investigation. It is wise to practise them so that they become 'second nature', i.e. familiar and automatic, thus enabling the student to work efficiently and to concentrate on the more difficult aspects of a case.

Later on, of course, other methods must be used in developing the case-materials and in critically evaluating them so that the most appropriate course of action can be adopted.

All these methods are intended to help the student to carry out better case-studies himself or herself and to evaluate (criticize, improve on) cases presented by other Investigators.

There is usually no difficulty in getting students interested in psychological case-studies when they encounter them for the first time, whether as young persons engaged in higher or further education of a general sort, or as post-professional people specializing in a particular area, such as nursing, social work, or management training. However, one can hardly have a specialized training course based on a series of unrelated case-studies. More usually, education and training are better served by presenting cases all of which are related to one or more common issues or themes, and yet different from each other in what they have to say about those issues and themes.

It is up to the individual instructor to decide which topics to study and which cases to use. Suppose, for example, an instructor wishes students to learn about the adjustment of frail elderly persons to residential care. Then cases could be drawn from different sorts of residential establishment, and the cases themselves selected according to criteria such as physical and mental health, family support, personality characteristics, institutional arrangements, and other factors affecting the quality of life—see Flanagan (1982).

Small-scale, informal surveys of special areas of interest, such as sheltered housing, drug abuse, and business failures, are almost as limited as single-case-studies in respect of statistical inference. This is not a serious flaw unless the Investigators attempt to generalize too widely, or too confidently. However, if their aim is more modest they can explore the similarities and differences between cases in their special area of interest, and then fairly claim to have established at least some interesting and useful 'prototype' cases. Their conclusions, in the form of low-level generalizations, would be firmly tied to empirical data and so fairly robust.

In some circumstances it might be more profitable to carry out a survey *before* conducting the case-studies in order to determine the most interesting or useful boundaries between types of case. Consider, for example, the problem of delay of discharge of patients from hospital for non-medical reasons. There are at least three parties involved—the medical staff, social services, and the patient and his or her family. How are individual cases to be assessed on a multilateral basis? What sort of assessment procedure will cater equally well for all parties? Is it possible, and would it be worthwhile, to identify 'types' of delayed discharge case? (see Eley and Middleton, 1984.)

Case vignettes

It is common practice to present case-studies in the form of brief reports or vignettes (word pictures). The vignette describes the kernel of the case, usually for the purpose of elaborating on a treatment method or introducing a more extended account, as in a case-conference or a journal report. Consider the following examples drawn from exercises in behavioural management.

(i) Mr X is nearly 80 years of age and has been incontinent of urine for four years following prostatectomy. His urinary incontinence is frequent and the smell offensive. He is disoriented for time and external events. Mrs X and the son have been concerned with his condition and want him to see a doctor, which he refuses to do. He is aggressive and will bang his cup or walking-stick to demand attention. Mrs X has become sick and tired of this state of affairs and in desperation has called for help, being unable to look after Mr X any longer.

The case is presented initially at face value in terms of how to persuade Mr X to seek help and of what advice and help to give to Mrs X. A psychological approach to the case, however, calls for a more detailed description, so that the problem(s) can be properly formulated. Obviously, a medical examination is central to the inquiry. What is not so obvious is that Mr X might very well agree to such examination when faced with someone acting in an official capacity—physician, nurse, or social worker—on, say, a routine visit. Mr X's symptoms—his incontinence, aggressiveness, and disorientation—are presented to us very indirectly and inadequately. What is needed is a more detailed account of these symptoms together with their antecedent conditions and consequences. Such an analysis can lead to proposals for behavioural management. A further set of issues are to be found in the family relationships. A chronic situation of this sort must derive in part from interpersonal factors and may be alleviated through family therapy and explicit advice to Mrs X and the son on how to cope.

(ii) Mrs Y is a 75-year-old widow. She is diabetic, and has suffered a mild stroke which has left her with slurred speech. The health visitor was called in about a year after her husband died.

Since that time Mrs Y had contacted the health visitor frequently to complain about all sorts of things, such as sore eyes and a sore back. She complains that she is very lonely and unhappy and she often weeps. Mrs Y is unresponsive to suggestions that she attend a day-centre or any other facility for enjoyment and companionship.

This case is presented at face value in terms of how to persuade Mrs Y to become more outgoing and self-reliant. A psychological approach to the case, however, would inhibit the tendency to jump to conclusions about remedies, and instead call for more details about Mrs Y and her circumstances. A more detailed medical investigation might reveal additional complications. Moreover, although physical ailments may be prominent, they may be aggravated by the social context in which they are set: self-neglect, unresolved grief reaction, iatrogenic disorder, and so on. The vignette makes no mention of the family or any social support system; it does not attempt to analyse the meaning of the various symptoms; it does not examine the possibility that Mrs Y may have led a very restricted social life and may need to be retrained in the basic skills of social interaction and communication.

(iii) Mrs Z is 74 years old and has been a widow for about 20 years. About five years ago she became convinced that she had a health problem. She started to read health magazines and decided that she had a vitamin deficiency. As a result, she took large quantities of vitamins and cut out sugar, carbohydrates, and fat. However, she felt no better, further modified her diet and took more vitamins. By the time Mrs Z came to the attention of the health visitor, her diet was very unbalanced. She was resistant to medical advice, believing that the doctors did not know what they were doing.

This vignette presents the case in terms of how to persuade Mrs Z to return to a balanced diet. A psychological approach, as with the two previous cases, calls for a more detailed description. For example, what about the family and social support system? Is it possible that Mrs Z has become socially isolated over the years and out of touch with the sorts of social influences that tend to inhibit radical departures from normal feeding habits? It might be possible, through a kind of diet-focused counselling, to redirect Mrs Z's thinking along more sensible lines. Of course, Mrs Z's behaviour might be symptomatic of an underlying psychiatric disturbance.

Case vignettes illustrate the extent to which case-studies can be shortened and simplified. However, the omissions may be so numerous or important that the logical structure of the case is distorted or incomplete. Decisions based on such partial accounts are likely to be inadequate.

Multiple case-studies

Normally, multiple case-studies—extended cases—need the cooperation of the organizations to which the Subjects of the case-studies are attached, such as Social Service Departments, industrial firms, HM Forces, churches, political organizations, and the like. Participant observation and other sorts of under-cover work may be used given the usual ethical justification, for example in situations where one suspects abuse of authority, sexual harassment, or other undesirable conditions.

It does not always matter that the evidence made available about a case is inconsistent, since such inconsistency may reveal important features about the social organization or the context within which the case exists. People may have access to different sorts of information; they may have different attitudes and values about what is important or relevant. These give rise to different perspectives on the case in question.

Multiple case-studies obviously require more time and resources than individual case-studies. But, as they are usually carried out for the purposes of research or teaching, the burden is accepted as normal; indeed, such work may be an integral part of the student's training. There might be some advantage in separating the data-collection function from the writing-up function, so as to neutralize the emotional involvement likely to result from the former. If the cases are to be dealt with as members of a set, e.g. occupational stress in nursing, then some effort should be expended in achieving a common framework of description and analysis and a common form of presentation.

The individual cases in a set can be used to demonstrate the same or different facets of the social organization or psychological process under examination, e.g. methods of referral, financial issues, or psychological coping mechanisms. The aim is to explore the ways in which social arrangements, behavioural management, or personal adjustment can be improved. Psychological counselling incorporates various techniques of communicating with and helping the Subject of a case-study and other interested parties—see Egan (1982a,b).

Case-studies are undertaken for specific purposes. Even a case-study carried out 'for fun' or for a class exercise has a purpose—entertainment, instruction, curiosity, or to satisfy an examiner. In professional and scientific work the purpose for which the case-study is carried out plays a fundamental role in determining the nature and scope of the exercise, the way the case-study is written up, the way the recommendations are implemented, and how and to whom the results are communicated.

An interesting feature of the case-study method is that it is reflexive—one can carry out a case-study of a case-study. See Chapter 11 for further discussion of second-order case-studies.

A case-study can be carried out, in effect, on virtually any circumscribed episode or state of affairs—land use (Williams *et al.*, 1983), library search procedure (Fidel, 1984), ageing and the public sector (Decker and Whelan, 1984), the development of language (Klein, 1984), for example. This reinforces the argument that the case-study method is basic to scientific inquiry generally.

WHAT IS TO FOLLOW?

The chapters that follow introduce a variety of concepts and methods for studying individual cases. The account is amply illustrated with case-materials showing how case-studies can be carried out. Teachers may wish to present case-material of their own to bring out the special features of their specialized area of work. The intention is to describe a set of guidelines for investigating and dealing with human problems rather than to provide a cook-book of recipes for instant decisions.

The abstract and general principles embodied in the guidelines for carrying out case-studies are best conveyed to the student and general reader through discussion and analysis of concrete examples. The examples to be described and analysed have been specially selected to show the diversity of cases that can be brought within one procedural framework. I call this procedural framework the 'quasi-judicial method' because it is modelled on ideas derived from jurisprudence (legal science). It is not to be confused with a judicial procedure proper (particularly the adversarial procedure in a British court of law), because it is also a 'scientific' procedure in the sense of using rational argument to interpret empirical evidence—a procedure which is essentially an exercise in problem-solving rather than an exercise in administering the law. Thus the emphasis is on the nature of evidence and argument—see Eggleston (1978), Nokes (1957), Twining and Miers (1976) and Stone (1984)—rather than on legal procedures.

As with the two brief examples already referred to—Case A and Case B—the case-studies to be presented in subsequent chapters will be identified by a letter of the alphabet. It will be necessary to refer back to cases from time to time. The cases are listed in the subject index. When a case is first presented it is considered mainly in order to illustrate just one aspect of the case-method. Each accompanying commentary is far from exhaustive. Each new case is used to illustrate different aspects of the quasi-judicial procedure.

Although each and every case-study presented is a selective account of the information available, it can be regarded, for the purposes of instruction in case-method, as complete. In other words, each case is treated as if all the information available at that stage of the inquiry had been presented. There is, however, nothing to prevent the interested student or teacher from speculating on or assuming, for the sake of argument, additional facts, or from dealing with aspects of the method other than the one the author happens to be dealing with.

SUMMARY AND CONCLUSIONS

It has been appropriate to consider an educational framework for teaching and learning about the case-study method at this early stage (before dealing with the complexities) because the intelligent lay person will already understand, in an intuitive rudimentary way, what the case-study method amounts to. The basic ideas are common knowledge. The framework has two aims: first, to assist the transition from this initial level of understanding to a more scientific and professional level by drawing the attention of readers to some of the wider and deeper issues in the study of individual cases; second, to enable students and teachers to share a common system of concepts and methods.

Consideration is given to the different forms that case-studies can take and to the different ways of using case-materials.

Curriculum development involves identifying the basic concepts needed in a particular area of interest, finding methods that will work effectively in relation to collecting information and managing cases, and evaluating the training programme.

A psychological case-study is an exercise in solving a human problem. Six stages can be identified: locating a problem; identifying the main issue(s); constructing a social context for the case; proposing solutions for the problem(s); working out the implications of proposed solutions; making the best decision and implementing it.

Communication plays a vital role in case-studies and, of course, in teaching. But communication has to be adaptive, it must take account of the different ways in which information and influence operate in social relationships.

Among the further issues in education and training are the following: hindsight and the limits of commonsense reasoning; the uncertainty of outcomes in real-life cases; the relationship between statistical and clinical reasoning; the problem of specifying predictions about cases; the nature of brief assessment; the need for a systematic approach to complex cases; and the use of multiple case-studies.

Attention is drawn to what is to follow in subsequent chapters in the way of selected case-material subjected to close analysis as regards content and logical organization, with a view to demonstrating how psychological case-studies can be carried out.

CHAPTER THREE

Identifying and Clarifying the Problem

CASE-RECORDS: A WARNING

The case-study is, in a sense, the means whereby an interpretation is placed on the case-material. The case-records document this material. Case-records provide valuable documentary evidence, but their objectivity and validity cannot be taken for granted. Moreover, case-records contain a variety of entries and documents compiled by different people for different reasons. Thus, even in a case-study where there is considerable documentary evidence, such evidence may need to be critically examined before being made use of in the case-report.

Case-records compiled by Investigators sharing the same concepts and methods can be expected to be extensively cross-linked and internally consistent. On the other hand, lack of consideration of alternative approaches makes such a case-study vulnerable in the event of external evaluation.

Holbrook (1983) draws attention to an interesting aspect of case-records— namely the possibility that, since they can be used in the managerial interest to supervise performance and set work-loads, there may be a tendency for the contents of case-records to reflect expectations regarding accountability rather than factual data and professional opinion. As Holbrook points out, social facts are not self-evident. The contents of case-records—what Investigators choose to record—are affected by a variety of considerations, such as their relevance, their apparent importance, their likely effectiveness in producing some desired result, e.g. control of the Subject or the implementation of a decision, and their function in enhancing the role and status of the person making the entry.

Entries in written case-records, whether couched in ordinary or technical phraseology, are forms of language and may fulfil the many different functions language is known to have apart from reporting observations or asserting matters of 'fact'. Even 'putting something on record' is a function over and above simply recording it, and omitting something from the record may occur for reasons other than irrelevance and unimportance. We should constantly bear in mind the complexity and subtlety of language as a means of communication and influence. This caution applies equally to the written records of the case and to the oral discourse among Investigators, the Subject, and interested parties, whether during a case-conference or at other times.

Case-records, therefore, are not necessarily simple straightforward accounts, even though their official format and professional aura may inhibit critical examination. They are compiled within an institutional framework, with its professional ideology, and by an individual with a particular kind of interest in the case. An individual contributor may or may not share the prevailing beliefs, values, and attitudes of other contributors or of the wider society. In some instances there may not be any well-defined rules that bear on the particular case. It is not surprising, therefore, that disagreement occurs, even between well-intentioned and well-informed professionals. It is not surprising, either, that the Subject of the case-study and his or her interested parties will sometimes disagree with the official assessment and the consequential decisions and actions. In some case-studies the reactions of the Subject and other participants to provisional results may help to determine the final form and content of the case-report.

Bush (1984) presents a highly critical account of the contents and functions of case-records in one area of professional work with people—namely, child welfare. It seems not unreasonable to suppose that analogous criticisms could be made of case-records in other areas, e.g. social and psychological work with the aged, education, personnel work. He illustrates the inadequacies of case-records and the many ways in which they can frustrate the interests of the client (child) whilst protecting or enhancing the interests of the professional worker. Of particular interest is the tendency of the Investigator to substitute the case-record for the Subject—that is, to base his or her assessment on possibly dated and partial information rather than on current and adequate first-hand evidence. Also of interest is the frequent apparent failure to question the worth of the information in the case-record.

Broadly speaking, Bush found that entries in the case-records fulfilled a number of functions other than those of recording good evidence and rational arguments. Forms of words were used which obscured the fact that failure had occurred, or that there was an unrecognized problem, or that difficulties could not be managed. Obscure and vacuous phraseology, untested speculation, and jargon provide a semblance of reasoning to justify self-serving conclusions and recommendations. Bush concludes that, in the area of child welfare at least, case-records need to be made more accessible, not least to clients, so that greater accountability will foster improvements in professional services.

Psychological work in educational and occupational guidance has been much concerned with systematizing the sorts of information that should be included in a case-study. This is, in a sense, a problem of content analysis. How does one define the scope of the information deemed relevant to the case, and how does one classify it, organize it, and interpret it? If one makes the convenient assumption that human problems in educational and occupational guidance fall into one or another of a limited number of *types* of problem, then it is not too difficult to list the sorts of information that will be likely to have a bearing on those problems. In practice, within a given area of behaviour, most problems do fall into one sort of category or another; and in time administrative conveniences and efficiency give rise to the systematic collection of the sorts of information that have proved to be useful—academic ability, interests, health, motivation, social background, and so on. However, it is unlikely that *all* the information relevant to a case will be available from routine records; and much information kept in routine records may never be used—because the Subjects never become a 'case' or never become a 'serious case' demanding exhaustive inquiry.

A minor point to note is that the *absence* of certain events, circumstances, actions, and so on may be as informative as the presence of other facts in enabling the Investigator to make sense of the Subject's behaviour. This sort of information is often assumed by 'default', or taken for granted, which is to say that if the information were otherwise it would have been provided.

Any critical point in the case-narrative should, methodologically speaking, be anchored to or supported by information in the case-records. These records, in turn, should represent, or enable one to represent, the real world to which the case-narrative refers. In many instances, however, such support is lacking; but this may not matter unduly if the overall structure of the argument is supported by sufficient evidence. The metaphor is that of the 'web' of argument, not the 'chain' of argument.

The time it takes to carry out a case-study, the fallibility of memory, and the confusions arising from disparate points of view about a case, underlie acceptance of the idea that case-records are essential for all but the most trivial of cases.

Case-records take many forms: handwritten observations and comments by Investigators, transcripts of tape-recorded interviews, psychometric measures, profiles and interpretations, routinely available documents, video recordings, progress charts, and so on. The main distinction is between items which purport to present facts or observational data (ignoring for the moment the admissibility, relevance, and reliability of such data) and items which present comments, interpretations, inferences, assertions, or other notions which go beyond the empirical evidence.

Within the broad category of observational data there is a wide variety of sources and types of information, as we have seen. Similarly, within the broad category of comments there is a wide variety of statements, questions, instructions, explanations, riders, forecasts, and the like. Often there is little or no attempt to keep these different categories and varieties of information separate in the case-record. Usually they are entered in sequence at the convenience of the Investigator or clerk. Some of the information may be located in subfiles elsewhere, e.g. medical records, educational and psychometric test results. Obviously, not all the information available will necessarily find its way into a case-report, simply because it is too detailed or too peripheral.

In theory, case-records should be functional in the sense of contributing to the overall purpose of the case-study. But, as we have seen, case-studies may be carried out for all kinds of reasons—and not necessarily for manifest or stated reasons. It follows, therefore, that entries and deposits in the case-records will be determined to some extent by administrative and procedural factors—for example, whose job it is to make up the records, the time available, and the layout of the record sheet. In theory, too, the function of the case-records should be reflected in the use made of them. For example, attendance records may be kept (because it is a rule) but ignored (because the information is trivial or arrives too late to be of use).

Among the many purposes fulfilled by case-records, some are fairly common or routine: (i) *aide memoire* for Investigators; (ii) historical record for Investigators coming to the case at a later stage; (iii) administrative record for managerial control, evaluation, and legal protection; (iv) illustrative material for training purposes; (v) research data.

Ideally, the information contained in the main case-record should enable a new competent Investigator to understand where the case-study is up to when he or she takes it over. The information should be relevant, correct, confirmable, as concise as possible, problem-oriented, and easily retrievable. Retrievability of information is hardly less important than comprehensiveness. The Investigator normally consults the case-records prior to making further inquiries, or in anticipation of a case-conference, or when preparing a case-study or progress report for official or training purposes. In those circumstances, it is helpful if the case-records are referenced or indexed in some way, e.g. by listing, grouping, or numbering, as discussed later.

Where certain kinds of case are a regular occurrence—for example in prisons, hospitals, schools and business organizations—case-records are likely to follow a standard pattern (see Raffel (1979) for a sociological analysis). This is important if different sorts of people need access to the case-record (file) for different reasons, and where different sorts of people have to make entries in the file independently of one another. Obviously, the task of compiling a case-study from a substantial case-record is made easier if the Investigator can easily locate the sorts of information he or she needs.

The focal point of the case-study is the 'problem' or 'issue' that gave rise to the investigation and/or keeps it going. The information in the case-records should justify the Investigator's formulation of the problem. For example, a case formulated as a problem of lack of achievement on the part of a sales representative should be backed up with evidence of comparative sales performance together with relevant personal and situational data.

Since case-records and case-reports can be prepared for different purposes and in different contexts, there is no standard format for recording and reporting cases. Even where some standardization has been introduced for administrative convenience, the framework should be flexible enough to allow the diligent Investigator to record or report what is important even if it does not fit neatly into the standard format.

If the problem has been adequately formulated (diagnosed) and if solutions to the problem have been suggested, then the next step is to collect further evidence to determine the most feasible solution. When this has been done the task is to implement that solution and to follow up the consequences in order to see whether or not the proposed course of action was actually followed and whether or not the problem was solved. In doing all this it is important to keep the case-record up to date, not only on matters to do with the treatment or management of the case, but also on any other matters which have a bearing on the case.

Certain forms of treatment or management are applied because it is expected that they will result in certain kinds of (beneficial) outcome. These expectations should be entered into the case-record as justifications for the action taken (no decisions or recommendations without good reasons). The expectations should be framed in as specific a way as possible so as to permit clear-cut confirmation or refutation of the prediction (prognosis). The general form of the prediction is that the Subject will behave in a certain kind of way provided certain environmental conditions occur. A new cycle of problem-solving may have to be started if the actions taken do not result in the expected outcome.

Even if published case-studies are not numerous, case-records and case-summaries are kept on a tremendous scale in large industrialized societies. There are a variety of professional and sub-professional groups whose job it is to compile such records and summaries—in industry, the Armed Forces, business, government, education, social welfare, the voluntary agencies, the police, medicine, and so on. Assessments and decisions of the utmost importance to the individuals affected are made on the basis of these records and summaries—see Bush (1984), Garfinkel (1974) and Wheeler (1969). As we have seen, there are reasons for supposing that case-work in many areas is not well done—not just because of lack of time or concern (Garfinkel argues that there are 'good' organizational reasons for 'bad' clinical records), but because of lack of understanding of the proper functions of case-records and lack of an effective system of evaluation and public accountability (including direct personal accountability to the client/Subject).

Obviously a prime requisite for improvement in case-work is a system of concepts and methods that goes some way to meet professional and scientific aspirations. Included in such a system will be the beliefs and values which provide the context for case-work, in all its varieties, including the notion of public accountability and client health and welfare.

Professionals concerned with human problems are expected to combine a scientific attitude with an ethical attitude in their approach to and their handling of a particular case. In this respect they are not unlike physicians who, in the public mind, can be trusted to deal with a medical problem scientifically whilst working within a commonly accepted ethical framework. The occasional lapses that are reported simply draw attention to this normal state of affairs. Professional case-work, of whatever variety, carries with it an obligation to behave according to the appropriate social expectations and values.

Case-records or case-materials can exist in several forms, and different forms of the same information may convey different impressions. For example, an informant or a Subject giving a verbal report (in a particular setting and with a variety of expressive accompaniments) may create a different impression from that of a tape-recording of the report played back later (or to another Investigator). A typed transcript of the recording conveys a different impression again. These different forms differ in status with regard to their acceptability as case-records: the Investigator's subjective recall of the informant's testimony is usually less acceptable than the typed manuscript. Of course, only *material* records can be archived.

CASE C

Case C is a greatly oversimplified case-study used to introduce the notion of reorganizing case-material.

After doing well at school, C took a university degree in Geography. However, she had a rather low opinion of herself because of her unattractive appearance and lack of social poise. After working for a number of years as a research assistant, she formed a relationship with a man. This resulted in more social interaction, but the sexual side proved unsatisfactory. The relationship deteriorated and after about two years her partner deserted her for another woman. C was by then nearly forty years old. Her reaction to the desertion was to feel depressed and self-critical; she tried to kill herself. She received in-patient and out-patient psychiatric care (medication and counselling) for some considerable time before being persuaded to return to work. She obtained a research post similar to the one she had previously held. C developed an interest in yoga and meditation, which was then fairly popular, and, whilst maintaining her interest, has not become too absorbed in it.

A crisis developed when her apartment was badly flooded and many of her prized possessions spoiled. She had been settled in her apartment for a long time and her adjustment to her new home was slow. She has come to feel at odds with people even more, and sees no future prospect of rewarding and fulfilling employment. Although she has continued to receive psychological counselling there seems to have been little improvement in her personal adjustment. She is pessimistic and unrealistic in her outlook; she is preoccupied with her own problems and has few friends. She continues to maintain contact with her family, but seems to derive little satisfaction from them.

The reader's first reactions to Case C are likely to be threefold. First, 'Yes I can understand what has been reported, although it is in summary form, and I could summarize it further if necessary.' Second, 'What other information is there that would answer the questions that come immediately to mind?' Third, 'The more I think about the case, the more open-ended it becomes. That is to say, there is not a single well-defined problem with one correct solution, but rather a fuzzy collection of issues that need much more clarification.'

There is clearly little to be gained by trying to find interpretations for C's behaviour, or recommendations about how she might cope more effectively, simply because there is insufficient evidence to go on. How then to proceed? For the moment, let us put to one side questions like, How was the information provided in the first place? Who provided it? When? For what purpose? How was the information presented? And so on. As we shall see, these are crucial questions which need to be asked early in a case-inquiry, but discussion of them is better left to a later chapter. Let us also put to one side the question of what other information is available. This too is a crucial question, and one that recurs throughout a case-inquiry.

Let us see what we can do with the information made available, assuming it to be reasonably accurate. Our aims are to examine the evidence carefully, to reorganize it if necessary, and to restate it as a scientific argument. This last-mentioned aim should be achieved prior to restating the case in a form appropriate to a case-conference or application for resources, where the professional worker has a particular aim and audience in mind.

There are several ways of reorganizing the case-material: indexing, restructuring, sequencing, filing, coordinating and reducing, and connecting.

INDEXING

This means listing, by brief title, the key features of a case, i.e. the essential points in the story or narrative. It makes summarization easy and may suggest key features that are missing. An index for Case C is listed in Table 3.1.

Indexing items of information is useful too for retrieval purposes. Now that case-materials can be stored on a computer, and reproduced by means of a word-processor, it is worth considering a numerical system for coding these items of information. An obvious technique would be to code the items arbitrarily in their natural order of occurrence; or, once some organization of the information had been achieved, they could be grouped and numbered within groups. Grouping can take place at several levels; so we might have a scheme like that in Table 3.2.

Table 3.1

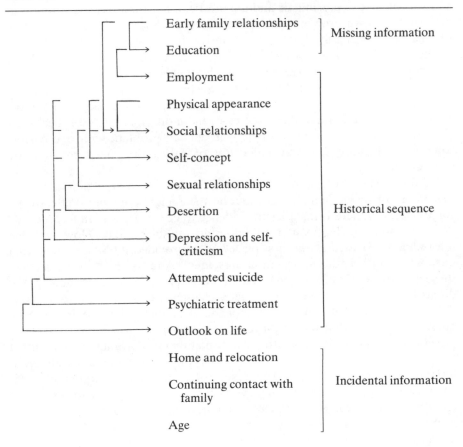

For convenience, many statements are made at a high level of abstraction and generality; they subsume a wide array—or set—of specific statements or items of information. This does not matter provided these specific statements (comprising the lower limits of case-materials) are recorded somewhere—in the interview-tapes or in the original written records, and can be traced if necessary.

There is as yet no acceptable general framework for organizing the information in a case-study. Bromley (1977) suggests one possibility, but makes it clear that case-materials and personality descriptions need to be adapted to their particular purpose.

One of the problems of classifying information describing personality and adjustment is that the same piece of information can be classified in different ways depending upon what significance or meaning one attaches to it. The

Table 3.2

Number	Statement or statement set
1.1.1	Personal characteristics. Appearance. Physically unattractive
1.1.2	Personal characteristics. Appearance. Physically unattractive
1.1.3	Personal characteristics. Appearance. Physically unattractive
1.2.1	Personal characteristics. Social relationships. Lack of social poise
1.2.2	Personal characteristics. Social relationships. Few friends
1.2.3	Personal characteristics. Social relationships.
2.1.1	Life history. Education. Did well at school.
2.1.2	Life history. Education. Graduate in Geography.
2.2.3	Life history. Occupation. Research assistant.
etc.	

sorts of information indexed for Case C above are just a few of the hundreds, thousands, of items of information that find their way into case-studies. We shall see later in this chapter that there is at least one sort of check-list Investigators can use to ensure that they have looked into all or most of the facts that might be relevant.

Another problem is that, as in a subject index in a book, a case-study index may have several entries under one heading. This does not matter unduly because in a brief case the separate items of information are likely to be closely connected, and in an extended case the Investigator can subdivide the entry if necessary, e.g. Education (Primary), Education (Secondary), and cite the appropriate paragraph number(s).

A third problem is that a simple index does not show the connections between the items. Indeed, an alphabetical index would break up even the chronological sequence (assuming the case-material is set out chronologically). This fault can be rectified by using lines and arrows, as above, to indicate the major associations and causal pathways—or rather to indicate the associations and causal connections that are implied in the case-material. As I have indicated, the argument which eventually imposes a coherent pattern of meaning on the case-material comes as the *culmination* of the case-inquiry, not as its opening statement. Successive attempts to make sense of the information provide closer approximations to this final pattern.

In summary, therefore, indexing the initial information provided about a case means making a short list of items (in their order of presentation), subdividing them if necessary, and linking them by lines or arrows to indicate possible associative relationships or causal connections.

STRUCTURING AND RESTRUCTURING

Case-material can be presented initially in very different ways—in spoken or written form, in an arbitrary way, or systematically. Material which is relatively unorganized is easier to structure since it implies no particular initial interpretation. Material which is organized in the sense of being coherent and interpreted, on the other hand, tends to pre-empt alternative interpretations. As we have seen, these initial interpretations, i.e. explanations, are likely to be the more obvious ones; alternative explanations will be more difficult to think up. Reorganizing or restructuring case-material implies the possibility of a different interpretation of, or a different perspective on, the available evidence.

The small amount of material for Case C makes it difficult to restructure. But consider how the case might look if the items were indexed and linked as shown in Table 3.3.

The effect of restructuring in this particular instance is to focus on the main issues affecting C's personal adjustment and to shift concern away from the historical narrative or life-history.

The distinction between a case-study and a life-history is an interesting one. This was dealt with in Chapter 1. Briefly, a case-study is about a person's

Table 3.3

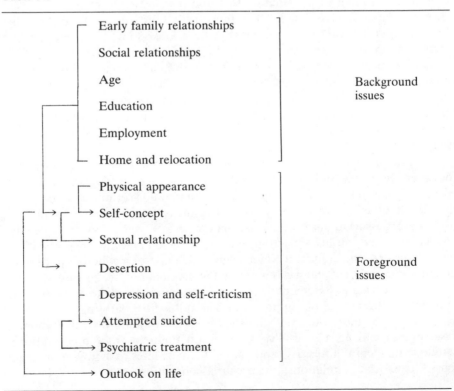

adjustment to a situation over a relatively short space of time. A life-history, by contrast, is a narrative account of the major formative and culminative events describing an individual's life.

In view of the small amount of material for Case C, and the vagueness of much of that material, there is little scope for restructuring. Given a more detailed case, as we shall see, there might be several ways of sorting and linking the various items of information. This activity has a parallel in exploratory data analysis in statistics whereby, through the use of visual modes of presentation and successive rearrangements, one may discover the best way to describe and interpret the data.

Other sorts of case might incline us to categorize some of the material in terms of 'symptoms' and 'underlying disorder' or in terms of 'predisposing factors' and 'precipitating factors' or in terms of 'psychological factors' and 'environmental circumstances'. These categories, however, are rather broad. If we wanted a more detailed and appropriate categorization we could apply a conceptual framework applicable to typical cases of 'attempted suicide', 'never married', 'poor self-image' or 'social isolate'. But the frameworks themselves show us what might be worth looking for in the way of further information, given the opportunity to explore the case further.

By far the most important consideration in relation to structuring and restructuring case-materials is the context within which the exercise is being carried out. Consider, for example, a military context, a business context, a social work context, an educational context; each of these contexts has a typical concern which largely dictates the categorization of data. A military case-study might categorize information in terms of the Subject's previous experience, relationships with superiors and subordinates, style of command, use of military intelligence, response to stress, political pressures, and so on. A business case-study might use categories like the Subject's access to finance, his grasp of the market and of the processes of production and distribution, his tendency to take risks, his independence of or dependence on business associates, his physical health, and so on.

The explanation for the differences between areas where case-studies are carried out is that cases within a given area tend to share certain family resemblances. That is to say, they have common features in virtue of the fact that the Subjects of the case-studies tend to be certain kinds of people in certain kinds of situations. It would be nonsensical, or at best comical, to describe and analyse a psychiatric case using a military framework, or a social work case using a business framework. Different games have different rules.

The main advantage of structuring and restructuring is that it discloses gaps in the data. What is missing from Case C? First, a lot of concrete detail is missing—the case is stated in vague, general terms. Second, there is no mention of female friends, no mention of C's physical health, leisure interests, and so on. The importance of concrete empirical data cannot be overemphasized. It is all too easy to state the case in abstract and general terms; such statements cannot be queried or used effectively until their empirical basis has been established.

SEQUENCING

Case-study materials often cover all three tenses: past, present, future. Information about the individual's life-history, by definition, is about the past. Information about current or present events encompasses the recent past and the immediate future. Information about longer-term actions, circumstances, consequences, and so on, with a range of outcomes and likelihoods, is about possible futures.

Readers may find a schematic illustration useful (see Figure 3.1). The horizontal blocks or sections represent the sequence of circumstances and psychobehavioural episodes making up an individual's actual life-path (life events in the general sense). The diagonal lines intersecting at the point marked 'present moment' represent the range of circumstances and actions that 'might have been' possible in the past or 'might yet be possible' in the future, at a given moment in time.

Notice that the possibilities close in as time approaches the 'present moment' and open up again into the future. The diagram can be thought of as representing a 'stream of behaviour' in time, not forgetting the stream of experience, the stream of circumstances, and the stream of physiological processes with which it is interlocked. A large-scale episode sequence takes in

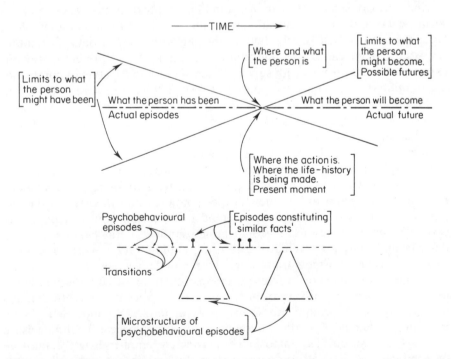

Figure 3.1 A schematic diagram illustrating the life-course as a series of psychobehavioural episodes

a long period of the life-history and each block represents a major episode or connected set of episodes; minor events would not be shown. A small-scale episode-sequence represents a shorter period of time and magnifies episodes that would not appear in a large-scale diagram.

We have to consider the possibility that there is no intrinsic 'plan', 'structure', or 'pattern' to a person's life-history, only that which the observer constructs in order to give it meaning (presumably for some purpose). The individual can be regarded as the locus of an infinite number of 'possible persons', namely those that he or she might have become had things gone differently. Only one outcome is selected in an evolutionary sense by force of (inner and outer) circumstances from the array of possible outcomes. In the life-history process, chance seems to play a major part—see Fiske (1961). Presumably, biological and ecological factors delimit the range of life-history variations, and no doubt interesting and important regularities can be established—see Horowitz (1979) and Runyan (1984). But the range of psychological and behavioural variations seems limitless.

Having said that, it is obvious that human beings have to impose some kind of meaning—structure or regularity—on human lives, otherwise they would be unable to interact effectively and unable to establish a stable social order. The notions of psychological 'types', sociological 'careers', and developmental 'stages' illustrate attempts to impose order and meaning on human nature.

Even a good life-history can establish only a tiny fraction of the empirical facts. There is often no way of telling which events have been unnoticed, forgotten, misconstrued, misremembered, or imagined.

At best, therefore, the life-history method can provide us with only rough approximations and inconclusive knowledge. However, it may be possible, through what we have called 'triangulation', to corroborate many aspects of a life-history even if the life-history as a whole cannot be verified.

The case-study, by contrast, is a much less ambitious enterprise than a life-history. It is usually more recent, the data relatively more plentiful and accessible, the findings more easily corroborated. Although it too can yield only an approximation to knowledge, the opportunities for verification or falsification are relatively more numerous than for the life-history, with the result that conclusions and decisions can be reached with greater confidence.

For both the life-history and the case-study the important thing is not the sheer amount of information (which may be excessive) but the availability of logically structured relevant and important information.

A psychological case-study is about a person in a situation (or in a system of interrelated situations). The events and behaviour described in the case-study occupy time, and the language used to describe those events—the narrative—determines the type and scale of representation (the behavioural map) by its choice of terminology and conceptualization and by the level of abstraction and generality adopted. For example, describing the minutiae of one's activities during the last twelve hours and forecasting the next twelve would constitute a small-scale behavioural map. By contrast, describing the last twenty years would constitute a large-scale map. Obviously, a statement like, 'Then he spent a week in hospital with a broken arm' is fairly abstract and general, i.e. it incorporates a host of subsidiary episodes—eating meals, sleeping, receiving visitors, and so on. By contrast, a statement like 'I telephoned my wife to tell her I would be late home' is fairly concrete and specific. Although it too contains a number of subsidiary actions—lifting the telephone, dialling, and so on (which could be subdivided even further by a motion-and-time-study expert)—such fine detail behaviour reports are rarely needed. They may be needed, however, in case-studies involving accidents (What happened exactly?), in interpersonal misunderstandings (What did you say exactly? What, precisely, did he do?), and in legal proceedings or other inquiries of a judicial sort (Did you make a written record of your conversation? Can you give me the exact dates and times of your visits?).

Sequencing is making out a chronology of the events referred to in the case-materials. For practical purposes the sequence can be set out as a vertical list (like the index list) but in chronological order. Where appropriate, the actual time and duration of each episode can be shown by a square bracket, together with a time marker. The episodes may be bracketed in various ways—see Barker and Wright (1951) and Barker (1963) where the method is applied to the fine details of the stream of behaviour. For Case C, the sequence is as in Table 3.4.

The temporal sequence of events in Case C is fairly straightforward, at least according to the available information. Sometimes, however, the exact temporal sequence may not be immediately apparent and may need to be worked out very carefully, otherwise important connections, hypotheses and inferences will be missed. In the case of C, for example, did the psychological disturbance precede, accompany, or follow the breakdown of sexual relationship? The information given does not enable us to answer this question, but examining the sequence at least enables us to raise the question and helps us to decide what further lines of inquiry to take up.

The duration of episodes and the intervals between episodes, as well as their chronology, may be important in helping to reveal their psychological significance. In Case C, for example, it is possible that the sexual relationship had lasted long enough to be more than a 'brief encounter', but not long enough to become 'stale'. In either of these two periods the relationship *might* have come to an end without catastrophic consequences for C.

FILING: CLASSIFICATION AND CROSS-CLASSIFICATION

In the subsection headed 'Indexing' we listed what was, in effect, a collection of 'files' of information. Effective filing is difficult, but unavoidable once the information about a case has built up beyond about a thousand words, or beyond the span of unaided memory. The reason for filing information is to be able to group it into a relatively small number of categories so that one can retrieve it as and when necessary—to explore possible connections, to make

Table 3.4

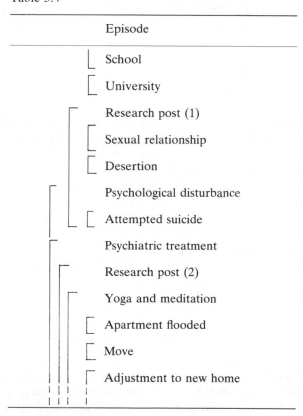

Episode
School
University
Research post (1)
Sexual relationship
Desertion
Psychological disturbance
Attempted suicide
Psychiatric treatment
Research post (2)
Yoga and meditation
Apartment flooded
Move
Adjustment to new home

inferences, to work out lines of inquiry, to write up the material in a coherent way. Items of information, however, can sometimes be filed under more than one heading, i.e. belong to more than one category of meaning. Hence, cross-classification becomes a help to retrieval when the Investigator has more than one use for an item of information. In Case C, for example, 'desertion' might be classified under 'Recent life stresses' or under 'Social relationships'. Other broad groups might be: 'Occupational history', 'Education', 'Family', 'Domestic life', 'Leisure activities', and so on.

Later in this chapter a comprehensive general system for classifying case-material is presented together with the questions needed to elicit that material. In practice some of the categories can be omitted, some can be combined, others can be subdivided. The important thing is to classify the information in a way that helps the Investigator to pursue the case, and to make sense of the information collected.

An Investigator soon finds that he or she has lots of information in some files and little or nothing in others. The reason for this is that the filing system, i.e. the set of content categories used in analysing the data, is the joint product of an inductive (empirical) and deductive (rational) approach to the problem. The inductive approach takes the available information and classifies it without too much concern for meaning and theoretical issues. The deductive approach, on the other hand, is theoretical, and tries to impose a comprehensive and coherent pattern of meaning on the data. The deductive approach, therefore, may raise pertinent questions about matters where information is lacking. This is all too obvious in Case C, because if we suppose, i.e. theorize, that C had not really intended to kill herself, but intended only to make other people think that she had, then we could create a file labelled 'Suicide gesture'. This would help us to look for relevant evidence, but initially the file would be empty.

Classes and lists are not the only way of systematizing data. One can use diagrams and other aids. For example, one might use a sociometric diagram, a family tree, a schematic situation network, or a causal path. Diagrammatic or tabular devices from social interaction analyses, such as scripts and plans, can be used to illustrate the fine detail of episodes in cases. The aim is to explore new possibilities for meaning and to help identify the most convincing interpretation. We shall see the usefulness of diagrams in the analysis of arguments in Chapters 7 and 9.

COORDINATING AND REDUCING

Several of the preceding aspects of the case-method bring about an extension and elaboration of the case-material. As the inquiry continues, however, it is necessary to reduce the accumulating information to a more compact form. This is achieved by coordinating related items of information, by imposing an appropriate 'structure' or 'pattern' of meaning onto the data, by keeping a moving summary which tells 'the story so far'. In the interests of convenience, data reduction necessarily forgoes a wealth of detail. In Case C, for example, a summary might report, 'C was deserted by her lover and reacted by trying to kill herself'. This summary may focus on the key issue, in which case it is useful. If it does not focus on the key issue it may be positively misleading. Consider, for example, the following summary, 'C's being deserted precipitated a depressive episode'. Notice that what the summaries do in these two examples is to link events in a *causal* sequence. This is not always possible, or even desirable, in the early stages of an inquiry.

In cases where there is a great deal of quantitative data one can obviously use statistical methods of a descriptive sort, or the newer so-called 'exploratory data analysis' methods. Case-studies of this sort are unusual, except where the data have been generated by experimental or quasi-experimental methods—as in single-case designs—see Hersen and Barlow (1976) and Cook and Campbell (1979).

Non-experimental cases generating quantitative data might be made, for example, of people who keep detailed diaries, records, and accounts, or write many letters. Analysing and summarizing the contents of such records might reveal interesting facts and relationships not immediately obvious from scrutiny of the raw data. Finding that a woman spends 12 per cent of her income on books and 1 per cent on clothes carries a different implication from finding that she spends 1 per cent on books and 12 per cent on clothes!

In personal relationships, people are quick to remark on what they see as quantitative changes in behaviour—decreased social contact, increased mistakes, increased alcohol consumption, more intense mood states—and to draw what they think is an appropriate conclusion, bearing in mind the context within which the behaviour occurs. Thus the notions of 'baseline behaviour' and 'baseline circumstances' are important even when no actual quantitative value can be assigned to them.

Regardless of whether the information is of a qualitative or quantitative sort, the aim of coordinating and reducing the data is to extract as much meaning as possible. When suitably summarized, data can convey a pattern of meaning that is easily remembered and communicated. Such summaries, however, are useful only to the extent that they truly reflect the data from which they were derived. Hence, it is essential to keep 'the story so far' under constant review. Information acquired later may force a revision of the interpretation put on data acquired earlier.

CONNECTING

Finding relationships between items and groups of items of information is a creative intellectual activity. For example, one may notice that two people are seen together quite often, or that a mood change precedes the start of a menstrual cycle. The effect of finding, or rather supposing, a relationship is to further the process of imposing a pattern of meaning on the available information. A relationship established in one area may lead to the formation of relationships in other areas, as in reasoning by analogy. For example, an observer may infer that a person's jealousy, like his aggressiveness, is a symptom of his insecurity.

Connections between quantified data can be explored objectively and systematically by means of statistical analysis. Connections between all sorts of individual facts, however, are explored in a more subjective intuitive way by a process that we shall call 'argumentation', meaning only that logical inferences can be drawn from case-materials provided a reasonable argument can be constructed. Arguments of the form, 'He refuses to back down because he is not prepared to lose face, although he knows he's wrong' show connections and generate inferences. But 'argumentation' in case-studies is by no means as simple as one might suppose—see Chapters 9 and 10.

In carrying out the sorts of case-study activities we are dealing with—indexing, restructuring, sequencing, filing, coordinating and reducing, and connecting—we are usually also making interpretations and inferences about the case-material. However, we must be careful to avoid possible errors.

First, we must not confuse the empirical data, i.e. our observations and evidence, with the inferences and patterns of meaning we have imposed on them. It is all too easy to take as true something which is merely consistent with the facts as known, as opposed to being independently verified or a necessary consequence of the facts as known. Evidence and inference complement one another. To misquote a well-known aphorism, 'Evidence without inference is lame, inference without evidence is blind'. Second, we must tolerate the uncertainty and ambiguity that accompany partial knowledge and partial understanding of a case. An important rule in problem-solving and creative thinking is not to foreclose one's solution options prematurely in spite of the strong need to do something about the case. One must learn to live with approximations to the truth.

Another possibility worth bearing in mind as one works over the case-materials—adding more information and meaning—is that changes in one part of the case may have repercussions in other parts of the case. For example, finding that Case C had hoped to stop working, get married, and start a family, might lead us to underestimate the importance of low self-esteem as a causal factor in her attempted suicide. The same finding might conflict with evidence of poor family relationships during her child-hood.

In a complete case-history, every fact should be related in some way to other facts in the pattern of meaning eventually arrived at. Ideally, this pattern should be 'overdetermined' in the sense that particular facts and their relationships should be supported and corroborated by a variety of other facts and relationships in the case-material. In practice, however, such complete-ness and consistency are rarely attained and the Investigator has to resort to criteria like the 'balance' or 'weight' of evidence and the 'cogency' or 'plausibility' of argument. Like a scientific theory, a case-study cannot be proved true, even though it may be accepted with some confidence; and it may, through further inquiry, be shown to be in error. Hence the need, mentioned above, to keep one's options on interpretation open for as long as possible.

One way of avoiding the tendency to make premature judgments about cases is to engage in the activities described above—indexing, restructuring, sequencing, filing, coordinating and reducing, and connecting—working on the assumption that 'There is more to the case than meets the eye' and that 'There are usually at least two sides to an argument' or, proverbially, that you should, 'Look before you leap'.

The widespread tendency to deal with cases briefly is partly a function of shortage of time and resources in professional settings, but also partly a function of a natural inclination to jump to conclusions and act on the basis of the first available evidence, as in 'first impressions' in social judgments, and in the formation of consumer preferences.

The main features of a case, then, should not be identified at the outset of an inquiry, but only at its conclusion. But, the reader may ask, 'How is the case to get started in the first place?' and, 'What about the point made earlier that the aim of a case-study is to settle certain issues which are in dispute, i.e. answer certain key questions?' The answer is that the inquiry into a case is often recursive. That is to say, consideration of the initial assumptions, facts, and arguments gives rise to inferences, conjectures, and further inquiries, which lead to a revision of the initial assumptions, and to further cycles of inquiry until the process of revision can go no further. Only at this stage in the process of problem-solving is it correct to aim for 'closure' by finally identifying the 'main issues' and 'basic problems' in the case.

It is worth noting that the methodology we are applying to the investigation of individual persons has a more general applicability to the investigation of social organizations—industrial, commercial, educational, governmental, military, political, and so on. This is not only because one can adopt a reductionist approach to the study of social organizations and see them, in part at least, as the product of the interactions of their constituent individuals, but also because a social organization can be seen as a singular entity having a particular sort of existence in a given context of circumstances. For example, a systematic analysis of the role-relationships in an organization may reveal self–other misconceptions which lead to unsatisfactory interaction and inefficiency. Also, one individual in a group may be a major source of discontent within an organization. Case-studies of persons can thus clarify problems of social organization. The main point, however, is that a social organization itself can become the focus of a case-study and be investigated in broadly the same way as other individual entities—see Easton (1982).

Even a little experience with the way case-studies are carried out will reveal the ease with which errors and omissions can creep into the case-records and into the subjective accounts that Investigators render. As time goes by, the information pertaining to a case goes through a series of revisions. Some new material is added, some old material is forgotten or revised. Even if the people responsible for managing the case are working in a responsible professional fashion, there is still some risk that relevant information will be lost or overlaid by more recent, possibly less relevant, material. If the case is in the hands of people who are incompetent, negligent, or corrupt, there is considerable scope for distortion, and the possibility of a catastrophic error of outcome. Cases based on unobtrusive surveillance and secret files, as in police work or counter-espionage, will be at considerable risk because the information collected about a case must, by its very nature, be indirect and difficult to corroborate. There is less likelihood that the case can be considered by independent impartial Investigators. Similarly, cases without advocates or resources are likely to fare worse than others, simply because those responsible for carrying out the case-study will either be honestly convinced of the validity of their assessment, or dishonestly prepared to see the Subject suffer.

Some readers may be dismayed by the prospect of the extra work entailed in identifying and clarifying the problem. Moreover, as we shall see in later chapters, there is considerably more to preparing a detailed case-study than

Table 3.1 A systematic semi-structured personal appraisal schedule

---

Identity and appearance: What is his/her name and address? Who is he-she? How can he/she be recognized and identified? Has he/she any special distinguishing characteristics?

Life-history: What is the story of his/her life so far? How did he/she come to be the person he/she is now? What formative experiences has he/she undergone?

Present circumstances: What are the main circumstances currently facing him/her? How have these circumstances arisen?

Future prospects: What does his/her immediate future hold? What opportunities and constraints are there in his/her circumstances? What possibilities are open to him/her? What will be the likely long-term consequences of his/her current actions and circumstances? What is to become of him/her?

Routine habits and activities: How does he/she live his/her life? How does he/she spend his/her time, money, and energies?

Material circumstances and possessions: What financial and material resources does he/she have at his/her disposal?

Actual incidents: What actual incidents reveal his/her psychological characteristics, and/or the circumstances in which he/she has been involved?

Physical and mental health: What is the state of his/her physical health? Is there anything unusual in his/her thoughts, feelings, desires, or actions?

General personality traits: How is he/she inclined, in general, to behave? What regularities and consistencies are there that characterize his/her behaviour in different situations?

Specific personality traits: How does he/she behave in these particular (specified) situations?

Expressive behaviour: How does he/she express his/her feelings? What is his/her usual manner or demeanour?

Motivation and arousal: What does he/she want? What is he/she trying to do? What are his/her hopes and fears? What does he/she like and dislike?

---

the simple measures described above. The point is that the Investigator has a responsibility to ensure that his or her conduct with regard to a particular case measures up to the professional and scientific standards appropriate to that case. The methodology proposed in this book is designed with the aim of achieving the highest possible standards in the study of individual cases. It is up to the individual Investigator, or critic, to decide whether the rigour of the method matches the importance of the case.

A SYSTEMATIC SEMI-STRUCTURED PERSONAL APPRAISAL SCHEDULE

The systematic semi-structured personal appraisal schedule in Table 3.1 shows the kinds of general questions needed to elicit information on

Table 3.1 *cont.d*

Abilities and attainments: What is he/she able to do? What is he/she *not* able to do? How competent is he/she to cope with this particular (specified) situation?

Orientation and feelings: How does he/she see this (specified) situation? What hoes he/she expect to happen? What options does he/she think are open or closed to him/her? How does he/she think and feel things are going for him/her?

Principles, character, and moral rules: What are his/her basic beliefs, values, and rules of conduct?

Self-concept: What is his/her attitude to him/herself? What does he/she think and feel about him/herself? What does he/she want of him/herself? How does he/she describe him/herself? To what extent is he/she the sort of person he/she ought to be?

Objects of interest: What things are important to him/her? How does he/she relate to them? How do they affect him/her?

Social position: What is his/her position in society? What do other people expect of him/her?

Family and kin: Who are his/her closest relatives? What is his/her family like? What are his/her relationships with them?

Friendships and loyalties: Who are his/her friends (or enemies)? To whom is he/she friendly and loyal (or unfriendly and disloyal)?

Subject's response to others: What is his/her attitude to people in general (and in particular)? What does he/she think of other people? What does he/she expect of them? What does he/she want of them? How does he/she react to them?

Others' response to Subject: How do other people in general (and in particular) react to him/her? What do other people think of him/her? What do they expect of him/her? What do they want of him/her? How do they react towards him/her?

Subject's interaction with others: What activities and interests does he/she share with other (named) people?

Similarities and differences between Subject and others: How does he/she compare with others? In what ways is he/she similar to and different from other people?

---

personal identity, and on a systematic and comprehensive range of well-defined aspects of the Subject and his/her circumstances. Various schedules can be compiled for special purposes, e.g. student selection, employment interviewing, marriage guidance, psychiatric screening. The method can be used to provide a basis for a case-study or individual counselling.

Table 3.1 shows only a selection of the general-purpose 'probe' questions that can be incorporated in a systematic semi-structured personal appraisal schedule. It will be seen that many of the questions are much less specific than their counterparts in personality questionnaires or interviews; they normally have to be modified to suit specific practical applications and individual cases.

The method is based on one approach to the problem of assessing personality (and the self) by means of the content analysis of personality-descriptions and self-descriptions in ordinary language. The questions listed in the table are adapted from a detailed analysis of the case-study method in Bromley (1977), and of the self-concept in Bromley (1978). They are derived from a set of thirty categories of information found in adult personality-descriptions in ordinary language. The list is illustrative rather than exhaustive, since different sorts of personal appraisal are required for different sorts of people and for different purposes.

Taken individually, the items show the kinds of questions any normal reflective individual asks himself from time to time and indicate the kinds of information a Subject can normally make available with help from the Investigator. It is easy to see that by rephrasing the questions slightly—'Who am I?', 'What formative experiences have I undergone?', 'How do I express my feelings?' and so on, the schedule can be transformed into a self-appraisal questionnaire.

SUMMARY AND CONCLUSIONS

Case-records do not necessarily provide a good guide to the facts of a case. This is because they are liable to a variety of accidental or deliberate omissions and distortions. Nevertheless case-records are essential in all but the simplest of cases and fulfil a variety of functions. The information they contain may derive from many sources and take different forms. Ideally, the information in the case-record should be complete and easily accessible to duly authorized Investigators (possibly including the Subject of the case-study) but otherwise confidential.

Case C illustrates how even a brief case-record containing only a few statements can be indexed, structured, and restructured in an attempt to make the most of the information available. Attention is drawn to the way in which episodes and sequences in the 'stream of behaviour' can be represented and analysed in greater or lesser detail. A case-study shows where the action is, or was, at some stage in the Subjects' life-history.

Items in the case-record can be classified and cross-classified for the purposes of interpretation and ease of retrieval. The categories used depend partly on the sorts of evidence made available and partly on the ideas the Investigator is using to make sense of the case, i.e. to put a construction on the evidence.

As the case-records increase it becomes necessary to find ways of coordinating and reducing this information so as to make it more manageable. This is usually achieved by summarization—identifying the main points and the connections between them. This necessarily reflects the pattern of meaning the Investigator has imposed on the case.

It is essential to keep fact and opinion separate, even though we must use opinions (theories) to interpret the facts. It is also important not to be unduly influenced by one's first impressions of the case, otherwise later evidence may be discounted or misinterpreted. Some types of case-study are particularly liable to error.

The quasi-judicial case-study method is not a description of how case-workers go about their business, but rather a prescriptive, normative procedure—a description of how we ought, ideally, to carry out case-studies if we claim to be scientists or professional practitioners.

Although there is no standard format for organizing the data in a psychological case-study, one option is provided in the form of a Semi-Structured Personality Questionnaire (SSPQ). It is based on a comprehensive system of personality description, and contains a variety of questions that can be employed in guiding an inquiry and interviewing a Subject. It can be adapted as required to suit the particular circumstances of the case.

CHAPTER FOUR

Description and Analysis: Some Complications

Introduction
Case D: R. W. White's 'Joyce Kingsley'
Commentary and Associated Issues
Summary and Conclusions

INTRODUCTION

The case-study described and analysed in this chapter is based on a chapter in R. W. White's book *Lives in Progress* (3rd edition, 1975). It is the case of Joyce Kingsley—housewife and social worker. White's aim in collecting and analysing the material on Joyce Kingsley was simply to illustrate the natural, 'real-life', development of personality adopting a psychodynamic approach to the study of personal adjustment. Full details of the case can be found in White's book. Our concern is to provide a commentary on parts of the case to show how the study of individuals can be improved through attention to the appropriate scientific methodology.

Case D (Joyce Kingsley), a college senior, volunteered to take part in a study of opinions and personality. The methods used to collect data about her were similar to those used in Murray's classic *Explorations in Personality* (1938). They included interviews with several Investigators, psychometric tests of personality and intelligence, projective tests, performance tests in a laboratory, free-association, and an assisted autobiography. Some of these methods of psychological assessment have come in for a great deal of criticism in recent years, and it is probably a mistake to suppose that the raw data derived from such methods will support the weight of inference carried in the case of Joyce Kingsley as reported by White (1975). Nevertheless the methods do include some still commonly found in psychological case-studies. The psychoanalytic approach too has become much less favoured.

Case D's initial assessment was followed up five years later when she was married, nineteen years later, and finally twenty-nine years later (by which time she was fifty years old). This span of time covers a good part of Case D's life-history. We have already drawn a clear distinction between the life-history and the case-study. A case-study deals with one major episode (or group of related episodes) within a relatively short period of the individual's life. We shall deal with only one segment of Joyce Kingsley's life—her years at college. However, it will be necessary to refer *back* occasionally to relevant life-history information, and interesting to refer *forward* to what actually happened to Joyce Kingsley later in life.

CASE D: R. W. WHITE'S 'JOYCE KINGSLEY'

Case D was the eldest of three children. Her father had a successful career in the ministry—first as a pastor, then as an executive. Her mother was a teacher. Both parents had strong religious affiliations, and both had experienced difficulty in breaking free of parental influences. Case D was brought up in a family environment that was financially secure, affectionate, strongly moral, and religious. According to her own account she was an able and obedient child who did well at school, possibly because she was able to transfer family values and attitudes to the school environment. On moving to a small private school, however, she encountered difficulties in personal relationships arising, apparently, from an inability to share the values and interests of her class-mates, especially with reference to males and to school authority. Fortunately, she met a young man with whom she could associate closely on her own high moral terms, and this seems to have made her feel secure, and able to maintain good social relationships, whilst enjoying positions of power and responsibility in student affairs.

The transition to college, however, brought with it more problems. First, that of competing academically and socially with people of comparable or higher abilities. Hitherto, she had been used to high academic grades and high social status. Second, unlike other students, she continued to live at home and yet knew none of the students attending the college. The academic demands were greater at college, and she experienced difficulty in relating to staff and taking part in extracurricular activities. To make matters worse, relationships with her boyfriend became temporarily less satisfactory. Fortunately, she was attractive to men and this helped her find acceptance among the female students.

Surprisingly, perhaps, after relationships with her boyfriend had improved they became secretly engaged—aware presumably of parental disapprobation of exclusive attachments and early marriage. The security this gave Case D enabled her to resume official activities connected with student affairs. She was aware, however, that she did not have close friends or confidants of her own age.

She had a wide range of extracurricular interests, some of which brought her into association with other people—for example in music, painting, and politics. Her social outlook was strongly conditioned by her family upbringing—liberal and democratic but strongly religious. Her academic environment provided support for all these expressions of her personality. At this stage her parents adopted a child, and Case D seems to have expressed considerable 'maternal' interest in him over a long period.

COMMENTARY AND ASSOCIATED ISSUES

(a) Evidence and inference

The information in our account of this case-study consists of a variety of statements organized in a particular way. The statements are not all of the same sort or equally precise. Some consist of simple or complex factual assertions, e.g. '. . . after relationships with her boyfriend had improved they became secretly engaged. . .'. Others consist of suppositions, inferences or interpretations, e.g. '. . .this seems to have made her feel secure', '. . .this. . .enabled her to resume official activities. . .'. Some are value judgments, e.g. 'To make matters worse. . .', 'Fortunately. . .'. Some are methodological, e.g. 'According to her own account. . .'.

In a long case-study we can expect to find sentences and other forms of words expressing questions, comments, reservations and qualifications, explanations, alternative views, conclusions, recommendations, and so on, interrelated in the complex grammatical ways necessary to convey the meaning and effect desired by the writer. Perhaps the most important distinction to make when examining case-material is that between factual information, i.e. empirical data, and inference, i.e. the construction or interpretation placed on that information. Notice that statements of an abstract or general sort may or may not go well with the evidence that can be cited in their support. For example, the statement in Case D that '. . .they became secretly engaged. . .' is not only vague (What does it actually mean?), but we have, apparently, only Joyce Kingsley's uncorroborated word for this 'fact'. It is not that there is any reason to doubt what is contained in Case D (although there might well be in other cases), but rather that case-material needs to be carefully analysed and evaluated if it is to be worth using.

Some statements found in case-materials are very precise and easily verified—statements about the case's name, age, appearance, for example. Ideally, an Investigator should be able to test the reliability and validity of all those statements in a case-study which are taken to be factual statements. The reliability of a statement can be 'tested' in a non-statistical way by examining the internal coherence of the network of statements of which it forms a part, or by rephrasing it or working out its implications to see whether the consequences are consistent with it. Thus, in Case D, the statement that 'she did not have close friends or confidants of her own age' might be found to be consistent with other remarks made by Joyce Kingsley about life at college. For example, if she had said, of the same period, 'I did not really have any girl-friends I could confide in', this would lead an Investigator to attribute greater reliability to each of these mututally supporting statements. Of course, the rule breaks down in cases where there is malingering, or conspiracy between informants.

The validity of a statement can be tested by observing its correspondence with the independent verifiable evidence. The statement that Case D 'had a wide range of extracurricular interests' would be confirmed if her specific extracurricular activities could be independently established and if they were diverse in the sense of covering several spheres of interest—cultural, social, practical, ecological, athletic, and so on.

Validity, like reliability, can be tested indirectly—for example by independent testimony rather than by direct observation. Where the evidence is restricted to one primary source, e.g. the Subject of the case-study, or to a few first-hand observers, it could be argued that the best one can do is to examine the internal consistency of the information available, its reliability. This is not unlike a legal or quasi-legal inquiry where the testimony of an informant can be reviewed under cross-examination.

Most case-studies are exercises in historical research rather than prospective inquiries. Moreover, many of the events and circumstances making up the case are, for the purposes of the particular case-study, unique, not replicable and not within the purview of people other than those present at the time they occurred. Such would be the case, for example, in Joyce Kingsley's relationships with her boy-friend.

As we shall see more fully in Chapter 11, a case-study is not to be judged by the extent to which it statistically 'represents' the population from which it is drawn. Indeed, its merit might lie in exhibiting a feature *not* shared by other similar cases, i.e. in its idiosyncratic features. In any event, a sample of one has no statistical merit. A case-study is to be judged by its internal coherence, by the extent to which its empirical content can be independently and objectively verified, and by the validity of its conceptual framework. An abundance of relevant data is important in this connection, but sheer quantity of information is less important than sufficient good evidence and ample corroboration. Since actual behaviour depends so much on a variety of contextual factors, prediction of behaviour is not a satisfactory test of the correctness of a case-study. Some of Joyce Kingsley's actions were unpredictable because the situations she faced were unpredictable. What one has to predict is whether a Subject's reactions in certain circumstances are 'in character' or 'compatible with the conclusions already arrived at'. This should be achieved without the introduction of new theories or suppositions 'to save appearances'.

These considerations impose considerable restrictions on the conclusions that can be drawn from case-studies. But one must not exaggerate the handicap. Experimental studies of human behaviour are also open to serious criticism on the grounds that, for various reasons, their results are not easy to replicate—see Epstein (1983).

Ideally, each statement in a case-study should be examined carefully to clarify its meaning, its reliability and validity, its role in relation to other parts of the case-material, and its general significance. One also needs to ask what difference if any its absence would make. It may be possible to improve the accuracy and precision of initially vague statements by giving actual names, numbers, dates, times, places, who said exactly what and in what circumstances, and so on. Attempts to clarify vague statements will often draw the Investigator's attention to missing information. Words and phrases like 'sometimes', 'fairly', 'reasonable', and metaphors like 'at my wits end' or 'over the moon' may convey a general impression well enough, but the problem is to identify more precisely the events, actions, circumstances, and states of mind to which they refer.

In a case-summary, as in a statistical summary, information is discarded in the interests of comprehension and communication. It is important, therefore, for the summary to be based on detailed and accurate information, otherwise it will reflect the biases and omissions in the case-materials. As the case proceeds, the information in the earlier case-materials tends to be further simplified and consolidated, its weaknesses and omissions forgotten.

One reason why the distinction between evidence and inference is sometimes lost sight of in a case-study is that we build up, in the course of experience, frames of reference, sometimes called 'schemata', which can be regarded as conceptual routines for handling familiar sorts of problem. By means of such schemata we learn to react quickly, economically, and effectively to situations which are like the ones we have previously encountered, e.g. a teacher dealing with a disruptive child, a manager dealing with a lazy worker, a doctor dealing with an anxious patient. In time, these frames of reference may become so overlearned, ingrained, that they can be regarded as habitual ways of thinking, no longer subject to critical reflection and doubt. The assumptions and modes of inference which govern these frames of reference for organizing our experience and action impose an immediate, automatic 'pattern of meaning' on the situation we face, thus strongly determining the course of action we are likely to take in response to it whilst remaining outside our awareness.

Clear and relevant examples of the role of immediate inference in our judgments of other people can be found in the way implicit theories of personality seem to operate. A person whose appearance is untidy and unkempt may be judged to be generally careless and untrustworthy and treated accordingly. A person who is 'known' to be intelligent, religious, and politically conservative is 'expected' to do well as a student, to conform, and to help promote the standards set by authority. We are not surprised when Case D—Joyce Kingsley—is upset by her husband's loss of religious conviction, but we feel the need for a special explanation to account for her reaction against authority in her first employment—see White (1975).

The point is that common experience, and even the way our language is structured, makes certain kinds of events appear natural or obvious, i.e.

immediately comprehensible and acceptable, whereas other kinds of events—those that do not fit any obvious patterns of meaning available from experience—appear unnatural or unfamiliar, i.e. not immediately comprehensible, and therefore puzzling. The difficulty is that the evidence available to us in everyday social interaction, and even in the course of a systematic case-study, is often incomplete, so that it is open to a variety of different interpretations or inferences. The danger then is that we pay attention to the more obvious familiar elements in our experience of the other person, and rely unthinkingly on our habitual frames of reference—our implicit assumptions and theories about human nature—in working out the implications of what we seem to 'know'. In this way the critical distinction between evidence (the observational data) and inference (the pattern of meaning, the construction imposed on those data) may be lost sight of.

Thus, case-studies are never merely a matter of collecting enough facts. The facts do not speak for themselves; they have to be spoken for. They are spoken for by what is, in effect, a 'theory', a form of argument by means of which the facts can be shown to be related to each other in a particular kind of way. To interpret facts in a particular way tends to rule out other interpretations and leads to implications which go beyond the information given. In this expression the term 'information given' refers to the facts of observation. Moreover, even the 'information given' is never simply that which is contained in the case-materials. A great deal of information is taken for granted as common knowledge about the world and about human nature. Added to this there are a great many reasonable assumptions which can be introduced as a matter of convenience to enable one to arrive at a satisfactory interpretation of a case. Consider, for example, the interpretation given to Case D's initial difficulty in coping with the transition to college.

Another way of thinking about this issue of the distinction between evidence and inference is to regard a case-study as the focus of an inquiry into a problem. The problem consists initially in establishing the meaning of a collection of data. The danger lies in jumping to conclusions about the solution to the problem or, worse, not even recognizing that a problem exists. This danger comes about, as we have seen, because of a natural inclination to rely on familiar conceptual routines—often operating outside of conscious awareness or critical reflection.

The problem at the focus of a case-study is a set of facts embedded in a context of 'further information'. This further information has to be explored and examined in order to discover what else is relevant to the case. As a rough rule of thumb, evidence becomes relevant if its inclusion makes a difference to the interpretation of a case, and irrelevant or superfluous if it does not.

One expects a scientific case-study to provide, as a minimum requirement, an interpretation that is a 'reasonable' interpretation of the evidence available. Ideally, it should do more; it should provide enough evidence to rule out competing interpretations. The 'weight of evidence' should be sufficient to make other competent Investigators confident that one of the interpretations is clearly superior to the others. In practice, of course, this may not happen, and the case is never satisfactorily resolved. The available evidence may not be sufficient to discriminate between competing theories, or Investigators may not be clever enough in interpreting the available evidence.

Further assumptions and more real-world knowledge enter into the case-study when it reaches the stage at which forecasts, recommendations, and courses of action are agreed. For example, in the case of a school refuser, the child's behaviour may be symptomatic of faults within a particular school (bullying by other children, fear of a particular teacher), not simply of the child's personality and home background. Therefore, recommendations for dealing with school refusal differ according to how the child's behaviour is explained. Similarly, the treatment of alcoholism depends on the assumptions introduced to make sense of the medical, psychological, and social data. An emphasis on social factors may point to family therapy, an emphasis on psychological factors to counselling and/or behaviour modification, an emphasis on medical factors to drugs and nutrition.

Initially, such recommendations and forecasts are based on 'case law', i.e. similar cases in similar circumstances. Such reasoning is liable to error because of the many personal and contextual factors which make one case different from others in spite of the similarities. What we have, in effect, is an argument by analogy. However, if some sort of action is taken, e.g. treatment administered, based on such reasoning, then the consequences of such action become directly relevant to the particular case. By definition, experimental and quasi-experimental studies of individual cases are confined to cases and circumstances over which the Investigator has considerable control—as regards both intervention and surveillance. Real-life case-studies, by contrast, are much less constrained; hence treatment outcomes in such cases should be interpreted with considerable care, since the Investigator cannot tell what might have happened if the 'treatment' had been withheld, or if a different treatment had been given.

The main point, however, is that one cannot proceed with a case-study without making use of indirect real-world knowledge, assumptions, and corrigible arguments. The case-materials are embedded in a sort of knowledge structure shared by a larger or smaller number of people. The size of this pool of knowledge depends upon the level of intelligence and education needed to acquire the knowledge (including the ability to apply or appreciate the relevant methods), the degree of technical specialization involved, and, of course, on the number of people involved in trying to understand a particular case.

The knowledge, the assumptions, and the arguments need to be made explicit. This can usually be done only by writing them out. The student will soon find that many of the actual cases he or she encounters are very incomplete. The details have to be worked out—by empirical research or by reasoning and the application of real-world knowledge. Investigators are free, in a sense, to speculate about the case they are dealing with—this is an important creative function in case-studies. But such productive reasoning must be followed up by critical examination of the empirical consequences and logical implications—by looking closely at the facts of observation and at the logic of the arguments used in the case-study. Only in this way can one see whether the desired internal coherence and external correspondence has been achieved.

(b) Four important questions

The separation of evidence and inference in a case-study, together with an initial lack of information and understanding, means that the Investigator has two immediate problems. First, he or she must add to the information initially available some 'obvious' further information. This means adding various facts and relationships which can be established without a great deal of effort or risk of error. In Case D, for example, the autobiography written by Joyce Kingsley might have omitted relevant matters which would have been noticed immediately by an interested Investigator, e.g. specific dates, social relationships, and circumstances. Such obvious matters would be easily dealt with in subsequent interviews with Case D. Other obvious facts might be public knowledge, e.g. the sexual mores, political attitudes, and educational standards prevailing at the time.

The Investigator's second problem is to consider the different ways of making sense of the information about the case. It is not difficult to appreciate that two Investigators might have rather different views on a case, particularly in the early stages when information is lacking. An Investigator has to exercise only a little ingenuity in thinking up obvious accounts of the case other than the one that comes most readily to mind. In ordinary circumstances there will eventually be several possible accounts which will have different degrees of likelihood. In Case D, for example, it was assumed that her apparent avoidance of sexual involvement with men was a natural but temporary consequence of a conservative religious upbringing rather than of lesbian tendencies or a neurotic predisposition. The assumption pointed to a common difficulty faced by young women like Case D at that time, whereas the other possibilities were less commonly reported and therefore less likely to be seriously considered in this particular case.

Lying behind the two immediate problems of filling in obvious information and thinking of the obvious reasons and causes, i.e. explanations, is the requirement to formulate the case as a 'case', i.e. to state it in the form of a problem or puzzle demanding a solution or an interpretation, usually so that some kind of action can be taken as a consequence.

Unlike a case that comes before a judicial inquiry in the United Kingdom, a case dealt with by means of a scientific quasi-judicial procedure is not constrained by the 'issues' identified at the beginning of the inquiry. It may be that findings at later stages of the investigation lead to a re-examination of what is at issue in the case. For example, a case which has its beginning in an inquiry into an individual's financial failure may, later on, shift its focus of interest to the individual's sex life. The financial failure might come to be seen as a fairly obvious logical consequence of a much less obvious and less well-understood pattern of sexual development and deviation.

We have already referred to this recursive character of the case-method.

Throughout the case-study, then, the Investigator should be aware of four important questions:

1. What is at issue?
2. What other relevant evidence might there be?
3. How else might one make sense of the data?
4. How were the data obtained?

So far, in this section, we have concentrated on the point that in the early stages of the inquiry at least there are some easy, obvious answers to these questions. As the case proceeds, however, additional relevant evidence becomes increasingly difficult to find and one begins to run out of ideas for interpreting the data, although this is compensated for by an increasing confidence in one of the interpretations. At the same time, what is at issue is likely to become more settled, if only because of the recursive character of the case-method.

Up to a point, each new item of information obtained, each new relationship established, each new line of inference examined, tends to alter the picture that is emerging—rather like putting together a jigsaw puzzle with little or no initial idea of what it will look like on completion.

The qualities to be cultivated by an Investigator are those of flexibility, ingenuity, thoroughness, patience, scepticism, rationality, empiricism—all the hallmarks of a scientist.

Where 'cases' are presented as part of a training programme in areas where the study of individual cases is important for theoretical or practical purposes—marriage guidance, self-destructive behaviour, educational and vocational guidance, and so on—it may be helpful to get students to distinguish between what can be squeezed out of the available information in the way of obvious internal implications and what can be added to it from obvious outside sources, e.g. common knowledge, accepted practice. An inquiry into an accident, for example, might well accept that a guard or a shopkeeper would behave in ways appropriate to that role, given that there was no evidence to the contrary. Obviously, Investigators differ in the extent to which they can import reasonable data into a case-study. A teacher who is experienced and successful with difficult schoolchildren might be more likely to introduce useful additional data to cases of that kind than would, say, a subject-teacher or even a professional social worker or psychologist. Knowledge of local circumstances and of the 'type' of individual under investigation could give additional advantage.

Unfortunately, case-materials are frequently very inadequate; so usually little is gained by close analysis of the initial data. Even so, it is worth considering what this analysis involves.

The provisional answer to the first question, 'What is at issue?' is found by determining how the case came into existence—Who raised it? When? How? In what circumstances? For what reasons? And so on. The answers to these questions might reveal that the 'real' problem was not a boy's bad behaviour but his bad behaviour in relation to a particular teacher.

The provisional answer to the second question, 'What other relevant evidence might there be?', is answered by identifying the more obvious missing items of information—'What did the Subject actually say or do?' 'What other circumstances should be taken into account?' 'Is there any documentary or corroborative evidence?' and so on. The answers to these questions are likely to reveal that one's initial reactions to the case stand on shaky ground, and that one needs to collect the information that is obviously needed if the inquiry is to stand any chance of success. The information that comes to light in this way—perhaps with no great effort—may reveal that a person's actions have been misreported or misunderstood, that it is one person's word against another, that there are apparent contradictions in the evidence available, and, almost invariably, that there are at least two sides to every question.

The provisional answer to the third question, 'How else might one make sense of the data?' is answered by identifying alternative 'patterns of meaning' or 'theories' about the case. This can be done by becoming Devil's Advocate—rejecting the obvious explanation and putting forward an alternative. It can be done more easily sometimes by sharing the case with colleagues and getting their reactions and suggestions. We saw, for example, that Case D's sexual inhibitions could have been construed differently. However, no attempt was made to test them, not because they were improbable, but because these other possibilities were not even raised (at least not in the published case-material).

The fourth question about the case-materials is 'How were the data obtained?' Each statement must have a source—an informant, a document, or some other trace. It may be possible to trace statements back through several stages of development, but they must have origins somewhere. The importance of this point for the case-study is that a piece of evidence may be only as good as its source. Obviously, an unreliable witness, an anxious informant, a Subject with much to lose by telling the truth, cannot be relied upon to provide 'good' evidence. A properly conducted case-study, therefore, will have some of its energies directed towards establishing the credibility or otherwise of the sources from which the case-materials were obtained. We have already had occasion, in relation to Case D, to question the value of projective test data and psychoanalytic theorizing; but this is not quite the same as impugning the credibility of the people who provided those sorts of materials. Rather, we would say that (with the benefit of hindsight) their views are less acceptable now than then, simply because of historical changes in the nature of scientific method and theory in psychology.

Such hindsight, by definition, is not available at the time when a case-study is being carried out; but this need not prevent Investigators from questioning the credibility of: (a) the participants, i.e. people who are involved with the investigation and are more than mere informants but are not part of the investigating team; (b) each other's views; (c) the Subject of the inquiry; (d) other witnesses and informants.

In theory, a case-study should examine the credibility of a source, and the credibility of the material regardless of source. In practice, a case-study may have to rely on the materials supplied by a source whose credibility has been established.

(c) Some cautionary remarks

The fact that obvious items of information are missing, or that obvious alternative interpretations have not been considered, may raise the question of the extent to which the initial case-materials are biased or even rigged. A certain amount of faking and deliberate distortion can be expected as part of life, and guarded against as far as possible—for example by asking whether any of the Investigators or informants have anything to gain (an 'interest' in) the outcome of the case-study. A nurse might want a troublesome patient discharged; a headmaster might 'help' a poor teacher to get a job elsewhere; one might omit from one's *curriculum vitae* items of information which would worsen one's chances of selection.

Information may be missing simply because it does not exist, or has not yet been disclosed. We know next to nothing of Case D's sexual problems early in her marriage; her phantasy world is largely unexplored (the projective tests are used to explore the possible psychodynamics of personal adjustment to the real world). In many instances, given the necessary time and resources, the missing information can be collected. For example, we may need to test a child's intelligence, refer to a person's medical history, obtain a student's academic record, or get referee's reports for short-listed candidates.

Information costs time and money; so it is not surprising that individual cases are sometimes dealt with in a very superficial way, without inquiring too deeply even into matters of direct relevance to the case. This happens when the pressures for rapid action are strong and where previous experience indicates that little risk will be incurred by not abiding by ideal standards of inquiry. Unfortunately, such lapses are likely to increase in frequency until a major misjudgment occurs, when those responsible for maintaining standards of assessment exercise their authority, or pass judgment on a case—see Department of Health and Social Security (1974).

The decision not to include information that is available has to be made often, otherwise the case-materials would become increasingly bulky and indigestible. The decision is based, as we have seen, on the 'relevance' of information (and on its 'admissibility' in legal hearings). If it makes a difference (to one's interpretation) it is relevant; if not it is irrelevant or at best superfluous. The recursive character of the case-inquiry, however, means that the Investigator deals with two sorts of information—foreground and background. The foreground information is that which, at a particular stage of the inquiry, seems most pertinent to the main issue(s). The background information is that which is known to the Investigator but not regarded as important enough to form part of the 'case'. It is information which, in a court of law, would be 'not in dispute', e.g. common knowledge or facts that no-one is denying.

Another distinction that can be made is between the 'manifest' and 'latent' content of the case-materials. One might describe this as the difference between what can be 'read out of' the materials and what can be 'read into' them. In other words, an Investigator brings a great deal of real-world knowledge to bear on the task of making sense of the information available. This real-world knowledge comprises both ordinary everyday experience—common knowledge or common sense—and the specialist concepts and methods derived from scientific training and professional experience. Thus a social worker might 'read into' Case D meanings about family relationships and social attitudes, a psychologist might 'read into' it meanings about emotional conflicts, strategies of adjustment, or contingencies of reinforcement. It may not be possible to 'read into' the case the kinds of meanings read into it by the original Investigators, since what makes sense and what does not changes with the times. For example, in Case D the Freudian interpretations look somewhat fanciful and irrelevant nowadays, whilst some environmental contingencies previously unremarked seem more relevant to understanding her relationships with her parents.

What can be 'read out of' the case-materials are only the literal meanings of the statements they contain; so that a passive mechanical sort of scrutiny or content analysis is not going to do much more than prepare the ground for the task of interpretation. The search for meaning is an active process; it depends on what the Investigator can bring to the task in the way of intelligence, experience, and methodological skill. As we have seen, however, it is essential to remain aware of the difference between evidence and inference (news and comment in journalism); evidence is data, inference is argument.

In making sense of a case-study, then, one is not entirely dependent on the case-materials (the observational data or evidence). One brings to the task other knowledge of the real world, particularly knowledge of human nature as we know it. This is most obvious in relation to comprehending the text (in a written case report), since the very words and phrases used in the text cannot be understood without reference to the reader's vocabulary and concepts— see Sanford and Garrod (1981). This issue is important for two reasons. First, it draws attention to the complex cognitive processes involved in understanding or carrying out case-studies. Second, it suggests that it will be far from easy to develop an 'expert' system (in the sense of a computer-assisted system) for dealing with psychological case-studies—see Chapter 11.

Our real-world knowledge operates in part by filling in the gaps in the case-materials, and by working out their 'obvious' or 'probable' implications. In Case D, for example, it seems obvious that Joyce Kingsley had a reasonable amount of money to spend on clothes, books, leisure, and so on—although we are given no details; also, she was probably careful in matters of personal hygiene and domestic cleanliness, although again we are given no information on this point. Sometimes the implications will be so immediate that we may not even be aware of the assumptions we are 'reading into' the case.

If a case-study is examined bit by bit, taking contextual factors into account, it is possible to explore implications revealed by the application of common sense or technical knowledge. For example, 'common sense' might lead us to suppose that Case D's sexual inhibitions early in her marriage would increase her dependence on her husband, reducing the risk of her seeking extra-marital male companionship.

There may be several angles to a case-study. It is up to the Investigator to decide which to follow up. It would be rare, perhaps even impossible in practice, to investigate all the 'angles' to a particular case, simply because the trails lead back into the obscurities of the life-history and forward into the uncertainties of future behaviour and circumstances. A case-study usually has an objective—to determine what action to take in relation to the focal issues. The study of individual cases for academic purposes—for fuller understanding, not action, as in Case D—is a relative luxury. The Investigator, or each Investigator on a team, considers a case mainly if not entirely within the terms of reference dictated by the purpose for which the case-study is being carried out. Unfortunately, there are usually too few resources to explore all the 'angles' fully. The resources deployed are likely to be a function of the importance of the case in the eyes of those responsible for deciding that a case will be investigated—a government department, a newspaper editor, a hospital administrator, a director of social services, an employer, a court, and so on.

It is from the intensive study of individual cases that the procedural steps—the methodology—of the case-study has been developed; but in everyday life, and in the bulk of professional work with individual cases, it is unusual to find case-studies being conducted intensively or exhaustively. The bulk of cases, even at a professional level, are dealt with relatively superficially. There are reasons for this. First, and probably most important, there is widespread lack of awareness on the part of professionals of the standards to be met in investigating individual cases. Second, there is often insufficient time and resources to study all the cases raised, i.e. too heavy a case-load. Third, there may be a disinclination or inability to assign priorities to cases, so that the resources available are not allocated in relation to the importance of the case. The importance of a case is part of its 'latent' meaning; it depends on what the Investigator tacitly understands to be important.

A case may be important because of the risks being run by the Subject of the study. It may be important because it will satisfy some other social need—contribute of one's dissertation, help a colleague, fend off a complaint, justify a decision, or simply make life difficult for someone.

If the time to be devoted to a case-study is to be measured in hours rather than in weeks or months, then there are obvious limitations on the scope and depth of the inquiry. This does not render methodological rigour useless. On the contrary, it demands even greater care, because there is so little time and opportunity for correcting mistakes and testing the validity to one's argument about the case.

At the lower limit of resources one has to admit that the information about a case is so inadequate that no reasonable person could offer a confident opinion. In these circumstances people have to decide whether the case is important enough to warrant further investigation. If not, then there is literally no case to consider. If the case is considered important enough, for whatever reason, to be worth devoting time and effort to, then it must compete with other calls on the Investigator's resources. Hence the need to arrange one's case-load so that resources are not spread thinly over many cases, but concentrated on important 'key' cases. One might use the so-called 20/80 rule, i.e. devote 80 per cent of one's time to 20 per cent of the cases. This would probably result in dealing much more effectively with the important or difficult cases, without abandoning the unimportant or easy cases altogether. The other advantage would be that the Investigator would learn more from his or her fuller understanding of the important and difficult cases and so be better placed for handling easier routine cases.

One must, however, guard against an obvious danger. One must not confuse cases which are rare and interesting in their own right with cases that are important, otherwise there is the risk that attention will be distracted from the main task—that of maximizing the effectiveness of the resources available. The importance of a case, therefore, is itself an important issue to be justified in the description of the case—both initially and in the final analysis. To the extent that a case can be shown to be a 'model' case, i.e. conceptually representative of a whole class of similar cases, then a thorough investigation can be expected to lead to a fuller understanding of, and a better handling of, cases of that kind. In other words the improved understanding and management is applicable not only to the case in question but also to comparable cases. The selection of a case on the grounds that it can be expected to provide a general model or solution, i.e. a conceptual routine for dealing with a certain class of human problems, then requires that the grounds for such selection be justified. If this can be done, then the importance of the case will have been established more fully, objectively, and explicitly. We can feel more confident that the case is not being studied for the wrong reasons.

Of course, case-studies can be obstructed, ignored, and neglected for the wrong reasons—fear of disclosure of malpractice, lack of resources, laziness, incompetence, and so on. Invoking the 20/80 rule means that the less important cases do get looked at from time to time, and may eventually surface as important. For example, circumstances may change or a case may develop in a significant way—a child's bad behaviour at school may reach the threshold at which the headmaster feels obliged to take firmer action; an elderly bereaved person becomes ill, forcing a reappraisal of her capacity for independent living.

Once a case has been deemed important enough to warrant investigation, a case-study is carried out and then written up as concisely as possible. Further details and discussion in the form of supplementary material can be made available as required to other people involved in the case. People familiar with cases of a certain kind, such as school refusers or alcoholics, may not need as much background information or technical explanation as other people. Similarly, they may share the same assumptions as the Investigator, whereas people who are unfamiliar with the sort of case under consideration may need to have these assumptions made explicit (and, in so doing, perhaps raise questions about the correctness of these assumptions). For example: the assumption that a child is refusing school generally (rather than a specific feature of a particular school) may be incorrect; the assumption that a person's alcohol intake is under control may be incorrect.

The main point, however, is that there is no one best way of carrying out and writing up a case-study. How the information is recorded, stored, written up, and presented depends on a constellation of contextual considerations, e.g. resources, regulations, skill, audience.

(d) Facts and opinions

Case-studies can be described in general approximate terms or in specific precise terms or in a mixture of both. Consider, for example, the following statements about Case D: 'She had unpleasant experiences in her first year at college', 'She looked to her boy-friend for help', 'She did not hear from him for three months'. It does not follow that more precise statements are more valid or even more accurate than statements couched in more general terms. Even a precise statement can be wrong or inaccurate. Indeed, part of the pressure for precision in case-study statements is to enable their accuracy and validity to be tested more readily. There is no point in assembling cloudy statements open to a variety of interpretations or, worse, no interpretation at all.

Sorting and examining the initial case-materials statement by statement, as described in Chapter 3, should generate many opportunities to clarify and validate them. Clarification is effected by answering questions like 'What does this statement mean?' 'How can it be stated more fully and more exactly?' 'How does it relate to other statements?' Validation is effected by answering questions like 'How does this statement correspond with what is already known, with some confidence, about this case?' 'How can we test the truth of this statement?'

As the statements are assembled and interpreted (remember that they include assertions about facts and assertions about inferences as well as a variety of other sentences and forms of words), they form an interconnected web of argument—see Chapter 9. To the extent that the elements within the network are mutually supportive, we can speak of the reliability or internal coherence of the case. Although the terms 'validity' and 'truth' are carefully distinguished in formal logic, in case-studies and in psychometric studies the corresponding distinction is between 'reliability' (internal consistency) and 'validity' (external verification). Thus the term 'validity' is often used to refer to the correspondence between what is asserted about the case and how that corresponds to the real world. But, ideally, what is asserted about the real world gets incorporated into the case-materials—provided it is true and relevant—as confirmatory evidence.

The solution to this apparent paradox is simply that the act of testing the validity of a statement in a case requires one to go to the real world to collect the relevant evidence. If this evidence confirms the assertions, it is added to the case-materials as corroborative evidence; if not, it obliges us to drop the statement, or at least introduce reservations about its validity.

It might be supposed that, by a process of logical deduction, some inferences could be drawn by a process of valid reasoning from initial premises known to be true, thus going beyond the information given and yet not engaging in mere speculation. If it is true, for example, that 'If Joan gets angry, then she will take a long time to calm down', then asserting 'Joan is angry' implies that 'She will take a long time to calm down'. This is a simple case of asserting the antecedent. There are, of course, many other logical forms which demonstrate valid inferences.

However, if one examines the sorts of arguments which are used to make sense of case-materials, one sees that formal logic plays only a small part. The rules of formal logic constitute a sort of minimum requirement to avoid the sorts of fallacies that can occur in reasoning generally. In practical logic, in the logic used in arguments about matters of substance (not just matters of form), the analysis of arguments proceeds rather differently. This matter is taken up in detail in Chapter 9, but it is worth mentioning that practical logic enables the case-presenter to incorporate relevant observational data, real-world knowledge, claims as to the points at issue, expressions of confidence in the correctness of the argument, justifications for drawing conclusions, and contextual considerations. In other words it is not simply a matter of separating 'evidence' from 'inference', but rather of putting together a complex structure of argument which carries conviction in virtue of the way the statements interlock to support the final recommendations or conclusions. There is no question of simply reducing the arguments in a case-study to their 'formal' equivalents and testing their validity. In any event, arguments about the truth or otherwise of those statements that refer to empirical matters are themselves incorporated in the case-study. They do not stand outside it, as it were. There are many different sorts of statement in a case-study, statements fulfilling different sorts of functions in the overall description and analysis. It is important to be able to identify these different components and to see how they connect one with another.

As we shall see in more detail in later chapters, asking critical questions about statements in the case-materials enables one to accept or discard some statements and to formulate others—partly by the application of real-world knowledge, partly by framing questions and finding the answers. For example, one might accept a statement about the way a person's actions were determined in part by expectations about the situation he or she was in. One might discard the view that an informant's testimony should be given some weight, on the grounds that he or she had given different accounts to different people. One might frame a relevant question about a person's attitude or ability and then set out to make the observations necessary to answer the question.

Reference to Case D in its more detailed form shows how the Investigators tried to build up a valid body of knowledge about Joyce Kingsley. They make statements at various levels of abstraction and generality, selecting and linking items of information and inference to achieve a high degree of internal coherence (reliability), and using a variety of independent sources (corroboration) to test the validity of their claims about the case.

It might be supposed that such care and attention makes the case of Joyce Kingsley proof against criticism. This is not so. Criticisms can be made in terms of undue reliance on self-report methods, uncritical acceptance of psychoanalytic doctrine and projective test data, neglect of the situational determinants of behaviour (reinforcement contingencies). Such criticisms, however, are rather obvious coming so many years after the original study. This is one of the benefits of hindsight!

It is not always easy to distinguish a factual statement from a mere opinion. A factual statement is an assertion with a firm basis in individual experience and verifiable through intersubjective agreement between competent observers. The 'fact' about which competent observers agree is the interpretation to be placed on evidence available to them all. An opinion is an assertion which may have some basis in individual experience but cannot be easily verified intersubjectively—it is not a 'fact' that independent observers can agree on, either because they cannot agree the evidence, or, having agreed the evidence, differ as to its interpretation.

One should not confuse intersubjective agreement (as the basis of factual knowledge) with agreement between Investigators sharing the same narrow frame of reference. A group of fortune-tellers might well agree on a reading of one's palm or tea-leaves. The strength of intersubjective agreement in professional and scientific work is derived in part from a comprehensive system of concepts, methods, and findings subject to continual validation.

People differ in the extent to which they commit themselves to their opinions. Some are quite dogmatic and find it difficult to believe that they are wrong even when there is strong evidence to that effect. Others are more dispassionate, and seem prepared to consider opinions and evidence which run counter to their own views. Readers should realize that in the exchange of opinions about a case, even in a scientific or professional setting, people may be doing more than merely providing information or interpretation. They may be defending themselves, making excuses, attacking others, showing solidarity, or engaging in other 'performative utterances'—see Smith *et al.* (1956) and Austin (1962).

It is essential for a scientific Investigator to adopt a dispassionate approach to cases. The only justification for strong commitment to personal subjective opinions is when, for one reason or another, the role of Investigator has been abandoned in favour of that of advocate. Perhaps the justification for holding an opinion on a particular case, in the absence of firm evidence for or against it, is that comparable cases in the past support it. Unfortunately, arguments based on 'similar facts' rest on rather insecure foundations, in law at least, and should be treated with care. Consider, for example, the argument that Case D's identification with the teachers in her school was a carry-over from her obedience to parents because it was 'similar' with regard to submission to authority.

Personal opinions are important whenever the case-study stands in need of new ideas. Active debate between Investigators, and active dialogue with participants, should generate numerous possibilities for further inquiry. This is the creative aspect of the case-study. A useful analogy can be drawn with natural selection. In the evolution of ideas about a case, many ideas can be generated but only a few will survive the selective effects of testing for validity.

In some respects a case-study is an exercise in intelligence-gathering. Indeed, in certain contexts it *is* intelligence-gathering! This notion reminds us of the devious, wide-ranging, and unobtrusive methods that can be used in collecting information about a case when the normal ethical prohibitions on certain kinds of scientific investigation are lifted—telephone tapping; intercepting mail and other communications; extensive direct and indirect (electronic) surveillance; the use of stooges, searches, positive and negative persuasion to disclose information; and so on—see Webb *et al.* (1966). At the same time, the secretive nature of such inquiries makes them more liable to abuse, error, and misdirection, since the case-materials are not protected by the usual scientific and professional standards or the right to reply leading, sometimes, to unfortunate consequences.

It is possible for ordinary case-studies to deal in the sorts of 'intelligence' referred to above—statements made under duress, documents improperly obtained, codes of conduct violated, the use of paid informers. Information like this must be handled with care. In one sense it should be rejected as inadmissible because it breaks the normal rules of professional conduct and possibly emanates from an insufficiently credible source. In another sense the information, once available, cannot be ignored and may lead on to further evidence from a credible source which is admissible.

A great deal of factual information, interpretation, and opinion may be packed into a case-study. This is done, where appropriate, by means of abstract general statements which summarize an array of particular facts and issues. Consider, in Case D for example, a statement like the one referred to earlier, 'She encountered major negative life experiences during her first year at college.' The statement is meaningful even without further elaboration, but becomes more so when one or two of the relevant experiences are cited as representative examples. In this way the general statement and its examples can summarize a large array of particular detailed experiences.

There are dangers, however, in going from concrete and particular instances to an abstract and general statement. In particular one may read too much into the general statement, supposing it to cover a wider range of instances than is intended. For example, to say of someone 'He supports the Conservatives' may be taken to mean that he supports all Conservatives on all issues—a most unlikely state of affairs. Such overgeneralized stereotyped assertions may be based on completely inadequate evidence; so we may have a judgment, an attribution, which looks like a generalized statement based on a range of particular facts but is in reality a vacuous opinion or prejudice.

General statements, therefore, should be met with questions like 'How do you know?' 'What evidence is there?' 'Can you give me some actual instances?' or simply 'What do you mean?'

One often-quoted advantage of the case-study method is the way in which multiple sources of evidence tend to point to a common conclusion. The best illustration of this process is detective work. Systematic observation yields valuable evidence and rules out certain possibilities until eventually, if all goes well, there is little room for doubt about the facts of the case and how they must be interpreted—the argument is internally coherent and corresponds with reality. Stone (1984) deals in detail with the problem of proof of fact in criminal cases.

From the point of view of scientific knowledge, in a 'good' case-study the issues will be clearly stated, the methods of inquiry unobjectionable, the evidence overwhelmingly in favour of one interpretation. The better the case-study, the less room there is for debate and criticism. Of course, from an instructional point of view, a 'good' case-study might well be a bad scientific specimen!

The observations and materials that enter into the case-record or function as relevant matters in the minds of the Investigators should be connected in some way with the theories which are, implicitly or explicitly, guiding their inquiries and reasoning. A fact which does not count, one way or another, for or against a particular interpretation is irrelevant. A relevant fact, therefore, is not neutral as between competing theories about a case.

The relationship between theory and evidence is not established simply by counting the number of findings for or against a theory. It is impossible to calculate the weight or value of any item of evidence. Consider instead the following 2 × 2 table (Table 4.1) which shows the four types of instance that can arise, together with the possible Investigator effects.

The individual case-study can be used as a method of explanation and discovery, but it can also be used as a method for testing hypotheses, i.e. as a method of proof. In neither method does statistical inference have any part to play. What is discovered or proved depends on the cogency of the substantive argument and on the available evidence.

Empirical data and logical reasoning are interlocked in the sense that certain sorts of empirical data may elicit certain forms of argument, and certain forms of argument may direct attention to certain sorts of empirical data. Conversely, evidence may prevent consideration of certain logical possibilities, and failure to consider certain logical possibilities may lead to the neglect of available evidence. The search for consistency should not be allowed to restrict the scope of the inquiry, particularly in the early stages.

In a well-constructed psychological case-report all the relevant information should be organied in a complete and explicit logical framework (the substantive argument). The rules covering the organization of this material are determined by the grammar of the language employed, which incorporates the terminology and 'logic' of the psychological theories used by the

Table 4.1 Four types of evidential data

		Evidence (Empirical data)	
		Relevant facts that fit the theory	Relevant facts that do not fit the theory
Theory (Explanation)	True	Type A: Confirming instances. The Investigator tends to overrate them.	Type B: Latent instances. The theory is true as far as it goes, but it does not go far enough. The Investigator remains unaware of these further implications.
	False	Type C: Coincidental instances. Relatively few in number, but the Investigator regards them as confirming instances. They would also confirm other theories including the correct one.	Type D: Falsifying instances. The Investigator tends to underrate them or to ignore them or to discount them.

Investigator(s). Our ability to make inferences depends upon our familiarity with the data and our skill in theorizing. Making a prediction is theorizing—working out the implications in our system of ideas. Unfortunately our theorizing is sometimes very primitive.

Psychological theories particularly rest on an infrastructure of common sense and ordinary language. An Investigator may not appreciate that the *specific* claims or implications of the theory should be kept separate from those that are associated with the wider context of the theory. Hence the value of counter-intuitive implications, i.e. predictions specific to a theory which run counter to what one would otherwise expect.

Accepting opinions from a credible expert source or authority may be necessary if the data are technical and need to be explained or interpreted, or if the case-investigator has insufficient time to make independent inquiries. It goes almost without saying that an expert or authority in one area of a case-study may have no expertise or authority in another area. The competence and credibility of an informant is an issue at every stage and point of an inquiry.

We must not forget that the case-investigator himself, or herself, may commit the sorts of mistakes or malpractices to which we have referred. So, when reading, listening to, or viewing case-material we must be constantly aware of who prepared the case and for what purpose. A case-study may have a latent function, e.g. to accuse a drug company of unethical practices or to deplore housing conditions, although its manifest function may be to illustrate a medical condition or an attempted suicide. Put another way, a case-study may be an exercise in propaganda, not an exercise in scientific research, professional help, or education.

Close examination of case-studies carried out and presented for ulterior motives usually reveals various kinds of faults—missing evidence, fabricated evidence, over-reliance on selected facts, neglect of alternative interpretations, and so on. Applying scientific and professional standards should help reveal such faults.

A case-study can be critically examined by asking whether the best evidence available is being used, whether the information can be corroborated, whether informants are credible, whether the arguments used to make sense of the evidence are the most convincing, and so on, through all the criteria governing scientific and professional merit.

SUMMARY AND CONCLUSIONS

A case-study based on parts of a detailed case published by White (1975) is used to illustrate a number of important aspects of the quasi-judicial case-study method. The relationship between evidence and inference is dealt with at some length because it draws attention to cognitive and language processes which are largely automatic, such as using background knowledge to 'read into' the case-record information which is not explicitly stated, attaching unwarranted meanings to words and phrases, and reasoning by analogy.

A case-study is judged partly by its internal consistency (reliability) and partly by the extent to which its argument can be empirically verified—in the sense of proving resistant to attempts to show it to be false.

Four important questions are raised: What is at issue? What other relevant evidence might there be? How else might one make sense of the data? and How were the data obtained? If these questions can be answered satisfactorily, the major obstacles to progress in the case-study will have been overcome.

Some cautionary remarks are offered in connection with the following matters: the risk of accidental or deliberate mismanagement of a case; the cost of information and the deployment of resources; and the wider context within which the case-study is carried out.

A distinction is drawn between the formal validity of arguments in case-studies and their substantive truth. Formal logic enables one to avoid the more obvious errors of inference, but case-study arguments must be assessed against additional criteria such as the extent to which they correspond to the facts of the real world, the extent to which they can be 'explained' by some kind of psychological theory, and the extent to which competent observers working independently can agree on the findings.

There is likely to be a conflict between the role of impartial Investigator and advocate. The way to deal with strong advocacy is to adopt an adversarial role, although scientific and professional work is usually best served by consensual procedures.

Statements of an abstract and general sort are useful for the purpose of summarization, but should be translatable into their concrete and particular counterparts.

A distinction can sometimes be drawn between the manifest (apparent) function of a case-study and its latent (deeper or real) function.

CHAPTER FIVE

Developing a General Approach to Understanding Individual Cases

INTRODUCTION

The previous chapter concentrated mainly on the complications involved in describing and analysing a case. The aim is to organize and, where possible, to simplify the case-materials. The present chapter moves on to the next aim, which is to explain and synthesize the case-materials. This means imposing the most appropriate pattern of meaning on the available information and arriving at decisions about the most effective course of action.

I have described a psychological case-study as an exercise in solving human problems, with special reference to the individual person. In Chapter 2 I said it was useful to define a problem as a discrepancy between a desired or possible state of affairs (hope, aspiration) and a current or actual state of affairs (present circumstances)—see Duckworth (1983). In order to identify the problem fully, we need to work out in some detail what it is that constitutes the current (actual) state of affairs and makes it less than satisfactory, and what it is that constitutes the future (possible) state of affairs and makes it so much more desirable. The problem, then, is not simply that of moving from a less to a more satisfactory state, but rather that of determining what options are available, what one feels and thinks about them, what particular moves would amount to, what benefit they would bring, what they would cost, and how the moves might be made.

Not unexpectedly, one finds that problems rarely occur singly and in

114

isolation, but present themselves in clusters or 'syndromes' because of their interconnected functional relationships. Thus, for example, excessive zeal by someone in a supervisory position at work might lead to complaints, a loss of production, work stress affecting family relationships, and so on. Similarly, marital disharmony arising from unnecessary dependence or dominance might lead to sexual coolness, loss of mutual friends, financial difficulties, emotional stress, and loss of working efficiency.

In some instances, where the functional connectedness of the problems is relatively weak, it may be possible to deal with the problems on a piecemeal basis. In other instances, where the problems can be traced to a single major root cause, a piecemeal approach may do little more than alleviate a difficulty for a time. In a given case, however, it is not always easy to separate out the superficial from the deeper-lying problems. The question is whether to deal first with the most obvious problem or withhold positive action until a more thorough assessment has been made of other, possibly more important or basic, problems.

So far, we have emphasized a strategic approach to solving human problems. This approach consists of a thorough examination of the basic issues followed by an assessment of the best means to achieve a relatively long-term settlement of those issues. However, in some cases a more opportunistic or 'tactical' approach might yield quicker and better results. This is where Investigators with training in particular methods and experience in particular areas have an advantage—see Egan (1982a,b), Krumboltz and Thoresen (1969) and Masson and O'Byrne (1984), for example.

Since solving human problems involves a comparison of 'undesired' and 'desired' states of affairs with a view to finding a means of moving from the former to the latter, it follows that a thorough assessment of the individual's aspirations and expectations is also necessary. Thus, for example, in the case of a problem associated with excessive zeal by a supervisor, we may find that, initially at least, the people involved have unrealistic expectations. The supervisor may be hoping for support from management and compliance from workers, the workers may see that the only solution is for the supervisor to be moved, the management may simply want a quiet life. All these 'desired' states of affairs may be unattainable. Part of the problem then is to enable the various people involved to recognize what can and cannot be achieved within an acceptable framework of circumstances.

It is possible to extend the notion of a 'problem'. Problems are usually thought of as undesirable states of affairs, usually associated with frustration, stress, disappointment, and other unpleasant experiences. Problems, however, can be viewed with excitement, hope, and anticipation as opportunities to achieve and do the things to which one aspires. Consider, for example, the 'problem' of getting married, of settling into a new job, of retiring, of using a financial windfall, and so on. An important feature of good personal adjustment is the willingness and ability to identify and make use of opportunities for constructive action.

In addition to the distinction between problems as 'constraints' or 'opportunities' one can distinguish constraints which simply withhold satisfaction from constraints which threaten harm. The effect of this second distinction is to draw attention to the relatively greater urgency for defensive or offensive action in situations which theaten harm as compared with situations which limit or deny satisfaction. If we draw an analogy with physical health, then 'opportunities' provide for the extension and exercise (enjoyment) of one's physical capabilities, whereas 'constraints' refer to limitations on them.

Of these constraints, those that constitute acute limitations and threaten serious reductions in life-satisfaction can be expected to provoke crises and emergency reactions. On the other hand, constraints that bring about gradual, but persisting, chronic limitations on action, and set limits to the range of our physical activity (without seriously reducing them in the short run), are likely to be accompnied by correspondingly more persistent, but less intense, emotional reactions.

Obviously, the emotional reactions that accompany behaviour in problematic situations are an important indication of what the situation means to the person, and of what they are inclined to do about it. Emotional reactions vary in the extent to which they help or hinder effective adjustment. It is not possible to generalize because an emotional reaction which is beneficial for one person may not be so for another, or one which is beneficial for a person in one set of circumstances may not be so in another. Description and analysis of a person's emotional reaction to a situation usually becomes a focal issue in a case-study, because emotional reactions indicate how the person views the situation and what he or she wants to do about it. That is to say, it brings into focus the cognitive, affective, and motivational aspects of personal adjustment.

A case-study must take into account the time-dimension of human problems and the emotional reactions that accompany them. For example, in the case of bereavement, there is, or may be, an anticipatory grief reaction, a reaction to the actual death, and a period of mourning afterwards. The problems of adjustment faced by the bereaved person, similarly, change over this time-period.

Let us consider a case in which the emphasis is on the problem-situation rather than on the psychological and other characteristics of the person being investigated. Readers may wish to speculate on the way different sorts of person could be expected to react in such circumstances.

CASE E

The Subject of the study was adopted soon after he was born. When he was in his late 'teens he became actively concerned to locate his biological parents. The adoptive parents had one child of their own who appears not to figure prominently in Case E's own account of his life with them. The adoptive father was a company director, the adoptive mother a housewife. Their socio-economic circumstances were good, and they made good financial provision for both their natural child and their adopted child for when they become mature and independent.

Case E went to the local primary school and enjoyed many of the further educational advantages that money can buy. His years at school were successful in that he took part in a variety of extracurricular activities and obtained good examination results. By the time Case E had left home to work in a branch of his father's business, he had a range of private and group interests, such as music, reading, and outdoor activities related to nature study.

His independence and reliability made him very suitable as an organizer and leader. However, he also displayed a tendency to withdraw at times into solitary pursuits as if avoiding social interaction.

Case E was, at the time of the study, somewhat preoccupied with his own sense of personal identity, and felt that ignorance of his true parentage hindered his understanding of himself. It was not that he was unhappy with his adoptive family but rather that he had not come to terms with the fact that in a very important sense his origins were something of a mystery and therefore different from those of most other people.

Further inquiries involving Case E and other informants revealed that E's social withdrawal had increased steadily over the previous years and was accompanied by a depressed mood and resort to alcohol. The social withdrawal, although by no means abnormal, had been aggravated by two factors. First, E's personal qualities and social background were somewhat different from those of his friends and acquaintances; second, E and his friends shared a common political outlook, but E was rather lukewarm in his support of them.

E's parents had handled the adoption well. They had explained the circumstances as fully as they could as soon as E was old enough to understand. They had treated him otherwise as their own child. E had little recollection of his adoptive status during his school years up to puberty and at times seemed to have derived satisfaction from it.

One of the difficulties, however, was that E's parents were not always able to answer the many questions about his parents that E raised in early adolescence. For example, there are many specific features about one's origins that one normally learns about and takes for granted—one's parents, grand-parents, where they lived, what they were like, whether there were any special circumstances associated with one's birth. Many such facts were not known to E's adoptive parents, so they were unable to satisfy his curiosity.

E's growing concern with his biological origins drew his attention to the fact that whereas his adoptive brother was similar to his parents, E was not. The two boys got on well together, however, and their physical dissimilarity appears to have been of little consequence. Also, like some ordinary children, E would occasionally have fantasies about his 'true' parents. In the early stages, at least, he seems to have avoided the risk of upsetting his adoptive parents by concealing the real depths of his interest in his biological parents, and the mother at least was against the idea of looking for them.

E's adoptive mother was, if anything, a little overprotective, perhaps trying to make up for not being E's 'real' mother, but also perhaps because of her own loneliness and lack of outside interests. The adoptive father was too busy looking after his firm to be able to spend a lot of time with E. As is often the case, this resulted in a less strained relationship.

When E found himself living away from home, working at a branch of the family business, he felt less reluctant about taking active steps to locate his biological parents, partly because of the less frequent contact with the adoptive parents, partly because of a growing independence of them.

Adopted children have some rights of access to their records. With the help of the Social Services, E was able to check the birth certificate and other official records. This information gave him his mother's name and address. He then used detective work to try to locate her physically. This proved to be more difficult and more time-consuming than he had expected, but the investigation developed a momentum of its own and a personal preoccupation to the extent of not keeping the adoptive family informed of progress, or rather lack of progress. The lack of progress was naturally depressing, and E's behaviour was misconstrued by friends as moodiness and over-work.

Eventually, however, E's persistence paid off, and further inquiries enabled him to meet an uncle. It had occurred to E that his search might result in unsatisfactory consequences for him and for his biological and adoptive families, but he had not given much thought to this possibility. Naturally, the prospect of meeting blood-relations face-to-face provoked strong and mixed emotions. When the meeting took place, however, the momentary shock and initial awkwardness gave way to harmonious relationships and a mutual exchange of information. The 'mysteries' of his origins and family connections were disclosed, and E was left with a better understanding but with no special wish to deepen or extend the attachment.

COMMENTARY AND ASSOCIATED ISSUES

(a) Rearranging the information

We have argued that, in many cases, human problems occur not as single issues but as interrelated clusters. It helps therefore to identify and list those problems; although, as we have seen, it is easy to misidentify and misconstrue them. Consider the list of problems derived from Case E:

1. Concern to locate his biological parents.
2. Independence increasing to the point of social withdrawal.
3. Preoccupation with personal identity (obscure origins and different social circumstances).

4. Increased alcohol consumption?
5. Coincidental disagreement with friends.
6. Hiding his feelings and actions from his adoptive parents.
7. Maternal overprotection; mother's vulnerability?
8. Neglect of the consequences of the outcome of the search for his biological parents.

If this case had arisen in a professional context before its happy outcome, the main problems would probably have been seen as the second and third: the second because of its immediacy and risk of worsening, the third because it appears to be a root cause of the other problems.

In Case E we have assumed that the account provided is the whole story. It is not inconceivable, however, that behind that story lies another—a broken romance for example, or homosexuality, or a problem at work—for which the first story is a screen or cover. There is a risk, therefore, in jumping to conclusions about the nature of a human problem. Things are not always what they seem. It is unlikely that the first few perusals of the case will disclose all or the most important issues it contains.

Cases come to one's attention in a variety of ways for a variety of reasons. It is necessary therefore to consider each case in the context in which it has arisen, because the more important issues may prove to lie in the context rather than in the problems as presented. For example, if Case E's preoccupation with his biological origins was not genuine, but rather an excuse to neglect a job which he was finding increasingly irksome, then one's assessment of the problem (in terms of personal/social identity) would be misleading, at least in part, since what appears to be merely a contextual matter, namely absence from and neglect of work, might really indicate a central problem—work-stress or occupational maladjustment perhaps.

Listing the problems provides one precaution against jumping to conclusions about what a case is about; it also helps one to think productively by providing a check-list of matters to be inquired into further. The exercise of listing can be carried further by grouping the problems into related treatment areas or by putting them in chronological order or in terms of their likely causal connections. For example, in Case E the chronological or historical sequence might be: 3, 1, 7, 6, 5, 2, 4, 8; the related treatment areas might be: A(1, 3, 8), B(2, 4, 5), C(6, 7); a possible causal network might be:

$$
\begin{array}{c}
4 \\
\nearrow \ \uparrow \\
3 \rightarrow 1 \rightarrow 6 \rightarrow 2 \rightarrow 8 \\
\uparrow \qquad \uparrow \\
7 \qquad 5
\end{array}
$$

The purpose of listing the issues and sifting through them in the ways suggested is to help the Investigator to impose a full and coherent pattern of meaning on a growing body of evidence. Rather like a jigsaw puzzle, one can sometimes see connections between the pieces, one can complete small sections of the puzzle, one can search for the missing pieces (those that we cannot identify right away, as well as those that are literally missing).

Although it is essential to be able to speculate freely, i.e. think creatively, about a case, it is also essential to assess the likelihood that the ideas thus generated are true. The rule here is to examine the more obvious possibilities before the less obvious ones, on the grounds that they are more likely to be considered reasonable by independent observers, more easily refuted if they are incorrect, and more easily confirmed if they are correct. The process is that of generating ideas, possible solutions to the problem or lines of inquiry to be followed up, and testing them against the relevant evidence. This is standard scientific procedure. Evidence which goes against one's expectations should force a revision of one's ideas about a case, failure to find supportive evidence should also force a revision of one's ideas. Confirmatory evidence, on the other hand, allows us to feel more confident, although we must always consider the possibility that subsequent findings will prove us wrong. Looking for evidence that runs counter to one's beliefs and expectations goes against one's natural inclination, but nevertheless constitutes a sort of scientific moral injunction.

Cases we have worked on for some time, cases with which we are over-familiar and have no more ideas about, may benefit from independent assessment. Investigators fresh to the case may view it in a different way and open up new lines of inquiry.

The first stage of a case-study is complete when the Investigator has made enough inquiries to form a provisional interpretation of the available facts. This is analogous to the physician's tentative diagnosis and the lawyer's tentative opinion. The next stage pursues the provisional interpretation with the aim of collecting further evidence which either supports or fails to support the tentative hypothesis. We shall soon see that, as far as psychological case-studies are concerned, there may be little chance of finding external points of reference for anchoring one's social judgment. In other words, there may be no available psychometric norms, survey results, and so on, but this should not deter one from looking.

Comparison between case-study data and external data need not be exact. Even rough approximations may offer some guidance. For example, the suicidal grief of a recently widowed woman has to be set against the general rate of recovery of widows; the bizarre appearance and behaviour of many adolescents has to be set against its absence in people a few years older. Case E's social withdrawal and solitary drinking might be seen as not so unusual by observers working in related areas. The minority report on the case of Maria Colwell points out that the behaviour of the stepfather is more comprehensible once cross-cultural differences in social attitudes are taken into account— see Department of Health and Social Security (1974).

The important thing is to collect enough evidence to rule out all explanations which cannot account for the facts, giving priority to what is called 'best evidence', which is evidence that competent observers agree is most directly relevant, is easily corroborated, and comes from highly reliable sources. It is necessary, therefore, to search for evidence which, if it can be found, goes *against* the various explanations put forward. As the evidence mounts up, in the early stages at least, it may increase the number and variety of problems in the case-study. This is all to the good, in a way, because it ensures that the case is investigated thoroughly. The more complex a case becomes, the greater the need for a systematic procedure to keep the case-materials and the lines of inquiry under control.

We saw earlier in this chapter that a list of 'problems' can be generated for a particular case-study. We also saw that such problems are likely to increase in the early stages of the inquiry, especially if multiple perspectives are used to explore the internal ramifications of the case, and if external (objective) points of reference are introduced to give substance to subjective impressions. The various facets and problems can be classified or arranged in various ways, e.g. historically or according to type, or shown as a balance sheet of constraints and opportunities or as foreground and background. This too may help to further the investigation by drawing attention to issues which might otherwise have gone unnoticed.

One of the difficulties with professional case-studies is that they tend to come into operation in response to crises; major problems of adjustment require urgent action. The consequence is that too little time is available to examine the case in detail, to work out what is likely to happen in the future, or to take preventive measures. A further consequence is a dearth of well-researched cases for teaching purposes.

In military and political policy-making we encounter the term 'scenario', which refers to a possible situation that can be constructed to test out the available military or political responses. A case-investigator, similarly, can construct possible 'scenarios' in an attempt to work out, perhaps with the help of the Subject of the case-study, what the response options are. Normal planning and fantasy provide examples of similar processes, albeit less systematic or explicit. An extension of the method is to generate a range of scenarios from the best to the worst case. Decisions about courses of action can then be based on the subjective probabilities one can assign to these possible outcomes, or on the need to prepare for the worst, even if that means not being able to make the most of a good outcome. Decision analysis is dealt with in Chapter 8.

One danger in case-studies is to overemphasize the negative characteristics of the person and his/her circumstances whilst neglecting positive characteristics and circumstances. In studies of elderly people, for example, when considering the problems associated with multiple infirmity, we tend to concentrate on the elderly person's deficits, when we should also consider ways of using the person's residual capacities and environmental supports.

Both of the above measures—constructing possible scenarios and devoting attention to the 'positive' features of the case—make it more likely that the Investigator will come up with more ideas for dealing with the problems and therefore be more likely to arrive at effective solutions.

The use of a team of Investigators may lead to initial disagreements, but this is all to the good since it will increase the range of actual and possible problems in the case, increase the amount of relevant evidence, and increase the range of suggested solutions. Subsequently, if the Investigators are rational and competent, there should be a convergence of opinion (to the extent that the evidence is unambiguous) about the case.

(b) Problems: Past, present and future

Cases vary according to whether they are studied retrospectively, prospectively, or concurrently. One can expect to have more control over a prospective study; retrospective studies may become partly concurrent. There is a time dimension to the Subject (or Object) of the case; it has a past, a present, and a future. The list of problems in a case-study can be considered in terms of these three broad categories.

1. Problems that have arisen in the past and have been resolved or coped with to the extent that they no longer constitute problems in the present. Such problems may give information about the Subject's personal qualities and circumstances as life-history data, but care is needed in using historical data and 'similar facts' as evidence relevant to current problems.
2. Problems that have arisen in the past and persisted to the present. These are relatively 'chronic' problems and it is likely that their persistence has given rise to further problems which would not have arisen had the problems been dealt with promptly or effectively in the first place. This second category also includes problems which have just arisen, in the very recent past, such that the person is still in the early stages of reacting to the problem. If the problem is severe we refer to it as a 'crisis', because it threatens to disrupt the person's whole life.
3. Problems that can be resolved or coped with only with difficulty and are likely to persist beyond the immediate future. These are the problems which occupy the foregound of a case-study. Additionally, however, in this category of current persisting problems, are problems which have not yet arisen but will arise, or may arise in due course, simply because one can forecast with some confidence the way things will go. The most obvious everyday examples are those associated with an excess of expenditure over income, keeping 'bad company', being on a poor or harmful diet, or working in stressful or dangerous conditions.

Investigators familiar with particular problem areas in human behaviour have expectations about the normal course of events, rather like a doctor has expectations about the course of an illness. One should not take this analogy too far, however, because human behaviour is so complicated, and contextual factors are so uncertain, that clinical prediction—forecasting individual behaviour on the basis of data about the individual—is hazardous, as discussed in Chapter 8. Nevertheless, an Investigator is duty-bound to examine the case-materials and to use his intelligence and experience to identify the problems that seem likely to persist or to arise in due course. These anticipated difficulties then became part of the problem-list, to be dealt with as appropriate, or preferably by preventing them from arising in the first place.

Consider the following examples based on a few of the cases already referred to. Case E will face the problem of how his adoptive parents will react to his finding blood-relations; he may have to deal with approaches from them since the relationship is not simply one-way. He may have to resolve conflicts of loyalty. If he gets married and has children he will have to deal with the complications arising from having two different sorts of relative. Case D—Joyce Kingsley—at one stage in her life-history had to face up to a problem that might have been foreseen by an experienced Investigator, namely the sexual difficulties that arose because of her moral training. However, her husband's loss of religious commitment was quite unpredictable, given the available case-material. Case C can expect to have to deal with the question of her parents' infirmity, although that is probably simply an additional problem and too remote a possibility to be relevant at this stage. She can be expected to develop some odd personal qualities and to become increasingly isolated socially unless she can be helped to form new relationships with others. She needs to find some way of keeping in touch with her line of work, otherwise she is likely to become less employable as time goes by.

Some problems disappear without any deliberate effort on the part of the Investigator or the Subject of the case-study. It is partly a matter of a problem 'solving itself in time', since with the passage of time there are changes in the person and in his/her circumstances. There are changes in attitudes, in the sorts of stress experienced, changes in opportunities for action, changes in the resources available to the person, and hence changes in the way the Subject's problem is defined. It follows that simply 'biding one's time' may sometimes be an appropriate course of action (or rather inaction!). The Investigator should resist the urge to 'do something positive' when a more passive 'wait-and-see' attitude might be more appropriate. This is not the same as ignoring the problem.

(c) Objectivity and case-law

The virtual absence of explicit case-law in most areas of psychology means that it is difficult or impossible to make the sorts of comparisons one would like to make between one person and those other people with whom he or she can be properly compared. The whole psychometric movement in psychology has been an attempt to come to grips with a similar problem in relation to the assessment of general-purpose characteristics such as intelligence, scholastic achievement, occupational aptitude, and various attributes of personality.

In many areas of professional work, references to psychometric norms are commonplace in case-studies, as in statements about a child's IQ or his reading age, or about an adult's vocational interests, life-satisfaction or capacity for independent living. Unfortunately, such isolated items of information, useful as they are in dealing with individual cases, are no substitute for psychological case-law. If such case-law existed, it would provide us with representative and model cases described in some detail, with particular reference to the key structural features of cases of a given kind.

The development of psychological case-law presupposes widespread agreement about the procedures to be used in carrying out case-studies, in compiling case-materials, and in publishing the results. No such agreement is apparent at present. This deficiency stands in marked contrast to the profusion of case-material available in law, in business studies, and in medicine.

Survey research archives and the results of experimental psychology provide further examples, rather like that of psychometric standards, of the way in which individual cases might be looked at in relation to relatively objective norms and standards, in respect of particular features of the case, such as spending patterns, housing amenities, and leisure activities, or emotional reactions, persuasability and learning. Survey and experimental research, however, is concerned mainly with aggregated data of a very general sort, and rarely deals with the issues central to psychological case-studies (apart from single-case experimental studies). One would usually have to look for specialized surveys on such issues as divorce, suicide and parasuicide, interpersonal hostility, crime, occupational adjustment, and so on, in order to find out whether they provide results relevant to forming an opinion about a particular case, e.g. the chance of remarriage, the likelihood that an attempted suicide was genuine, the prospect of advancement in a particular career. Stone (1984) argues that experimental psychology has contributed little to the analysis of criminal cases.

The virtual absence of case-law and the irrelevance of much experimental and survey data to the study of individual cases does not mean that the Investigator should not search for such material. There may well be published data which have a bearing on the case in question. The difficulty is simply that of finding the information or even learning where it is likely to be found.

In cases where the central problem of adjustment seems to be rather rare, as in Case E's search for his biological parents, one would not expect to find published source materials of a directly comparable sort. If, however, such cases are redescribed in more general terms, as Case E might be redescribed as a problem of 'personal identity', then one is more likely to come across relevant normative data in published sources.

As we have seen, identifying the basic issues and problems is a major achievement in carrying out a case-study. Being able to identify a general (basic) class of problems of which a specific problem is a member is part of this achievement. Investigators should remember that cases sometimes turn out to be different from what they seem initially to be.

The main reason for looking for external, public, objective points of reference for a case-study is that one does not want to be confined to one's subjective experience, which is liable to misleading heuristics and biases—see Chapter 10. We can make our assessments more objective by calling on competent independent Investigators for assistance and by searching for published materials relevant to the case in question.

It is, of course, necessary to make one's standards of judgment—whether subjective or objective—explicit in the write-up of the case, otherwise the reader may be misled about the validity of one's inferences and recommendations. If there are no comparable cases available for comparison, and no relevant survey results, experimental data or psychometric norms, then the 'procedural' or 'methodological' features of the case are likely to determine the acceptability of its findings. This book is an attempt to show the sorts of procedural or methodological features a case-study should have if it is to be regarded as a scientific study, even if it is, to all intents and purposes, a unique case. To say that science is not concerned with the individual case is simply to ignore the empirical and applied aspects of science in order to focus attention on its conceptual and theoretical aspects. The individual and the general case walk hand-in-hand.

STANDARDS AND JUDGMENTS

In making judgments about what constitutes a 'case' or a 'problem', we refer to certain standards of comparison. The most obvious standard of comparison is the 'norm'. We form, out of personal experience and the shared experience of others, subjective standards or frames of reference which enable us to make judgments—for example, judgments about whether people are tall, short, bright, stupid, rich, poor, well-adjusted, or poorly adjusted. A great deal of effort has gone into the task of refining and standardizing psychological judgments, mainly through the use of psychometric measures of characteristics applicable to everyone, e.g. life-satisfaction, neuroticism, interests.

For the moment, however, let us consider some relatively simple and obvious standards of comparison. First, historic baselines or trends. If a person has been doing his job well for many years, then a change in his normal efficiency or work-satisfaction could give rise to concern. If a child's progress at school begins to fall behind or to move ahead of the other children with whom he is normally compared, then this may raise questions in the minds of his teachers. These examples illustrate our tendency to expect people to behave consistently. If they do not, then we feel obliged to explain their behaviour by attributing it either to a change in their environment or to a change in their personal characteristics. Thus, we may attribute a change in working efficiency or job satisfaction to a change in working conditions or to a change in the person's attitudes and values. We may attribute a change in a child's rate of progress at school to greater parental supervision or to a shift in the child's interests. These sorts of judgments are common and form the basis of our expectations about how people are likely to behave in future circumstances. These beliefs, judgments, and expectations, however, are normally latent or implicit. We tend to make statements explicit only when called upon to justify our actions or to communicate our views to others.

Normative or actuarial standards of judgment are appropriate when we need to compare an individual's characteristics or circumstances with those of other people, e.g. a child's intelligence, attendance record, or school behaviour, a doctor's career progress or prescribing patterns. Negative deviations from the norm may indicate the nature of the problem.

Ipsative standards of judgment are appropriate when we need to compare an individual's characteristics in relation to each other, e.g. his values and preferences, or his behaviour on one occasion with his behaviour on another, e.g. before and after marriage or the birth of a child, before and after a treatment programme. Again, negative deviations such as reductions in life-satisfaction, achievement, progress, output, and so on, are usually indicative of personal problems.

The historical trends on which judgments are based may occur naturally in real life or be artificially induced by experimental or quasi-experimental treatment conditions. Controlled quantitative studies of single cases are commonly reported in the literature. They constitute a rather distinct type of case-study associated with a special sort of methodology and confined to issues that can be studied in an experimental or quasi-experimental way—see Stanley (1985). A single-case experimental study may well form part of a comprehensive case-study, but should not be confused with it conceptually.

An interesting feature of historical trends in personal adjustment is that adaptation tends to take place in response to changes in characteristics and circumstances. For example, people can 'get used to' being widowed, out of a job, or in the public eye. Similarly, people can get used to asserting themselves more vigorously, feeling hungry, organizing their time more effectively, or being depressed—in the sense that their 'adaptation level' shifts to a new norm. Adaptation and habituation are particularly easy if the changes are small and gradual. Not only the person, but also the observer, tends to adapt in time to the individual's changed patterns of adjustment. Hence our surprise when we encounter someone after a long interval of time during which they have changed gradually but substantially in appearance, manner, or in other ways. Our expectations, based on out-of-date baselines, are not borne out.

It is sometimes said that the best single predictor of future behaviour is past behaviour, i.e. historical baselines and trends. There are, however, other ways of making predictive judgments. Forecasting future behaviour in the context of a case-study is dealt with in Chapters 8 and 10.

Ideal standards of comparison are used when making judgments in relation to model or perfect cases. For example, a frail elderly person may be performing at a level well below what is possible given her physical and mental condition and the sort of environent she is in. This 'excess disability', as it is called, represents the discrepancy between what the person could achieve—in this case in relation to the ordinary activities of daily life, especially self-maintenance—and what the person is actually achieving. This discrepancy reveals where effective remedial action can be directed.

Another example of the use of ideal standards would be the common practice of setting goals in behavioural management—performance appraisal exercises in industry, behaviour modification techniques in the treatment of obesity, smoking, and so on.

As already mentioned, it is possible to make comparisons between 'what is' and 'what ought to be' in relation to a person's adjustment to his or her environment. Many of these standards are derived from prevailing social prescriptions—for example, with regard to marital relationships, occupational effort, scientific or commercial honesty. Such normative prescriptions— about how people 'ought' to behave—must be distinguished from actual social behaviour, which may be very different. Also, the internalized standards of conduct characteristic of a particular person may be at variance with those of other people, and this may lead to conflict and stress—as in the case of Joyce Kingsley.

Comparisons and contrasts with other people who are similar in certain respects is possibly the commonest sort of social judgment in case-studies. Self–other comparisons are familiar in ordinary everyday experience and play an important part in the formation of the self-concept and in feelings of self-esteem throughout life. Whether in relation to appearance, social attractiveness, intelligence, health, competence, or whatever, we experience on countless occasions the differences between ourselves and others. These differences lead to feelings of satisfaction or dissatisfaction depending upon whether we judge ourselves to be better or worse in relation to the comparison-other for the attribute in question. Similarly, we make discriminations between other people, leading usually to evaluative categorical attributions—'He is a good golfer', 'She is a good cook', 'He cannot be relied upon', 'She lacks insight'.

Case-study materials abound with judgments about the personal qualities of the individal concerned—his or her traits, abilities, attitudes, and so on. These judgments are usually based, either implicitly or explicitly, on normative expectations about other people with whom it is thought the individual can be usefully and fairly compared. Often, such comparisons name a specific other person—another case perhaps in the experience of the Investigator. Here, the form of reasoning is by analogy: P_1 is like P_2 in respect of characteristics D and E and therefore in F and G. Comments like 'This case is very similar to that of. . .' or 'She is like her sister. . .' illustrate the pervasiveness of reasoning by analogy in case-studies, and in the informal social judgments of everyday life. Even the choice of the characteristics mentioned in discussing a case is determined to some extent by normative expectations about what is relevant, by the availability of the conceptual and linguistic frameworks for expressing one's views, and by the vividness of our recollections.

Although there are usually superficial or obvious similarities between the person in question and the person with whom he or she is being compared, the risk in reasoning by analogy is that there are also dissimilarities—see Hesse (1963). At best, such reasoning is heuristic and tentative, not compelling. The danger is that the cases which come to mind when making comparisons will come to mind just because they were striking and memorable, not because they were representative of the class of cases with whom the individual in question might be fairly compared—see Chapter 10.

PROCEDURAL FRAMEWORKS

A case-study which is methodologically correct from a scientific 'quasi-judicial' point of view must incorporate a great deal of formality in the sense of following procedural rules in a systematic way, and making issues explicit. A case-study which lacks formality is likely to suffer from omissions, distortions, and other errors.

The same sorts of 'proper procedure' are found in other contexts—from landing an aeroplane to sorting out one's financial affairs with an accountant. The nearest familiar analogies are with medical or legal advice. The doctor takes account of the signs and symptoms of your disorder; the lawyer listens to your account of the difficulty you are in. Both doctor and lawyer then go on to examine your case more systematically, using the procedures appropriate to their professions. The doctor carries out certain tests, the lawyer identifies appropriate documents and witnesses. Both doctor and lawyer try to see whether your 'case' fits one or other of the general classes of case with which they are familiar, e.g. stomach ulcer, trespass. There may be complications to take account of, special circumstances affecting the way in which the health problem or the legal difficulty can be dealt with, such as dietary habits, rights of way. Such complications can usually be dealt with by following the rules of procedure appropriate for medicine or the law respectively. In these well-worked professional areas most problems have been encountered before, and there are fairly standard ways of dealing with them. Only rarely is it necessary to devise a new solution for an otherwise intractable problem—as when a doctor identifies a new illness or a lawyer senses a 'precedent'—a case that will serve as an example for a new ruling.

Each scientific and professional discipline employs general and specific conceptual and methodological frameworks in dealing with its problems. A case-study can be examined in a variety of such frameworks. For example,

Case D—Joyce Kingsley—can be looked at from both a psychological and a sociological perspective. A marital problem might be looked at biologically, psychologically, sociologically, and in accountancy terms. Each perspective requires a particular sort of selection, organization, and interpretation of the relevant data (evidence). Such multiple perspectives generally provide a richer, deeper understanding of the case than one could get from any one perspective alone. The same general point was made many years ago in an article by Jocher (1928) which demonstrated considerable insight into the scientific character of the case-study method and argued, as I have done, that its roots reach far back into human history. Thinking in terms of particular cases and learning from examples seems to be a fundamental cognitive process.

MANAGING AND EVALUATING CASES

So far, we have neglected the 'management problems' that can arise as a consequence of dealing with the various people who contribute to a case-study. They are relevant in so far as mismanaging them may retard the progress of the case-study, lose relevant information, and so jeopardize the outcome. Mismanagement may arise from being too critical or too casual or too demanding of time or inquiring too closely into private affairs, being impatient and not establishing rapport, not helping the other person to come to terms with his or her own mistakes or deficiencies, not communicating effectively with people, not showing consideration or thanks.

Problems in a case-study do not necessarily arise independently of the person(s) charged with dealing with the case, since the Investigator(s) can, to some extent, choose to formulate and deal with the case in a particular way. For example, in the case of an employee whose style of interaction with others is abrasive and dominating, a manager might choose to deal with the problem in terms of redeployment or a change in job-content, or he might choose to deal with it by means of counselling and training the employee in social relationships, or in terms of modifying his behaviour in the natural work environment by encouraging others to adopt unrewarding modes of response to that employee's dominating and abrasive manner. Each of these different ways of dealing with the basic problem—say low morale—introduces its own problems of implementation and subsequent evaluation of the outcome.

The investigative process, problem-solving, can incorporate, or be incorporated in, the therapeutic (treatment, management) process. We must not neglect the possibility that the Investigators themselves may create problems within the case.

It is not necessary to go into the details of evaluation research, except to say that only under very closely controlled conditions can rigorous and precise assessments of the effects of a course of action, e.g. a form of treatment, a change in working methods, an environmental change, be monitored and assessed. Most professional case-studies usually involve recommendations as to the course of action to be taken as a consequence of the findings, but much less usually follow up its effectiveness.

Evaluation means testing whether the course of action recommended was actually taken, and if so whether the outcome was as expected. In practice, things are not so simple. The course of action implemented may differ somewhat from that recommended, it may be difficult to monitor what is happening, and outcomes may be affected by factors that the Investigator has not considered or are outside his control. See Cronbach and associates (1980) for a general perspective on programme evaluation. See also Levine and Levine (1977).

Case-studies carried out in an experimental or quasi-experimental context are more likely to incorporate techniques for evaluating progress and outcome than are case-studies carried out in more natural, less constrained, circumstances. It is important, from the point of view of case-study methodology generally, that some form of evaluation be incorporated as a matter of course, and that the data collected find their way into the case-record. Among the more usual sorts of single-case evaluation techniques are the following: standardized behavioural reports and checklists, personal questionnaires and rating-scales, performance and goal attainment measures. Naturally, the sorts of evaluation methods used depend upon the nature of the case and the context within which it is investigated. The aim is to generate objective quantifiable data—good evidence—so that the problems can be properly assessed at the outset and so that the effects of intervention from initial baseline levels can be demonstrated.

Gingerich (1984) deals with the question of the extent to which single-case evaluation techniques taught in training are subsequently used in professional practice. He found considerable diversity depending upon factors like prior training, agency policy, and area of application.

SUMMARY AND CONCLUSIONS

Human problems are usually thought of in terms of chronic life difficulties or as crises and stresses arising from life events. But some problems can be regarded as positive challenges and opportunities for personal development. One must always be alert to the positive features of a case even though most 'cases' arise because of their negative features.

Case-study problems can be dealt with in different ways ranging from a piecemeal approach, which gives priority to those aspects of the case which are easy to deal with, to a more fundamental strategic approach, which attempts to identify and deal with the basic problem(s). Human problems can be usefully thought of in terms of how to move from a less desirable to a more desirable state of affairs, how to manage environmental constraints and opportunities, and how to manage personal assets and liabilities.

The central problem in a psychological case-study is likely to be an emotional upset related to the individual's self-regard and social relationships, as illustrated by Case E.

The information in the case-record can be rearranged and possibly extended in the process of identifying the focal issues. It would be useful to be able to use normative data from psychometric norms, social surveys, and experimental investigations, so as to determine how the Subject compares with other people in respect of relevant matters, such as social values, defensive reactions, and self-regard. Unfortunately it is usually difficult to locate relevant normative data, except in specialized areas such as clinical and educational psychology. The difficulty is that normative standards established in a particular way under closely controlled conditions may not apply to particular cases in special circumstances. The way forward, in the absence of objective external standards of comparison, is to search more thoroughly for relevant evidence within the particular case and to maintain high standards of investigative procedure.

Case-studies can be carried out retrospectively, prospectively, and concurrently. Each case has a past, a present, and a future. The time dimension is usually important especially in relation to the practical management of the case, since the character of the case is likely to change over time even without deliberate intervention by the Investigator.

Common knowledge and professional experience provide a basis for subjective judgment. We commonly assess people in relation to deviations from their normal baseline behaviour, as when we judge someone to be angry, productive, ill, or 'losing ground'. We also commonly assess people in relation to 'comprison others'—particular persons with whom they can be usefully compared—reasoning by analogy.

The psychological study of individual cases follows a procedure which is logically comparable with that used by a lawyer or physician. Reasoning in terms of particular cases, and learning from examples, especially by a process of comparison and contrast, appears to be a fundamental cognitive process and to be a method of reasoning with a long social history.

No attempt is made to cover specific problems and techniques associated with the *management* of individual cases, for example in counselling or behavioural management, except by way of injunctions about maintaining scientific and professional standards. We are not in a position to report on how psychological cases are in fact conducted. Studies of this sort generally arise only in response to serious derelictions of professional duty which come to light because of socially unacceptable consequences. Nevertheless, evaluation is a difficult but increasingly important aspect of the work on individual cases and social programmes, for example in education, medicine, and human services generally.

CHAPTER SIX

Finding Relationships

INTRODUCTION

Previous chapters described how to identify and list the many particular features to be found in a typical case-study. Some of these features lie at the forefront of a case; others, less important, fall into the background. Some of the features are clearly defined; others are not. Some need to be dealt with right away; others can wait. This chapter deals with the relationships *between* the features of a case: how they influence each other; how they can be grouped into broad problem areas.

The normal individual's adjustment to his or her environment can be thought of in terms of a delicately balanced ecological system, and it is the essence of such a system that a change in one part tends to induce changes in other parts. For example, an increase in the time required to deal with one aspect of one's life means a reduction in the time available to deal with other aspects. Loss of employment brings about reduced income and status, loss of social contacts, relief from certain responsibilities, shifts in the use of time, and so on.

It follows that one problem in a case cannot be adequately defined until it has been examined in relation to other problems in the case. Similarly, one should not take remedial action in relation to a problem before considering how such remedial action might affect other features of the case.

The problems in a case may lie, like Russian dolls, one inside the other; dealing with one discloses another. Or, by contrast, the problems can be thought of in terms of the 'domino effect'—the solution to one problem may trigger solutions in a series of others. Probably the most appropriate metaphor to use when considering the relationship between problems in a case—a metaphor which we shall use again in connection with the analysis of arguments—is that of the web or network. Removing one of the strands (problems) weakens the web (of difficulties) a little; removing several strands, especially key strands, weakens it considerably; remove enough strands and the whole web (of difficulties) falls apart or comes adrift. The same metaphor can be used in relation to providing supports to establish and maintain a Subject's readjustment to his or her environment.

The Subject at the centre of a case-study is often a person in difficulties. His or her maladjustment can be thought of in terms of an ecological system which has been disrupted and has so far failed to return to its normal state. The risk is that dealing with one aspect of the system may make matters worse rather than better. For example, in the case of a girl who is at risk sexually, instructions and warnings may increase rather than decrease her sexual interest and involvement. Thus, the order in which case-problems are dealt with may be important. In the case of the girl just referred to, unobtrusive surveillance, restriction of opportunities for sexual involvement, contraceptive measures, instruction and warning to potential violators, may be more effective. If this particular problem is the key to the case, and if the measures to deal with it prove successful, some of the related problems—misbehaviour, parental anxiety, lack of progress at school—may disappear.

In the case of a single-parent student whose family commitments are in conflict with her academic commitments, simply increasing the pressure for academic progress may aggravate the problem by raising her level of anxiety and further disrupting an already unstable organization of behaviour. A better solution, probably, would be to counsel the student, exploring in detail her use of time, her sources of social and financial support, and her hopes and aspirations. It may be that some reorganization in these areas would increase the amount of time available for academic work sufficiently to ensure satisfactory progress. Or it may be that examination of the case would reveal the need for much more drastic action—perhaps withdrawing from academic study for a year or so, perhaps fostering the children temporarily, because of irreconcilable factors in the case.

Failure to think problems through tends to lead to inadequate solutions. As we have seen, some of the difficulties listed initially may be merely symptomatic of a deeper-lying problem, as in Case E's social withdrawal and solitary drinking. Solving the basic problem eliminates its adverse effects, like curing a disease removes its symptoms. This 'medical model', however, can be misleading. Specific behavioural difficulties may be associated with specific causes and conditions, and not be symptomatic of any deeper-lying problem or disorder. In such cases, specific remedies for specific difficulties, e.g. shyness, sexual inhibitions, school refusal, interpersonal conflict, or over-spending, may be all that is required.

It is probably best to assume initially that a closer study of a case may reveal problems of different sorts—acute as well as chronic, current as well as pending, superficial as well as deeper-lying. The procedure for organizing one's understanding of them is as follows:

First, list the features of the case and sort them into groups which seem to belong together in a functional sense, i.e. to be causally connected with one another. The reasons for sorting the features into groups need to be made clear. These reasons provide a provisional definition of the major issues of the case.

Second, follow up this tentative grouping by collecting further evidence, by developing interpretations, and by regrouping the problems if this seems appropriate.

Third, when no further ideas of a creative or critical kind are forthcoming, and the empirical findings are sufficiently substantial, the case-materials settle into a fairly firm pattern. At this juncture one redefines the major issues and justifies this account of the case. This needs to be made explicit not only to clarify one's own ideas but also to communicate them to other people.

Let us consider these three steps in relation to another case-study.

CASE F

Case F was for a time a member of a religious order. After leaving, he worked in local government, married, and raised a family. The case-study concentrates on the circumstances and events associated with the transition from life in a religious institution to life as a lay person.

His father was a miner, his mother a housewife. His parents were devout catholics, and religion was a major influence in his upbringing at home and at school. At the age of sixteen he started to train as a Brother. On completion of his training he was occupied with youth and community work for about ten years until he left the Order at the age of thirty-two. F's father died while F was at school; his mother was a domineering sort of person and F did not get on well with her. The family had friends in the Church who suggested that F might join an Order. The religious training F received was strict and authoritarian, but he was well-liked by his superiors and enjoyed the limited freedom he was granted and a sense of security in a large community setting. F subsequently moved to a smaller establishment where his work involved him more with the lay community. It was at this stage that he became more aware of the contrast between communal and lay styles of life. He knew of individuals who had left religious orders to marry and lead a secular life. However, he was strongly committed to Christianity, celibacy, and the Order, and derived considerable satisfaction and security from his life as a Brother. Consequently, he was relatively unaffected by his first encounters with the lay community, and continued with his training. F's doubts about his vocation emerged subsequent to the Second Vatican Council which promoted liberal and democratic principles. This event brought about major changes in social organization and in the attitudes of many individuals in the Catholic Church. F was unhappy with the liberalization, having been brought up and trained to operate in a hierarchical system, where one accepted certain assumptions and traditional practices. He obtained little help and guidance from others, since they were faced with similar problems of how to behave and what to accept. At this time F had moved to another part of the country and had taken his solemn vows. The sexual temptations he encountered in his new location overwhelmed F's moral defences, partly because he was physically attractive to women and had little experience of relationships with members of the opposite sex. To some extent, therefore, F's religious commitment was made without full knowledge of what it might entail. F was transferred to another area. His superiors were aware of his 'failings' and arranged for him to be trained in social work so that he could still work 'professionally' in the event of his leaving the Order. This illustrates F's continuing dependence on his superiors and his apparent lack of insight into his own character. After some time a close relationship was re-established with one of the women with whom F had been friendly. Since this was incompatible with his religious vows, F applied to have them revoked. Soon after F left the Order, he first lived with, and then married, the woman with whom he had become involved. He found employment in community work, set up a home, and lived as a lay person, although he still experienced difficulty in dealing with members of the opposite sex. There are indications that for a time F felt guilty about his behaviour and could not discuss it openly or honestly. Paradoxically, perhaps, he was reluctant to participate in lay social organizations outside his area of employment but retained an association with his former religious Order.

COMMENTARY AND RELATED ISSUES

(a) Listing, grouping, and redefining

The problems in Case F can be listed, as follows:

1. The Subject's ambivalent attitude to women in general.
2. His attitude to his wife in particular.
3. His relationship to the Catholic Church and to his former Order.
4. His religious beliefs.
5. His attitude towards himself and his past, i.e. his self-concept.
6. His attitude towards his mother.
7. His ability to cope without the protection and support of a large organization.

I have omitted from the above list any mention of 'procedural problems', i.e. problems associated with the methods used to collect the information, to establish the reliability of information, to validate the information provided, to counsel and advise F, and so on.

If we now sort these problems into functionally similar or related sets, we can see three broad categories: Set A—problems 1, 2, and 6 (Attitude to the opposite sex); Set B—problems 3 and 4 (Religion); Set C—problems 5 and 7 (Personal identity and social relationships). If we consider the case in terms of past, present, and future phases, we could identify other problems, e.g. how his mother will react to him and to his wife, how he will cope with inevitable marital tensions, what he will do about having children, and their moral training. For present purposes, however, we can ignore them. The reasons for grouping the problems in this way are as follows: Set A—problems 1, 2, and 6—raise the general issue of the Subject's relationships with members of the opposite sex. Some of the case-materials (not included above) indicate that his mother was a domineering figure that F had no great affection for. His commitment to a religious order may have derived in part from a desire to get away from his mother and 'women in general'. Having spent so many years in all-male organizations it is not surprising that F might have some difficulty in establishing sexually neutral relationships with women. Although his marriage appears satisfactory he may continue to be susceptible to the attractions of other women. His wife appears to be a dominant figure and she may well have some of the attributes of his mother. This might lead to an abrupt change of attitude in the event of marital conflict.

Set B—problems 3 and 4—relate to the issue of how the Subject is to stabilize his religious beliefs and practices, having been unable to adjust to the changes that followed the Second Vatican Council, and having abandoned what had been a firm commitment to a religious way of life. Although the case-materials are short on information about this area, in spite of its central importance to the case-study, identifying religion as a major issue at least serves to remind us of the need for further evidence in this area.

Set C—problems 5 and 7—raise the related issues of personal and social identity, i.e. how the person sees himself in relation to other people. Within the religious Order, his role, status, and functions were very well-defined and regulated. From the time he exchanged the routine, status, and security of the Order for the freedom and uncertainty of the wider society, he has had to cope on his own, with whatever support he can obtain from family and friends. The increased tolerance of people like F by the Church meant that the break was not as severe as it might have been had liberalization not taken place. His continued association with the Order and the continuation of friendships he had made during his religious career could be further investigated to see what part they played in the transition to ordinary life—the transition being the ecological process of establishing and maintaining the Subject's readjustment to his environment.

In the Introduction to this chapter I said that the third step in reorganizing the information in a case-study is to redefine the major issues and to justify this account. With F, then, we have the case of a man who, partly through family circumstances, was easily persuaded to embark on a religious career. His progress was good, helped in part perhaps by an aversion to women acquired in response to his mother's domineering ways. However, exposure to the wider world through religious work in the community stimulated hitherto inhibited aspects of his psychological make-up; in particular, sexual desires. His religious convictions and vows were further weakened by radical changes within the Church, which included changes in the traditional practices of religious orders. His religious Order could no longer provide the authority and support he had grown used to. The incompatibility of his sexual desires and his religious vows and duties forced a decision to leave the Order and, eventually, to marry and to try to establish himself in the outside world.

The justification for this account is that it makes reasonable sense; it fits the facts, in so far as these are known; there is nothing in the case-materials to suggest equally convincing interpretations. It seems unlikely that sexual temptation alone, without the crisis of conscience, would have led to his leaving the Order. Similarly, it seems unlikely that the crisis alone, without the sexual temptation, would have been sufficient.

The problem of transition that we have been describing and discussing was solved by the Subject of the case-study in association with friends, colleagues, and superiors, and the woman who was to become his wife. The problems that remained at the time of the study were speculative—they lay largely in the future. His attitude to his wife and to women in general had to stand the test of time and circumstance. His religious beliefs and practices appeared to have relaxed sufficiently to allow him to make the transition without losing contact with his religious brethren. His personal identity and social relationships will have undergone some change, as for everyone. A further follow-up study would show whether his readjustment has been successful in the long term as it seems to have been in the short term.

(b) Making the account explicit

The foregoing case illustrates the point that different Investigators may impose different sorts of emphasis on its various aspects. A religious counsellor would probably see F's religious beliefs and practices as central, whereas his supervisor at work would focus on his effectiveness as a community worker. There is no single obvious focus for this particular case-study. Nor is it clear how changes in one area of adjustment—say marriage—would affect other areas—work, religion, leisure activities. In other cases, however, it is often possible to forecast, with some confidence, how changes in one area of adjustment will affect other areas. Case E had a number of difficulties which flowed from a single source; once that source was removed, the difficulties disappeared. In Case D—Joyce Kingsley—difficulties associated with college adjustment could be traced to her living arrangements, moral principles, and academic standards.

The theoretical (supposed) relationships between causes and effects can be expressed in terms of a graph, rather like causal paths in statistical analysis. Such a graph can be used to represent the strength and direction of the factors in the case—see Baruch (1952) for an early example. If the various factors are connected in a multiplicity of ways, then it becomes difficult to predict how a change in one part of the system will affect another part. The thought required to actually compose the graph often has the effect of clarifying and developing the analysis. For Case F, the sequence of events and their relationships are shown in Figure 6.1.

We have drawn attention to the difference between an historic sequence of events (the narrative account), such as that described above for Case F, and a dynamic/causal account which explains how the factors at work at a given time result in a particular pattern of behaviour. To use the medical analogy again, one can describe the course of a disease historically from the stage of infection to the stage of full recovery; but one can also, given sufficient understanding, describe what is 'going on' at each stage. What we lack in F's case is detailed information on what was going on when he became disenchanted with the religious life. Presumably he was required to revise his assumptions and habitual practices because of the radical changes in the

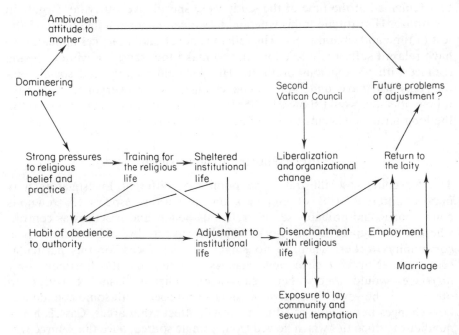

Figure 6.1 Case F events and relationships

organization of religious life in the Church and his Order. It is clear that he felt anxious, resentful, insecure, and confused at times. Many of his religious brethren would feel the same way. His superiors would possibly feel under greater stress. Much of the security and satisfaction associated with life in a religious institution would be removed. His disenchantment was aggravated, as I have mentioned, by his growing awareness of the advantages of life as a lay person. This is a very general speculative account, however, and good evidence is lacking. His action in leaving the religious life was not taken on the spur of the moment; several years intervened between the Second Vatican Council and his leaving. The woman he married had been known to him over that same period; he had been familiar with life beyond the Church for many years, having worked in and with its communities.

An analysis of the historical connections between problems may be appropriate for a life-history (as compared with a case-study), but a functional analysis is the main requirement for a case-study. One can use diagrams to illustrate functional connections, just as one can use them to illustrate historical sequences. Naturally, the diagrams should make clear that causal factors precede their effects in time. A functional diagram, however, may contain feedback loops, implying that the system operates in time although time as such is not represented. Consider the example of Case C (Chapter 3) shown in Figure 6.2. The diagram illustrates the difficulty of disconnecting the factors that maintain a chronic state of depression and social isolation. It also illustrates the dependence of surface characteristics on more basic factors, such that if one could improve C's physical appearance, or enable her to have positive social experiences, then the effects of these factors should diminish or disappear altogether. However, it is always possible that a case has been completely misconstrued. How do we know that Case C is not temperamentally disposed to depression independently of her physical appearance? In some cases quasi-experimental methods can be used to examine hypotheses of this sort. In non-experimental cases the same logic of inquiry is used, but the unavoidable lack of controls in its application means that much less confidence can be placed on the conclusions reached. Practical considerations may also prevent or offset action intended to improve the case. For example, cosmetic improvements may be expensive and regarded by C as artificial; improvements in outlook may not in the end lead to improved employment because of external circumstances. This reminds us that in dealing with a case-study we must not expect a complete solution to all the problems it presents. Nor must we assume that our solution to one problem will not create others—perhaps worse. The aim of intervention is to minimize constraints and stresses on the one hand, and to maximize opportunities and satisfactions on the other. Exchanging one set of problems for another more preferred set is the aim of the exercise.

Diagrams do not necessarily tell us more than can be said in words, but the act of constructing them amplifies and clarifies our understanding, and they can be an aid to communication. So far I have used diagrams for three purposes—to interconnect problems in a list, to show historical sequences, and to show possible functional (cause–effect) relationships. In Chapter 9 they are used to display the structure of arguments in a case-study.

It is well-known, but worth reminding ourselves, that the same effect (or type or effect) can arise from different causes (or types of cause), and that different effects (or types of effect) can arise from the same cause (or type of cause). This is because in carrying out a causal analysis we are interested in identifying the major or critical factors. In practice, contextual factors and minor contributory factors can alter the effects of a major cause. Many of the effects we are interested in in case-studies are also the outcome of a multiplicity of factors and conditions. The examples already given illustrate these points. The following example illustrates another point: that the functional relationship between factors in case-studies may be that of competition or opposition.

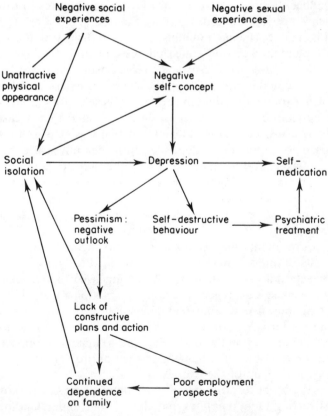

Figure 6.2 Case C events and relationships

CASE G

Case G is a fifty-year-old man who runs a small home-based business supplying specialized printed materials direct to individual customers. He has built the business up over a number of years and it keeps him very fully occupied—he handles all aspects of it himself without help from others. He has not sought to employ his skills more advantageously, since he prefers to be his own boss. His overall income from his business is only enough to support a moderate standard of living. He is married with three children. Relationships within the family are strained, partly because the youngest child is backward. G refused to acknowledge this for a long time and devoted himself to the child's upbringing to the extent of neglecting the other two children, who were perforce closer to the mother. G and his wife became emotionally estranged, but the family lived together through habit and force of circumstances. G had always been a hard worker and a highly practical individual, but he had not had a high level of education or the benefit of parental support in setting up his business. He was extroverted and impetuous. His disinclination to reflect on the long-term consequences of his behaviour led to a pattern of adjustment in which three main areas of activity—his work, attending to his backward child, and other domestic matters—competed for his time and attention. His lifelong habit of working hard and his over-involvement with his backward child left him very little time to devote to his wife and other children, who had in any event learned to live without his close involvement. As these children grew more independent, and as the mother began to think more about her own future, the family moved closer to disintegration.

COMMENTARY AND RELATED ISSUES

(a) Competing factors

In this case the contrasting factors are business pressures and the demands of the child on the one hand, and the needs of the other family members and other routine activities of daily living on the other. Figure 6.3 illustrates the situation. The hierarchical level of the statements in the diagram shows their relative importance and why the needs of other family members are unlikely to get much of G's time. The problem can be seen as a two-fold one: first, modifying G's temperament and lifelong habits of adjustment; second, reorganizing G's priorities and use of time. However, one cannot ignore the problem of family income, or the problems of each other member of the family. At first glance, a number of 'solutions', i.e. courses of action, seem possible, but as we have seen, they may bring other problems in their train. If Mrs G were to find paid employment outside the home this would supplement the family income but possibly increase the time G spends with the backward child and on the routine activities of daily living. If G were persuaded to

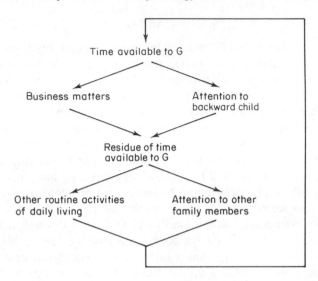

Figure 6.3 Case G factors and relationships

devote more time to his wife and the two normal children this would reduce the income from his home-based work and probably disrupt the backward child's behaviour, at least in the short run. It might also decrease G's life satisfaction and increase his level of anxiety, depending on the psychological functions fulfilled by these two major emotional investments. Such 'solutions' seem superficial and it is likely that only intervention in the form of family therapy would help avert disintegration here. Expert advice might help deal with the management of the backward child; psychological counselling and training in self-management might help G to revise his beliefs, values, habits, and feelings. Family therapy would help the other family members to support each other, and possibly to increase the degree of interaction with G and the backward child by working cooperatively in the ways agreed between family members and therapists. The time allocated to family therapy would probably come out of that previous allocated to the backward child, routine activities and other family members; so that the only real adjustment would be in areas like holidays, meals, sleep, household maintenance, and so on, assuming that G's normal life-style allows no slack time or daily leisure.

Case G illustrates not only the sort of counterbalancing that can occur between features of a case, but also the multiplicity of causes underlying a particular problem. For example, it would not necessarily follow that a reduction in G's time with the backward child would be compensated for by an increase in the time he spends with other family members. He might very well use the time in business affairs or in sleeping. In other words, removing one source of difficulty does not necessarily lead to changes of the sort one desires. Spending more time and money on social activities does not necessarily increase the number of friends one has, although it may be a prerequisite for such increase.

Case G, above, was presented in brief. A more thorough investigation would need to delve more deeply into the family history and into G's life-history. These further inquiries would probably reveal useful leads for psychological counselling and family therapy.

Case G illustrates the sort of case in which problems cannot be dealt with on a piecemeal basis because the factors at work are so closely interrelated. Neither is it the sort of case in which there is just one central problem, which, when it is dealt with, clears up all the other difficulties associated with the case.

The advantage of elaborating the problematic nature of a case-study is that it inhibits the 'rush to judgment' and oversimplification characteristic of naïve problem-solving.

CASE G (continued)

G has an aggressive, opinionated style of social interaction and gives the impression of wanting to manage his affairs without help or advice from others. It is not clear to the Investigator that this represents G's underlying qualities of temperament and personality, since on the few occasions when G has found time to talk about family matters he has given the impression of listening and understanding the Investigator's interpretation of the family's situation.

However, G's own upbringing and education were adversely affected by his mother's death, his father's remarriage, and his own unsuccessful early attempts to become independent. G and his wife present themselves to others as normal parents and spouses. In fact they sleep separately, have not had sexual relationships for many years and have not discussed what is to happen when the two normal children become independent. G's wife feels that part of the difficulty with the youngest child is that it has been 'spoiled' by the father, who perhaps recognizes something of his own character, since the child is said to be very like his father. Before long, unless G's business improves substantially, G and his family will be forced to realize some of their assets and move house. This will suit everyone except G, who has invested a great deal of time, effort, and money in the property in which the family live and in which he runs his business. As the backward child grows up he is becoming more disruptive and wayward outside the home. It is becoming increasingly likely that legal action will oblige G to submit to whatever course of action is thought to be in the child's best interests—a course of action that might very well conflict with G's wishes.

COMMENTARY AND RELATED ISSUES (continued)

(b) A diagram of Case G

Figure 6.4 represents Case G diagrammatically. The further information on Case G, above, enables us to use the sorts of diagram found in 'systems

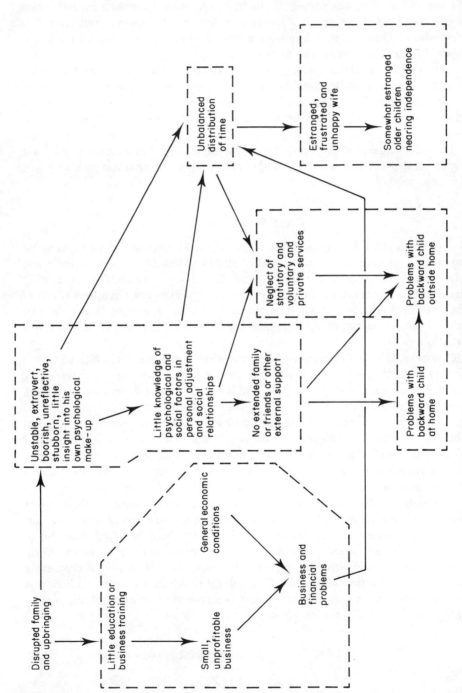

Figure 6.4 Case G factors and relationships; problem sectors (---)

analysis' to organize and clarify the undesirable states of affairs and trace the factors responsible for them as a preliminary to taking remedial action. The limitations of brief case-studies should now be abundantly clear.

The main advantage in representing case-studies in diagrams is to secure a systematic view of all the information available, and to organize it in a way that summarizes it, reveals its internal relationships, and makes it easier to understand and communicate. These are exactly the same advantages that we derive from data reduction and exploration and pictorial representation when dealing with quantitative and statistical data. The difference is that the case-study functional diagram, based on systems analysis, represents a dynamic situation not a static one. It represents a system of interrelated factors and conditions giving rise to a variety of possible observable effects, depending on the overall state of the system and the cause–effect relationships at work.

A life-history diagram fulfils a different function since it represents mainly a narrative sequence.

(c) Levels of abstraction and generality

The main benefit of a diagram is derived from actually carrying out the exercise on real case-material. The diagram itself is simply the visible end-product of a long process of thinking about the case, which may also, incidentally, be useful in communicating one's ideas to others.

Diagrams, like textual statements, can represent things at various levels of abstraction and generality. For example, in Figure 6.4 the box representing the estranged, frustrated, and unhappy wife does not reveal the particular features of the estrangement, frustration, or unhappiness. The question of whether there is good evidence to justify the state of affairs represented by the box should either be settled before that part of the diagram is introduced or it should have a question-mark attached to indicate that its validity is still open to doubt.

In relatively simple cases the contents of such boxes would be 'unpacked'. The case-materials would be set out in smaller packages, at a level of detail appropriate to the purpose for which the diagram has been constructed. In more complex cases, on the other hand, the diagrams would become large and confusing if the same low-level detail were displayed.

Fortunately, ordinary language enables us to move up and down the ladder of abstraction/generalization with no great difficulty. It also enables us to partition a case-study into distinct areas of interest which can nevertheless be related to each other in pairs, in groups, or as a whole.

Complex cases can be simplified in the above ways or by simply omitting peripheral issues from consideration. For example, Case G had a minor physical ailment which bothered him from time to time, but there was no indication that it had any bearing on the central issues in the case, so reference to it was omitted. The risk, of course, is that the initial judgment to exclude some fact or other as irrelevant or trivial might distort the picture, although important facts have a sort of insistence that is difficult to ignore if we are sincere and thorough in our scientific work.

As work on a case progresses, the amount of information available to an Investigator increases, and his or her ideas as to how the case-materials are to be organized change. Consequently, systems analysis diagrams drawn early in the investigation have to be redrawn so as to correctly represent the updated situation. The process works in two complementary directions. One direction is towards greater detail in matters of empirical evidence: this inevitably enlarges the scope of the inquiry. The other direction is towards the grouping of material into meaningful sectors. Each of these sectors provides a relatively self-contained issue, or set of issues, which takes its meaning in part from the context provided by the rest of the case-materials. In Case G, for example, the problem of that particular backward child makes sense only in the context of that particular case-study, although the child may have features in common with other types of backward child. Similarly, G's behaviour 'makes sense' only in the context of what we know about the rest of the case, although the case as a whole may have features in common with other types of problem family.

The distinguishable sectors of a case-study can be represented in the systems analysis diagram by using large boxes to enclose the statements—see the dotted lines in Figure 6.4. Each box represents a sort of partial framework within which a group of related issues is to be studied or dealt with.

As pointed out in Chapter 2 and elsewhere, problem-solving is a recursive process. One moves from problem-detection to a proposed solution to data-collection and inference to evaluation to problem-revision and through the cycle again and again until the problem is resolved or abandoned.

The procedure for exploring a particular sector of a case-study is virtually the same as that for dealing with the case-study as a whole; it is the recursive process of problem-solving. The difference lies simply in the specificity of the case-material. In Case G, for example, we might concentrate on the issue of Mrs G, or on the issue of the backward child's disruptive and wayward behaviour outside the home. It so happens that we have little information on these particular sectors of Case G, but it does not require much imagination to figure out what sorts of questions to ask, what sort of evidence to look for, and where to look for it. The aim would be, as it were, to pack (rather than unpack) the appropriately labelled boxes with the evidence relevant to its main issue. The unpacking occurs when we are called upon, as responsible Investigators, to describe and justify our account of a particular sector of the case-study.

Further study of these sectors of Case G might show that Mrs G's frustration and unhappiness were as much a function of the way she viewed her future prospects living apart from G as of the current and earlier stresses within the family (stresses to which she had, to some extent, adapted). The backward child's disruptive behaviour might be traced to an obscure physical condition or to inappropriate management within the family. One needs to establish the facts, finding corroboration where possible, not take them for granted or assume too much. One needs to consider all sorts of possible relationships, not just the obvious ones that first come to mind. Causal connections are likely to be complicated and multiple. Mrs G's behaviour may be influenced by a variety of extra-family factors. The procedure is designed to help unravel these complications—not just by examining the available evidence (the case-materials) but also by collecting more good evidence of the kind indicated by the analysis.

In principle it is possible to consider relationships between all pairs of problems in a case-study. For example, in Case G we could consider the problem of the backward child's behaviour outside the home in relation to the low profitability of G's business. One would not normally think of trying to relate such disparate issues, yet doing so might well affect one's interpretation of the case. In this example our attention would be drawn: first, to the unbalanced distribution of G's time, which we had identified anyway; second, to the increasing likelihood of outside intervention compelling G to accept a solution which might have financial implications and which would force him to deal with the psychological factors that underlie his excessive involvement with the child. This last-mentioned eventuality might or might not help him to rethink his whole way of life.

A systematic comparison of pairs of problems need not be particularly time-consuming in most case-studies because the number of problems, initially at least, is usually quite small. As the case-study progresses, although the number of specific problems increases, they are grouped into sectors, and it is these sectors that enter into the comparison exercise.

The point of the exercise is to explore, in a systematic and comprehensive way, the factors and relationships that make up the case. Although we normally consider the 'obvious' factors and relationships early in a case-study, and pursue the relevant lines of inquiry, these obvious issues are not necessarily the ones that prove to be important. There may be other issues more basic and central to the case. Suppose, for example, that G's devotion to his backward child is in part a way of avoiding discussion or acceptance of the idea that his business venture is a failure (in the sense of not providing a secure and sufficient income for the family) which he might also have to attribute to himself rather than to circumstances outside his control. This supposition might have been raised without formally comparing G's business problem with the backward-child problem, but the formal comparison makes it less likely that the possibility would not have been considered at all. The possibility is represented in diagrammatic form in Figure 6.5.

This is an example of how a case-study can be developed and of how the systems analysis diagrams can be segmented and redrawn. Naturally, this means collecting additional empirical evidence, not just speculating about what is going on. The method helps to identify the problems but does not establish their importance; that is a matter for subsequent analysis and judgment.

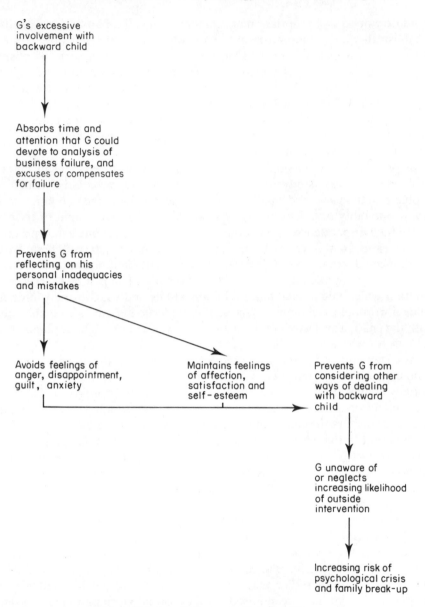

Figure 6.5 Case G factors and relationships

(d) Four further questions

The analysis of a case can be carried further by asking four basic questions. First, what factors gave rise to the issues (problems) in the first place? Second, what maintains these problematic states of affairs? Third, how did these issues come to the attention of the Investigator, i.e. what is the purpose of the case-study? Fourth, how can the problems be dealt with? These questions are appropriate only in cases where the problem is how to move from a less desirable to a more desirable state of affairs. In case-studies which describe achievement and success, the emphasis is on how that came about.

The first question is answered by describing the history of the events leading up to the case. This can be helpful in identifying relevant issues. The second question is answered by a functional analysis of the factors at work in the case—why do people behave in the way they do in the circumstances described? The third question, as indicated in an earlier chapter, is designed to forestall oversimplified and hasty solutions or solutions proposed for ulterior motives. The answer to the fourth question depends partly on the ingenuity of the Investigators, partly on the resources available to them.

In Case G there is clearly a lot of work to be done tracing out the family history and G's personal history. This would say quite a lot about the personal qualities and circumstances of the people involved, and help to organize our ideas about the current family problem. The functional analysis would concentrate on current circumstances and behaviour, trying to find out what reinforces G's behaviour in relation to his work and his child, and what might reinforce more adaptive behaviour. The factors which raised G's case in the first place, e.g. marriage guidance instigated by G's wife, or educational guidance instigated because of the disruptive behaviour of G's child, tend to emphasize some issues more than others. The systematic case-study procedure we are advocating should minimize this. We have concluded that Case G, in virtue of its complexity and chronicity, is likely to be dealt with effectively only by means of a family therapy service with ample resources.

We must be wary of making false attributions by neglecting to examine all the relevant evidence critically. For example, it would be easy to see G as a hard-working individual pushed to the limits of his ability to cope by an unfortunate set of family circumstances—a difficult backward child and a rejecting or unsupportive wife. This is not to say that these views should not be entertained. On the contrary, if there is some possibility that they are true, then they need to be tested and compared with the other interpretations that can be made of the facts.

SUMMARIZING THE CASE

When the further analysis needed to answer the four questions posed above has been carried out, the Investigator is in a position to review the case-materials, reorganize them, and present them in summary form. What we then have is a description and an analysis (explanation) of the main facts of the case. It is also useful, at this stage, to summarize any procedural matters which might affect the validity of the decription and analysis.

The Investigator usually needs to discuss the case with other people and to review the case periodically to establish what progress has been made. Reports to colleagues and interested parties may be needed, for example, at case-conferences. These reports need to be in summary form for ease of understanding, rather like a mass of statistical data needs to be reduced to summary form.

There are two ways of arriving at a case summary. One is to express the information in a systems analysis diagram of the sort already described. Another is to work out the 'informal' logic of the case and to express it in the form of an argument. The advantage of this latter method is that it forces the Investigator to make his conceptual analysis explicit. The analysis of informal, substantive logic in case-studies is dealt with in detail in Chapter 9.

At the intermediate review stages, issues relating to intervention—how the case is to be dealt with—can usually be deferred until one is reasonably confident that the more important problems have been identified.

As we shall see, the arguments for or against particular courses of action with regard to a case can be separated from the arguments which draw conclusions about the nature of the problems. Indeed, the end-result of an argument about a problem becomes, in effect, the starting point for an argument about how to deal with it.

Reviewing a case after a further period of investigation is rather like rehearsing a song or a theatrical performance after making a number of changes designed to improve the production. The case-materials should have increased in amount and quality, and the case may need to be extensively rewritten.

The statements contained in the systems analysis diagrams are titles or summary statements. They make sense only because the reader is fully aware of the body of knowledge from which they arise. There may be some advantage, therefore, in making an intermediate statement which summarizes those parts of the case-material bearing directly on the problem. This sort of intermediate statement is much longer than the diagrammatic statement, but much shorter than the case-material description.

Consider our understanding of the main problems in Case G. How would we summarize them? Perhaps as follows.

G is the central character in a family crisis. His personal qualities, upbringing, and habits of adjustment in adult life have interacted with his life circumstances to produce an unsatisfactory state of affairs; namely, excessive and unproductive time spent with a backward child to the virtual exclusion of time spent with other members of the family. His preoccupation can be seen in part as a barrier to the realization that his unprofitable business venture is, to a large extent, attributable to his personal failings. He attempts to make up the lack of quality in his business activities by working long hours. This further diminishes the time he has available for other family members. This too is a form of defence, because closer contact with them would inevitably raise questions about their life-style, particularly his preoccupation with the child, and the unprofitability of the business. The problem is further complicated by the probable irreversible estrangement of G's wife and the threat of outside intervention because of the backward child's disruptive behaviour if G and his family do not solve the problem themselves or move voluntarily to obtain help from others.

The documentary evidence which supports this sort of summary of the problem is normally to be found in the case-materials. In the case of G, all the information to be made available has been presented. The case-materials given there are fairly brief anyway, and the reader is invited to identify the statements which are summarized above. Technically speaking, the 'evidence' one points to in support of a summary statement of the problem is not the text of the case-records, but rather the actual events and circumstances referred to in the records—people's actions, words, and states of mind, the opportunities and constraints of their environment, the things they refrained from doing or saying, their relationships with other people, and so on. In many cases such evidence is indirect and not easily corroborated, and it is usually not too difficult to criticize the amount and quality of the evidence available.

ASSIGNING PRIORITIES TO PROBLEMS

The summary statement of the problems in Case G, above, corresponds to the 'sectors' or 'problem areas' referred to in connection with the systems analysis diagrams. If the case-review seems to be definitive—in the sense that all the major avenues of inquiry have been explored and all reasonable interpretations have been considered—then we have reached a critical point in the case-study, for now the Investigator can turn to the question of how to deal with them, assuming that resources are available.

This question is answered by considering first of all how the problems differ in importance. Problems which are thought to be central and basic to the case are, by definition, more important than peripheral or superficial problems. It might also be thought that problems which, for one reason or another, do not require urgent action can be regarded as less important. But this is to confuse two sorts of importance. One is the intrinsic importance of the problem in the case; the other is the importance of the problem in the context of the action to be taken by the Investigator. For example, an Investigator might regard G's attitudes to himself, his family, and his work, as the central and most important problem (or set of problems) in the case, but not a problem that can be dealt with quickly or easily. He is likely, therefore, to choose some other problem in the case as the one to deal with first.

Are there any criteria for deciding the order in which the 'treatable' problems should be dealt with? One criterion is the ease and promptness of a proposed remedy. The application of this criterion has the advantage of ameliorating the situation. The problems which are easy to deal with, however, are likely to be the superficial, peripheral ones; so the effect of intervention is likely to be small. The main advantage is in signalling that something is being done to deal with the case.

Another criterion is the intrinsic importance of the problem, as already mentioned. Supposing G's wife has already used a marriage guidance service, it might be possible to persuade G to make use of the service himself. This would open the door to outside support and intervention; it would ease the transition to more substantial intervention by social, family, and medical services, since such intervention seems inevitable anyway.

Consider another case, that of A, described briefly in Chapter 2. The problem can be summarized as follows: 'A has been redeployed because his behaviour was a cause of discontent to other workers. It would suit the management of his firm to make him redundant. A cannot come to terms with his predicament.' If further investigation confirms the original 'diagnosis' in this case, the question arises as to what to do about A. The central problem is that A's personal qualities are unsuited to relationships where he has to exercise authority. The prospect of modifying long-standing qualities of temperament and character is poor, although counselling and training in social skills might go some way to improve A's ability to get on with other people.

The firm is unable to provide the sort of supervision necessary to keep A's behaviour under surveillance, much less to modify it. Since A possesses an industrial skill which can be exercised without his having to occupy a supervisory position, the firm might be persuaded to maintain his redeployed status for a time on the understanding that the post was temporary and that A would obtain vocational counselling with which the firm's management would cooperate. The use of an independent third party to act as arbitrator and channel of communication is important if A is to learn anything of value from this experience. In this case, therefore, the most important course of action from the Investigator's point of view is that which will delay redundancy, give time and opportunity for counselling, and maintain continuity of employment.

There are cases in which drastic action is deemed necessary; action which changes the situation completely. The consequences of such action are difficult to predict, however, because of the complex and interacting factors involved. Marital separation, removing a child from parental care, changing or leaving one's job, these are examples of drastic action to solve a problem. But such action is usually the last in a series of actions taken in response to a problematic situation. Where possible, case-studies should be instigated and carried out in the early stages of a human problem, so that preventive action can be taken to avoid desperate consequences and desperate remedies.

A cautious, piecemeal approach to dealing with a problem has much to recommend it, provided it is not avoiding the main issues. It has the advantage that little or no damage is done if one's assessment of the case is wrong. It has the disadvantage of not having an overall strategy and therefore runs the risk of not being able to maintain the initial sense of progress.

SUMMARY AND CONCLUSIONS

The individual's adjustment to his or her environment can be compared to an ecological system in which various factors operate in relation to each other to produce stability, gradual change, or rapid disruption. A change in one part of the system induces changes in other parts. Underlying the surface characteristics of the system are more basic structural arrangements and functional relationships.

Case E is used as an example to demonstrate the interconnectedness of factors in a case-study. The problems in a case can be listed and grouped into sectors. This facilitates understanding and summarization, and makes it more likely that investigative and remedial resources will be deployed more effectively. Diagrams in the form of graphs can be helpful in 'structuring' the case; their main advantage is that they oblige the Investigator to provide a complete and explicit account of the case in a form which is readily communicated. Diagrams are constructed for cases F, C, and G. They illustrate a sort of intermediate stage between the raw data and case-records on the one hand and the final explicit argument (which organizes and explains the facts) on the other.

Among the persisting questions in a case-study are the following: How did the problems in this case arise? What maintains them? Why is the case-study being carried out? How might the problems be dealt with?

Eventually the Investigator may have to review, reorganize, and summarize the case. Most cases are communicated in summary form, so this aspect of the case-study is most important. The summary should state the essential points of the case in an explanatory framework. This is more difficult than one might suppose and further discussion of the 'grammar' of case reports is presented in Chapter 11.

Decisions about what action to take in relation to a case depend on how the Investigator assigns priorities to problems. Subjective judgments are liable to a variety of errors—see Chapter 10, whereas objective judgements usually require more information and time—see Chapter 8.

Some rules for arranging the case-problems in order of priority are as follows:

1. Unless one can think of a sensible strategy for dealing with the case-problem as a whole, one should deal with the more obvious, easier, more manageable problems in a cautious, piecemeal way. This will give an immediate sense of progress and time to think up a more systematic approach. It may also reveal the more central, basic problems more clearly.
2. Give high priority to problems which are central and basic to the case (usually the most difficult). If the most important of these intrinsic problems cannot be dealt with, then of those that remain choose the next most important problem that looks as though it can be dealt with promptly and effectively.
3. Give high priority to problems which threaten serious consequences in the short run.
4. Give some priority to problems where outside help will be accepted or

    where a third party can act as arbitrator and channel of communication, e.g. in interpersonal conflicts.

5. Give some priority to problems whose solution helps uncover more basic issues in the case.

6. Give low priority to problems which look insoluble or whose solution would require drastic action, unless inaction threatens equal or worse consequences.

7. Adjust your priorities according to the time-scale of future prospects for the case. The effective use of time and resources by the Investigator(s) and by the Subject(s) of the case (and the others involved) is a major determinant of success.

8. Give no priority to problems over which neither the Investigator nor the Subject have any control, except to establish the limits of remedial action.

Nothing we have said about the criteria for choosing which problems to deal with affects case-studies carried out for instructional purposes, except at advanced levels where a student is a co-investigator. Case-studies dealt with in educational courses include discussion of appropriate courses of action to be taken in relation to the case-problems. But, since the proposals do not result in actual intervention, the question of priorities becomes, literally, an academic issue.

CHAPTER SEVEN

Finding Solutions to Problems

INTRODUCTION: BASIC SOURCES OF UNDERSTANDING

Solutions to human problems are derived from three main sources: first, general knowledge of human behaviour; second, scientific knowledge and professional expertise in particular areas of human affairs; third, administrative procedures which exist independently, as it were, of the individuals who implement them. The first and the second sources comprise the individuals participating in a case-study—the Investigator(s), the Subject(s), informant(s), advisor(s), and other interested parties. The third source comprises the cultural and administrative framework within which a case-study is carried out. An obvious example of this third source would be the handling of a case of social deviance in a democratic as compared with a single-party authoritarian regime. Another example would be a case of single parenthood nowadays as compared with a generation ago. In other words, the behaviour of people who are involved in case-studies is influenced by the prevailing attitudes, values, and practices of the community to which they belong. This influence is usually profound and not readily brought under critical scrutiny. It leads to conservative forms of interpretation and management of cases, and while it sometimes acts as a brake on useful innovation it also serves to restrict the lunatic fringe.

The process of psychological development which enables us to understand ourselves and other people is dealt with in detail in Livesley and Bromley (1973) and Bromley (1977). This process is described briefly in Chapter 1 of the latter book, since it explains a great deal that is otherwise puzzling about personality description at a common-sense level in ordinary language; Chapters 8, 9, and 10 are more concerned with professional and scientific levels of understanding human behaviour. It should bring home to the reader the fact that while self-understanding and understanding others—as in the study of individual cases—is grounded in common sense and ordinary language, this level of understanding is limited and sometimes misleading. It can be greatly improved by the acquisition of well-founded scientific concepts, methods, and professional practices. It can also be greatly improved by careful analysis of what common sense and ordinary language can provide in the way of an infrastructure for scientific understanding and professional or semi-professional management.

Case-studies are best carried out by Investigators who can combine the personal characteristics needed to cope with disturbed and confused people under stress and in quandaries with the characteristics needed to cooperate with colleagues in understanding and dealing with cases. The cooperation of others is essential if the pool of 'objective knowledge' is to be maximized. What needs to be avoided is the unwitting or slavish conformity to majority opinion or authoritative opinion—in group situations—when one's own intelligence and knowledge indicate a different interpretation or course of action.

There are serious weaknesses in individual subjective judgment—see Chapter 10; there are difficulties with group decisions too—see Janis and Mann (1977).

THINKING CREATIVELY IN CASE-STUDIES

Identifying problems in a case-study is like being faced with a tangle of wool. One's task is to unravel the tangle, to separate the individual strands, to sort them out into their appropriate categories. Interpreting findings and implementing solutions is more like knitting—one selects the required strands and knits them together systematically so as to achieve the desired pattern or effect.

Before solutions can be implemented, they obviously have to be proposed and made available. Proposing solutions for case-problems can take two forms. First, where there is a limited set of standard solutions, one can select the most appropriate and apply it. Second, where there are no standard solutions, or where the standard solutions do not apply for some reason, then novel solutions have to be developed. There are many areas of case-work where problems occur as a matter of routine—marriage guidance and family therapy, bereavement, performance appraisal, single parenthood—and where routine solutions, developed through case-law over many years of professional or semi-professional experience, can be applied. Even here, however, there is room for innovation and ingenuity in those cases which present problems outside the normal range.

The first task in finding solutions to the problems presented by a case-study is to try to match the central and basic problems that have been identified with a known and available solution, e.g. intrapersonal conflict with psychological counselling, severe neurosis with psychiatric referral, redundancy with retraining, social deviance with social restraint and guidance.

Where possible, one should think of several possible solutions to a problem. It is a principle of creative problem-solving that one should not be critical of new suggestions until one has run out of ideas. Critical appraisal begins when one works out the implications of the proposed solutions to the problems. One can use both a piecemeal approach—looking for tactical solutions to specific problems, and a global approach—looking for a strategic solution to whole problem areas. This should maximize the range of proposed solutions. The essential point is to feel as free as possible of constraints in generating ideas about how to deal with problems.

It is not necessary to describe the psychology of problem-solving. There are several useful textbooks—see, for example, Lindsay and Norman (1977). I have concentrated on those psychological processes most relevant to solving human problems. However, it is worth emphasizing the creative aspects of problem solving. The creative stage can be distinguished from and contrasted with the critical or evaluative stage. The former is concerned with exploring the problem conditions and the possibilities for progress towards a solution; the latter is concerned with testing the correctness of the proposed solutions.

There seems to be little doubt that many of the techniques advocated for stimulating creative thinking can increase the number and diversity of ideas generated in response to a problem. There are various techniques. Brain-storming means withholding criticism, free-associating, hitch-hiking (using one idea to carry another), thinking laterally, pushing ideas to their limits, making random connections, inverting and reversing ideas, and so on. Structural analysis means taking the main features or dimensions of a problem and looking at them systematically in relation to each other, e.g. making comparisons between pairs of problems in a case. Rethinking the problem means revising the original definition or description of the problem. This may suggest a larger, different, or more important problem. For example, rethinking a problem originally defined in terms of school refusal may redefine it as a problem about ethnic relations in a school. Using images, e.g. analogies and metaphors and fantasy generally, sometimes has the effect of triggering new ideas. We used the metaphor of 'counterbalancing' in Case G, and the trick of 'making a virtue of necessity' in Case G, and the trick of 'making a virtue of necessity' in Case C, in the sense of emphasizing the benefits whatever the outcome. Reviewing the problem from different perspectives means asking questions like, 'How would such-and-such a person see the problem? How would it look from another point of view?' Linking with arbitrary ideas means using chance factors to stimulate thought. For example, consider a problem looked at in relation to the contents of a book opened at random. In Case G, for example, this manœuvre raises the possibility that the wife's estrangement is a consequence of something she has done, to which G cannot be reconciled—a completely new possibility. Examining the assump-tions underlying the problem means questioning the foundations of those initial claims which gave rise to the problem. For example, in Case A we can question the assumption that it is A's behaviour as such that caused the discontent, and speculate that it is being used as an excuse by a clique of workers to avoid interference in cosy but unproductive working arrangements.

Given the relative lack of case-law in relation to the psychological study of individual cases, it is not surprising that more depends on the Investigators' professional training, experience, scientific knowledge, native intelligence, and ingenuity than on their ability to apply a set of routine logical procedures in a mechanical way. In other words, we are not yet in the position of developing an 'expert systems' approach to psychological cases—but see Chapter 11.

A neglected aspect of solution-finding is that some solutions not only solve the problems they were intended to solve but others also; or they may create opportunities that work to the benefit of the case.

Let us consider Case C again (Chapter 3). This is the case of the unattractive forty-year-old woman who had an unfortunate love-affair and subsequently attempted suicide. The case was handled in a fairly routine way via psychiatric referral, counselling, and medication. What solutions might one propose regardless of one's first reaction to their feasibility or suitability? (a) Cosmetic treatment or even surgery might help, depending on the nature of her physical unattractiveness. (b) Further counselling on this specific issue, coupled with greater willingness to associate with physically unattractive men (if this was something she had avoided). The aim would be to increase the amount and range of her social contacts, with both men and women. (c) Re-examination of her academic and professional talents with a view to retraining for interesting employment which might help to compensate for lack of a male partner. (d) To move away from her parents and the locality of her unhappiness, and to move, possibly, into a more communal life-style simply to explore its advantages and to break away from old habits. (e) Do nothing, and let events take their course, relying on chance circumstances and self-help to secure an adequate (if not optimum) level of adjustment at least until a new personal crisis threatens.

Other solutions to C's problems may occur to readers if they suspend, for a while, the tendency to reject an idea simply because their first reaction to it is negative. What is required is an effort to search for the *advantages* of a proposed solution, and to use it as a stimulus or stepping-stone to yet other proposed solutions. In this way one may succeed in finding ingenious solutions to what appear to be quite intractable problems.

In some ways, finding the solution(s) mirrors the process of finding the problem(s). For example, one can take the individual problems and the problem areas in a case and list all possible solutions. The emphasis at this point is on generating a large number of possible solutions with little regard to their feasibility. We want to avoid the error of excluding some possible solutions even if it means entertaining a large number of inappropriate or impractical solutions; hence the need for creative thinking. Critically evaluating and choosing the best of the many solutions proposed comes at a later stage of the problem-solving process, when it is necessary to find a solution or make a decision.

Let us consider some of the cases we have described so far, with special reference to proposed solutions. In each case some of the major problems are presented as sub-headings, and the solutions listed below.

Case A (Chapter 2)

Case A is a worker facing redundancy as a consequence of economic recession and the antagonism of other workers.

Problem 1:	A is still a potential source of discontent in the organization.
Solution (a):	Sacrifice A's feelings and welfare in the interests of the organization—make him redundant as soon as possible at least cost.
Solution (b):	Delay A's redundancy giving him time to reorganize his affairs and plan his future, and giving the organization time to arrange to get along without him.
Solution (c):	Reconsider A's abilities and potential contribution to the organization, and whether he could be usefully employed in a different capacity or in a different department.
Solution (d):	Re-examine the complaints against A; use the opportunity to explore other ways of improving relationships within the organization, and of changing work practices.
Solution (e):	Try again to reconcile A with the people he used to work with—making clear their role-relationships and working activities.
Problem 2:	A is anxious about his future and seems unable to cope with his situation.
Solution (a):	Persuade A to see his doctor so that his doctor can arrange for him to receive professional help—psychological counselling and medication as appropriate.
Solution (b):	Refer A to one or other of the various private, statutory, or voluntary agencies that provide advice and information, e.g. Professional and Executive Register, counselling agencies, singles' associations.
Solution (c):	Assign someone to look after A's welfare—counselling and advising A even after his contract has been terminated.
Solution (d):	Let A sort out his own problems.

Case B (Chapter 2)

Case B is a student who has lost interest in his course.

Problem 1:	How to help B decide what he wants to do.
Solution (a):	Let him work it out for himself and take the consequences of any delay or mistake.
Solution (b):	Refer him to the student counsellor.
Solution (c):	Use problem-oriented counselling and one's experience of similar cases to help the student work through the implications of the choices that are open to him.
Solution (d):	Persuade him to talk things over with the people that matter to him and work out a decision with them.

Solution (e):	Refer him to the careers officer.
Solution (f):	Review with him his educational and personal history to see whether he was badly advised to take up the subject he is studying.
Solution (g):	Arrange leave of absence to give him time to work things out.
Solution (h):	Let him transfer and take the consequences.

The reader should note that, in the interests of brevity, I have not listed all the problems in the cases above, and I have not listed all the solutions to the problems mentioned. The reader should also note that the solutions are not all mutually exclusive, that some proposals could be tried out without jeopardizing the implementation or effectiveness of others. By contrast, some solutions are drastic and pre-empt any subsequent attempts at solution.

The various solutions are not listed in any particular order; so, assuming we have exhausted our store of ideas, we can begin to examine the proposals— group them, arrange them in order of merit, and generally sort out our priorities for action.

DECISION-MAKING WITH THE AID OF DIAGRAMS

One way of dealing with the list of solutions generated is by the paired comparisons technique already mentioned. This procedure is practicable if the list is short—say about six solutions—for then the number of comparisons between pairs of problems is $(n^2 - n)/2 = 15$. If the comparisons are consistent with each other, then the solutions can be ordered from most to least preferred. However, if there are many solutions the task becomes tedious and the ordering inconsistent. The method also breaks down if there are several criteria for making comparisons.

A complication in deciding which solutions to implement is that, as we have just seen, some solutions are not independent of one another. For example, solution (a) may rule out solution (b); solution (c) can be implemented only after solution (d) has been made to work.

In some cases a provisional sorting of solutions may be possible. For example, proposals may be categorized as follows:

(i) Feasible and probably effective in a limited way, no obvious drawbacks, leaves other options open, simple.

(ii) Moderately complex and fairly difficult to implement, some obvious drawbacks, closes several other options, only moderately effective.

(iii) Very complicated, difficult to implement, serious drawbacks, pre-empts many other solutions but could be very effective.

This would give a rough order of preference based mainly on ease of implementation and preservation of options.

Another way of choosing between alternative courses of action is derived from business case-studies—see Easton (1982). It consists of a series of 'evaluation cycles' whereby one considers the more general solutions earlier in the series and moves on to the more specific solutions at each complete cycle. This procedure complements that described earlier in connection with problem-finding whereby problems could be reformulated at successively higher levels of abstraction and generality. Just as problems can interact with each other and be grouped into more general 'problem areas', so solutions can interact with each other and be grouped into more general 'solution areas'.

A more general solution is obviously one that subsumes a wider variety of particular solutions over a longer time-scale. Some solutions can be regarded not as ends in themselves but as means to some other end. For example, in Case G, persuading G to cooperate with the marriage guidance service could be the means whereby other outside agencies could be introduced.

The relationships between means and ends, and between lower-order and higher-order solutions, can be represented by means of a network or dendrogram, i.e. a branching diagram. These can take many forms—decision trees, means–end chains, flow diagrams, critical path analyses. A left to right diagram is useful if it is important to refer to a time-base. The diagrams simplify and clarify the connections between events, and so help an Investigator to choose between different courses of action having traced out the likely consequences of each. The diagrams may also fulfil a heuristic function in drawing the Investigator's attention to problems and/or solutions that he would not otherwise have thought of. As with the diagrams referred to in Chapters 6, 8, and 9, dealing with the way cases can be analysed conceptually, the main advantage is that actually constructing the diagram forces the Investigator to clarify his ideas and make them explicit.

Consider the following dendrograms or decision-trees (Figures 7.1–7.3) for the three cases referred to earlier in this chapter. These representations go beyond the earlier statements to illustrate their heuristic function.

In certain cases an examination of the branches of the dendrogram or decision-tree clarifies the merits or otherwise of the various courses of action, and so enables one to define the more preferred paths through the network. Once these preferred paths are decided upon, the non-preferred paths can be ignored, thus saving the time and resources that would otherwise have been expended in exploring all possible courses of action.

A cycle of evaluation consists in working through the decision-tree, from the general to the specific issues, cutting out the non-preferred lines of action. Eventually, in some cases at least, one is left with one preferred course of action which incorporates a basic strategic decision and its anticipated consequences. Naturally, one may have to make tactical adjustments to unforeseen circumstances as they arise.

Some cases do not have one most preferred path, partly because of lack of information and uncertainty about future conditions and the consequences of

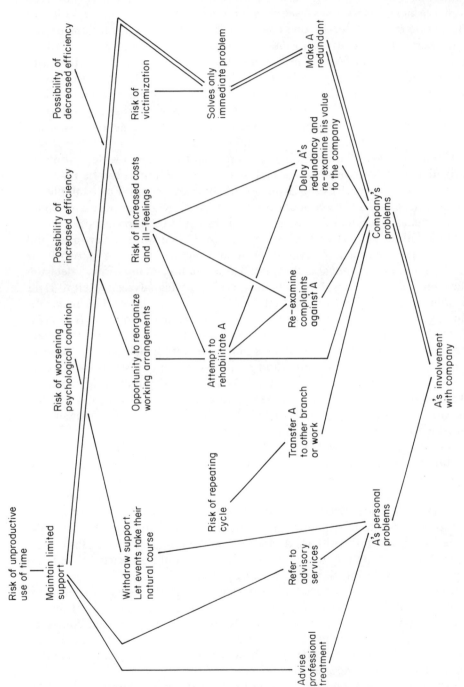

Figure 7.1 Case A decision tree

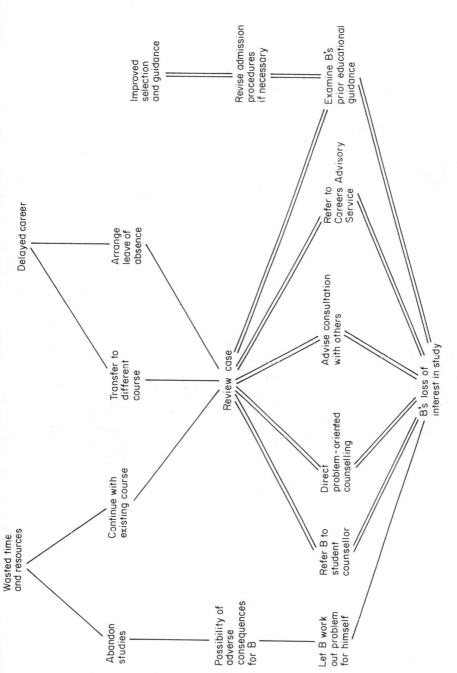

Figure 7.2 Case B decision tree

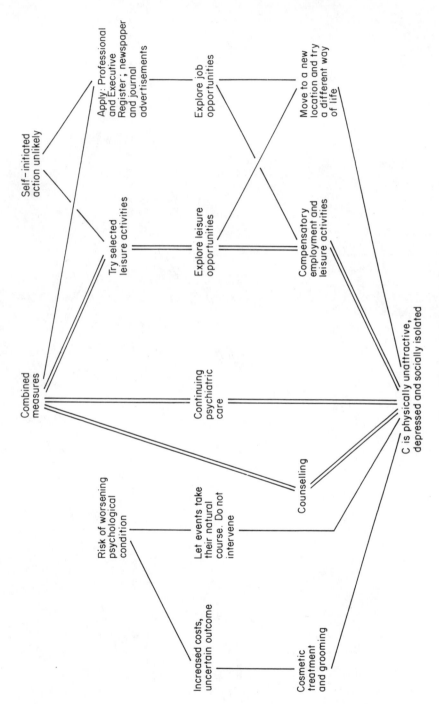

Figure 7.3 Case C decision tree

any action taken. In Case A, for example, much more information is needed about A's relationships with others, about his conditions of service, legal matters, his employability elsewhere, and so on. The double line shows a path which cuts the firm's losses without abandoning all interest in A's health and welfare. Any lessons learned about industrial relations can be applied the next time a similar problem arises. The dendrogram helps draw attention to the lack of information. In Case B there are several paths, shown as double lines, which are all compatible with one another up to the point where more information is needed, or where one needs to await the outcome of earlier actions. In Case C the indications, shown by the double lines, are that continuing psychiatric care and positive counselling are needed to safeguard C's health and welfare over a long period of readjustment, and that this should be combined with new leisure activities rather than seeking new employment and relocation, since this seems to be less risky and could pave the way for more radical change later.

The dendrogram can be simplified by grouping some actions and eliminating others. For example, in Case B we could group the referral actions and eliminate the proposal to let B work out his own problems and the proposal to look into the whole question of student admission procedures. The dendrogram would then be as shown in Figure 7.4. Further reflection might result in the decision-tree shown in Figure 7.5.

This makes it clear that although a strategic decision has profound implications for the handling of a case, in particular it may pre-empt

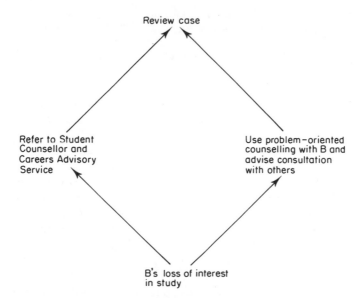

Figure 7.4 Case B simplified decision tree

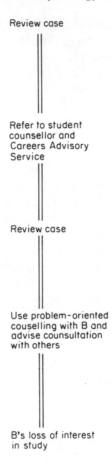

Figure 7.5 Case B simplified decision tree

alternative courses of action, this does not mean that the case cannot be reviewed from time to time or that tactical adjustments cannot be made if needed.

Rather than simplifying a dendrogram by grouping and pruning, one may wish to elaborate it—again, the dendrogram provides a useful heuristic.

In implementing decisions we must remember that some solutions are mutually exclusive, and we must take care not to go into a 'blind alley'. We must also remember that different solutions might achieve the same result, so our choice can be made in terms of economy, speed, or simplicity. In Case B, for example, it might be wasteful to refer B to both the Careers Advisory Service and the student counsellor, since they are likely to duplicate each other's work, at least in the early stages.

Mention of waste should remind us that case-investigators do not have unlimited time and resources at their disposal. Consequently speed and economy can become important considerations in decision-making. For example, in Case B the Investigator should ask whether his time would be better spent in counselling B or in reviewing the admissions procedure.

As a case is being dealt with, the various courses of action taken have consequences; sometimes they pay off, sometimes not. In the process we learn more about the case and the circumstances with which we are dealing. This may have the effect of changing the nature of the case and its problems. This can be taken care of by means of periodic case-reviews. As information and insight accumulate the possibilities for action should become clearer.

INDIVIDUAL AND SUPRA-INDIVIDUAL CASES: A PHILOSOPHICAL REMINDER

Case-studies are carried out for a purpose and in a particular context. For example, students carry out psychological studies of individual persons in the context of an academic course in personality or a professional course in clinical psychology or social work. They find that case-studies illuminate and bring to life matters which might otherwise seem dry or 'academic'. It is not part of our purpose to deal with supra-individual case-studies, which refer to social organizations, institutional processes, or to complex incidents rather than to individual persons. They deal, for example, with problems in politics, industrial enterprises and conflicts, architecture, and planning, with major accidents or disasters, disability and disadvantage, military operations and so on—see Easton (1982), Pauls and Jones (1980), Doig (1984), Locker (1983), Dixon (1976), Moore *et al.* (1976), and Lane and Roberts (1971).

Although the psychological study of an individual case may refer to the industrial, environmental, or military context in which it occurs, its primary focus is the person. When it deals with more than one person its focus is on each person in turn. Conversely, although a case-study in management, building, or economics may refer to individual people, its primary focus is on the organization or the wider set of events, i.e. it is supra-individual.

This is not to say that there are two quite distinct sorts of case-study—individual and organizational. On the contrary, these various sorts of case-study share a common scientific methodology. Much of what we have said about the psychological study of individual cases has its counterpart in the study of particular social organizations, processes, and events. The logic of the case-study is the argument which enables one to make rational inferences about the empirical evidence one has collected. Our philosophical position is the belief that even a case which is apparently unique is not scientifically useless, because it must eventually be accounted for in terms which make it possible to compare and contrast it with other cases if only as an exception. In judicial and quasi-judicial science, individual cases are assimilated through the establishment of general principles in case-law. As we have seen, the logic and the procedure of the case-study are different from those in experimental investigations and in statistical surveys, but this does not detract from its status as a scientific method.

In each of the many areas where case-studies are carried out, whether individual or supra-individual, there are basic concepts, methods, and bodies of knowledge that one can refer to in order to understand the particular case one is dealing with and comparable cases. This is, in a sense, 'case-law', although the information is not usually systematized and retrievable in the orderly way it is in jurisprudence. The information is available—from books, technical reports, journal articles, and by word-of-mouth from well-informed practitioners in an area. There are, for example, bodies of knowledge about personal adjustment, psychiatric disorder, interviewing and counselling techniques, psychometric assessment, behavioural management, self-control, time-scheduling, financial budgeting, interpersonal relationships, social skills training, family therapy, attitude change, marriage guidance, and so on. This is not to say that one should search for ready-made solutions to one's case; recipes, where they exist, need to be adapted to the particular features of the case one is dealing with.

With increased training in, and experience of, his or her main field of work, an Investigator accumulates much of the relevant knowledge and skill. The Investigator encounters similar sorts of problem and develops conceptual and methodological routines for handling them. The training Investigators receive should enable them to deal with routine cases with a minimum of supervision. Help should be needed only with cases that fall outside the normal range, cases which are so rare that little or no case-law exists (where there is no substantial body of experience to refer to). These are the sorts of cases which call for the problem-finding and problem-solving approach we have been describing, whereas the easier cases fall into familiar common categories where little effort is required to find an appropriate solution.

The advantage of systematic training and wide reading in one's area of interest is not simply to accumulate knowledge of specific cases, but rather to build up general categories and principles derived from systematic comparisons and contrasts between a variety of cases. Investigators should have, at the back of their mind, 'model' or 'prototypical' cases which refer not to one particular case but to an array of similar cases which contrast in some way with the array of cases for a different model. For example, Jamil (1985) describes some 'model' cases of Arab students at British universities. One contrast is between students receiving a grant from their Government and students privately financed. The difference is thought to be associated with a range of differences in personal adjustment. In a large well-controlled statistical survey this would correspond to demonstrating the main effects of an independent factor on a number of dependent variables. This correspondence deserves closer examination. First, unless the possibility of the contrast (between state-financed and privately financed students) arises as a consequence of a pilot study or exploratory case-studies, the factor may not be included in the design of the main investigation. Second, if the main investigation is not large enough or sufficiently well-controlled (for reasons outside the Investigator's control), the contrast may lack statistical validity while yet making good psychological sense. Third, in communicating the findings about the contrast, statistical data may be much less meaningful than 'model' cases based on the data, rather like statistical data can be made more meaningful when expressed in a pictogram.

Our philosophical position, however, as previously stated, is more radical than this because we do not regard case-studies as pilot cases for, or mere illustrations of, statistical surveys. We regard case-studies, and the case-law conceptualizations they give rise to, as a basic form of scientific inquiry.

SUMMARY AND CONCLUSIONS

The basic sources of understanding human problems are to be found in common knowledge, scientific research, and professional experience. In order to deal with human problems we also normally need to operate through established social and administrative arrangements. These different sources and arrangements are not sharply distinguished from each other. Scientific and professional work with people depends heavily on an infrastructure of common sense and ordinary language. Social and administrative arrangements make it possible to pool ideas and resources so that solutions can be devised and implemented that would be beyond the power of one Investigator acting alone.

Creative thinking in case-studies should be engaged in separately from critical thinking, otherwise original and useful ideas may not emerge. Case-studies are exercises in problem-solving.

Possible solutions to problems can sometimes be compared and arranged in order of preference—in terms of their likely effects, feasibility, and cost. Diagrams provide a useful way of exploring the ramifications of proposed solutions. They sketch the various 'scenarios' that can be envisaged. The aim is to find the most preferred path through a series of actions and eventualities towards the most appropriate goal.

Having concentrated for some time on the psychological case-study, it is worth reminding ourselves that there are other sorts of case-study. One can carry out case-studies of major events, like battles or disasters, or of large organizations such as firms or schools, or of social processes such as trade or crime. Case-studies in these areas share a common logic with psychological case-studies, although they rely to some extent on different sources of common knowledge, scientific research, and professional experience, and are governed by rather different social and administrative arrangements.

Case-studies do not play a subordinate role in the advancement of knowledge.

CHAPTER EIGHT

Making Decisions About Cases

INTRODUCTION

The psychological study of individual cases is carried out more often than not for practical reasons, for the benefit of the Subject of the case-study and other interested parties. Investigators try to find solutions to problems which are causing distress; they make decisions and recommendations in the hope that beneficial consequences will follow from their implementation. How are such decisions and recommendations arrived at? Are there any ways in which such decision-making can be improved—that is to say, made more rational, more realistic, and so more effective?

The first of these questions is answered in part by describing the psychology of problem-solving as it applies to the psychological study of individual cases in various professional contexts, such as probation, marriage guidance, or bereavement counselling. The bulk of this book is concerned with the methodology of solving human problems.

The second of these questions is answered in the same way, because what we actually do, or try to do, when we study individual cases, cannot be considered apart from what we ought, or think we ought, to be doing.

Strictly speaking, the first question is an empirical one, the second procedural or normative. The differences between what we actually do and what we ought to do (as scientists and professionals) are referred to throughout this book, and particularly in Chapters 1, 10, and 11.

The purpose of this chapter is to explain and illustrate, as simply as possible, some of the methods used in what is called 'decision analysis'. Such methods can greatly improve practical decision-making, and are extensively used in much more elaborate forms in business studies and elsewhere. As we shall see, it is not easy to quantify the factors commonly found in psychological case-studies, and therefore it is not easy to use formal decision-making methods. Nevertheless, understanding the reasoning behind such methods should help readers to arrive at, and critically evaluate, decisions about individual cases.

ELEMENTARY DECISION ANALYSIS

Let us consider a decision in which we are required to adopt one of two or more possible courses of action. The consequences of each course of action depend on circumstances. We cannot be sure what those circumstances will be, but we can make a reasonable forecast. We can define a small set of mutually exclusive conditions (circumstances or situations), where each set is assigned a probability (chance) of occurrence, and where the sum of the probabilities is equal to unity (1.0). We can also attach personal utilities (subjective values) to the consequences expected to occur in each set of circumstances. The subjective values express, on some kind of scale, the relative desirability of each possible outcome.

Let us take an oversimplified problem to begin with. We are considering the advisability of buying a house. We have to decide whether to buy a house or not (ignoring other options). An important consideration is whether house prices will rise, fall, or stay the same (let us ignore all other considerations, such as the time-scale or local variations in price change). We reason that we shall gain if we buy and house prices rise, and lose if we buy and house prices fall, and vice-versa. We can estimate these subjective utilities on an arbitrary scale to represent the six possible gains or losses—see Table 8.1. We confine ourselves to one or other of three possibilities: house prices will rise, fall, or stay the same. We think the first is most likely and give it a probability (P) of 0.5, the second next most likely $(P = 0.3)$ and the third least likely $(P = 0.2)$. The sum of these probabilities is 1.0.

The question is, given the utilities of the various outcomes and the probability of each of a mutually exclusive set of contingencies, which decision, 'Buy' or 'Don't buy', is the best? The decision is arrived at by multiplying the estimated utility of each outcome by its probability, and then summing the products for each decision to find its subjectively expected utility (SEU). The decision which yields the highest expected utility, 'Buy', is in one sense the best decision.

The anticipated consequences of each course of action under the different conditions can be represented as a 'pay-off matrix' or decision matrix, as in Table 8.1.

This sort of decision-making, based on SEUs, thus comprises three distinct sets of factors: (i) the options for action open to us; (ii) the values we place on each possible outcome, and (iii) the probabilities associated with the situations that might arise. Remember that the *actual* outcome is uncertain, otherwise the choice would be so obvious that it would not involve a 'decision' in the proper sense of that word.

Table 8.1. A simple 'pay-off matrix' or decision matrix illustrating options for action, the circumstances that might arise (together with their probabilities), the utility of each possible outcome, and the subjectively expected utility (SEU) of each course of action

Options for action	Circumstances and probabilities			
	Prices rise $(P = 0.5)$	Prices stay the same $(P = 0.3)$	Prices fall $(P = 0.2)$	Subjectively expected utility (SEU)
Buy	Utility: $+5$ $P \times U = +2.5$	Utility: $+1$ $P \times U = +0.3$	Utility: -5 $P \times U = -1.0$	$+1.8$
Don't buy	Utility: -5 $P \times U = -2.5$	Utility: -1 $P \times U = -0.3$	Utility: $+5$ $P \times U = +1.0$	-1.8

Where investigators can think of several criteria for evaluating the consequences (costs and benefits) of different courses of action, they can apply what is called 'multi-attribute utility theory' (MAUT)—see Edwards and Newman (1982). Let us consider a relatively simple case. Suppose a person is trying to decide what sort of career to enter. Given the appropriate information, guidance, and opportunity, he or she could assign subjective numerical values (degrees of preference) to each of, say, six independent criteria, e.g. security, prospects, interest, working hours, social life, and pay, relevant to a number of career possibilities, such as journalism, teaching, social work, and politics. The subjective numerical values could be assigned by means of ratings or magnitude scaling or some other method—see Lodge (1981), Wooler and Lewis (1982). Phillips (1980) presents a simple case-study in decision analysis together with comments on subjective scaling and decision-trees (sequential decisions).

Next, the Subject assesses the relative importance of the criteria chosen to compare and contrast the four career options. If we now multiply the values of the subjectively scaled judgments by the associated indices of relative importance we are, in effect, weighting the original subjective values for their importance to the Subject. If we sum these weighted values across the six criteria we arrive at a relative overall preference value for each career option.

Table 8.2 shows that, in this particular example, journalism is well ahead of the other three career possibilities, which are not very different from each other.

The numerical values assigned to each of the four career options for each of the six criteria could have been assessed more objectively by experienced careers guidance counsellors. In fact, now that computer-assisted careers guidance is possible, a Subject is encouraged to use careers guidance as a

Table 8.2. A simple decision matrix illustrating career options, criteria for comparison between options, subjectively scaled value-judgments, indices of relative importance of options, in brackets—the values obtained by multiplying subjectively scaled values by the associated index of relative importance, and summed values indicating relative overall preference

				Criteria for comparison				
Options	Security	Prospects	Interest	Working hours	Social life	Pay		Relative overall preference
Journalism	50 (6.0)	60 (12.6)	70 (16.1)	20 (2.0)	80 (17.6)	60 (7.2)		61.5
Teaching	90 (10.8)	50 (10.5)	30 (6.9)	90 (9.0)	50 (11.0)	50 (6.0)		54.2
Social work	80 (9.6)	50 (10.5)	50 (11.5)	50 (5.0)	50 (11.0)	50 (6.0)		53.6
Politics	10 (1.2)	70 (14.7)	80 (18.4)	10 (1.0)	70 (15.4)	40 (4.8)		55.5
Relative importance	0.12	0.21	0.23	0.10	0.22	0.12		

form of education about the world of employment, and as a way of improving self-understanding. The Subject's criteria, career options, and subjectively scaled preferences can be examined and discussed, and iterated until they stabilize. This is important because the Subject's initial thinking about possible careers is likely to be erroneous.

Case-studies in career choice can now be carried out with the aid of computers—see *Journal of Counseling and Development* (1984). For example, the client's subjective estimates can be optimized by modifying them in relation to any available objective estimates and additional criteria, such as personality characteristics and the probability of succeeding in gaining entry (obviously there are more openings in some careers than in others). However, it may be difficult to obtain objective estimates uncontaminated by subjective factors.

At the end of the exercise the career options can be listed in order of the magnitude of their subjectively expected utility (SEU). The best option, in terms of decision-analysis, is the one that gives the highest overall combination of desirability and realism. If, for some reason, this option is not acceptable, the exercise can be repeated using fresh options, probabilities, and utilities. The aim of the exercise is to fully explore and systematize the decision-maker's reasoning.

For example, among the relevant criteria in considering a career are the Subject's personal qualities: intelligence, emotional stability, sociability. These might be included in the decision matrix. Similarly, if we estimated the relative opportunity for entry into journalism, teaching, social work and politics at $P = 0.2, 0.3, 0.4$, and 0.1, respectively, then we could readjust the relative overall preference accordingly, as shown in Table 8.3. Thus, consideration of the factors affecting access to these various professions could bring an even stronger note of realism into the process of decision-making (assuming the factors affecting access are realistically assessed). Journalism becomes the third preference and social work the first, in this hypothetical example.

It is obvious that some types of psychological case lend themselves to rational decision-making of the sort we have been considering—case-studies

Table 8.3. Adjusted overall preference rating

Career option	Preference value		Probability of entry		SEU
Journalism	61.5	×	0.2	=	12.3
Teaching	54.2	×	0.3	=	16.3
Social work	53.6	×	0.4	=	21.4
Politics	55.5	×	0.1	=	5.6

in career guidance are good examples. Other types of case, however, lack the sort of data-base and expertise available in careers counselling. Nevertheless, the basic principles of decision-analysis are the same. That is: (i) consider what the options are as regards possible courses of action; (ii) establish several independent criteria to be used in comparing the different courses of action; (iii) evaluate each course of action in relation to each criterion on a common scale; (iv) establish indices of relative importance for the criteria; (v) calculate the relative 'pay-offs' for each course of action; (vi) evaluate each course of action in terms of its relative chances (probability) of success; (vii) calculate the subjectively expected utilities for each course of action; (viii) either select the option that has the largest subjectively expected utility (SEU) or (ix) critically examine the decision-process and revise it if necessary.

The above oversimplified examples demonstrate that decision-making can be rational even when subjective rather than objective numerical estimates are used. Although even a moment's thought reveals a host of difficulties—such as what factors to take into account, how to weight their importance, how to combine factors in decisions about situations involving several attributes—developments in decision-analysis have succeeded to some extent in coping with these difficulties—see Phillips (1980, 1982 and undated), Wooler and Lewis (1982), Wright (1984), and Easton (1982). The multi-attribute utility theory (MAUT) approach helps decision-makers to analyse their experience and reasoning so as to take account of many sources of information and lines of argument without losing track of their relative importance.

It must not be supposed that the utilities and the probabilities together exhaust the considerations to be taken into account when arriving at a decision—whether in business, or in one's personal affairs, or in connection with a case-study. A further obvious factor, well-recognized in the psychological study of human and animal behaviour, is the delay—the time interval between the onset of the required behaviour (course of action) and the associated consummatory activity. For example, a person who wishes to obtain an academic qualification or a professional position should, rationally, weigh up not only the likelihood of success and the anticipated benefits but also how long it is going to take to achieve this aim and what it will cost in money, effort, alternative satisfactions forgone, and so on. These considerations can be handled by means of the SEU model in deciding whether an action is worth taking or not. In business decisions the time between incurring the cost and yielding the profit is crucial, for delay means increased interest charges and cash-flow problems.

There is usually some sort of psychological or situational pressure to find a way of dealing with a case—business competition, professional pride, fear of the consequences of failure, the requirements of one's role, the limitations in one's resources. Pressures like these force practical and approximate solutions. One cannot wait indefinitely for the best or the correct answer. Notice that 'academic' questions, so-called, tend to be about abstract and theoretical issues which call for consensus and not for urgent practical action. In business decision-making, as well as in psychological case-studies, one finds a conflict between the need for more thought and information on the one hand and the mounting need for decision and action on the other. There comes a time when the benefits of a better-informed, more-considered, decision are outweighed by the costs (the disadvantages) of the delay in reaching it.

The more one searches for a rational basis for decision-making, the more complex that basis seems to become, even when the 'affective' issues are de-emphasized. For example, does the disincentive of delay increase in a linear fashion with time, or exponentially? Lengthy time-intervals between action and outcome provide opportunities for changes in the individual and his or her circumstances, making the original calculations less appropriate.

The term 'satisficing' has been coined to refer to the first solution which meets the minimum requirements for a decision. It enables a prompt response to be made, a fact which may be of the utmost importance in business or military decision-making as well as in other areas. Such a solution gives time to consider other courses of action without seriously limiting subsequent choice. On the other hand, an early response based on insufficient information may preclude a change of course.

The term 'incrementalism' has been coined to refer to piecemel decision-making. That is, dealing with small, relatively separate, more manageable aspects of the larger problem without necessarily solving the problem as a whole. Incrementalism has advantages and disadvantages: it enables one to make a start on a problem, especially a large, complex long-term problem that one knows will otherwise persist in one form or another, e.g. domestic overspending, school indiscipline, staff morale; but it may simply mean tinkering with minor difficulties instead of getting to the root of the problem.

When dealing with problems in a constructive but critical way one goes through a series of stages. At each stage, including the proposed solution stage, one may revert to an earlier stage including the first (formulating the problem). Problem-solving is an iterative process—in moving forward and searching for the best solution we may reformulate the problem, modify the procedures, and take different steps at successive iterations or trials. Initially, we need to know the aim of the exercise. What are we trying to do and why? Next, we have to consider the possible solutions or courses of action that would meet this objective. What *can* we do? What is possible? Next, for each possibility, consider what the outcome(s) would be under various conditions: good? bad? or indifferent? and what are the probabilities of those conditions: high? moderate? or low? Next we must decide on the criteria to be used in choosing between the various courses of action. The criteria chosen should be independent of each other and be applicable to all courses of action. They are used to evaluate the *relative* worth of the options open to us in relation to a case.

This method of analysing decision-making can be used to decide whether it is worth waiting for more information or whether it is worth spending money on research or expert advice. The method makes the reasoning explicit so that it can be shared among people in a way that makes it possible for solutions to be agreed collectively, even when Investigators see the problem from different perspectives because of their different backgrounds, interests, values, and assumptions—see Phillips (undated and 1982).

PRACTICAL CONSIDERATIONS IN DECIDING ABOUT CASES

The method of rational decision-making we have been discussing does not rely wholly on the availability of precise numerical estimates. Simple ratings, rankings, or even simple +/0/− values can be handled. The main lesson we want to learn from this exercise is that decisions can be made rationally, with due regard to the facts of the case. There may be no need to rely entirely on guesswork or intuition. Decision theory obliges us to provide data and explicit reasons for the decisions we reach in psychological case-studies. Although clinical experience provides the necessary information and hypotheses, decision analysis is often necessary to handle the information and the logical implications.

A quantitative approach to decision-making is well-established in many fields, such as business, industry, government, and military affairs. In the psychological study of individual cases the quantitative (actuarial) approach to decision-making was originally contrasted with clinical decision-making— see Meehl (1954 and 1955, 1956, 1957—reprinted in Meehl (1973a))— although Meehl (1973b) has emphasized the essential role of clinical judgment in rational decision-making. The quantitative approach has been explored in other areas, e.g. delinquency, vocational selection and guidance, but the general impression seems to be that the approach is by no means well-established in the psychological study of individual cases, even in clinical psychology.

Meehl's (1973b) paper on 'Why I do not attend case conferences' is not an attack on the clinical or case-study method. On the contrary, he is at pains to confirm the fundamental importance of clinical observation and inference. His attack is concentrated on the low level of scientific and professional reasoning he encountered in case-conferences, which he attributes to factors such as inadequate intelligence, education, and training; ideological blinkers; lack of critical acumen; and social inhibitions. He provides a list of faults to be identified and eliminated together with a number of recommendations for improving case-conferences; see also Compher (1984).

A clinical, rather than an actuarial, method is unavoidable in certain circumstances. If there are few or no actuarial indicators then the Investigator must of necessity rely on clinical experience and common sense. Or, if there are rare but obviously important features which have no actuarial basis then the Investigator's clinical judgment can override an actuarial calculation. Ideally, a combination of reliable clinical and actuarial indicators will secure both statistical probability and psychological confidence. The danger lies in not using the best evidence and procedure.

The main reason for introducing the topic of decision analysis is to illustrate the assumptions and thought processes involved in rational decision-making, even when it is not possible to quantify the probabilities and outcome values with any great accuracy. We can ignore the method in those cases where the considerations are so simple and straightforwrd that there is no problem about what decision to take.

The consequences of actions spread out into the wider environment and forward into the future. In dealing with a case-study we must try to foresee as much as possible. In Case A, for example, the Investigator must try to work out what effect A's redundancy would have on A and other workers in the firm. Suppose, in Case A, management agreed to assign the chances of rehabilitating A at 0.2 and the value of successful rehabilitation at 70 (as compared with $P = 0.8$ and $V = 30$ for an unsuccessful attempt at rehabilitation). The subjectively expected utilities become $0.2 \times 70 = 14.0$ and $0.8 \times 30 = 24.0$ respectively. This argues against trying to rehabilitate A. Sometimes the outcome of such calculations, especially when a series of probabilistic relationships are involved, is such as to persuade Investigators to rethink the subjective probabilities and values that they are using in their decision-making.

Ideally, one would like to be able to assign values and probabilities to all the foreseeable possibilities in a case-study. But actual outcomes, i.e. consequences, may interact with one another, sometimes in ways one could hardly have foreseen. For example, in Case B, B may receive conflicting advice from different sources and become further confused. In Case C, C might miss a good job opportunity because she is concentrating on her leisure activities.

In making forecasts we are in the realm of possible worlds. The recurring question is, 'What might happen if—?' The question needs to be asked repeatedly—for each problem and problem sector, in relation to all the contextual factors that impinge on the case, such as the availability of time and resources, the effect of external events (sickness, changes in staff or policy), and so on.

A useful technique is to take each proposed solution to a problem and list the possible consequences under two headings (+, positive or −, negative). These advantages and disadvantages should be listed where possible in order of magnitude of effect (bearing in mind the ramifications that can occur in complex cases). Consider this technique as it applies to Case C:

(a) Concentration on leisure activities.
    Advantages (+):
    (i) Minimum disruption to existing life-style.
    (ii) Leaves C 'in control' since the activities are voluntary.

   (iii) Low financial cost.
   (iv) Permits contact with a wide range of people, some with compatible interests and characteristics.

  Disadvantages (−):
   (i) Only a substitute for or means of reaching close attachment to a male partner.
   (ii) Possibility of unrewarded effort.

(b) Concentration on relocation and change of life-style.
  Advantages (+):
   (i) Removes current constraints and contingencies reinforcing maladaptive behaviour.
   (ii) Opens up a new range of opportunities of all kinds.

  Disadvantages (−):
   (i) Loss of support and rewards available locally from family, friends, and colleagues.
   (ii) Major life-stress will aggravate current maladjustment.
   (iii) Temporary loss of control over events because of unfamiliarity and uncertainty of the new environment.

Some consequences will be neutral in the sense of neither adding to nor detracting from the favourability of an outcome, i.e. they make no difference. There is therefore no point in entering them into the equation. If their effect is neutral because the good effects and bad effects cancel each other out, then one should consider how these effects might be disconnected through some other course of action so as to maximize the positive consequences.

When one is comparing the advantages and disadvantages of different courses of action, one should check to see whether any of the pros and cons of one course are applicable to another. This should help to ensure that the final decision is a 'balanced' one. If it is possible and sensible to assign quantitative values to the advantages and disadvantages, one could find the total number of points credited (or debited) to each possible course of action and select the one with the highest score. Another method is to identify only major advantages and disadvantages, or assume each has unitary value (+ or −), and select the one with the largest positive score.

One's estimate of the value of an outcome should be kept separate from one's estimate of that outcome's probability of occurrence. Probability of occurrence can be expressed in exact quantitative terms or in approximate terms such as: likely, as likely as not, unlikely. Numerical probabilities are used to multiply the subjectively judged value of an outcome to find the expected utility.

The point to be made clear is that, in areas where we have some experience of outcomes, a number of different considerations enter into a decision. It is possible to 'calculate' the relative contribution that each consideration, i.e. variable, should make in relation to an outcome, although the considerations themselves may well have been arrived at through clinical intuition. The calculation combines several weighted variables in an optimum way to arrive at a decision or prediction which is better than the prediction that would have been achieved without the benefit of calculation. This is called 'bootstrapping'—see Lovie (1985).

Note that the utility of an outcome is expressed relative to other outcomes in terms of a subjective scale, e.g. 1 to 10 or 1 to 100, and not in terms of some absolute magnitude such as time or money.

Subjectively, it may be difficult to make one's estimate of the probability of an outcome independently of one's estimate of its worth. Consequently it is important to be clear and consistent in the way one uses the terms in decision analysis: options, conditions, probabilities, weights, valuations (worths) or utilities, expected utilities, and outcomes.

Options are the possibilities for action, including taking no action. Conditions are states of affairs that might arise. Valuations or utilities are subjective estimates of the relative worth of particular outcomes. Probabilities are the chances that certain conditions will arise. Weights are the importance we attach to different criteria. Subjectively expected utilities (SEUs) are the product of the utility of an outcome and the probability of its associated condition (or the weight attached to its associated criterion). Decision analysis provides a means whereby an Investigator, or a group of Investigators, can arrive at a decision (argue a case) in a rational way, in the sense of using an explicit, precise structure of inference. In Chapter 10 we consider some of the weaknesses of ordinary reasoning which decision analysis helps to overcome.

In practice, decisions may not be implemented, or not implemented in the appropriate way, in which case the action taken cannot be expected to produce the required result. Moreover, all sorts of contingencies can arise to upset even the best forecasts and plans; such contingencies do not fault the decision analysis, they simply remind us of life's uncertainties.

Each set of mutually exclusive possibilities is associated with a given decision, although the decision may have consequences other than those listed in a particular set. For example, the possibilities of being happy and productive, unhappy and unproductive, neither, or a little of each, are associated with the decision whether to retire or not. Assuming the first of these is the most preferred outcome (possibility), one looks to see whether it is more likely to follow one course of action, retirement, than the other, non-retirement. The four outcomes listed above are general statements; they need to be translated into specific effects—into concrete 'performance' statements rather than abstract 'achievement' statements—before they are evaluated, otherwise the decision will be based on vague and uncertain considerations.

As we have seen in connection with time perspective in case-studies, the foreseeable consequences of actions do not normally extend far into the future, hence case-reviews should be carried out, if at all possible, at suitable intervals to keep the effects of intervention under control. Solution-finding, like problem-finding, is a recursive process.

The sequential nature of causes and effects (actions and their consequences) means that there is an evolving network of interrelated events moving through time. It is our ability to understand these events and their relationships, to see the way things are moving, and to intervene in the right way at the right time that enables us to influence outcomes. We need to be able to assign probabilities and values to outcomes in order to make sensible decisions and recommendations. We need to have command of the resources necessary for their effective implementation.

There are obvious limits to the accuracy with which we can make forecasts far ahead, and equally obvious limits to our ability to invervene effectively in cases. A rational approach to case-studies helps us to move closer to these limits.

Contingency planning is a term used to refer to consideration of the action to be taken in the event that certain eventualities occur. Contingency planning is usually thought of in connection with the management of serious undesirable outcomes. For example, one might want to have a course of action prepared in the event that a schoolchild's disruptive behaviour continues beyond a certain date or exceeds a prescribed limit. Other examples would be plans prepared to cope with loss of employment, bereavement, the granting of parole, attempted suicide, or marital separation.

MORE PRACTICAL CONSIDERATIONS

A simple way of explaining the decision process is to think in terms of a two-by-two table which generates a four-fold classification of the advantages and disadvantages of a course of action. The basic questions are 'How likely is it?' and 'How important is it?'

	More likely (+)	Less likely (−)
More important (+)	A	B
Less important (−)	C	D

The advantages and disadvantages are listed for Case C (Chapter 3) can be classified as follows:

(a) Concentration on leisure activities.

Advantages:

	Importance	Likelihood	Category
(i)	+	+	A
(ii)	+	+	A
(iii)	−	+	C
(iv)	+	− ?	B

Disadvantages:

	Importance	Likelihood	Category
(i)	−	−	D
(ii)	−	−	D

(b) Concentration on relocation and change of life-style.

Advantages:

	Importance	Likelihood	Category
(i)	+	+	A
(ii)	+	+	A

Disadvantages:

	Importance	Likelihood	Category
(i)	+	+	A
(ii)	+	−	B
(iii)	+	−	B

This procedure directs our attention to the items in Category A, since these are thought to be both important and likely to occur. So it is a way of simplifying the decision process.

The methods we have been considering should not be used unreflectively. They are, after all, based on practical experience and intelligent reasoning. They are essentially heuristics or aids to creative and critical decision-making in case-studies. However, the mechanical process of calculation is an essential part of the overall procedure designed to improve our success rate.

In order to put a value on an outcome it is necessary to know in what ways the outcome is important, i.e. worth bringing about. Remember that outcomes do not usually come free of charge; they need time and resources to bring them about. If the possible outcomes are mutually exclusive, the time and resources employed in relation to one outcome cannot be used for another; choosing one outcome means not choosing another.

Although it is easy to say, in general terms, what outcomes one would like to achieve (or avoid), it is more difficult to say, in concrete terms, what it would amount to. What one needs here are behavioural and environmental definitions or specifications of exactly what one has in mind. Thus, for example, what does it mean exactly to say that C's relocation and change of life-style would:

(a) 'open up a new range of opportunities' or
(b) 'remove her from current constraints and contingencies of reinforcement'?

Such statements must be translatable into observable events or at least into more specific expectations, such as: (a) 'having new neighbours and other social contacts in new settings at work or in leisure time; encountering new situations and ideas; finding new job vacancies; getting fresh independent advice if needed'; or (b) 'fewer reminders of her unfortunate affair; less criticism from her family; fewer rewards for avoidance behaviour'. These statements could be made even more specific given more information about Case C and the available options.

An Investigator needs to know what empirical facts would have to be established in order to establish the claim that a particular outcome had been achieved. He should not be content with vague generalities of the sort expressed in phrases such as 'making progress', 'adjusting well', 'less depressed', 'more sociable', 'getting on better with his wife', or 'settling in', unless they can be backed up by specific observational reports.

It is a feature of language that we can express ideas at various levels of abstraction and generality. The danger in case-studies and personality descriptions is appearing to say something meaningful only to find, on closer examination, that the phrases we are using are vacuous, empty of content. Not that the phrases are meaningless in themselves, but rather that they can be given different meanings depending upon the context in which they are used. Until we specify the meaning we wish to attach to a phrase, uncertainty and ambiguity remain.

It would be unusual for a case-study to be dominated by just one criterion for success—employment, better use of time, marriage, improved living standards, discharge from care, recovery from bankruptcy, self-reported life-satisfaction or job-satisfaction, or whatever. We have emphasized the complexity of the case-study—the different facets of the Subject's personality, the various sets of circumstances that make up his or her environment, the context in which the case-study is carried out. All these considerations point to the need for multiple criteria to test progress in a case-study. Nevertheless, the more coherent and simple the criteria, the easier it is to choose between the available courses of action.

One assumes that success in the short term, as judged by clear empirical criteria, is a step along the road to successful adjustment in the long term. It is a great advantage to know what successful long-term adjustment would amount to—again in clear empirical terms, for this helps one to decide on short-term objectives.

The use of the word 'objectives' should remind us that much of what we have had to say about the analysis and management of case-studies—identifying problems, finding solutions, making decisions—bears a close resemblance to management by objectives as practised in industry, commerce, the Civil Service, and the Armed Forces. Management by objectives is closely related to the business of performance evaluation, to which we have already referred. In other words, the scientific study of individual cases is one aspect of a general method, or collection of methods, of solving human problems. It uses a recursive technique in which questions are formulated, lines of inquiry are developed, new findings emerge, new questions are asked, or old questions reformulated. Eventually, solutions are proposed, their implications examined, their merits assessed, and a rational decision based on empirical evidence is reached. That decision takes into account the relevant objective and subjective (social and psychological) considerations and is implemented as and when appropriate.

SEQUENTIAL DECISIONS

It is important to bear in mind that, even in a relatively short sequence of related outcomes (where later events depend on what goes before), the probabilities of the outcomes at the end of the sequence—the outcomes of major interest—are conditional probabilities in the sense of being dependent on the earlier outcomes to which they are related.

Consider the simplified dendrogram in Figure 8.1. It represents a case-study in pre-retirement planning. Note that each outcome has been assigned an associated subjective probability. We see that, in this particular example, the conditional probability of the person enjoying a very productive life

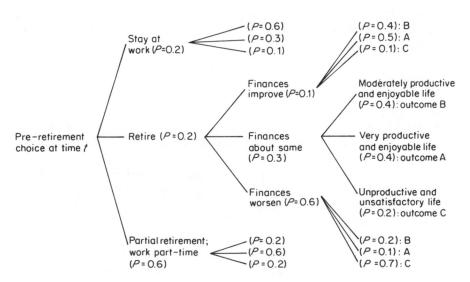

Figure 8.1 Subjective probabilities associated with various outcomes following a pre-retirement decision

following complete retirement is 0.2×0.3 (if his finances stay about the same) $\times 0.4 = 0.024$. This superficially pessimistic prospect must be looked at relative to the other outcomes in the set. Thus the conditional probability of moderate enjoyment and productivity is $0.2 \times 0.3 \times 0.4 = 0.024$, i.e. the same. The conditional probability of an unproductive and unsatisfactory retirement is $0.2 \times 0.3 \times 0.2 = 0.012$, i.e. half as likely.

If we consider other possible sequences of events we can calculate the likelihood of other outcomes. Consider the likelihood of an unproductive and unsatisfactory retirement if he decides on partial retirement and part-time work, and if his finances worsen. With this prospect the conditional probability is $0.6 \times 0.2 \times 0.7 = 0.084$. This is substantially greater than the conditional probabilities calculated earlier. But it is coincidentally the same as if he retired ($P = 0.2$), suffered worsening finances ($P = 0.6$) and suffered an unproductive and unsatisfactory retirement ($P = 0.7$), since $0.2 \times 0.6 \times 0.7 = 0.084$. This comes about because the person concerned judges that retiring completely will increase the likelihood of worsening finances as compared with partial retirement and continuing work part-time. But this is counterbalanced by a relatively higher likelihood of the latter course of action.

What we are doing, in these examples, is finding a numerical way of calculating the likelihood of these particular combinations of events. We are connecting an opportunity to decide about retirement with a range of foreseeable outcomes. The probabilities reflect the person's attitude to retirement. They are highly subjective. They take into account his health, domestic circumstances, working conditions, and so on. The probabilities assigned to his financial situation in retirement are more objective in the sense that he can calculate his income, expenditure, and tax fairly accurately (but not with absolute certainty). The subjective probabilities he associates with different degrees of enjoyment and productivity in life are largely a function of the importance he attaches to financial security. It may be that closer examination of the non-financial benefits he hopes to gain by retirement would reveal that a worse financial situation (within limits) would not seriously affect his preferred life-style. In that case his subjective estimates of what might happen could be revised, leading perhaps to a reconsideration of the decision to retire or not. This would be analogous to what is happening in modern computer-assisted career counselling, in which actually carrying out an exercise in this kind of decision-making gives the person more insight into his own beliefs, attitudes, and values.

The pre-retirement dendrogram above is grossly oversimplified. One could add many more stages and branches to the system, such as relocation, health status, domestic circumstances, and so on. The problem then is to systematically eliminate the less preferred outcomes to find the best sequence of decisions—see Phillips (1980) and Easton (1982).

The retirement decision can be represented in the form of a matrix, as in earlier examples—see Table 8.4. In this table we assume only three options: retire early, continue to work full-time; take partial retirement and work

Table 8.4. A simplified decision matrix for a retirement decision, assuming the options are equally available

	Criteria					
Options	Financial resources	Health	Personal interests and activities	Family considerations	Facilities for productive work	Subjectively expected utility
Retire early	50 (15.0)	100 (24.0)	60 (6.6)	80 (19.2)	60 (6.6)	71.4
Continue to work full-time	100 (30.0)	80 (19.2)	80 (8.8)	100 (24.0)	100 (11.0)	93.0
Work/retire part-time	70 (21.0)	90 (21.6)	100 (11.0)	90 (21.6)	90 (9.9)	85.1
Relative importance	0.30	0.24	0.11	0.24	0.11	

part-time. We look at each of these options in relation to five criteria: financial level, health, personal interests and activities, family considerations, and facilities (meaning facilities for personal activities). Using the magnitude scaling method, values are assigned to each option on each criterion. The relative importance of the criteria is indexed (the indices sum to 1.0) on the bottom row of Table 8.4. The subjectively expected utilities are calculated in the usual way (the sums of the criterion values weighted for importance), on the assumption that all three options were equally possible. We find that the best decision, in this particular example, is to continue to work full-time.

The use of numerical estimates in decision-making is exceptional in the psychological study of individual cases. What usually happens is that the Subject of the case-study, or the Investigators, or both, develop images or 'scenarios' representing possible outcomes. These images fluctuate, depending on the particular aspect of the case under consideration; it is difficult to hold them in mind and compare them. As a result, decisions are often made arbitrarily—on the basis of momentary feelings, salient experiences, pressure of events, reliance on other people's recommendations, and so on. Phillips (1980) provides an introduction to decision analysis which shows how such 'scenarios' can be transformed into sequential decision-trees.

Bayesian statistics are commonly used to revise opinions as further information becomes available. However, we are not concerned with the more technical aspects of decision analysis. For a still useful early reference to decision analysis in psychology, including a discussion of the concept of rationality and an account of Bayesian statistics, see Edwards *et al.* (1965). For commentaries on recent developments see Lovie (1985).

Each series of decisions results in an outcome. The different outcomes have associated costs and benefits such as time saved, money spent, changes in self-regard, stress, inconvenience to others, and opportunities forgone. Sequential decision analysis shows how to identify the route to the preferred outcome, provided one can estimate the various chances of success and the utilities of the various outcomes. Consider, for example, how you might decide to deal with a windfall of £5000 (after tax). You would consider first of all whether to spend it or save it. If you spend it you could purchase one major item like a new car or a house extension, or you could purchase a number of minor items like a hifi system, a desk, new clothes, and so on. If you save it you could go for a high-risk high-profit scheme or for a low-risk low-profit scheme. The actual outcomes would be determined by the degree of success or failure of the investments or of the purchased items. In order to reach a sensible decision in the face of uncertainty about the outcome you would have to decide what factors are relevant and important to you in relation to using the windfall. For simplicity, let us suppose you give equal weight to four criteria: (a) the need for ready money, (b) comfort and convenience in daily life, (c) increased assets, and (d) protection against inflation. You must then estimate the relative value of each possible outcome on each criterion and calculate the utilities. Next, you must estimate the chances of success or failure following the two sorts of investments and two sorts of purchases. Note that expert advice as well as ordinary experience can be used to help estimate the various values, weights, and probabilities. As we have seen, the product of the weighted subjective value and the probability gives the subjectively expected utility for each possible outcome. By 'averaging out' the expected utilities and 'folding back' or 'pruning' the decision-tree, i.e. blocking off all the paths except the one that leads through to the highest value, one can find what seems to be the best solution to the problem.

If one is not satisfied with the decision arrived at in this way, then the analysis has at least drawn attention to some inconsistency in one's reasoning. This calls for a further step known as 'sensitivity analysis'—a procedure which tests how robust the decision is in relation to variations in the subjective judgments that enter into the decision process. In practice, decision analysis is useful mainly because if helps Investigators to clarify a problem and to consider the consequences of alternative courses of action. The benefits are derived not only from the explicit numerical and logical features of the procedure but also from its heuristic function. In the process of constructing the matrices and decision-trees, thinking up options, finding criteria, assigning values, and choosing weights, Investigators are forced to make clear much that might otherwise remain obscure or be left out of consideration.

It is not sufficient to ask 'What is the value of this course of action in relation to the problem it was intended to remedy?' Outcomes have repercussions beyond their intended effect. Indeed some solutions are proposed *because* they not only solve the main problem under consideration, but also promise to solve subsidiary problems or to bring secondary benefits. It is one of the principles of systems analysis that changes in one part of a system are likely to induce changes, sometimes unintentional changes, in other parts of the system. Hence the need, in a complex case-study, to trace out the possible ramifications of the proposed courses of action. Otherwise, one runs the risk of what in operational research is called 'sub-optimization'. Decision analysis guards against this.

PSYCHOLOGICAL AND SOCIAL VALUES

Where several Investigators are involved, there is room for diversity of opinions about the case based on different value-judgments. Case conferences provide opportunities for such differences to be aired and settled. Decision analysis provides an appropriate framework and procedure whereby a collective decision can be reached.

Another point worth bearing in mind is that although the Subject of a case-study is its central character, he or she is usually not the only person whose health and welfare are affected by the outcomes in the case. Decisions about which courses of action to take should take these additional effects into account by listing them and organizing them, and by assigning values and probabilities as for the other more obvious effects possible in the case. This means having some idea of the values that should be attached to outcomes affecting persons other than the central character in the case-study. The Subject of a case-study exists in a context of social, environmental, ethical, and financial considerations. The possible effects of a decision about a case on these contextual factors are part of the process of decision-making.

In some cases the attributes of the Subject and of the context will be such that only certain kinds of recommendation can be implemented. A Subject may refuse help; a service may be unavailable; there may be rules which limit the extent of service provided; public opinion may force a particular decision.

The effect of an Investigator's own values depends in part on the role he or she plays in the case-study. If Investigators carry the responsibility for the outcome they are likely to adopt a conservative approach to intervention. If they are advisors or consultants they can afford to adopt a more adventurous approach.

More often than not, an Investigator is not only the Subject's agent, but also society's agent. Hence, he or she may experience a conflict of interest in trying to reconcile different evaluations of the worth of a particular course of action. This is clear in the case of G, since the Investigator has to try to reconcile an array of conflicting interests—social and individual.

DECISIONS AND AFTER

We saw in earlier sections that one should expect to use several criteria in evaluating the progress of a case-study once one has reached the stage of implementing decisions. Since a case changes in response to changing conditions over time, the criteria for evaluating progress must also change. Also, the reasons for continuing the case-study may change, putting it into new contexts. This too affects the way progress is evaluated.

Using more than one criterion to evaluate progress is a form of insurance. Instead of focusing exclusively on one particular course of action or on one particular aspect of the case, we choose to consider wider issues and alternative decisions. For example, although a child's academic progress may be the central issue in a case, we may choose to take social relationships into account when evaluating progress.

Long-range goals or outcomes can generally be broken down into subgoals and sequential stages by identifying the appropriate means–ends relationships. Thus, in Case F, F's vows had to be nullified before he could feel free to rejoin the laity and live a 'normal' life. This act had to be preceded by other inquiries, discussions, and procedural formalities. There is no indication that the long-term outcome for Case F was not the best possible in the circumstances. The difficulty, of course, is that one never gets to know 'what might have been' had some other course of action been taken. Case-studies are not normally controlled studies, comparable cases are usually in short supply, and hindsight is misleading.

The process of identifying subgoals and sequential stages in achieving long-term results may show that the same end-result might be attained in different ways. For example, if F had been converted to a different religion or had become politically committed he might have circumvented the regular procedure for leaving the Order. In Case E a family friend might have acted as intermediary between E and his adoptive parents, so that a more concerted effort to find his biological parents could have been mounted.

The essence of practical management of a case is to specify, in concrete terms, the realistic goals to be aimed at and the means whereby these goals are to be attained. A prerequisite is that the various courses of action considered earlier in the case-study have been narrowed down to a relatively small set of measures likely to lead to favourable results, as described earlier in this chapter. We can construct a provisional matrix for Case C. The results are shown in Table 8.5.

Clearly the decision matrix needs to be revised and stabilized. It should be regarded as a heuristic, at least in its initial stages. The act of constructing the matrix is likely to reveal a serious lack of information and ideas. This should be a stimulus for further work on the case until, after a number of revisions, the matrix comes to represent one's firm plans for, and expectations about, the case.

The + and − entries in the cells of the matrix indicate whether or not a particular option would improve the situation (+), worsen it (−) or leave it unchanged (0). Doubt is indicated by a question-mark. If one course of action looks as if it would produce more overall improvement than any other, then the more elaborate decision analysis may not be needed. At this stage one is trying to simplify and clarify the situation so as to be able to concentrate one's limited time and resources. The matrix as it stands points to compensatory employment and leisure activities as the course of action which most satisfies the criteria laid down. What this means is that C should try to find work (if necessary on a voluntary basis) and leisure interests which satisfy *some* of her aspirations and utilize *some* of her abilities, thus going some way to compensate for the non-fulfilment of other aspirations and the non-utilization of other abilities. Engaging in compensatory activities is a normal, common way of coping with deprivation and frustration, and can become rewarding in its own right and self-maintaining.

In applying criteria and choosing among possible courses of action it is usual to avoid high-risk options and options with little pay-off. For example, to discontinue the case and take no further action seems to have nothing to recommend it except the saving of time and resources. By contrast, for C to move her home and try out a new life-style is a considerable risk, and there are many uncertainties associated with this option.

It remains to be seen whether these methods of decision analysis applied to individual case-studies will result in more systematic case-law and psychological theory. At the very least, however, consideration of how a wide variety of considerations can be handled rationally and quantitatively once the

Table 8.5. A provisional decision matrix for Case C

Option	Relief from stress	Fulfilment of potentialities	Self-esteem	Security and comfort	Freedom	Need satisfaction	Active emotional involvement	Advantages to others	Use of time and resources
								Criteria	
Discontinue; no intervention	−	−	−	−	+?	−	−	0	+
Cosmetic treatment, etc	+?	0	+?	0	0	+?	0	+?	−?
Counselling and continuing psychiatric care	+	+?	+	+	−?	0	0?	+	−
Compensatory employment and leisure activities	+	+	+	+?	+	+	+?	+	−?
Relocation and new life-style	−	+?	+?	−?	+	0?	+?	0?	0?

necessary information is available should provide a sort of ideal standard for decision-making in psychological case-studies.

Among the issues that we have not drawn special attention to, but are worth emphasizing, are the following. First, timetabling work on the case-study so that events take place in the correct sequence, opportunities are not missed, and contextual factors are catered for. Second, assigning work and delegating responsibilities among the people who are actively engaged with the case; this avoids conflict and duplicated effort and makes for effective role relationships. Third, mobilizing the resources necessary to carry out a case-study; unless the resources (time, money, people, materials) can be guaranteed there is little point in embarking on the exercise; cases carried out on a shoe-string are likely to be unsatisfactory and wasteful. Fourth, reviewing the progress of the case provides the feedback or knowledge of results necessary for corrective action to avoid unwanted outcomes and to assess the need for further information. Fifth, minimizing the disadvantages and maximizing the advantages of a course of action leads to the optimization of results; this is achieved by monitoring progress and making tactical adjustments as necessary to one's plan of action. Sixth, contingency plans can be made to cope with major foreseeable setbacks. Seventh, making the decisions at the right time; there is no point in finalizing a decision prematurely, but it is a mistake to delay a decision beyond the point where it can have the maximum effect.

Some case-studies constitute stressful situations for Investigators in the sense that they may have to deal with people who are aggressive, emotionally disturbed, unreliable, unappreciative, and otherwise difficult to work with. In addition, Investigators may find themselves facing difficult choices and conflicts of interest. In other words, although case-studies can be regarded as exercises in solving human problems and making sensible decisions, they are not entirely rational in character since they can evoke strong emotional reactions on the part of the Investigators. Consequently, problem-solving and decision-making can be distorted, for example, by impatience, by avoidance, by guilt or hostility, and so on—see Janis and Mann (1977).

SUMMARY AND CONCLUSIONS

The culmination of an exercise in problem-solving is arriving at a solution or decision. Decision analysis as a logical, quantitative method for optimizing decision-making has been developing over many years. Perhaps the best-known applications of decision analysis in relation to psychology were reported by Kelly and Fiske (1951) and Meehl (1954). Actuarial predictions have been shown to be at least as good as, and usually better than, clinical predictions. The advantages of the so-called 'linear model' of estimation appear to be widely accepted in areas where it is possible to assemble the same sorts of data for many Subjects and to enter the results into a previously validated prediction equation.

In business too, and more recently in careers counselling, for example, decision analysis has been used very effectively to explore and improve the logic of the reasoning that Investigators use in reaching their decisions.

Briefly, decision analysis is the process whereby we identify certain options for action, estimate the chances of certain conditions arising, work out a pay-off matrix (the value to us for each option under each condition), and calculate the subjectively expected utilities. The results may induce a reconsideration of the factors affecting our decision. Decision analysis provides a common framework for discussion where more than one person is involved in making the decision.

Examples are given of house-buying, vocational choice, retirement choice, and Case C.

The method can be used not only to find the optimum decision in a static situation but also to find the best route through a sequence of decisions in a dynamic situation where decisions earlier in the series limit the availability of subsequent options.

A related but simpler technique for working out decisions in a case-study is to list the proposed solutions to the problem and count up the expected positive and negative consequences of each solution. A simple four-fold categorization quickly identifies the most important and probable consequences and enables the Investigator to concentrate on those key sectors of the case. Decision analysis proper introduces more refined forms of quantification and analysis.

In spelling out the possible courses of action and the various conditions that might arise, it is important to be as specific as possible, using concrete behavioural and situational terminology rather than vague abstractions. Objective statements are unambiguous and readily agreed between different Investigators.

Decision analysis makes it possible to convert a vague 'scenario' into a much more rigorous framework for understanding cases, making predictions and recommendations. Decision analysis can take account of subjective factors such as personal values and expectations.

Even optimum rational decisions may prove to be wrong. That is natural in view of the intrinsic uncertainty of events. It is wise, therefore, to devote some time and resources to contingency planning, so that if things go badly wrong one is not completely unprepared.

There are many minor ways of improving the management of case-studies. Emotional stress may diminish the ability of Investigators to think rationally and impartially.

CHAPTER NINE

Reasoning About Case-Studies

AN INTRODUCTION TO TOULMIN'S APPROACH TO THE ANALYSIS OF ARGUMENTS

A case-report, like many other sorts of technical report conducted according to professional and scientific rules, tends to have a logical structure. That is to say, it contains statements of various sorts: statements which describe how a problem arose, statements which describe how the problem was investigated, what empirical facts were established, how these facts were interpreted, why they were interpreted in this way, what conclusions were reached, what confidence can be attached to them, what course of action is recommended, what other factors were taken into account, and so on. It is not possible to provide a definitive list of all the types of statement a case-study might contain. Any assertion which is relevant and makes a worthwhile contribution to understanding and dealing with the case can be included.

The logical structure of the arguments in case-studies can be analysed by a method developed by Toulmin (1958) and recently updated by Toulmin *et al.* (1979). Further discussion of the method and examples of its application can be found in Bromley (1970, 1977). Toulmin's approach to the analysis of logical relationships is radically different from the traditional and modern approaches to formal logic. Toulmin is concerned with what can be called the logical 'substance' or 'content' of arguments about matters of fact, in contrast to the 'formal logical validity' of arguments like those in geometry. The formal validity of arguments is, of course, not irrelevant. It needs to be confirmed. The difficulty is that many important arguments in scientific and professional work do not lend themselves to formal logical analysis. I shall refer to Toulmin's approach variously as 'Toulminian analysis', 'substantive logic', 'practical logic', or 'informal logic'.

Toulmin's approach identifies six basic types of statement in a rational argument:

Label	Name(s)	Logical Function
C	Claim or conclusion	States a claim or a conclusion.
D	Data, evidence, or foundation	Offers data or foundations, i.e. relevant evidence, for the claim.
W	Inference warrant	Warrants or justifies the connection between data (D) and claim (C) by appealing to a rule of inference, such as an operational definition, a practical standard, or an analogy.
Q	Modal qualifier	Qualifies a claim or conclusion (C) by expressing degrees of confidence and likelihood.
R	Rebuttal or reservation	Rebuts a claim or conclusion (C) by stating the conditions under which it does not hold; or introduces reservations showing the limits within which the claim (C) is made.
B	Backing	Backs up, justifies, or otherwise supports an inference warrant (W) by appealing to further evidence (empirical data, common knowledge, professional practice, scientific theory and so on).

Colloquially speaking:

C answers the questions 'What are you saying?' 'What is it you are claiming?' 'What is your conclusion?'

D answers the questions 'What have you to go on?' 'Where is your evidence?' 'What data do you have?'

W answers the questions 'How do you make that out?' 'What is the connection?' 'Why are you entitled to draw that conclusion?'

Q answers the questions 'How sure are you?' 'What confidence you do have in your claim?' 'How likely is it that what you say is correct?'

R answers the questions 'What are you assuming?' 'Under what conditions would your argument break down?' 'What reservations would you make?'

B answers the questions 'What proof have you?' 'What is the justification for your line of reasoning?' 'Is there any support for the connection you are making?'

The logical structure of a case-report is most easily established form the case-summary or from summary sections of the report. Unfortunately, however, in real life many case-reports are seriously deficient in that they do not present anything like a complete and valid account of the case. Much has to be assumed or 'read into' the case-report in order to carry out a 'Toulminian analysis'.

Although the following case is artificially simple and brief, it nevertheless illustrates the general structure of arguments in psychological case-studies.

CASE H

H, a nine-year-old adopted child, was referred to an educational psychologist because he was not making satisfactory progress at school. His teacher thought his intelligence was below the average and that he should be in a lower stream. The educational psychologist interviewed the teacher, observed H briefly in class, interviewed him, and administered several tests of ability and attainment. On examination, H was found to have a mental age of nearly nine years. He was a year behind in his attainments in reading and arithmetic. The educational psychologist reported that in his opinion it was most unlikely that H's backwardness was a consequence of low intelligence. He recommended remedial work, closer supervision, more parental involvement, and a more encouraging (less disciplinary) attitude towards the boy. The teacher thought that H's ability might have been overestimated and that H's parents were already sufficiently involved in the child's educational progress. The school decided to accept the psychologist's other recommendations and to review H's progress in six months time.

ANALYSIS AND DISCUSSION OF THE LOGIC OF CASE H

The above extract contains a number of statements of the sorts listed above. The reader is invited to identify the function fulfilled by each statement.

The extract is worded in a way that obscures some of the underlying logic; but, if we carry out a 'Toulminian analysis', we can make it explicit and complete. We begin by asking what conclusion (C) was arrived at. It appears to be as follows:

C: 'H's intelligence is about average.' This claim or conclusion is not actually stated in the extract, but it is implied by a number of considerations. Consider first the psychologist's opinion that 'It was most unlikely that H's backwardness was a consequence of low intelligence.' This contradicts the teacher's belief that 'His intelligence was below the average' (meaning so far below the average as to produce slow learning). Consider second the psychologist's report that 'On examination, H was found to have a mental age of nearly nine years.' This second consideration, however, forms part of the data (D) in the underlying argument, together with the statement that H was nine years old at the time. Note that this statement is not attributed to anyone

Table 9.1

| D: | H is nine years old; H has a mental age of nearly nine. | ⟶ | C: | So H is of average intelligence. |

in particular. One assumes that whoever wrote the report can vouch for its accuracy.

We continue by connecting the conclusion (C) with the data (D) as in Table 9.1.

The next question is, How do we derive this conclusion from these data? Or, better, Why are we entitled to put this particular construction on the data? What justifies the step from D to C? Why, in other words, do we say that the data mean that H is of average intelligence? In order to answer what is basically the same question phrased in different ways we need an inference warrant (W), a logical rule or line of reasoning, that connects D with C, as follows:

W: Young persons whose mental age and chronological age are equal or nearly equal have average intelligence.

To those readers with some psychological training this may seem blindingly obvious, but the conclusion to the argument is by no means as obvious as one might suppose, as we shall see. Also, the example was deliberately arranged to be brief and simple so as to facilitate the exposition of Toulmin's approach to the analysis of 'substantive' arguments.

Diagrammatically, the argument now looks like Table 9.2.

Table 9.2

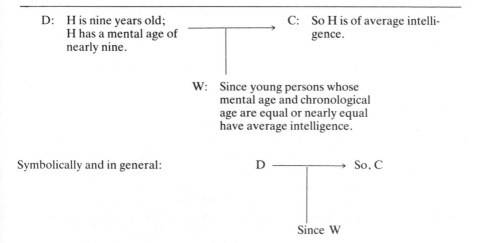

Another way of putting the argument would be, symbolically:

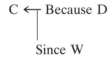

Or, in ordinary language: 'One concludes that H's intelligence is about average because he is nine years old and has a mental age of nearly nine years, since children whose MA and CA are similar are of average intelligence.' Note that the word 'because' is used in an 'evidential' sense, not in a 'causal' sense, in this context.

The next question to ask is, What confidence can be attached to the claim that H's intelligence is about average? Looked at from the psychologist's point of view 'It was most unlikely that H's backwardness was a consequence of low intelligence.' Notice that the claim 'H is of average intelligence' is not stated explicitly in the extract. It has to be inferred, assumed, or found elsewhere in the case-report. On the evidence available it can be assumed, because the psychologist does not confirm the teacher's estimate, and no-one is suggesting that the child's intelligence is *above* the average. It can also be inferred from the relationship between chronological age and mental age, as indicated above. Thus the psychologist seems to be saying:

Q,C: So, it is likely that H is of average intelligence.

The phrase 'it is likely' assigns a high degree of confidence and likelihood to the correctness of the claim. Note that the modal qualifier (Q) can express likelihood in indirect ways, for example, 'so, it is reasonable to suppose that. . .' or 'so, maybe. . .' or 'so, possibly. . .'.

If we turn to the teacher's opinion, she thought that, 'H's ability might have been overestimated.' She is making a different claim—that H's intelligence is below average. This is based on evidence that she could make available about H's classwork, his behaviour, use of language, and so on. So when she considers the psychologist's report, she is not convinced, and seems to be saying:

Q,C: So, I am not convinced that H is of average intelligence.

The phrase 'I am not convinced' assigns a low degree of confidence and likelihood to the correctness of the claim.

When the psychologist and the teacher discuss Case H and find themselves disagreeing about what the problem is and what should be done about the child, the scene is set for a deeper inquiry into the logical structure of the account extracted from the case-report.

The next question is 'What assumptions are being made?' 'Does the psychologist have any reservations to make about his verdict?' These sorts of questions have a bearing on the quality and the amount of evidence available about H, its relevance, the reliability of the sources of that evidence, H's health and state of mind when he was being assessed, and so on. So, for example, the argument rests on the assumption that H's age is nine years. But where did this information come from? Is it correct? Was his chronological age (CA) recorded accurately to the nearest month? Another assumption is that H's mental age (MA) was correctly assessed. But who assessed it? When? How? Were the results checked? Yet another assumption is that H's test performance was a reliable index of his mental ability. But was he feeling well? Did he cooperate? What does 'nearly nine years' mean? Did he really understand the instructions?

Diagrammatically, the argument now looks like the scheme in Table 9.3.

The sixth and last question to be answered in order to complete this miniature Toulminian analysis, is What justification is there for the rule that defines intelligence in terms of a relationship between mental age (MA) and chronological age (CA)? The ultimate justification, of course, is the whole theory and practice of intelligence testing as currently expounded in leading texts and by respected practitioners.

For readers unfamiliar with mental measurement, we should explain that during childhood intelligence normally increases steadily with chronological age, so that a child of a given chronological age will, if he or she is of normal intelligence, pass those intelligence test items up to and including those appropriate to its chronological age—the test items having been selected and standardized on the basis of extensive research. The ratio of mental age (determined on the basis of how many test items the child passes) to chronological age (in years and months) multiplied by 100 gives an intelligence quotient (IQ), i.e. $MA/CA \times 100 = IQ$. Also, traditionally, normal or average intelligence is said to lie between, say, 85 and 115. That is to say

Table 9.3

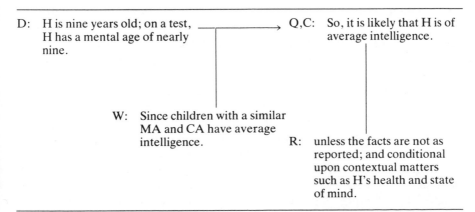

| D: | H is nine years old; on a test, H has a mental age of nearly nine. | → | Q,C: | So, it is likely that H is of average intelligence. |

W: Since children with a similar MA and CA have average intelligence.

R: unless the facts are not as reported; and conditional upon contextual matters such as H's health and state of mind.

within one standard deviation on either side of the mean of 100. Thus H, with an MA of nearly nine (let us say eight years ten months) and a CA of nine (let us say nine years two months) has an IQ of 8, 10/9, 2 × 100 = 96, well within the average range.

Expressed rather formally and using key words to identify the types of logical function used in Toulminian analysis, the argument now is as follows:

D: H is nine years old and has a mental age of nearly nine.
Q,C: So it is likely that H is of average intelligence.
W: Since children whose MA and CA are similar have average intelligence.
R: Unless the evidence is incorrect or unreliable; and conditional upon the circumstances of the case, such as H's health and state of mind.
B: On account of the theory and practice of intelligence testing which defines intelligence in terms of IQ.
      Symbolically:

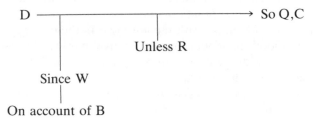

If we now refer back to the original extract we can see that (a) it contains some statements that do not enter into the logical structure we have identified, and (b) some of the statements that we have incorporated into the logical structure do not appear in the extract. How does this come about?

Consider first of all the statement that H was an adopted child. This statement appears to be irrelevant to the argument about the child's intelligence; so it has not so far appeared in the analysis. But suppose the teacher were to say 'H's father and mother are not very bright' (meaning they are below average intelligence), we might be inclined to give some weight to this fact (another datum) until we are reminded that the child was adopted, and that in any event parental intelligence is a poor guide to a child's intelligence.

Consider next the statements about the child's being referred to an educational psychologist who interviewed the teacher, observed the child in class, interviewed and tested him. These statements tell us something about the history of events in this case, and the circumstances that gave rise to it. They are even relevant, in a sense, because they describe some of the contextual factors, although not all, that might make a difference to the argument. As it stands, however, these further statements do not make any 'material' difference. That is to say, they are not worth including in the analysis. The statement about H being a year behind (children of the same age) in reading and arithmetic confirms the teacher's assessment of the child's progress at school (and incidentally lends credence to other statements she makes), but refers only to circumstantial evidence of H's intelligence. Note that the actual evidence, or the best evidence, of the child's progress at school would be the child's scores on scholastic achievement tests administered routinely to him and other children in his class. It is assumed that this is the evidence on which the teacher bases her opinions. The evidence is circumstantial because it has only an indirect bearing on the question of H's intelligence. There are many reasons why even a normal or bright child might make poor progress at school.

The statements involving recommendations could form the conclusions of another argument, but a different argument from the one we have been considering. In other words, those statements are not *immediately* relevant, because we have not yet expanded the web of argument to take in questions about what action should be taken to remedy H's backwardness. The extract goes on to describe the teacher's reactions to the psychologist's report and the school's decision about the case; but, again, these statements are not germane to the argument we have been analysing.

Consider now those statements that appear in our analysis of the argument but do not appear in the extract from H's case-report. In fact, only the statements labelled D appear in the extract, the remainder are implicit or expressed indirectly. As we saw, the component C: 'So . . . H is of average intelligence' is expressed indirectly in the psychologist's opinion that H's backwardness was not a consequence of low intelligence. The components W, R, and B are completely implicit. They constitute part of the background knowledge that is often taken for granted in arguments dealing with professional and scientific matters. This dependence on background knowledge and background procedures—field-dependence—is not peculiar to rational arguments in the psychological study of individual cases, it is *characteristic* of semantics and reasoning in professional and scientific matters, and in the kind of rational discussion that goes on in law, in business, in literature and the arts, and in moral reasoning—see van Dijk and Kintsch (1983). It is *not characteristic* of field-independent reasoning in so-called normative or formal disciplines, like mathematics and logic, where one is dealing with closed systems of clearly defined symbols and operations which permit complete, exact, and definite implications.

A simple example of a field-independent system would be the game of noughts and crosses (tic, tac, toe), or draughts (checkers) since most people can understand the aim, follow the rules, detect errors in moves, and agree the outcome. Arguments about people are rarely, if ever, like this.

The whole point of Toulmin's approach to the analysis of logic in arguments is that it enables one to deal with matters of substance about real-world issues. It is not concerned so much with the formalities characteristic of traditional and modern logic or with the exact procedures and calculations found in the physical and mathematical sciences. Toulmin's approach recognizes that there are ways of establishing the logical validity of arguments couched in symbolic (content-free) terms, and that in practice one must avoid the many sorts of fallacies found in rational argument. Note that I am using the term 'rational' here to mean reasonable; I am not contrasting it with 'irrational' meaning emotive and unrealistic. Thus, it is possible to fall victim to fallacies even whilst being rational. But being rational also means recognizing the fallacy you have fallen victim to when someone points it out to you. Since it recognizes the nature and scope of formal logic, mathematics, and the logical fallacies, Toulminian logic is widely applicable. But it is most useful in those areas that do not lend themselves to formal logical analysis, experimentation, and mathematical analysis, namely, vast areas of psychology and the social sciences generally, jurisprudence, and the arts.

Before embarking on a further exposition of Toulminian logic let us look at one or two more examples of the way the logical structure of arguments in case-studies can be analysed. There are, of course, many instances where the forms of argument are similar to those found in traditional logic.

'If Mary isn't careful, she will get into trouble.
Mary isn't being careful,
So, she will get into trouble'.

'All headmasters tend to put on an act,
John is a headmaster,
So, he tends to put on an act'.

'Some old people are mentally confused.
Joan is old,
But it doesn't necessarily follow that she is confused'.

Where an argument in a case-study can be formulated according to rules of formal logic, it is easy to demonstrate whether it is valid or not. Similarly, if one can show that an argument contains one or other of the familiar fallacies, such as affirming the consequent in a conditional proposition, or begging the question, then it is easy to demonstrate that the reasoning is faulty, as in the following examples:

'If he's good at politics, he's a good talker.
He's a good talker,
So, he's good at politics'.

'Peter is the most unpopular boy in the school,
Some of his teachers say so.
These teachers know an unpopular boy when they see one'.

It would take far too long to give even a simple outline of formal logic and the logical fallacies—but see Chapter 10. Interested readers are referred to some of the many introductory books on the subject: Shaw (1981), Hodges (1977), Alexander (1971), Thouless (1974), Bell and Staines (1981).

Even without the benefit of training in formal logic, intelligent and educated people can recognize many of the more obvious faults in reasoning about case-studies. Equally, however, if the material is lengthy and complicated, or presented rapidly and disjointedly, as at a case-conference, then even the best case-worker is likely to make mistakes and fail to detect errors.

Toulmin's point is that considerations of formal logic, including the traditional fallacies, are less important than considerations of 'substantive' logic. Because the formal logic of arguments in case-studies is not particularly elaborate or subtle, and because the material does not lend itself to 'formal' logical analysis, therefore all one needs to do is to ensure that the formal requirements of logic are met before going on to deal with substantive issues. It is careful and thorough reasoning about substantive issues that leads to improved understanding.

Willard (1983) pushes the notion of 'fields of argument' to the limit by seeming to accept even irrational forms of dispute as legitimate. He rejects the idea of a universal principle of rationality but accepts the practical necessity of using procedures for settling disputes which are comparable in the sense of operating across field boundaries. This means working out and testing the presumptions of arguments and counter arguments in a dispute and so finding common ground. He believes that this policy would lead to more coherent (compact) frameworks of understanding. Such coherence is lacking in psychology. Willard refers arguments to actual social practice, which is more inclusive than Toulmin's 'courts of reason', to determine what is to be regarded, temporarily, as knowlege. He agrees with Toulmin, however, in rejecting formal propositional logic as the sole criterion of rationality.

Mitroff *et al.* (1982) analysed a social policy argument (about the counting of minorities in the US census) by means of Toulmin's method of substantive logic. They showed that it was possible to convert this ordinary language argument into the Toulminian categories (data, claims, qualifiers, warrants, backing, and reservations) and relationships. This procedure then made it easier to develop the argument in the form of predicate logic and linear programming. Their procedure is not immediately relevant for our present purpose, but it is taken up by Locks (1985) who compares Toulmin's substantive logic with a Boolean system of analysis by re-analysing the same policy argument. Both articles appear to offer ways of formalizing some arguments normally couched in ordinary language. Locks reminds us that truth statements derived from propositions refer to possibilities not certainties. These ideas are relevant to the section in Chapter 11 where we consider the possibility of using artificial intelligence in the analysis of psychological cases.

The next section presents a more complicated case-study. It is set out as a series of numbered paragraphs for ease of reference in the subsequent discussion, and is followed by an analysis and discussion of its logic.

CASE I

1. Case I was born and brought up abroad. She left school at sixteen and worked as a teaching assistant for a few years; then, with support from her parents, she came to Britain to train as a nurse. Although she felt that she was making good progress, she failed an examination and was transferred to the less demanding SEN (State Enrolled Nurse) course. On completion of the course she worked briefly in a large hospital, but resigned to take up casual work. During this time she lived with relatives.

2. After a holiday abroad, where she was joined by her parents, she returned to this country to work as a hospital night nurse. She resigned from this post after about six months, worked casually again for a few weeks, and then settled for more secure but lower-paid work in the National Health Service. At the time the case-study was carried out she had been working in a large NHS hospital for about two years, living in comfortable quarters and enjoying the amenities.

3. The question is whether the changes in I's training and subsequent career are indicative of personal dissatisfaction or occupational inadequacy, or indicative merely of an unsettled period characteristic of late adolescence and early adulthood.

4. She maintained that she had no clear idea of the nursing career she wanted to pursue, or whether she even wanted to continue to work as a nurse. Also, the friends she made during training went on to work elsewhere and she soon lost touch with them.

5. It is possible that she might have abandoned nursing earlier had she not felt under some obligation to her parents who had helped to finance her travel and training. There were also rules governing immigration and work permits, which meant that she did not have a free choice of what to do with her life in this country.

6. Case I confessed that she had often contemplated giving up nursing training—usually as a consequence of disputes with people in supervisory or managerial positions in the hospital. This pattern of behaviour was confirmed by one of her friends at the time. It is not clear that she would have been as easily upset and discontented in another kind of work.

7. Case I appears to be more settled and contented in her present job—perhaps because she is more mature, or because she has very satisfactory accommodation, or because her work has displaced other sources of satisfaction, or for all these reasons. She appears to be highly regarded by the sisters and nursing officers in the hospital, who raise no objection to her occasional requests for favourable treatment.

8. Case I is very fond of holidays and foreign travel. This may be a sign of her restlessness, because on several occasions a break in her employment has been associated with an extended holiday.

9. Relationships with the opposite sex seem not to have played a prominent part in I's adjustment. She had one 'steady' relationship during nursing training; this was not a deep attachment and was terminated on I's initiative.

She then entered into a longer and deeper attachment. When her partner broke off the relationship she was very upset, although the relationship had been far from smooth. She still feels angry over what happened.

10. Unfortunately there is very little evidence available to throw light on I's personal qualities—her basic values, beliefs, abilities, motives, and coping strategies. There is no evidence of major changes in personality over the years. Her friends report a tendency on her part to blame other people or circumstances when things go wrong, rather than examine her own responsibility for what has happened. This would fit in with the idea that she is an extroverted individual, of perhaps little more than average intellectual ability. There was also some indication that she would try to manipulate other people in a selfish way.

11. Although, as mentioned above, she has no complaints about her work or her accommodation, yet she is not happy but can see no point in moving. It is characteristic, perhaps, that she should react to vague feelings of dissatisfaction by thinking of moving to where she has a close family friend rather than by reflecting on her feelings, expectations, and circumstances.

12. Running counter to the idea that I is strongly extroverted is her own statement that she finds it difficult to make friends, does not enjoy parties, and spends a lot of time alone. She is physically attractive, but does not respond to approaches from men—presumably because she is still angry and mistrustful after being rejected by her second boy-friend, or possibly she is just not interested—lacking the usual sexual or maternal drives.

13. Surprisingly, perhaps, I has recently applied for a post in the hospital which will allow her to work normal hours regularly, so that she can study and improve her educational qualifications. It is not clear what triggered this move or what the underlying motive is. The move has been accompanied by an apparent increase in her interest in leisure activities. The prospects are not promising, since the moves she is making would seem to require a more routine self-organizing style of life, when I seems to be a creature of impulse and circumstance.

ANALYSIS AND DISCUSSION OF THE LOGIC OF CASE I

The above account of Case I has been shorn of all sorts of information that one would normally expect to find in a case-study in order to make it simple, brief, and easy to analyse logically. The account says nothing about how the problem arose or how it was investigated. Little indication is given as to what actual observational data were available, or who provided the information. Nothing is said about what ought to be done. The account given of Case I nevertheless contains the sorts of statements one might find in referees' reports, in comments by colleagues, or in comments by the Subject about herself.

What logical connections can we identify? The first paragraph is largely descriptive and historical; its logical structure is partly implicit, as shown in

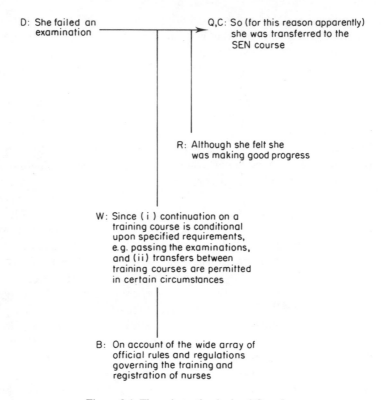

D: She failed an examination

Q,C: So (for this reason apparently) she was transferred to the SEN course

R: Although she felt she was making good progress

W: Since (i) continuation on a training course is conditional upon specified requirements, e.g. passing the examinations, and (ii) transfers between training courses are permitted in certain circumstances

B: On account of the wide array of official rules and regulations governing the training and registration of nurses

Figure 9.1 The substantive logic of Case I

Figure 9.1. Of the logical elements in Figure 9.1, only D, R, and C are stated explicitly in the case-material. The remainder form part of the background knowledge and assumptions that the reader has to bring to the case-material in order to understand it.

The statement R is not a rebuttal, but rather a reservation or reminder about I's responsibility for her failure. Consider the argument in Figure 9.2. The inference warrant, W, introduced here is clearly an oversimplification, but the general sense of how it applies in the particular case is understood.

The second paragraph of the case-material contains only narrative data, with no logical structure. The third paragraph states the central issue or question in Case I. Questions are often phrased in a way which allows one to rephrase them as hypotheses, or, less grandly, as expectations, claims, or guesses. If we examine the question raised in the third paragraph of Case I we find that it is a complex set of hypotheses (guesses or expectations) about what might be the case. They can be stated in the form of a complex claim (C) or conclusion, as follows.

C: The changes in I's training and subsequent career can be attributed to: (a) feelings of dissatisfaction on her part, (b) lack of the personal qualities

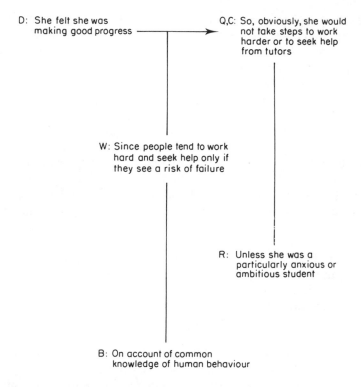

D: She felt she was making good progress

Q,C: So, obviously, she would not take steps to work harder or to seek help from tutors

W: Since people tend to work hard and seek help only if they see a risk of failure

R: Unless she was a particularly anxious or ambitious student

B: On account of common knowledge of human behaviour

Figure 9.2 The substantive logic of Case I

necessary for successful nursing, (c) temporary developmental difficulties, or perhaps (d) some combination of these.

Paragraph four gives some self-report data, and some further information of undisclosed origin. This information is relevant perhaps to the claim that Case I felt dissatisfied with her life as a nurse. Paragraph five helps to explain why she persisted with nursing training in spite of her feelings of dissatisfaction. Paragraph six gives further information which could be construed as relevant to any of the hypotheses (a), (b), (c), or (d) mentioned above. The last sentence in this paragraph cautions against attributing the cause of I's difficulties to I herself rather than to her situation.

Paragraph seven starts with statements relevant to hypothesis (c) above, but then goes on to raise another issue altogether—namely, the issue of why she is now more settled and contented than she was. Paragraph eight presents another item of data relevant, although indirectly, to hypothesis (a).

Paragraph nine presents a series of statements, with their own small logical substructure, running parallel to the main theme. They have the effect of introducing data relevant to hypothesis (c) and at the same time discounting it as of no great importance.

Paragraph ten introduces, in an apologetic way, some general statements about I's personal qualities—mainly to help create a consistent impression of the sort of person she is, and the sort of behaviour she has engaged in.

Paragraph eleven returns to the theme of dissatisfaction, i.e. hypothesis (a), and seems intended to maintain consistency in the account of her personality and behaviour.

Paragraph twelve introduces evidence which runs counter to the argument in paragraph ten, but is consistent with what was said in paragraph nine.

Paragraph thirteen introduces entirely new and unexpected information and concludes with a pessimistic forecast—partly, perhaps, because I's latest behaviour can be construed as yet another example of her unsettled nature.

It is not usual to introduce new and unexpected material late in an account of a case; the tendency is to write an account which is largely, if not entirely, consistent throughout. This is not to say that case-records rarely or never contain statements about unexpected actions and outcomes; of course they do. But when these accounts are written up, the actions and outcomes are described within an interpretive framework which has the effect of eliminating inconsistencies. Thus consistency is not so much a fact of human behaviour as a presupposition about human behaviour, without which behaviour would be incomprehensible.

Figure 9.3(i) to (v) portrays the structure of inference in the argument contained in or implied by the account of Case I. It is not absolutely complete, but the parts omitted are relatively trivial. It can be seen that the argument as a whole is formed by a number of interconnected subsidiary arguments, some of which have been linked by the capitalized word BUT to indicate relationships of a more tenuous sort than those identified by the logical functions D, Q, C, W, B, and R.

The startling fact is the complexity of the structure of inference in what is, after all, a very simple straightforward account of an ordinary person in a situation which is not particularly unusual. Readers are invited to study the diagram closely and then reread the narrative account of Case I. This exercise should help the reader to appreciate the ways in which natural language and ordinary thought can impose a logical structure on case-studies without resort to formal or symbolic methods of analysis and representation.

A few comments may assist readers in understanding Figure 9.3(i) to (v). First, some of the logical elements are not stated explicitly in the material for Case I; these elements have to be introduced in the form of real-world knowledge or theoretical assumptions, to make the argument complete, so that it can be properly evaluated.

Second, some statements fulfil more than one function depending upon how they are used. For example, the statement 'She did not work hard enough or seek help from her tutors' functions as a conclusion (C) in relation to the datum (D), 'She felt she was making good progress in training.' But it also functions as a datum (D) itself in relation to the conclusion (C), 'She failed the examination.'

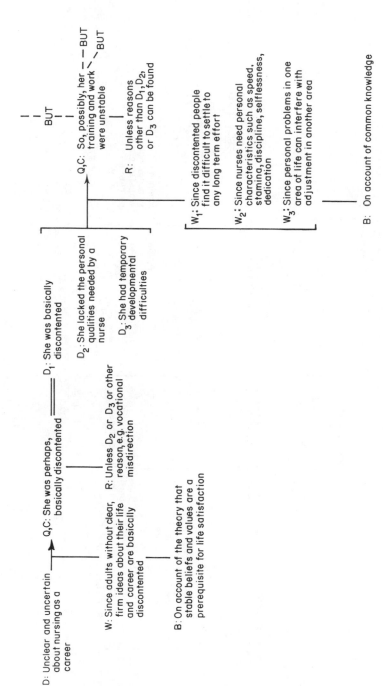

Figure 9.3 (i) to (v) The substantive logic of Case I

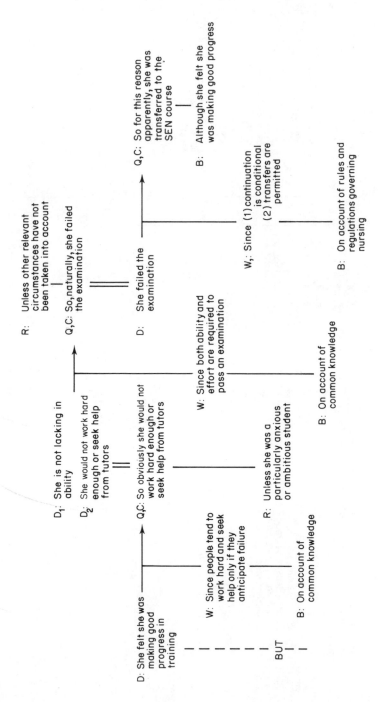

Figure 9.3 (ii) Case I

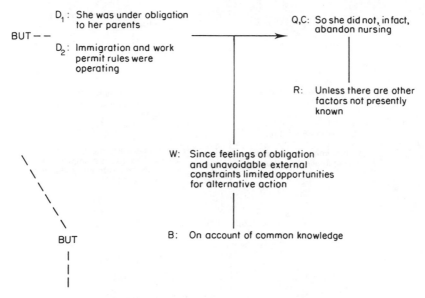

Figure 9.3 (iii) Case I

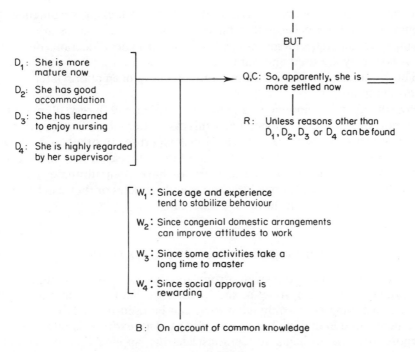

Figure 9.3 (iv) Case I

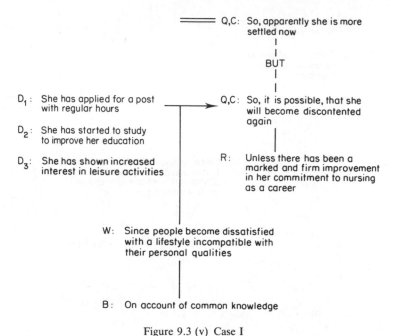

Figure 9.3 (v) Case I

What we see in Figure 9.3 is a network of interlocking arguments. The arguments interlock because they have elements in common, as in the above example. In general, statements can fulfil various logical functions depending upon how they are used and phrased.

Third, some of the statements in Figure 9.3 have been abbreviated for ease of presentation.

Fourth, all the component arguments in Figure 9.3 rest ultimately on 'common knowledge'. Understanding this case, after all, does not require any special scientific knowledge or professional expertise. In other cases, however, an argument may rest on, or be anchored to, scientific, technical, or professional knowledge. It is necessary to have such ultimate anchorage points for arguments, otherwise they go round in circles or they can be shown, by a persistent sceptic, to have no foundation.

A DIFFERENT SORT OF CASE-STUDY

We have borrowed extensively from the business studies approach to individual cases (firms); so let us see whether we can repay some of the debt by demonstrating how Toulminian logic can be used to analyse the logic of arguments used in making business decisions. This exercise is relevant to our purpose because it helps to demonstrate the applicability of Toulmin's approach to yet another area of human interest. The behaviour of indivdual persons in relation to each other in the world of business is important, and close to the heart of what we mean by the psychological study of persons in situations.

The example is adapted from the case referred to by Easton (1982, pp. 43–76). I have described it in a way which makes the account comprehensible without having to consult the original details. Readers may wonder why an example like Case J is being considered when it makes no reference whatsoever to the behaviour of individual persons. But readers who refer to the more detailed information in Easton (1982) will find many references to the individuals in Spanline Engineering Ltd. It is their behaviour in relation to the business conditions that confront them that generates the Case J described below. Easton describes several other business cases which make sense only when the psychological characteristics of individuals in the firms are disclosed. Case J, however, presents no particular 'psychological' problems; it is analysed simply to show the general applicability of informal logical analysis.

CASE J

Spanline Engineering Ltd. found that their sales of hoists to small-scale customers had suddenly levelled out after several years of rapid growth. Most of these sales were through another firm, Century Steel, marked with their brand name. The levelling-out of hoist sales was the result of an inadequate marketing programme, which was itself the result of lack of marketing expertise in that area. These factors were connected with, and partly responsible for, lack of knowledge about the purchasers and users of hoists. The marketing programme was failing worst in the area of distribution, since Spanline had only one distributor serving a limited range of customers and working on a low profit margin. This had resulted in poor coverage of too small a proportion of the replacement market and almost no coverage of the new market. Spanline Engineering had no brand image, did not advertise, and had little in the way of selling skills. The design of the hoist might have contributed to the levelling-out of sales. The low selling price of the hoists contradicts the reputation for quality that Spanline wish to foster. The marketing programme is inconsistent and unplanned and not based on a proper understanding of consumers.

ANALYSIS OF THE LOGIC OF CASE J

Figure 9.4(i) to (iv) portrays the structure of inference in the argument contained in or implied by this brief account of Case J. The statements labelled D, Q, C, W, B, and R are either taken directly from the brief account, or slightly rephrased to give freshness, or introduced in order to complete the Toulminian network. As with previous examples, it can be seen that the argument as a whole is formed by a number of interconnected subsidiary or component arguments. As a system it goes well beyond what is actually said in the brief account because the whole point of a Toulminian analysis is to explore and demonstrate the details and limits of an argument—and, in particular, to reveal the presuppositions, implicit rules, and real-world knowledge on which the explicit argument depends. The argument just presented is merely the tip of an iceberg of reasoning, most of which is normally out of sight; or, to use a different analogy, the summary account provides only a few pieces of the jigsaw puzzle; a fuller picture emerges as more pieces are added to those already available.

Again, readers are invited to study the diagram closely and then to reread the brief account of Case J and ask themselves whether their understanding of the case had improved.

FOUR DIFFERENT TYPES OF ARGUMENT

We can define 'reasoning' very broadly as the process whereby we search for and set out the evidence and rules of inference which support or justify a belief, decision, or action.

It is convenient to distinguish several kinds of reasoning in case-studies. There is, first of all, the sort of reasoning that goes on when a dispute arises and the parties to the dispute take up adversarial positions—see Levine (1974), for example. Each party is concerned to settle the dispute in its own favour because of the consequences that follow from winning or losing the argument. This sort of reasoning is essentially competitive; it concentrates on defending one line of reasoning and attacking the other. It is seen most clearly in courts of law in the cases put by the prosecution and the defence, which must be settled one way or the other, according to clearly defined rules and procedures.

There are limits to what can be regarded as 'reasonable' behaviour or 'reasoning' in a dispute. Obviously, physical superiority, bribery, threats, and other means may oblige an adversary to withdraw, but we are concerned only with rational and equitable forms of argument.

There is, secondly, the sort of reasoning that goes on after a dispute has arisen, and after the two or more parties to the dispute have done all they can to make the best case for their own claim and to weaken the case put forward by other parties. This sort of reasoning is essentially impartial arbitration; it concentrates on finding a compromise conclusion which satisfies (or dissatisfies) each party about equally.

Thus, if the parties to a dispute cannot settle matters between themselves but can agree to arbitration, or if the dispute is one which can be dealt with in the courts, that is how it can be settled.

The third kind of reasoning is the sort that goes on when a person is trying to reach a conclusion on the basis of facts and inferences which he or she finds convincing and expects other competent observers to find convincing. Although this sort of reasoning is often a solitary pursuit, as when we form

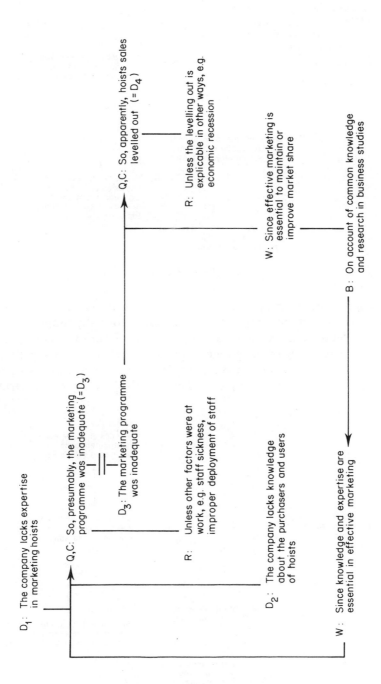

Figure 9.4 (i) to (iv) The substantive logic of Case J

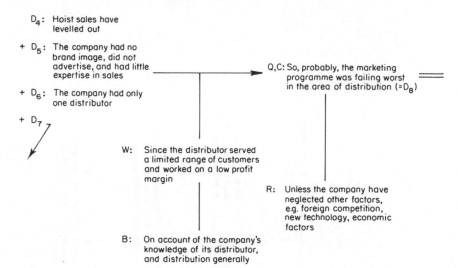

Figure 9.4 (ii) Case J

private impressions of people in daily life, it is in principle a collective or consensual activity in the sense that the individual normally supposes that his impressions (arguments) would stand up to public scrutiny. These personal impressions actually become public when we exchange views with other people on matters of common interest. Of course, gossip and casual exchanges of opinion are not subject to much control as regards the truth of

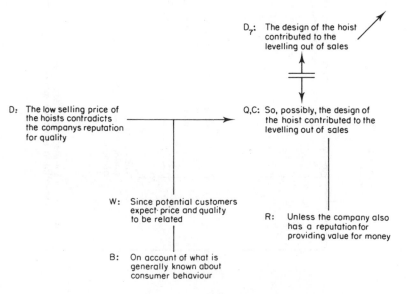

Figure 9.4 (iii) Case J

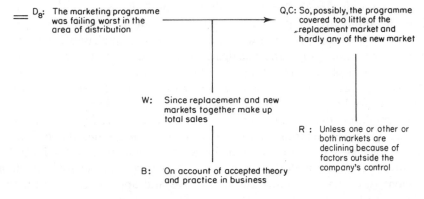

D_8: The marketing programme was failing worst in the area of distribution

Q,C: So, possibly, the programme covered too little of the replacement market and hardly any of the new market

W: Since replacement and new markets together make up total sales

R : Unless one or other or both markets are declining because of factors outside the company's control

B: On account of accepted theory and practice in business

Figure 9.4 (iv) Case J

statements or the validity of arguments; and casual social exchange constitutes a sort of lower limit to what can be regarded as 'reasonable' behaviour or 'rational argument'.

When this third kind of reasoning takes place in a professional or scientific setting—in a seminar or case-conference for example—this setting provides the occasion for a more rigorous assessment of the facts and inferences of interest. We shall be discussing professional and scientific levels of understanding other people in much more detail in later sections of this chapter.

In the meantime, let us bear in mind that what we mean by objectivity in science is really intersubjective agreement between people willing and able to assess the available evidence and arguments in a mutually agreed rational way. In other words, professional and scientific case-studies are part of a public or collective enterprise working towards improved knowledge and management of human affairs. One of the features of this enterprise is the injunction to look for and take account of evidence that runs counter to one's theories—an injunction absent from many religious and political enterprises. By definition, reasonable people are willing to listen to an argument that runs counter to their own, and are able to change their point of view if the counter-argument makes better sense of the evidence.

The fourth kind of reasoning is the sort required when circumstances call for prompt action, often on the basis of insufficient information. This sort of reasoning is typical of that called for in making decisions in business, medicine, politics, and warfare. This contrasts with investigations in science and law, where the emphasis is on getting the correct or the best decision eventually. Although time and resources cannot be ignored in science and the law, no-one supposes that the solutions or decisions arrived at within the time available and within the resources available are anything other than temporary or approximate ones. In business, medicine, politics, and warfare, however, the aim of an investigation and the point of an argument is to get the best decision in the circumstances at the time. Thus, even a relatively poor decision taken in time will be better than a 'good' decision taken too late.

For the moment, then, we have identified four very different types of argument: adversarial (competitive), arbitrational (equalizing), consensual (cooperative), and pragmatic (tactical). It can be seen that each kind of reasoning has a place in the study of individual cases.

As we have seen, solving problems in scientific and professional work with people calls for both imagination and critical evaluation. Imagination is called for in formulating the problem and developing the inquiry. Critical evaluation is called for in eliminating faults and omissions, including the traditional logical fallacies—see Chapter 10. One basic fault, found more often in spoken than in written case-material, is to assume that a rhetorically convincing argument (one that is emotionally expressive and appealing) is better than one conveyed less effectively. A related fault is to assume that the feelings of confidence one has about one's argument is a measure of its correctness.

Once a rational argument has begun, it is necessary to clear the ground of initial misunderstandings as to what is at issue in the case, to define terms, to disambiguate meanings, and to establish the appropriate frame of reference for the case in question—cases are dealt with differently in different contexts.

SOME FAMILIAR MODES OF REASONING

Toulmin *et al.* (1979) suggest that we can classify arguments in the following ways.

  (i) By analogy—arguing, for example, that because an individual is like his brother in respect of some personality characteristics, therefore he is like his brother in other characteristics. What one should do is examine both the positive and the negative parts of the analogy—see Hesse (1963).

 (ii) By sample and generalization—arguing, for example, that because some students complain about a course therefore all the students are dissatisfied (forgetting that while dissatisfied students tend to complain, satisfied students do not). What one needs to do is to ensure that the evidence one has is sufficiently large and representative to support such a generalization, as in statistical inference.

(iii) By objective signs and subjective symptoms—arguing, for example, that a certain facial expression or a particular action 'signifies' hostility; arguing that personal disclosures about feelings provide a correct account of the individual's state of mind. One should ensure, first, that one is aware of the signs and symptoms one is reacting to, since it is all too easy to be influenced by them without realizing it, and second, that one can interpret the signs and symptoms reliably and validly. Arguing diagnostically by reference to signs and symptoms is different from arguing by sample and generalization in the sense that one assumes an established causal connection between a sign or a symptom and the condition it signifies, whereas in arguing from a sample, one simply regards the observed sample of behaviour as characteristic of a larger set.

(iv) By cause—arguing, for example, that a person's stupidity or ignorance caused an accident, or that stress at work caused a nervous breakdown. The psychological study of how we attribute causes and responsibility goes back at least as far as Heider (1958), and has become a major area of interest in social psychology—see Jones *et al.* (1972), Shaver (1975), Jaspars *et al.* (1983). The area is now too large to be conveniently summarized here. Students of individual cases will frequently encounter arguments in which causes and responsibilities are assigned without sufficient regard for the factors which lead us, and sometimes mislead us, into making such attributions—for example attributing an outcome to one's own intervention when it might equally well be assigned to chance or to some other circumstance.

(v) By exclusion—arguing that there are only two (or three, or four) possibilities, so that, through a process of exclusion, only one remains. For example, we could argue that a person was either drunk or sober, and that if he was drunk he was irresponsible and if he was sober he was malicious, in that his behaviour harmed someone. This dilemma neglects the possibility of other interpretations of the person's behaviour, including the possibility that, although he had been drinking, he was not 'drunk', and that, although he disliked the person harmed, he was not 'malicious'. Thus a more reasonable explanation might be that the person was less inhibited than usual because of the relaxing effects of alcohol, and made remarks under provocation that he might otherwise have kept to himself, thus damaging someone's reputation. Argument by exclusion therefore works only if one has the right answer in one's list of options.

SOME CHARACTERISTICS OF ARGUMENTS IN PSYCHOLOGICAL CASE-STUDIES

According to Toulmin (1958) and Toulmin *et al.* (1979), one would not expect an argument in, say, economics to use the same sorts of facts and rules of inference as an argument in anatomy, literary criticism, or psychological analysis. Each field of inquiry, each 'universe of discourse' has its own characteristic forms of argument, its own settings, boundaries, and procedures.

Arguments in psychological case-studies have their characteristic features. To begin with, they often contain a mixture of common knowledge and scientific knowledge; they are not stylized (as in geometry or jurisprudence) except to the extent that 'due procedure' has to be followed for bureaucratic or other technical reasons. Naturally, they refer to the sorts of facts and theories found in the social and behavioural sciences, as well as those found in the biomedical sciences. Arguments in psychological case-studies do not often refer to very general and abstract principles. Since they are concerned with particular actions, circumstances, relationships, and so on, they tend to employ relatively low-level generalizations and statements hedged about with qualifications and reservations because of the lack of comprehensive and reliable theories about human behaviour.

Arguments in psychological case-studies are likely to contain some key concepts found in psychological explanations. The best known are those already familiar from ordinary experience—the concepts of role, motive, trait, habit, attitude, expectation, and constraint—see Bromley (1977) and Antaki (1981). The following phrases exemplify the use of these explanatory concepts in warranting (W) a connection between data (D) and conclusion (C): '. . . since he is a teacher', '. . . since he wants to get on with his work', '. . . since she is generous', '. . . since he always plays golf on Sundays', '. . . since he does not like pop music', '. . . since he expects to fail the examination', '. . . since they would not let him leave'.

In addition to these common-sense forms of explanation expressed in the ordinary language of daily life, there are various behavioural science concepts expressed in the technical language or jargon of the professions: conflict, ambivalence, reinforcement, defence mechanism, alienation, dyslexia, self-concept, alcoholism, amnesia, avoidance behaviour, compliance, demand characteristics, endocrine functions, excess disability, maturation, menopause, neurosis, psychosis, reinforcement, stress, to name just a few.

Effective argumentation at a professional level means having access to the requisite scientific explanations for the case in hand, as well as being able to build these into the infrastructure of common knowledge.

Case-study arguments, like other substantive arguments, may need to integrate concepts from several related disciplines, e.g. educational psychology, personality study, psychiatry, social psychology. Case-study arguments may also need to be incorporated into disciplines of a rather different sort, e.g. business studies, jurisprudence, sociology, history. This can be achieved only if there is agreement as to the terms of reference of the case-study, the way key terms are to be defined, what constitutes the best evidence, and the proper way to proceed with the inquiry.

Formal rigour and quantitative precision are not the exclusive hallmarks of logical quality in all disciplines and fields of discourse. The worth of an argument, according to Toulmin, is to be judged by the criteria appropriate to the area in which it applies—the ground rules so to speak. So legal arguments are judged by the sorts of criteria used in jurisprudence; business arguments by the criteria used in business decision-making; psychological case-study arguments are expected to meet the criteria used in professional and scientific work with individual people.

There are some criteria of logical quality that apply across all disciplines and fields of discourse, namely the canons of formal logic; but these are relatively few; they have to be met, obviously, but meeting these criteria does no more than clear the ground for the task of constructing a particular *type* of argument—a legal argument rather than a moral argument, a psychological rather than a sociological argument.

BEGINNING, SHIFTING, AND ENDING ARGUMENTS

Arguments get started in the first place because one person doubts and questions the opinions, beliefs, and actions of another. Such questioning can sometimes be brushed aside as irrelevant or of no consequence, as in law, for example, if the defence say 'There is no case to answer.' The person who puts forward an argument in the first place takes on the 'burden of proof', i.e. accepts that he or she must provide evidence and reason in support of the claim. When this claim is challenged, however, the burden of proof is transferred to the person who is raising doubts and questions.

Obviously, it is not good enough to reject an argument simply because one does not like the conclusion it leads to. So, when challenging an argument, one must raise substantial matters—like the key questions associated with D, Q, C, W, B and R. In a reasoned argument between people, one person raises questions, doubts, and criticisms, but is obliged to show that they are justified. He must have 'grounds' for his objections in order to make his opponent answerable. Otherwise his opponent can retort that there is no reason for raising the objection, and therefore no reason why he need retract his conclusion or modify his argument.

It is an important point in legal argument that a *prima facie* case be made out before an argument can be proceeded with. That is to say, one must present at least the beginnings of a reasonable argument before one can be taken seriously. For example, the argument that Joan is dispirited today because she was born under Capricorn would not be taken seriously by a scientific psychologist because it does not make out even a *prima facie* case for its conclusion. It is worth bearing in mind, however, that if one chose to conduct the argument *within the framework of astrology* (and so outside the framework of professional and scientific psychology) a *prima facie* case might be made.

This point leads on to a major feature of Toulmin's approach to substantive logic, namely the comparison of arguments involving different sorts of conceptual framework. As I have just mentioned, one can conduct a reasonable argument within the framework of astrology, but that same argument would normally be inadmissible within the framework of behavioural science. Similarly, one can argue within a religious framework, or a legal framework, or in the context of business, aesthetics, morality, sport, fashion, or technology. All these different areas of interest have their own specialized concepts, values, beliefs, data, rules of inference, procedures, settings, and so on. So an argument will normally make good sense only in its appropriate context. You cannot argue a moral issue in scientific terms, in the sense of deriving 'ought' from 'is'. You cannot argue an issue in sport, e.g. the relative merits of two football players, in aesthetic terms; or argue about a woman's academic capabilities by introducing matters to do with her dress sense. We are not saying that these conceptual boundaries preclude attempts to find common ground. What we are saying is that an argument makes sense only if the elements in it are logically compatible.

Suppose I argue that Joan is depressed because her husband no longer spends much time with her, and that the reason for this is that she feels emotionally deprived. The worth of this argument can be judged by the usual psychological criteria: Does the statement that Joan is depressed fit the facts? Could some other inference fit the facts equally well or better? She might be angry rather than depressed. Does the statement that '. . . her husband no longer spends much time her her' fit the facts? How reliable is this evidence? Is emotional deprivation a necessary precursor of depression? What other theory might apply? Perhaps the connection between her husband's neglect and her depression is the other way round—he neglects her because she is such a misery?

It would be difficult and inappropriate to apply sociological criteria to the above argument because it is not formulated as a sociological argument. We cannot ask whether the statement 'Joan is depressed about her husband's neglect' represents a middle-class interpretation of what is going on; not unless we want to move the whole argument out of its original psychological context. If we do want to do this we have to reformulate the argument, perhaps as follows: 'The idea that Joan is depressed because her husband no longer spends much time with her is a naïve middle-class interpretation of Joan's behaviour; so it can probably be rejected, since, in cases of this kind, one must take into account working class attitudes to marital relationships.' The effect, therefore, in moving across the boundary between psychological and sociological discourse is to leave the psychological argument behind (or rather to encapsulate it in order to reject it like a foreign body!) as a preliminary to reformulating the whole issue of Joan's behaviour. See Edmondson (1984) for an account of the way in which sociological arguments are actually presented.

Questions, puzzles, doubts, and so on provide the preliminaries for rational arguments about empirical matters. The question is answered, the puzzle or problem is solved, the doubt is removed, when a convincing argument has been formulated. The alert reader will have detected that the previous sentence is a circular argument, but it provides a convenient definition of what we mean by a 'convincing argument'. The term 'argument' can be used in its popular sense to refer to a controversy or dispute between people holding different points of view. As we well know, such arguments can be settled by force or bribery or trickery, as well as by the persuasive powers of reason. We are using the term 'argument' with reference to the structure of rational inference which can be imposed on case-material, and of course on other sorts of information. We are referring to persuasion by reason.

This raises the further point that some quite rational arguments can be conducted on an adversarial basis, as in legal disputes or college debates. In settings like these the aim of the argument is to show that one's own case is better than that of one's opponent. One is not required to show that one's argument is completely watertight or takes account of all the opponent's facts and inferences, only that it is better than its competitor. As previously explained, where adversaries will not yield to their opponent's reasoning an arbitrator may intervene to decide for one side or the other or find a compromise solution acceptable to both sides.

Contrasting with arguments of an adversarial sort (which are likely to degenerate into non-rational disputes unless presided over by an impartial judge or arbitrator) are arguments of a consensual sort. Consensual arguments are characterized by an attempt to find a form of reasoning, a structure of inference, which is acceptable to all the people involved and leads to a solution or a conclusion that all the people involved can agree with. In theory, consensual arguments are found in the deliberations of scientists and professionals and democratic groups of intelligent and educated people. In practice, such is human nature, rationality often breaks down under the strains of self-interest, emotional involvement, impatience, ignorance, and lack of intelligence.

A professional and scientific approach to the psychological study of individual cases is one which relies on reason and empirical data in its deliberations. It prefers consensual rather than adversarial decisions. Where an adversarial situation is unavoidable it prefers arbitration and conciliation rather than force, bribery, or deceit.

In addition to (a) maximizing consensus or (b) overcoming an adversary or (c) finding a compromise solution through arbitration, rational-empirical arguments can be used (d) to reach decisions in situations where time and resources are in short supply. The last-mentioned function refers to the sort of argument constructed in order to arrive at a business or military decision.

Ideally, arguments about case-studies have functions (a), (c) and (d); but, because participants in a case-study sometimes have a vested interest in the outcome or are less professional or less scientific than one would wish, one actually finds arguments about case-studies also having function (b), overcoming an adversary.

THE LIMITS OF ARGUMENT

If one were to push the argument in a psychological case-study to its limits, one would have to anchor it to certain 'primitive' or 'ultimate' grounds. These grounds are of four sorts: normative standards (statements about social values), observational evidence (statements of fact), theoretical concepts (statements which organize and interpret data), and methodological assumptions (statements about procedure). I have excluded philosophical grounds, for this would take us too far into ethics and epistemology.

Maddi (1980) has provided a particularly interesting comparative analysis of the theoretical concepts used in the very relevant area of personality study. With reference to psychological case-studies which result in recommendations for treatment one ultimate consideration in the argument might be the survival of the Subject, as in dealing with elderly people at risk, or the selection of personnel for dangerous work, or in the management of patients with suicidal tendencies. In general the professional case-worker bases his or her recommendations on an argument which takes account of the 'best interests' of the Subject in the context of the interests of the other people involved in the case. How these 'best interests' are to be defined and looked after is, of course, itself a matter which has to be determined for each particular case, in the circumstances prevailing at the time, and in relation to the appropriate professional and ethical standards. One would expect them to include things like: health, social and economic welfare, education, safety and security, happiness (life-satisfaction), and productive (useful) activity. Maddi lists the central features of human adjustment as follows: the resolution of conflicts, the fulfilment of potentialities, and consistency (the integration of behaviour and experience). One might add the avoidance of harm. These 'best interests' and 'central features' constitute some of the ultimate psychological grounds for justifying a particular argument—for example the argument that a woman should seek divorce rather than continue with her marriage, or the argument that a man should retire rather than continue working. Often such ultimate grounds are taken for granted, and do not appear explicitly in a case-report because they are tacitly acknowledged by all concerned.

Another sort of ultimate warrant has to do with what might be called 'organizational considerations'. These express the limits of what society can offer or put up with in relation to the Subject of the case-study. For example, one might argue that there are only two sorts of treatment available, or that a particular recommendation is not permitted by the rules.

The practical task, in rational argument, is to consider an array of relevant facts about an issue, and to interpret those facts by applying appropriate rules of inference. The task may be difficult if some facts are missing and if some contradict each other, or if one cannot think of the appropriate rules, or if the rules one applies lead to different conclusions. Nevertheless, even under these conditions it is possible to proceed in an orderly way—by collecting further evidence, bringing in new theories, working out the implications and ramifications of the argument. Eventually one will formulate an argument which is more convincing (or less unconvincing) than any other competing argument. This requisite argument is recognized by the achievement of consensus among the participants and by the absence of further improvements. Of course this argument remains final or closed only until someone chooses to reopen it, with new ideas or fresh evidence. A complete or requisite argument, i.e. an argument which is accepted for the time being, must be consonant with the prevailing system of ideas that provides its context (its conceptual framework). A psychoanalytic account, for example, must fit in with the accepted theory and practice of psychoanalysis. If it does not, then it is not valid as, by definition, it is not a correct psychoanalytic account. The same applies to other conceptual frameworks: neuropsychological, developmental, psychometric, ethical, and so on. Ideally, in the context of scientific inquiry, it is not a crime to be wrong, but it is a crime to do wrong. That is to say, one is not criticized for getting the wrong answer, but for using the wrong methods (even if one gets the right answer!). In practice, unfortunately, one cannot always see immediately which is the right and which is the wrong solution to a problem; so people with new ideas and new procedures may have to suffer criticism and ridicule for seeming to go about things in the wrong way. History has the last word in such matters.

FURTHER POINTS OF INTEREST

Before embarking on a further discussion of Toulmin's approach to the study of arguments of the sort found in psychological case-studies, let us consider briefly some other points about problem-solving and decision-making.

(i) The difficulty with informal problem-solving and decision-making is that we are too ready to jump to conclusions on the basis of insufficient evidence. We recognize the appropriateness of methodical reasoning in some areas, especially those where we know there is only one correct answer. But because of the need to react promptly or because we do not have the resources to carry out a methodical inquiry, or simply because the problem is not important enough, we tend to make do with a rough approximate solution. In practical situations one has to balance the costs of finding a better solution against the costs of further delay.

(ii) Problems and decisions which are normally regarded as 'clinical' or 'subjective' in character, as depending upon personal experience and intuition, can sometimes be handled more effectively by objective and quantitative methods. These rational and empirical methods can be made explicit, and people can be trained to use them. The debate on clinical versus statistical prediction in psychology goes back at least as far as Meehl (1954). Since then there have been considerable developments in psychological scaling, statistics, decision-making, expert systems, and, more recently, social judgment (heuristics and biases). All these developments have a bearing on problem-solving and decision-making in relation to the study of individual cases. Even when it is not possible to use the full rigour of modern mathematical techniques, as with many psychological cases, the logic of those procedures provides a useful model of how to go about solving problems and making decisions. By contrast, studies on social judgment demonstrate how risky it is to rely on unaided personal experience and subjective opinion.

(iii) In situations where there are uncertainties and inaccuracies in our understanding, as in most case-studies, these very uncertainties and inaccuracies can and should be examined in an attempt to improve our understanding and management of the case. We need to know in what ways and to what extent our grasp of the problem is less than perfect.

(iv) A rigorous and systematic approach to case-studies usually enables one to identify a relatively small number of major issues or factors about which competent observers can agree. One is no longer faced with a multitude of factors whose importance depends on personal guesswork. When the case has been clarified and simplified the resources available to the Investigator can be concentrated more productively on fewer but more important topics.

(v) A rational-empirical approach diminishes or even puts an end to the puzzlement and difficulties associated with the problem. Uncertainties and inaccuracies in understanding and dealing with the problem diminish. There is less scope for differences of opinion. Interaction—through case-conferences, for example—should increase the extent of each individual's awareness of other people's understanding of the problem and bring about a greater degree of consensus or conformity (partly through social psychological processes, partly through the forces of logic and empirical facts, i.e. reality). Unfortunately, if the case is argued out in an adversarial manner, then polarization rather than consensus is likely to ensue.

(vi) Time should be found for doubts and second thoughts to be expressed before a final decision is arrived at. To the extent that participants in a case-study no longer feel puzzled or frustrated, the problem or difficulty has been dealt with. Of course, if the participants are not sufficiently intelligent or knowledgeable, their solution may be judged unsatisfactory by a more competent body of people, or, more likely later, with the advantage of hindsight.

(vii) The image of a substantial logical argument as a web, network, or tissue of facts and relationships is useful because it gets away from the traditional image of an argument as a 'chain' of reasoning. Chains are only as strong as their weakest link; so obviously a chain-like sequence of argument can break apart if just one of its statements is wrong. Informal networks, however, if well worked out, are composed of interconnected statements, such that failure in one part of the argument may weaken, but not destroy entirely, the argument as a whole. A 'strong' argument is one which puts its conclusion at the centre of a large, strongly interconnected web of facts and relationships, a web which is firmly anchored at its periphery to solid foundations.

(viii) A successful outcome in a case-study does not *prove* the validity of the associated argument; it merely supports it. Similarly, an unsuccessful outcome does not *disprove* the validity of the argument, it merely casts doubt upon it. The reason for this is the intervention of unknown factors, especially if the case is a complex one or if there is a long period of time between the implementation of the decision and the subsequent evaluation. In any event one has to establish the *validity* of an argument separately from the *truth* of its premises or conclusion. The business of evaluating case-studies is complex because it must deal not only with the particular problem of the validity of the analysis, and the technical problem of following up the outcome, but also with the whole complex, cultural, and organizational framework within which the case-study is carried out. The evaluation of individual cases has to take account of political and administrative considerations—see Cronbach and associates (1980).

(ix) If we consider the sorts of statements that enter into the arguments found in case-studies, and, for that matter, into arguments from all areas of professional and scientific work, we find the six basic elements listed below:

Code letter	Type of statement
D	Data or evidence, statements of particular facts
Q	Modal qualifier or comment
C	Claim or conclusion, decision or recommendation
W	Inference warrant or specific reason
B	Backing or support of a more general sort
R	Rebuttal or reservation or objection

We also find the following elements: prescriptive judgments (should, ought), criticisms, wonderings (guesses, speculations), normative statements (rules, definitions), comments and asides, proposals (recommendations), instructions, promises, hopes and fears, excuses.

In order to appreciate the richness and complexity of discourse about psychological case-studies, consider more of the categories of information one can easily identify: common knowledge, expert knowledge or opinion, witness testimony, personal disclosures by the Subject of the case-study, reports of the actions and expressive behaviour of people involved, references to documents, physical traces, material evidence, rules of procedure, precedents, historical facts, future possibilities.

The problem is to sort out those statements that contribute to the structure of inference from the mass of spoken or written case-material, and from the practical circumstances that provide the context of the study. For example, I am likely to look very closely at an argument that affects my interest; I may be reluctant to put in writing what I am prepared to say in confidence to a colleague.

(x) As we can see more clearly in the pages devoted to the decision-theory approach to individual cases—see Chapter 8—it is not good enough, by professional and scientific standards, to think that one 'knows', or 'understands', a case on the basis of personal experience and subjective feeling (intuition) alone. One should be able to make the logic of one's argument explicit. One should be able to present the empirical data and the pattern of meaning one has imposed on those data in the public forums where it is of interest. One should be able to modify one's views in the light of what other people think about the case. In this way, what starts out as a fairly subjective and approximate account of the case finishes up as a more objective (intersubjectively agreed), fuller and more realistic account. Of course, different public forums require different statements of the case; the case one presents to an academic audience is different from the case one presents to the Subject of the study or to a professional practitioner who is taking over the case.

It should be obvious that the context in which a case is being considered affects the logic, the structure of inference, one is dealing with. For example, a summary account of a performance appraisal of a policewoman would describe and explain the extent to which her behaviour met the requirements laid down in a job description. But if she is being assessed in relation to more general considerations, such as how best to deploy her, whether to promote her, or her relationships with other people, then new facts and considerations would enter into the account.

We have seen that the contents of a case-report and the pattern of meaning that emerges because of the way the material is organized vary a great deal, even for the same case, because of the demands of the situation. There is often room for misunderstanding, since if one participant takes the context for granted he may very well omit information that another participant, who is not fully aware of the contextual considerations, needed to make sense of the report. Naturally, if all participants share a common frame of reference, then the case-report can be stated very concisely. One of the main functions of modern business decision-making is to establish a common frame of reference for all participants in a business venture, so that no relevant considerations are neglected, and so that the problem and the decision process can be set out clearly and concisely.

(xi) We have seen that claims (Cs) need to be supported by reasons (Ws) and statements of fact (Ds), although one and the same statement can fulfil different functions in an argument depending upon its role in relation to other statements.

The main function of an inference warrant (W) is to interpret the evidence (D). It is one thing to know that something is the case; another to see what that *means*. An inference warrant imposes a pattern of meaning, puts a construction, on the data. Notice that W introduces a general rule into the argument; it brackets D and C as an instance of a more general class of connected events, for example, symptoms with diseases, traits with behaviour, pay with productivity. Warrants are what make sense of evidence.

If an argument in a case-study can be shorn of its particular identity it can then represent a *class* of similar cases. This gives us a kind of case-law, or at least a precedent and the possibility that other cases can be similarly construed.

Warrants need not stand alone. They are derived from wider and more general bodies of knowledge or belief. Thus they can be justified or backed up by reference to their origins, for example in psychometric theory and practice, decision theory, psychoanalysis, neuropsychology, epidemiology, or in common knowledge. The backing (B) provides an assurance that the general rule or inference warrant (W) is legitimate, sound, valid, applicable in this case, and so on.

The general rule (W) and its support (B) create a presumption (Q) in favour of what we can call the normal or obvious conclusion (C). But there may be exceptional features about the particular case, or some failure of the usual assumptions in cases of this kind, that rebut (R) the argument altogether, or make it highly conditional or restricted. Notice that R can be phrased as a conditional statement, e.g. 'D → So, C, depending on R', 'D → So, C, on condition that R', 'D → So, C, unless R'. This is done when R is at least moderately likely, but not when it is unlikely. That is to say, the limits within which the argument holds have to be made explicit, built into the argument, when there is a reasonable possibility that the limits will apply. One need not introduce highly unlikely contingencies, e.g. '. . . depending upon his not falling ill', '. . . on condition that he works a 60-hour week', '. . . unless war breaks out'.

(xii) One argument is 'better' than another in a narrow logical sense when its various component statements can be referred to acceptable grounds deeper in the argument, where the evidence is stronger—more fundamental—and where there is likely to be more agreement about it. But one argument may be 'better' than another simply because it is more effective in the context in which it occurs—a case-study argued with psychologists rather than with social workers, for example, or viceversa.

Some case-studies—namely those dealing with technical matters or involving special circumstances—may require considerable commentary to clarify the argument. The commentary then is not essential to the argument: it is more in the nature of instructional material or background information for the less well informed. The sorts of thing one finds in commentaries are definitions, amplifications, examples, explanations, and references.

PRESUMPTIONS AND THE STRUCTURE OF ARGUMENT

In all areas of scientific and professional endeavour there are presumptions that such-and-such is the case, unless otherwise stated. For example, it is presumed that someone is sane rather than insane, normal rather than neurotic, honest rather than dishonest, happy rather than unhappy, healthy rather than sick, and so on. Such presumptions reflect the normal and expected course of events, and make for economy of effort and rapid reasoning. They put the 'burden of proof' on to the person who questions the presumption. The difficulty, however, is not so much in dealing with a questionable presumption but in recognizing the existence of the presumption in the first place. The manifest content (the explicit part) of an argument rests upon the latent content (the implicit part) of which we remain unaware until we make the effort to explore the infrastructure of the argument, as we do when we carry out a Toulminian analysis. For example, in a case of marital disharmony the question of the wife's infidelity may not be raised until several other more obvious lines of inquiry have proved inadequate to the task of understanding what is going on. The question reveals a presumption (an implicit assumption) deeper in the argument.

The statements in an informal argument are interlocked in a system of inference or pattern of meaning. The structure of an argument is weak if its constituent elements (statements) are not well interconnected, or if the facts and reasons given are not convincing to an impartial and competent judge, or if the attached reservations and conditions of rebuttal severely constrain the acceptability of the conclusion. Unlike arguments in formal logic, informal arguments are open-ended. Their ramifications extend into our knowledge of the natural world as well as into the man-made world of signs and symbols (language, images) and social systems (laws, rituals, and rules generally).

Toulmin's method of analysing the substantive logic of arguments has been applied to a major theory in sociology. Bromley (1970) has shown that the so-called 'theory of disengagement' in social gerontology can be analysed into six separate subsidiary arguments or logical networks. The overall system requires 327 statements making up 42 distinct but interconnected basic arguments. A basic argument (an argument in standard form) in the present context is one which contains the essential ingredients: D (data), C (conclusion), Q (qualifier), W (warrant), B (backing), and R (reservation). The analysis revealed a number of weaknesses and omissions in the theory of disengagement and was intended to illustrate some of the problems of theory construction and explanation in the social and behavioural sciences.

We have little difficulty in thinking up all kinds of plausible accounts and explanations for people's behaviour. The ability to think in this way is an important aspect of problem-solving in case-studies. The danger lies in not following up this creative work by the critical work of testing these plausible explanations against the evidence. The important thing is to try to *refute* an explanation, not merely to find evidence in *support* of it. A good explanation is one which fits all the evidence and is contradicted by none of it, one which exhausts all the possibilities and leaves the Investigators satisfied, temporarily at least, that that is the best they can do.

Regrettably, even in professional and scientific writings, arguments are often incoherent and incomplete; and many facts, assumptions, and relationships are not stated explicitly. The following informal argument in standard form taken from Bromley (1977), illustrates one of several possible 'constructions' imposed on an actual case-study. It should be noted that the argument is stated in general terms that could be applied to a class of similar cases.

CASE K

D: There was no evidence in the life-history data on the patient to indicate any predisposition to neurosis, and the presenting symptoms did not clearly fit any of the standard patterns. The patient's condition did not improve over a period of time.

Q,C: So, presumably, the patient was not suffering from a neurosis precipitated by the stress of the accident (a head injury) and the subsequent circumstances (absence from work, boredom).

W: Since stress reactions tend to decrease with time after the stresses are removed, and neurosis is usually associated with a predisposition to maladjustment.

B: On account of the accepted concepts and findings described in the literature of psychopathology.

R: Unless the term neurosis is taken to include the condition referred to as 'compensation case'; or unless the cumulative effects of ageing, alcohol, and occupational stresses have lately increased the patient's predisposition to neurosis; or unless the patient's life-history and present circumstances have not been adequately investigated.

PRESUMPTIONS AND THE STRUCTURE OF ARGUMENT (continued)

Arguments in ordinary language can be transformed into their explicit 'standard form' and connected with one another to form a 'network' by virtue of the fact that some of them have statements in common. For example, the C of one argument is the D of another. Each of the six component parts of an argument may consist of several sentences. Taken together, the component statements form a complex logical network or structure. Some of them may be accepted without question as assumptions; others may be disputed. Disputes give rise to further arguments until the parties to the dispute can find common ground for agreement. Such 'disputes', of course, may take place within the mind of one Investigator as he or she works out the implications of his or her own theories and observations. Eventually, some of the statements come to be regarded as established or not in dispute, or used simply as assumptions or definitions, and these provide anchorage points for the system as a whole. The problem is to develop the network of argument so that it is capable of dealing with the 'facts in issue'—capable, that is, of leading to a reasonable conclusion, either by finding evidence and arguments which deal with the problem directly or by finding circumstantial evidence and indirect arguments.

In theory, this approach to the analysis of case-material is an informal, open, logical system capable of assimilating all kinds of data, definitions, and concepts. In practice the problem is to derive, from the ordinary language of the case-study, those propositions which form the component statements in C, D, W, Q, R, and B. Actually, the explicit or manifest argument is usually derived from a much larger system of implicit or latent arguments, and the validity of the main explicit argument can be established only by working through the ramifications of these subsidiary arguments.

Statements about personality and adjustment may have quite complicated syntactical structures, expressing complex logical relationships—see Bromley (1977). The connection between the sentences in the case-materials and the logical argument is fairly straightforward. A statement of the form: 'P_i is A only when S_j is X', e.g. 'He is depressed only when there is pressure at work', might operate as a component in an argument about a person's occupational adjustment. As we have seen, a simple 'argument' in 'standard form' consists of a sequence of statements, as follows: D, so Q, C, since W, on account of B, unless R. A 'network' of arguments is an interrelated system of arguments in standard form, usually arranged so that the key issues can be settled by reference to them.

This method of analysing the logical structure of a complex argument goes well beyond ordinary language and common sense in the degree of explicitness, precision, and comprehensiveness that it calls for. Nevertheless, it does not have the exactness or completeness characteristic of formal logic; and for want of a better name it can be referred to as 'informal logic' or, to use Toulmin's original term, 'substantial logic'—see Toulmin (1958). It does, however, suggest the possibility for a computational, i.e. artificial intelligence, approach to the analysis of case-study arguments—see Chapter 11.

Our aim in this chapter has been to examine, in considerable detail, the logic of arguments of the sort found in case-studies. We want to be able to examine the contents and organization of any case-report with a view to identifying the structure of inference used in reaching the conclusions on the evidence presented. Whilst examining the nuts and bolts, as it were, of the structure of arguments about cases, it is as well to remember that arguments in case-studies can be regarded as sound, ultimately, only to the extent that they fulfil, at the very least, the basic aim of improving our understanding and/or management of the Subjects of those case-studies. Ideally, the arguments should illuminate and be applicable to whole classes of cases. In other words, the correctness and usefulness of arguments in case-studies depend on the whole enterprise in which the case-studies participate. If this enterprise is professional service or scientific research, then the arguments in the case-studies should reflect the standards and procedures of professional service or scientific research.

Another general point worth bearing in mind is that an argument about an issue in a case-study may change from one context to another. For example, the same point may be argued differently depending upon whether it is raised in a case-conference, in a private conversation, or in an official report. The reason is that these different contexts are governed by different norms, values, procedures, requirements, and so on; and the argument must be constructed in such a way as to fit the context in which it occurs. A comparable state of affairs is found when we look at an issue from different perspectives. For example, an argument about a child's intelligence will be constructed differently depending upon whether one is concerned with the medical aspects, educational aspects, social and family aspects, or legal aspects of the case. Indeed, all these different points of view may have to be incorporated into the case-study.

It is not usually possible to spell out an argument exhaustively, in all its details, because the ramifications extend deeply and widely into our knowledge of the real world, including our knowledge of human nature and its possibilities. All that is expected of professional and scientific arguments is 'reasonableness', i.e. a willingness and ability to be self-critical, to deal sensibly with justifiable objections and queries from others. In this way, a *basis* for agreement can be reached even if no *final* agreement can be reached on particular issues. Then, at least, points of disagreement can be explored more fully, or settled by arbitration, or simply left unresolved for the time being. All interpretations of a Subject's actions are liable to continual revision in the light of additional information. The aim is to collect data in such a way as to *eliminate* inadequate interpretations.

OPENNESS TO ARGUMENT

It is important for scientific and professional Investigators to be 'open to argument'. They should take account of the critical and constructive comments made about their arguments. This is possible only if their arguments are, in the first place, expressed openly in the appropriate public forums to those people who are concerned with the particular case or with the general issues raised by the case or with the maintenance of scientific and professional standards generally.

Openness to argument has a major role to play in the evolution of scientific knowledge—see Toulmin (1972) and Popper (1973). By developing new ways of thinking about phenomena, new ways of dealing with practical problems, and testing these out in public debate and applying them in real-life conditions, we find that some are successful and some are not. The process is analogous to the selective effects of competition in the evolution of adaptive behaviour.

With reference to psychology, openness to argument means being willing and able to evolve more adaptive frameworks of understanding and action in relation to the study of individual cases—better concepts, better methods of inquiry, more systematic and substantial bodies of knowledge, and more effective ways of managing people and organizations.

At any particular time, however, there is usually an agreed framework of understanding and action within which rational argument takes place. Unfortunately, in the case of psychology, it is difficult to define what this agreed framework is, because psychology is not a coherent system of concepts, methods, and findings related to human behaviour, but rather a loosely organized, widely scattered family of studies with few common interests.

Ideas can evolve not just because of, or within, the findings of scientific research and reports of professional experience. Historical changes—cultural changes, technological developments, political conflicts (including wars and revolutions), and so on—can bring about major changes in the climate of opinion about human nature. These can have a profound influence on scientific and professional work in psychology. Consider, for example, changes in society's attitudes towards slavery, racial differences, sex differences, intelligence, social class, human thought and judgment (i.e. 'mind'), morality, free will, abnormal behaviour, crime, and so on—Curti (1980). In other words, even without being fully aware of the factors which constrain and shape our thinking, we tend to approach the individual cases we study within a social and an ideological framework which is shared, largely, by the people with whom we associate.

A distinction has been drawn between 'normal' and 'revolutionary' changes in the way scientists conceptualize their problem—see Kuhn (1962) and Toulmin (1972). This is an issue which belongs to the history, philosophy, and sociology of science, and we cannot take it up here, except to mention that, in psychology, psychoanalysis brought about a revolution in the way we conceptualized abnormal behaviour, psychometric studies revolutionized our notions of intelligence and individual differences. There is no reason to suppose that comparable revolutions will not occur in the future, and no reason to suppose that we should, in the meantime, ignore the more gradual, 'normal' improvements in understanding that take place within a particular psychological 'paradigm'.

We can draw a similar distinction between 'regular' arguments, which are basically conceptual routines for dealing with routine cases, and 'critical' arguments, which are more like arguments about arguments. What happens in a 'critical' argument is that the whole structure of an argument is brought into question—perhaps because it uses obsolete procedures or is presented in the wrong context or can be replaced by an argument using different concepts.

SUMMARY AND CONCLUSIONS

It is possible to examine the logical structure of a case-report by means of a method developed by Toulmin. This method is concerned not so much with the formal logic of an argument as with its substantive logic, which depends to a large extent on the content and context of the argument.

It is possible to identify six basic components or types of statement in a substantive argument: C (claim), D (data), W (inference warrant), Q (modal qualifier), R (rebuttal or reservation), B (backing). An argument in 'standard form' contains each of these components. Arguments in standard form can be interlocked in a complex web or network of argument in virtue of the fact that one and the same statement can function in different ways depending upon how it is related to other statements in the network.

The analysis of substantive arguments is difficult because the manifest or stated argument is usually incomplete. The latent aspects of the argument have to be made explicit by introducing assumptions and real-world knowledge. Case H is analysed in considerable detail and shows that even an apparently simple argument may be difficult to explicate. Case I is a more complex case which is nevertheless susceptible to substantive logical analysis. This form of analysis, like the diagrams used in previous chapters, fulfils a heuristic function in the sense of forcing the Investigator to make the case-study clear and complete.

The method is shown to be applicable to cases and arguments in areas other than psychology, as in Case J, and in relation to the sociological theory of disengagement.

Four rather different types of argument can be described: adversarial (competitive), arbitrational (equalizing), consensual (cooperative), and pragmatic (practical). Ideally, scientific and professional arguments about case-studies should fit the consensual (cooperative) type; in practice, all four types can be found.

It is possible to identify a number of common forms of reasoning—analogy, statistical inference, diagnosis, attribution, and exclusion.

Arguments in psychological case-studies have their characteristic features. They tend to contain a mixture of common sense and technical notions, including a limited number of explanatory concepts. Their relationship to psychological theory is often tenuous.

Different areas of interest require different sorts of contents in the six basic components of substantive arguments. There are conceptual and methodological boundaries to these areas which make it difficult to argue a case in the same way when it is looked at from these different perspectives.

The limits to arguments in psychological case-studies are found in the ultimate grounds to which Investigators have to appeal if their arguments are persistently challenged. A sound argument must be anchored at its limits to firmly established facts and assumptions, although these basic facts and assumptions may not be expressed initially in the manifest argument.

A number of further points of interest are raised briefly, some of which are dealt with in more detail in other chapters.

An argument relating to Case K is introduced to illustrate a form of argument which could apply to a class of similar cases and not just to the particular case on the basis of which it was constructed.

The need for scientific and professional workers to be 'open to argument', tolerant of opposing lines of reasoning, is emphasized.

Psychology, like other sciences, can expect to change its concepts and methods in an adaptive, evolutionary way.

CHAPTER TEN

Sources of Error in Reasoning About Cases

Introduction
Heuristics
Some Forms of Reasoning Used in Making Predictions about People
Subjective and Intersubjective Factors
Further Liabilities and Limitations in Reasoning
Logical Fallacies and Other Mistakes
Summary and Conclusions

INTRODUCTION

Human beings have certain natural cognitive capacities which are exercised in everyday engagement with the real world. In addition, our cultural inheritance—our education and training—provides us with specialized technical (scientific and professional) concepts and methods which amplify and correct these natural cognitive capacities. Experimentation, formal logic, and statistical inference are obvious examples. Case-studies at a scientific and professional level require technical and expert forms of reasoning, and data collection, depending upon their content and complexity. For example, case-studies in psychopathy (personality disorder), early dementia, business failure, industrial conflict, and scientific achievement incorporate technical concepts and methods, although it is usually possible to write accounts in ordinary language which can be understood at a common-sense level. We shall assume that the scientific concepts and professional methods we use in dealing with individual cases rest on an infrastructure of common sense and ordinary language.

We have already had occasion to refer to some of the mistakes and fallacies that can occur in reasoning about psychological case-studies. Recently there has been a considerable growth of interest in the strategies of human inference, with particular reference to heuristics and shortcomings in social judgment—see Nisbett and Ross (1980), Kahneman *et al.* (1982), and Wheeler and Janis (1980). Although some criticisms have been made of the assumptions and empirical investigations in the work on biases and heuristics in social judgment, e.g. Smith and Miller (1978), Rich (1979), White (1980), there is sufficient evidence to show that in some circumstances a person may think or act in ways which are determined by factors outside his or her awareness, and which he or she attributes to factors which played no part in that particular episode (although the person may have good reason for supposing that the attributed factors normally determine his or her thoughts and actions in situations of that sort). For example, a person might recommend a book to someone, thinking that the reason for the recommendation was to increase the other person's enjoyment, when the 'real' reason is to ingratiate himself or to secure confirmation of his evaluation of the book. The problem, of course, is, how such 'real' reasons are to be identified.

Our purpose in this chapter is to describe and discuss only those heuristics and shortcomings which are particularly relevant to the way we reason about individual people. Our examples, naturally, are drawn from this particular area. Readers are strongly urged to read more deeply in the general area of social judgment.

A particularly subtle source of error in case-study materials is the *absence* of information and ideas. The possibilities that no-one thought of, and the facts that were not known, must have invalidated numerous case-studies, simply because people's attention tends to be concentrated on the information actually presented. It is important in case-studies and in problem-solving generally to go 'beyond the information given' to 'what might be' the case. Naturally, such speculations need to be backed up by reasoned argument and by a search for relevant evidence. Sensitivity to the absence of relevant evidence seems to depend on having an explicit theory about a case which, if it were true, would indicate the nature of such evidence. One can then look to see whether such evidence can be found. Our theories provide us with the rules of inference we need in order to explain the subject's behaviour and circumstances.

It is not always easy to ascertain whether we have applied a rule of inference correctly or not, especially when engaged in complex or unfamiliar forms of reasoning, and when the topic we are dealing with is emotionally loaded or needs urgent attention. The more we are aware of the rational procedures appropriate to problem-solving and decision-making, e.g. formal logic, substantive logic, statistical inference, the more likely we are to appreciate the need for them when faced with human problems. Similarly, the more we are aware of the fallacies and mistakes to which we are liable, the more likely we are to guard against them.

We have already seen that the connection between a conclusion or decision (C) on the one hand, and data or evidence (D) on the other, is justified by an inference warrant (W). The inference warrant is the sort of 'ticket' or 'licence' we need to demonstrate that we are logically entitled to make that connection. In the ordinary affairs of daily life we often omit to mention the inference warrant, taking for granted that other people will adopt the same line of reasoning. One needs time to reflect on incomplete arguments, because it is all too easy to miss opportunities to question implicit, unspoken, doubtful lines of reasoning. However, we are not particularly concerned with the 'performance' aspects of argumentation but rather with 'competence'—

with what people can and ought to do rather than with what they actually do when reasoning and arguing.

One aspect of social judgment has to do with attributing causality and moral responsibility. In the case of a motor-vehicle accident, for example, who or what caused the accident, who or what is to blame? If most people in a position to have an opinion on the matter say it was the driver's fault, this shows that the claim (C) that it was the driver's fault is not idiosyncratic (peculiar to whoever puts the claim forward). This provides corroborative evidence (D) in the form of *consensus* opinions between observers for the claim. If it is a fact that the driver regularly or repeatedly makes mistakes of this kind, these 'similar facts' show that the claim is *consistent* with other relevant facts. This too provides corroborative, if indirect, evidence for the claim. If the driver is one of the few or the only person who makes mistakes of this kind, then his *distinctiveness* greatly increases the likelihood that the claim will be accepted, because it tends to rule out other possible claims. Thus the consistency of a person's behaviour, its distinctiveness, and consensus among observers, all contribute a measure of confidence to social judgments that attribute blame and praise.

The dangers lie in emphasizing one aspect of attribution whilst neglecting others, and in relying on these kinds of indirect evidence when better evidence might be available. Exactly the same sort of attributional judgment would be at work if we claimed that the car, not the driver, was at fault. To take a rather different example: how does one decide whether a person's complimentary remark should be attributed to that person's good manners or to the social deserts of the recipient?

Some attribution studies show a tendency to explain one's own behaviour in terms of surrounding circumstances, and to explain other people's behaviour in terms of personal qualities. A thoughtful, informed explanation should, of course, take into account both personal factors and situational factors. Behaviour is a function of the complex interaction between the person and his or her environment. The relative importance of personal and situational factors in any given explanation depends on the nature of the phenomenon to be explained, the predilections of the explainer, and the nature of the puzzlement that generates the need for an explanation.

In understanding and dealing with other people we can be thought of as using mental representations or 'schemata'. The phrase 'plans and scripts' has also been coined to refer to the way in which mental and symbolic representations are used to guide our behaviour, particularly in familiar routine situations. Thus, a physician has a schema (plan or script) for understanding and dealing with one sort of patient, and a somewhat different schema for understanding and dealing with another type of patient. He has a schema of a completely different kind for dealing with his mother-in-law's week-end visit or the drug company representative's call.

Thus, when we are carrying out a case-study we call upon whatever schemata we have available for dealing with this particular sort of person in these particular sorts of circumstances. For example, the way we conduct our first interview with a depressed elderly person, or our final interview with a couple following marriage guidance counselling, or the way we administer a psychometric test to a language-disordered child, depend in part on our mental schemata. In some instances, therefore, the script or plan is a detailed, well-rehearsed scheme for dealing with routine cases in familiar situations. In other instances the script or plan is a vague, more tentative, problem-solving sort of scheme for dealing with non-routine cases or unfamiliar situations; it is a scheme which contains self-instructions like 'Use bland opening remarks', 'Wait and see what happens', 'If he responds normally, ask if he understands the reason for meeting', and so on. Although we rarely use explicit self-instructions like these, except perhaps during training, we often behave as if following such instructions.

Since a great deal of social interaction is 'rule-governed', it follows that a great deal of the business of carrying out a case-study is rule-governed. Behaving in a scientific and professional way means following the sorts of rules prescribed by the appropriate reference group for that sort of be-haviour. These rules govern both the ethical character of professional behaviour (conduct) and its practical character (skill).

We tend to attribute the consistency in a person's behaviour to characteris-tics within the person, neglecting the important persisting effects that the environment has on shaping and constraining the individual's actions. A high degree of consistency and regularity in a prerequisite for orderly social living and for satisfactory personal adjustment. This means we predict an indi-vidual's behaviour, to some extent, by assuming implicitly that he or she will behave in the same way in comparable circumstancs in the future. Such expectations are derived from the common-sense scripts and plans—schema-ta—we use to organize routine forms of behaviour in standard situations in daily life. The expectation that people will conform to role expectations is a common experience and basic to everyday social interaction. This relieves us of the burden of making clinical judgments based on particular facts about individual persons—a procedure which would lead us to make poorer judgments on average!

The scripts, frames, plans, conceptual routines, and other schemata we use in case-studies can be thought of as maps, guides, or instructions used in organizing our behaviour in relation to our goals and circumstances. Obvious-ly, faulty and misleading maps are likely to lead to inadequate performance. Heuristics can be thought of as exercises in map-making. An appropriate and valid heuristic is a sort of mental map or guide which is effective in enabling us to approach our goal.

Through everyday experience and ordinary language we acquire a variety of common-sense notions (schemata) about human nature in general—about social relationships, children's behaviour, feelings and desires, personality characteristics, and so on. Through scientific education and professional training we acquire a variety of technical concepts and methods for understanding and dealing with some of the more puzzling, difficult, and unusual aspects of human nature, as well as its more normal aspects. For example, we may study emotional development, stress, psychopathology, behaviour in organizations, ageing, and other special areas.

Implicit, then, in our common-sense understanding of ourselves and other people are structured systems of ideas called frames and scripts that enable us to follow certain fairly typical sequences of behaviour in relation to fairly standard circumstances. For example, we could, if asked, describe in general terms and with appropriate examples, what is meant by a lovers' quarrel, treachery, moral courage, professional jealousy, or moving house. We could construct a typical scenario (frame) and a story (script) to illustrate a typical sequence of events. Projective tests like the Thematic Apperception Test tap a subject's tendency to formulate frames and scripts with particular features when that subject is shown an ambiguous picture and asked to construct a story around it.

Similar structured systems of ideas are developed at the scientific and professional level of understanding and dealing with people. For example, with the benefit of training and experience we can understand, anticipate, and deal more effectively with cases which are difficult but nevertheless conform to fairly standard patterns—the recently widowed, the abruptly disabled, the long-term prisoner, the newly arrived overseas student, and so on. Each of these broad categories, of course, can be subdivided in various ways to achieve a narrower focus of interest and so a higher degree of similarity between cases, i.e. a smaller 'frame' a more specific 'script' for a narrower range of cases. The individual case is, by definition, unique—and so may not conform exactly to the plan and script we have worked out. We must be ready, therefore, to make tactical adjustments to the plan for dealing with the particular case.

The language we use to communicate our ideas to other professionals, e.g. 'This is a case of a subnormal girl in danger of being sexually abused', 'This is a case of a terminally ill man whose wife cannot cope with the situation', enables them to tune into an appropriate, shared, script. They can also follow it critically and constructively if they have the ability, training, and experience. The exchange of common-sense, scientific, and professional facts and ideas creates pools of shared information (and misinformation), so that 'tuning in' to a discussion or talk in one's own area of interest is fairly easy.

HEURISTICS

Among the processes that contribute to the formation of schemata (mental representations) are forms of reasoning called 'heuristics', which a dictionary would define as methods for finding things out or techniques of search and discovery. Thus heuristic reasoning does not mean using 'trial and error', to take one extreme, nor does it mean using formal logical deduction or computation, to take the other. It means, rather, using a rule of thumb, or informed guesswork, or a scheme of successive approximations, to find the solution to a problem. It means using a method of inference, which *could* lead to the wrong logical solution but which we believe will not. This sort of reasoning should not be confused with logical implication, which by definition *must* be right, i.e. valid, even if the conclusion is not true.

Two basic heuristics have been identified: resemblance (or representativeness) and salience (or availability). The resemblance heuristic relies on reasoning by analogy. For example, we might argue that a child with some delinquent tendencies should be regarded as delinquent, regardless of other considerations like the proportion of children who become delinquent, or the possession by the child of non-delinquent tendencies.

The availability heuristic relies on reasoning by subjective association of ideas—a common feature of stereotyped judgments. If a particular association of ideas is strong, for whatever reason—frequency of previous occurrence or emotional intensity, for example, then this association is salient; it is a high probability response. For example, to associate stammering with nervousness means tending to conclude that people who stammer are nervous, and that people who are nervous are likely to stammer. But subjective associations often overestimate the objective degree of association. We tend to neglect counter-examples—stammerers who are not nervous and nervous people who do not stammer. A good way of testing a rule of inference which states an association is to look for counter-examples.

Reasoning by analogy and reasoning by subjective association of ideas are not the only sources of error in social judgment. Errors can occur at every stage in the process. Selective attention may ignore relevant information. The information we attend to may be misinterpreted. We may forget things and make mistakes in recognition and recall. We sometimes fail to produce a correct version of what we have learned. Such errors can arise because of lack of ability, lack of interest, lack of training or experience, fatigue, distraction, anxiety, and so on.

Many people, even many professionals who work with people, have no training in formal logic (inductive or deductive) and the detection of fallacies; so they are liable to these sorts of errors too.

A simple way of looking at one kind of social judgment in relation to the study of individual cases is to think of it as requiring (a) a description of specific instances of behaviour (including absence of behaviour), (b) a summary of that sample of instances, and (c) an inference or generalization about the general category of which the specific instances are exemplars. Thus, we could describe some actions by a person, categorize and summarize that sample of his or her behaviour, and infer that the person possesses certain personality characteristics. But at each stage (a), (b), and (c) errors are possible. We may have a biased sample of the individual's behaviour. We may misinterpret the psychological significance of the actions. We may fail to appreciate the circumstances that gave rise to the behaviour.

Many social judgments depend on the idea of correlation or covariation—the extent to which two variables or factors are associated. Suppose, for example, we have two factors labelled A and B, and each can be either present (+) or absent (−). If we count the number of instances of each type of occurrence then we can separate out the four possibilities involving both A and B, viz. (++), (+−), (−+), and (−−). An example of the usual sort of display is a fourfold table (Table 10.1). Imagine that the numbers in this table relate to the occasions a report has been made on stock either missing (+), presumed stolen, or not missing (−) from premises B, when person A was known to have been either present (+) or not (−). What conclusion if any can be drawn from the figures?

There is a strong tendency for us to base our inferences on the extent to which A and B are present together, i.e. the (++) possibility. In fact, as elementary statistical reasoning shows, knowledge of the extent of the remaining possibilities, (+−), (−+), and (−−), is also needed before a correct estimate of the degree of association can be made. Superficially one has the impression that person A is often present when stock goes missing, but what about the other numbers? On 30 per cent of the occasions when stock goes missing A is not present; on 50 per cent of the occasions when A is present, no stock is missing; and on 50 per cent of the occasions when A is *not* present, no stock is missing. If we look only at the occasions when A was *not* in the premises (25), on 60 per cent of these occasions stock went missing. A statistical calculation taking account of all the data show $\chi^2 = 2.49$, a value which could reasonably be expected to have occurred by chance. In other words, the connection between person A and the state of the stock B is not established.

Not only are the figures misleading when looked at separately, as we have seen, but there are wider considerations to be taken into account. Who provided the figures? On what basis? Did persons other than A have access to stock? And so on.

Table 10.1

		Person A		
		Present +	Absent −	Total
Situation B	Stock missing +	35	15	50
	Stock not missing −	10	10	20
	Total	45	25	70

In any event, even if the data had established a statistical relationship beyond chance expectation, this does not actually *imply*, although it might *suggest*, a causal connection. The common error of confusing correlation with causality is too well known to deserve further comment, except perhaps to remind ourselves that this tendency is a fundamental, primitive sort of inference, not without its advantages. Experimental and quasi-experimental methods of inquiry can be used to establish the controls necessary to pursue questions of causal analysis. In natural circumstances where controls are not very adequate, one should take particular care to look for evidence which runs counter to one's expectations and beliefs.

Paradoxically, perhaps, human beings do not appear to be very good at detecting actual correlations between variables unless the correlations are very high. Oddly, we sometimes assume that variables are correlated when they are not. For example, we may think there is a connection between speech fluency and intelligence, or between physical attractiveness and sexuality. What we may fail to appreciate, on the other hand, is the correlation in intelligence between husbands and wives or the correlation between age and political values in adult life.

In situations where the consequences of social misjudgments make no material difference to the outcome, social consensus still provides a common framework for beliefs and practices—certain aspects of religion, politics, magic, medicine, and law, for example. In situations where the consequences affect survival, health, and welfare, then social consensus is not enough, and countervailing influences responsive to real-world effects must eventually emerge, and in the process give rise to more adaptive modes of thought. We have reason to believe that these modes of thought will be scientific (rational and empirical), technical, critical (sceptical of existing forms of understanding), and innovative.

The tendency to classify, order, and see connections between things is a fundamental process in human adjustment. We have a need to impose consistent patterns of meaning on what we see around us, and on our own behaviour and experience. We can impose order and meaning even on random events, and where the connections are spurious—for example, in astrology, palmistry, gambling, accidents, and illnesses.

The problem is to know when we have imposed the wrong meaning on events. What we must not forget is the extent to which we, the Investigators, tend to impose our interpretations on the available evidence. The facts do not speak for themselves, they have to be spoken for. A scientific or professional inquiry is one that pays as much attention to the reasoning—the theories, assumptions, and inferences—of the inquiry as it does to the empirical data.

In some situations, informal social judgment works well simply because it just happens to represent the real situation very well. For example, a single observation will be sufficient if all observations give the same result!

In arguing a case, we are inclined to use concrete examples not simply to illustrate the point we are trying to make but to prove a point. Particular instances of, say, child abuse, poverty, or racial discrimination are more easily grasped and more psychologically convincing than abstract and general facts derived from official statistics or social surveys. Nevertheless the latter may be more logically probative. If personal experience with particular cases, and illustrative case-studies from other people, are more psychologically convincing than abstract and general findings, then this helps to explain why we are impressed by the case of the man who died from a heart attack whilst taking exercise, the lifelong smoker who did not die of cancer, the lady who did not lose weight on a diet. Faced with vivid evidence of this sort, the thing to do is to examine the appropriateness of one's reasoning in the given circumstances. Is the case typical? What counter-examples are there? What is the statistical evidence?

Statistical reasoning reveals two common sources of bias in informal inference. One has to do with what are called 'base-rates'. A base-rate is the actual rate of occurrence of a class of events—holiday coach crashes, car thefts, actual suicide following threats of suicide, pregnancies following first intercourse. The actual base-rate is unknown unless someone has carried out the research necessary to establish it; so, if our subjective estimate of the base-rate is wide of the mark, it follows that we may completely misjudge the likelihood of an outcome. For example, if a girl believes that no-one gets pregnant 'the first time' without contraception, and if the actual base-rate is, say, 2 per cent (author's guess), then one such girl in fifty is going to be surprised.

We live in a large, complex, technological society and we cannot hope to learn all about it through personal experience. Consequently, we have to rely to a large extent on experts, and on the information made available by others—consumer reports, public inquiries, the media, government statistics, social surveys, and the like. Scientific and professional data are available in many areas to lessen our dependence on subjective judgment, although in psychology, unfortunately, our sources are far from satisfactory. We have not developed the kind of behaviour ecology that Barker (1963) advocated. Standardized test materials and norms leave a great deal to be desired. Survey and experimental results have limited applicability. There is virtually no case-law in psychology. Hence, we still have a long way to go in developing norms, standards, and base-rates that will help us to deal more objectively with individual cases, even in relatively circumscribed areas such as family relationships, occupational adjustment, and juvenile delinquency.

Another source of bias in informal inference is 'statistical regression', a phenomenon which arises when two variables are imperfectly correlated. Under this condition when we predict the value of one variable from knowledge of the other, the values lying outside the middle range tend to be overestimated if they are high and underestimated if they are low. In the case of a follow-up or repeated measure, the higher values tend to decrease, the lower values tend to increase, and the middle values stay about the same. For example, if we carry out a follow-up study of dieting to reduce weight or a repeat study of school attainments, what we find is that those subjects with high initial scores tend to get lower scores on follow-up, whilst the subjects with low initial scores tend to get higher scores on follow-up. Note that this does not indicate a persisting trend, otherwise all the subjects would eventually become average! What produces the effect is the unreliability of the measures and the shape of the sampling distribution at different levels of ability (assuming upper and lower limits of weight or ability). It has been suggested that ignoring this effect leads us to criticize poor performers to make them improve, but to be wary of praising good performers in case they get worse.

Also in the study of individual cases, we tend to judge people in terms of their initial performance, for example in a job or in a treatment centre. First impressions set our expectation about the individual's future performance. This line of reasoning is sensible when the individual's initial performance is near the average, but if it lies towards one or the other extreme of the range then, as we have seen, the chances are that it will revert to a level closer to the overall norm, i.e. to the average of the people with whom the individual is being compared.

We have seen that some implicit assumptions and rules of inference (heuristics) can lead us to make mistakes. We can ask the wrong questions, use poor evidence, confuse supposition with observation, forget or misremember what we knew, attach the wrong weight to evidence, and so reach the wrong conclusion or decision. These errors and omissions may be aggravated by emotional involvement—self-seeking, avoidance of blame—and by incidental factors, such as inexperience or carelessness. Even the order of appearance of material in a case-study may affect the impression one forms. There are many ways of influencing people through their feelings and personal involvement in an issue. Hence, when discussing a case, we must be alert to persuasive influences that are not part of rational argument and empirical evidence.

We seem to have a natural tendency to be more strongly influenced in our social judgments by our preconceptions and the availability of our subjective experience than by at least some of the objective facts (consensus, base-rates, survey data, and so on). So, for example, we may rate a person's chances of becoming rich or famous much higher than we should because we neglect the fact that only a tiny proportion of people succeed in doing so, i.e. we neglect the base-rate. Similarly we may encourage a person into a particular career path because he has a few of the characteristics we associate with that career, forgetting that the proportion of people who qualify fully is quite small. Failure to appreciate the odds against success may account for some of the persistence we observe in the behaviour of certain kinds of people—artists, writers, scientists, businessmen, politicians. On the other hand, appreciation of the significance of base-rates perhaps accounts for certain types of offence—drunken driving, shoplifting, fraud, tax evasion, for example—where the common belief that 'most people get away with it' is perhaps true.

Vivid instances in one's personal experience—contact infection, for example, or a road accident—seem to have the effect of increasing one's estimate of the relevant base-rate, temporarily at least.

In the study of individual cases we are not often in the position of having to calculate combined and conditional probabilities, although we may very well try to work out what is likely to happen in an intuitive non-quantitative way. For example, we sometimes find ourselves trying to forecast an outcome on the basis of several items of information. There is a rational way of dealing with this situation, but it has a place in professional and scientific reasoning rather than in lay reasoning—see Chapter 8. Our intuitive judgment is not capable of estimating or predicting an outcome when the outcome is a function of several interdependent variables. We are inclined to overestimate the importance of poor predictors and to neglect the interactions between predictor variables. Multiple regression methods can be used in cases where the appropriate information is available, but that is a specialized and technical area of statistics beyond our immediate concern. The attempt to combine information clinically (intuitively), especially when the relevance of the information is uncertain, can lead to peculiar judgments. For example, the information that a man is aggressive when drunk might raise our expectation of his physically abusing his child; the information that a man is aggressive and a good darts player might lower our expectation!

Our preconceptions and implicit theories about people's behaviour incline us to take account of evidence in favour of our ideas but not of evidence which runs counter to them; so we are more sceptical of counter-evidence and more likely to ignore or misinterpret it. Readers who have tried to convince anyone that their strongly held views are mistaken will be aware of this common human tendency.

Subjective estimates of the frequency or strength of a particular characteristic or circumstance are prone to errors of various sorts—for example, range effects, and the variety and distribution of instances of that sort of characteristic or circumstance. Our estimate of someone's intelligence or educational level or social background depends on the range and representativeness of our experience of such characteristics, on the sorts of cues we pay attention to, and on how such cues are interpreted. Similarly, our assessment of a home, a school, a business, or a military operation depends on the intelligence, interest, and available background knowledge we bring to the task, as well as on all sorts of accidental factors affecting the way the situation presents itself to us—the order in which events occur, their psychological impact, their context, and so on.

We tend to neglect the fact that the reliability of an estimate based on a sample of observations increases rapidly with the size of the sample, for samples of small to moderate size at least, provided the sample is representative of the population about which the estimate is made; so that even small representative samples can be remarkably accurate. Many forms of psychological assessment can be thought of as based on systematic sampling of the

Subject's behaviour, e.g. intelligence testing, educational attainment, and personality assessment. Social assessments can be made of Subjects in an institutional environment by time-sampling their daily activities and social interactions. A medical examination takes a sample of the more important indicators of health. A life-history examination takes a sample of the more obvious indicators of subjective self-awareness. It is assumed, with some justification, that multiple indicators give more accurate and more reliable estimates than a single indicator or impression.

It is important to recognize the extent to which strong evidence, i.e. evidence which is logically probative, can be overshadowed by evidence which is psychologically convincing but logically weak. For example, an argument based on school records and teachers' reports may be overshadowed by an argument from authority citing a dramatic personal experience involving a 'similar' case.

If sampling does not provide a feasible way of arriving at an estimate, one can use a heuristic which, in another field, is called 'triangulation'. The word is used to refer to the idea that if one makes several estimates based on different and independent, but relevant, criteria, then these different estimates should converge and make it possible to arrive at a result which satisfies each criterion about equally well. So, for example, opinions from three or more independent referees should enable one to form a better (convergent and more reliable) judgment about a candidate than an opinion from only one referee.

Psychologists have spent many years trying to develop valid and reliable methods for assessing psychological characteristics. The efforts have not been without limited success. We need not survey the psychometric methods available for assessment purposes, as these vary greatly from one area of interest to another. Nor need we enter into questions of reliability, validity, and utility, since these issues too constitute a large complex technical field of inquiry. Readers should be reminded, however, that the results of a psychological test are meaningful only when the test has been administered in the correct way to the sorts of people on whom the test was standardized. The fact that a test 'looks valid', looks as if it should give relevant results, is no guarantee that it is valid. Also the fact that a test gives 'reliable', i.e. replicable, results, does not mean that it measures what it is supposed to measure. The whole area of psychological assessment is a minefield for the unwary.

We are sometimes in the position of being able to provide an algorithm—a mechanical step-by-step procedure—for solving a case-study problem. The importance of algorithms in other areas of problem-solving—medical diagnosis, electrical and mechanical fault-finding, and administrative routines—shows that algorithms are powerful aids to reasoning. Some attempt should be made to routinize the process of problem-solving in situations where problems of the same sort recur. In psychological case-studies in areas such as management selection, military or other disciplinary hearings, or child abuse, there are often routine procedures to be followed which result in conclusions or decisions which allow the case to progress. These procedures include: the appointment of duly authorized Investigators, the submission of essential documents, examination and cross-examination of witnesses, tests to rule out certain possibilities, majority decisions, and so on, depending on the sort of case under investigation. Investigators familiar with a particular sort of case—say elderly people at risk—will tend to know what to look for, what the possibilities are, and how to move through the various stages of the inquiry to the point at which the case is closed.

When these procedural considerations in case-studies are made explicit and systematized, they constitute a sort of algorithm, but not an algorithm which leads *necessarily* to the correct solution. This is because it is not likely to incorporate all possible eventualities. A procedural algorithm is a conceptual routine—a plan or script that provides us with a guide to action but not necessarily with a computational routine. A computational routine is a logical device that enables us to 'calculate' a solution correctly. Where we can develop a computational routine that can be applied to certain classes of cases, this reduces the risks of faulty inference to zero and improves the scientific and professional quality of the case-study because it systematizes the investigation and makes it complete. A computational routine gives us the solution to a problem. It is possible that developments in artificial intelligence in relation to natural language processing and problem-solving will lead to 'expert systems' in certain areas of case-study. Expert systems are computer-assisted algorithms that aim to develop computational routines for solving problems of certain kinds—see Chapter 11.

SOME FORMS OF REASONING USED IN MAKING PREDICTIONS ABOUT PEOPLE

Some standard forms of argument are typically used in forecasting how people are likely to behave. The problem of predicting individual behaviour, however, is fraught with difficulties. There are usually too many interacting variables—personal and situational—and too many chance factors to make predictions reliable. In order to test whether a prediction has been borne out, it is necessary to carry out some sort of evaluation or follow-up. Here, one finds problems in defining one's predictions. What is to count as successful rehabilitation, recovery from disability, improved work, or better marital relationships? One has to state the prediction in a fairly general way in order to include all the different ways in which an acceptable outcome could occur. At the same time one has to define the outcome behaviourally so that independent observers can agree on the observed outcome.

One form of prediction uses knowledge of social role prescriptions and predicts that the person will do what is expected of him or her. For example, teachers are expected to prepare their lessons and keep records of their pupils' progress. In selecting candidates for teaching posts, these are among the things that we 'predict' they will do. But we probably do not even reflect on the matter, since our expectation is normally implicit, i.e. unspoken. So pervasive and so powerful are the social expectations and sanctions governing role behaviour that we do not normally need to make individual assessments in order to forecast what other people will do. Most people generally do what society expects of them. Unfortunately, we do not necessarily have good access to information about what people actually do, as opposed to what they are expected to do. Also, it is not always easy to discover the extent of a person's conformity to role-expectations, especially when there is unacknowledged collusion among people to hide what is going on—as in neglecting precautions against accidents, engaging in petty pilfering, or faking records.

Perhaps the next most common form of forecasting the behaviour of individuals is the principle of constancy, namely that the person will continue to behave in the same sorts of ways as before—the best predictor of future behaviour is past behaviour! Surprisingly, this is a useful form of argument. It is likely to be more often right than wrong, rather like forecasting that tomorrow's weather will be like today's. The reason for its success is that human actions are subject to a wide variety of influences which, in normal circumstances, lead to fairly stable circumstances and consistent patterns of behaviour. Major shifts in behaviour tend to come about only in unusual, i.e. unpredictable, circumstances, or over longish periods of time through the accumulation of minor modifications.

A variation on the theme of forecasting constant conditions or consistent behaviour is the argument that a pattern of change—a trend—in a person's behaviour will continue. We extrapolate from an existing trend. So, for example, we might argue that a person's adjustment will continue to improve, on the grounds that it has been improving, or that a boy will get into worse trouble because his offences have been increasingly serious.

Arguments of a formal sort, using logical classes and relationships, can be used in prediction. For example:

Joan is young and attractive.
Young attractive women get married,
Joan will get married.

If John is appointed, he will work hard.
John is appointed,
So, he will work hard.

Many sorts of clinical predictions rest on logical reasoning of this sort. But of course clinical and social judgments are also subject to fallacies and biases.

Predictions based on actuarial calculations are more widely appreciated nowadays than formerly. Such predictions apply to a class of individuals, not to one particular individual; but if 70 per cent of a class of students complete a course and 30 per cent drop out, then individuals on average have a 0.7

probability of succeeding, and one can predict success for a typical individual with a 70 per cent level of confidence. Furthermore, if I know that women have a higher success rate than men, and that students who pass the mid-course test have a higher success rate than those who fail, then, knowing these further facts about a person, I can greatly improve the success rate of my predictions, by setting up the appropriate prediction equation.

There is no doubt that actuarial methods of prediction are usually much more effective than clinical methods of prediction. The difficulty is that the sorts of data one needs in order to make actuarial predictions are often not available. Hence the continued reliance on more subjective clinical appraisals. However, professional and scientific workers have a responsibility to seek out the sorts of information that have a bearing on the predictions they are trying to make. For example, if one is trying to predict whether a student will get a first-class degree, it is as well to know that on average the probability may be less than 0.05. Consider also predictions about: passing a driving test, getting divorced, earning an income higher than £20,000, getting killed on the roads, being interviewed by a market-researcher, being the victim of a crime, or benefiting from psychotherapy. It is reasonable to suppose that we underestimate the likelihood of some of these possibilities and overestimate others. These sorts of subjective expectations are likely to influence our clinical judgments even when we are trying to take base-rates into account. Base-rates refer to the proportion of a population that has a particular characteristic, e.g. the proportion of people aged 65 years and over who are depressed, the proportion of people in their late teens or twenties suffering from schizophrenia, the proportions of BA graduates going into certain occupations, the proportion of 'difficult' primary school children who become 'maladjusted' in secondary schools.

SUBJECTIVE AND INTERSUBJECTIVE FACTORS

As soon as we begin an inquiry we bring into operation certain personal beliefs, expectations, and rules of inference. These assumptions and tendencies almost certainly bias our attention and our appreciation of a case. This can easily be confirmed by talking to independent Investigators, each of whom is likely to have a different perspective on the case in question.

Our personal biases are partly a consequence of our pre-existing attitudes and partly a consequence of having too little information. In addition, the information we have may be unbalanced or we may be unduly influenced by information which makes a strong impact, such as information which is dramatic (emotionally arousing), surprising (rare, running counter to strong expectations), or personally relevant (value-laden). Thus, for example, if we are dealing with a case of marital disharmony our approach is governed initially by our attitude towards marriage in general. Our subsequent thinking will be conditioned, obviously, by the amount of information made available, by whether we have equal access to all the relevant sorts of evidence, by whether the case involves dramatic features, e.g. suicide threats, or surprising features, e.g. a wide age disparity between the partners, or features that are personally relevant, e.g. involving one's friends or one's livelihood.

The cases that make an impact on us, the cases that we find 'memorable', will figure prominently in our thinking about cases in the same area in the future, rather like our experiences with a particular motor car conditions our attitude towards cars of that sort.

Recall of, and reflection upon, one's personal experiences has the effect of consolidating them and making them more consistent with our other ideas and feelings. Over time, therefore, our beliefs and values tend to become more stable. Our subjective preferences and judgments are backed by readily available key items of experience. Consider statements of the form, 'In my experience . . ., for example . . .'.

We share many of our thoughts and feelings with other people in matters of common interest, and so contribute to a sort of pool of 'common knowledge' (or rather 'common belief'). We often fail to realize how profoundly our attitudes, i.e. our values, beliefs, and intentions combined, are influenced by the sorts of social interaction we engage in. Consider, for example, one's attitude towards headmasters, tax officers, nurses, disabled children, or unmarried mothers. How are one's reactions to persons of this sort likely to be influenced on the one hand by shared social attitudes and on the other by salient personal experiences with individual persons of that sort? How, if at all, can we validate such beliefs and attitudes?

As we saw in connection with our analysis of the logic of case-studies in Chapter 9, 'common knowledge' or 'common sense' often provides the bedrock, the basic anchorage points, for arguments about people's behaviour; but it does not follow, of course, that what passes for common knowledge is true.

Our tendency to rely on personal experience, and on what seems to be a pool of common, shared experience, can lead to errors in social judgment, as we have seen. It is, however, possible to guard against these errors. First, by becoming aware of their existence (as we have just been doing) we become forewarned and therefore forearmed. Second, we can become more critical of subjective sources, and avoid being overconfident about the accuracy of our estimates and judgments. Third, we can pay more attention to whatever relevant 'objective' evidence is available, e.g. demographic data, survey results, psychometric norms, insurance figures, research findings, local records.

The difficulty is that psychological case-studies tend to be carried out because the problem is relatively complex and rare. If it were relatively simple and common, it is likely that hard data on cases of that sort would be available, reducing the scope for subjective judgment. The point, however, is that one should not neglect to look for hard, objective data when dealing with an individual case, even though the chances of finding any may be small.

Specialists in given areas should know where to search for such evidence.

We often react in a particular way as a consequence of a critical experience, like driving more carefully after noticing a police car or after seeing the results of an accident. An advertisement or a casual remark may jolt our memory and trigger an action, like making a purchase or telephoning a friend or making a charitable donation. Examples like these illustrate the ways in which chance factors influence our thinking and behaviour—see Fiske (1961).

There is no reason to suppose that accidental circumstances and momentary states of mind do not affect our reasoning in case-studies. Consider, for example, what is likely to happen to the way our ideas are moving with reference to a particular case if someone reminds us of a previous case we prefer not to think about, or if we had just attended a conference on another case where we were impressed by a novel approach or line of inquiry. Ideas and feelings can be induced in all sorts of ways quite apart from any deliberate voluntary control we may exercise. Such thoughts and feelings can influence our behaviour unconsciously, that is, without our being aware of the factors which influence us. The price of freedom from accidental and irrational forms of thought is constant critical reflection on the objectivity and effectiveness of one's scientific and professional work. That means being prepared to take account of disagreements expressed by others and being prepared to consider independent evaluations of one's peformance.

Through personal experience, we build up subjective frames of reference for judging all manner of things—people, institutions, consumer goods, and so on. Our personal preferences are often based on vivid and easily remembered experiences rather than on objective evidence. To that extent, therefore, the basis for our preference is psychologically compelling but logically weak. For example, a single personal experience of service in a particular type of store, or of a particular make of car, may lead us to generalize and to recommend that type of store or that make of car to other people. In the study of individual people we are constantly forming impressions on the basis of personal experience. Indeed, first-hand experience counts for a great deal even in judicial investigations. But we often neglect the possibility that our personal experience of a case is very limited, highly selective, and biased, i.e. unrepresentative, in a word, subjective. This subjectivity applies not just to our experience of single events, but also to our experience of classes of events. If my experience as a manager is limited to workers in one small rural firm, I may completely misjudge the behaviour of workers in the larger urban firm to which I have moved.

In so far as people share their experiences with others, there evolves a sort of collective or 'intersubjective' agreement. In the absence of other ways of arriving at realistic assessments, such consensual agreement can be regarded as 'objective'. Intersubjective agreement plays a major role in scientific and professional work, but it is by no means foolproof, as social history and the history of science show. The main point, however, is that the subjective views of *one* case-worker are not a reliable basis for judgment. What is needed is an objective (intersubjective) view of the Subject of a case-study. Differences between people in their assessment of a case are easily demonstrated—for example by getting them to make ratings of the Subject's characteristics, or by getting them to estimate the likelihood of certain outcomes. Indeed, one can turn these differences to advantage by pooling and averaging the results. This technique often results in more accurate assessments.

Subjective factors—beliefs, personal experience, values, presuppositions, and so on—are not 'illogical' in themselves. Indeed, one could not begin to reason without them. They are illogical only if we regard them as leading to definite conclusions rather than to possible conclusions. These possibilities are expressed as expectations or hypotheses. One must not confuse subjective confidence with objective fact. One must not confuse a real possibility with a real factuality. One must not confuse plausibility with confirmation.

Even bias has its place in decision-making. For example we may want to guard against one or other of the two sorts of error: asserting something to be true when it is false, and asserting something to be false when it is true. The obvious example is guarding against finding a person guilty when he or she is innocent. A less obvious example would be guarding against rejecting a radical but workable proposal.

A pernicious type of preconception is one which no amount of evidence can refute, i.e. which is 'unfalsifiable'. Prejudice and dogmatism provide many examples of closed systems of thought and feeling, largely impervious to counter-argument. Prejudice and dogmatism masquerading as scientific and professional expertise is particularly pernicious. It can be found in groups as well as in individuals. The way to deal with it is to expose the circularity of such reasoning, and the inadequacies of the evidence used in the arguments. The role of 'Devil's advocate' has much to recommend it.

FURTHER LIABILITIES AND LIMITATIONS IN REASONING

The fallacy of arguing that an outcome 'could have been' forecast or that a decision 'could have been' seen to be wrong rests on hindsight; that is, on interpreting the evidence *after* the problem has been solved. It is relatively easy to explain something when all the evidence is available and when there is a clear indication of what was happening. The difficulty is to find a solution or make an accurate forecast at a time when there is little evidence and no obvious construction to put on the facts. With the benefit of hindsight, therefore, some outcomes seem to have been inevitable—divorce, job failure, suicide, for example. In committing this fallacy we forget that the key piece of information—the outcome—was not available at the time; other outcomes were possible then. Also, if the case was handled correctly, these other outcomes must have looked more likely given the available facts and interpretations.

Another interesting fallacy in social judgment is supposing that complex or major outcomes must have complex or major causes. We are reluctant to believe that a major fire with multiple casualties could have been caused by anything as trivial as a child's carelessness or an exposed wire. We are likely to search for more serious causes—parental neglect or arson. We are warned against this particular fallacy by the lines, 'For the want of a nail . . . the rider was lost'. We are encouraged to fall victim to it by the saying that. 'Desperate problems need desperate remedies'.

Allied to this source of error perhaps is our tendency to think in metaphorical terms, as an examination of ordinary language will show—see Lakoff and Johnson (1980). The best way to deal with metaphorical expressions in a case study, once one has noticed them, is to secure a literal or more factual translation of the image. For example, on hearing that a person is 'living on a knife edge' or is 'tied in knots' one should ask the simple question 'What do you mean?' in the hope that the person's circumstances, behaviour, and state of mind will be described in literal terms. Some metaphors are like 'frames and scripts' in the sense that they refer to a sequence of events that occurs under certain conditions. Consider, for example, phrases like 'sell-out', 'domino effect', 'bluffing', 'too many cooks', 'too much to lose', even 'Murphy's law'. These are commonly used in daily life and are well understood. One encounters metaphors in case-studies, e.g. 'bad apple', 'emotional blackmail', 'boxed in', 'case-hardened', 'cool off'. These are used to draw attention to the possibility of a familiar sequence of events. The problem is how to decide whether or not the metaphor (which is serving a heuristic function) applies, and, if so, how it applies in the particular case.

One problem with heuristic inference is that it can work well in some circumstances and badly in others. The point is to check that one is using an appropriate heuristic. For example, having had a series of reliable items of information about one case from a colleague provides a strong warrant for accepting another item of information on the same topic from the same source; it does not necessarily provide as strong a warrant for accepting an item of information about a different case.

Another subtle feature of social judgments, even when based on inadequate evidence and argument, is that they tend to be self-fulfilling. Many social judgments take the form of predictions or expectations. If there are few or no substantial constraints on the outcome, our own actions may be instrumental in bringing about the result we anticipated. Persistence plays a part, no doubt, but in situations like school discipline the expectation that a boy will make trouble may induce behaviour on the part of a teacher that increases the likelihood that the boy will make trouble (or that any behaviour he engages in will be construed as making trouble). If we believe someone can be persuaded, we persist in our efforts and increase the likelihood or persuading him. If we expect people to be aggressive and competitive, we tend to behave in ways which make such behaviour more likely. In the study of individual cases, therefore, we should not be surprised to find that our judgments seem to be borne out (but not for the reasons we suppose!).

The realization that much of one's reasoning about other people is implicit or tacit may come as a surprise to many readers. But when we consider other aspects of our behaviour which are largely automatic (normally outside awareness)—language, for example, where we follow complex rules of syntax, semantics, and pragmatics often without knowing what the rules are—perhaps we need not feel so surprised. One can improve one's command of language by reflecting on one's use of language and by becoming more scientific and more professional in one's approach to language. Similarly, one can reflect on one's understanding of oneself and other people and one can become more scientific and professional in one's approach to the logic and psychology of individual cases, although common sense and ordinary language are sufficient for understanding normal behaviour in every-day life.

Ordinary language and common sense make it possible, for example, to shift the focus of one's analysis from the person to the situation, i.e. from dispositional factors to situational factors, from 'He is aggressive' to 'He is being provoked'. A logically complete explanation of a person's action, however, is not possible because any explanation could, in theory, be embedded in a fuller, more inclusive explanation. In practice, all that is needed is an explanation that satisfies the person who is puzzled by the person's actions. The merit of a scientific and professional case-study is that it goes deeper into the puzzle, as it were, than common sense and ordinary language will permit. This is because it can make use of technical concepts and methods not available to the lay person, and because its function is to explore the limits of psychological analysis (within the resources available and within the overall institutional framework)—see Chapter 9.

Many of the terms we use in the social and behavioural sciences are derived from ordinary language and defined in common-sense terms, unlike many of the technical terms we use to refer to the physical world. Thus, terms like 'fair', 'reasonable', 'promising', and their opposites, as well as terms that describe people, like 'shy', 'difficult', 'aggressive', 'devious', cannot be used effectively in discourse about individual cases unless there is explicit agreement on their meaning. The meaning of the word depends upon the situational context and the sentence in which it is used. A useful defence against the power of words to mislead is to check constantly on what the words actually refer to: In what ways exactly is a person being 'difficult', 'aggressive', or 'devious'? Could those sorts of behaviour be interpreted differently—for example, as 'confused', 'resentful', or 'mistrustful'?

The mental processes we call reasoning are by no means always conscious and under voluntary control. We also sometimes credit ourselves, wrongly, with reasoning in a certain way. Freudian rationalizations and self-justifications are the clearest examples of this phenomenon. It follows, of course, that the accounts we obtain from the Subject of a case-study, and from other informants, do not necessarily correctly represent those individuals' states of mind, even when they give their account in good faith. One should try to find evidence independent of subjective reports. We are not arguing against the use of subjective reports; psychological case-studies could not proceed without them. All we are doing is counselling caution: do not accept them at face-value and do not rely on them exclusively. This is particularly important in situations where the subjective accounts of informants are confounded with one another, that is, where they have shared the same pool of information and exchanged views on the issue. In some cases, everyone can be wrong!

When making decisions about cases we typically think in terms of 'family resemblances'. In other words, whilst recognizing a wide array of instances as belonging to a particular category, such as 'good mother', 'efficient secretary', or 'difficult colleague', we have in mind a sort of 'prototype' or modal image of members of a category. When we make judgments about individual people we compare them with this prototype to see whether they possess sufficient characteristics to be regarded as a member of that category (family). Thus, in selecting a candidate for a job, or in looking for a sexual partner, or choosing the best treatment for a patient, one tries to estimate the extent to which the person matches one's prototypical image. This type of thinking obviously has similarities with what we commonly call 'pigeonholing' or 'stereotyping'.

The difficulties we encounter as a consequence of mistaken social judgment may be attributed in part to emotional and motivational factors—selfishness, anxiety, and so on. But perhaps some of our emotional problems are traceable to the shortcomings of social judgment? It may be extremely difficult to extricate ourselves from misleading and damaging patterns of thought, especially if such ways of thinking have hitherto been successful and if, for one reason or another, our ideas are supported by other people. The examples which suggest themselves are members of political and religious sects, scientists not yet converted from a demonstrably outdated theory, children who resist genuine efforts to help them. Since their ideas relate to values of central psychological importance to them, it is not surprising that their social misjudgment and emotional involvement go hand in hand. The illusion of being right is easily sustained, as may be seen by the way most people vigorously defend their points of view. Indeed, a person who is rationally diffident about his theories and judgments is likely to be dismissed as vague and ineffectual—a liberal or a 'wet'.

We are probably better at identifying the biases and limitations of other people's thinking rather than our own, as may be observed in any argument or case-conference.

Informal social inference, with all its biases and limitations, is so widespread and natural that we must regard it as normal. It is the scientific and professional approach to human problems which is unusual. It is unusual because it is not commonly observed! It is technical, difficult, laborious, and not immediately rewarding. It is likely to remain a minority interest. What is puzzling is the evolutionary advantage of the forms of reasoning we have criticized so severely. Perhaps these forms of thinking worked well enough in mankind's early days but are not so well-adapted to modern needs. If so, we obviously need a 'science' of human nature more than we thought.

LOGICAL FALLACIES AND OTHER MISTAKES

No account of the logic of any area of human thinking would be complete without some reference to the fallacies that abound there. The fallacies I shall briefly describe and illustrate in this section are the sort referred to in standard introductory textbooks—see Chapter 9.

There are so many ways in which reasoning can go wrong that it would be difficult, perhaps impossible, to enumerate and classify them. The errors we are concerned with are those to which reasoning about people seems particularly prone. We deal with seventeen of them in this section.

   (i) Failing to register that a significant element in an argument is missing. This can occur when one assumes or feels confident that an argument is complete and correct, when making the latent structure explicit reveals its weakness, omissions, and perhaps its falsity. For example, 'Joan is very intelligent, so she should do well at university' neglecting that Joan is not interested in study or has heavy family responsibilities. Our preconceptions may introduce bias into our interviewing of the Subject and informants in a case-study. For example, if we think that a person is an ineffective manager our inquiries may be biased in that direction (neglecting inquiries we might make to establish that he is an effective manager).

  (ii) Making unwarranted assumptions. This is similar to (i) except that the assumption is introduced explicitly if mistakenly. For example, 'Joan is generous so she must be well-paid, since she needs a high salary to pay for the style of life she leads.' But in fact Joan is not particularly well-paid; she has private means and invests her money effectively.

 (iii) Overgeneralizing from small or biased samples. This is a previously mentioned error to which we are particularly prone. We are likely to form impressions from brief encounters, or in unrepresentative circumstances. For example, we ride as a passenger in a person's car; she drives fast (on that occasion); we conclude that she is a fast driver. We hear someone tell a funny joke; we conclude that he is a humorous, sociable person. The error lies in not recognizing the difference between an isolated incident and a reliable, representative sample of observations.

　　We fall victim to this common fallacy by not taking the trouble to test for exceptions (negative instances). Thus, for example, we may conclude, on the basis of single instances, that teachers at a particular school are not very good, that social workers are of no help, or that general practitioners have no time for drug addicts. It should be obvious that such generalizations would not stand up to critical examination, no matter how strong the conviction. Vivid, compelling instances play a major role in the heuristics and biases associated with social judgment.

  (iv) Failing to detect ambiguities and vagueness. For example, if I am told that 'Joan is a lovely girl', I may conclude that she is beautiful, only to find she is just good! Some psychological terms are ambiguous, many are vague. Consider, for example, the meaning of the following terms: aggressive, nice, well-read, cold, clever. A useful procedure in a discussion is to ask the question 'How do you mean—aggressive? nice? clever?', and so on. This obliges your informant to give you more factual data, which you may then prefer to label differently—as resentful, obsequious, fast talker, and so on.

(v) Using a general rule which is not applicable to the particular case. It is well known that 'circumstances alter cases', that the context of an event helps to determine the meaning of that event. Failing to bear this in mind can lead to errors in reasoning. For example, if, as a general rule, supervisors can be relied upon to deal fairly with their subordinates, it does not necessarily follow that this particular supervisor dealt fairly with this particular subordinate on this particular occasion. Of course, the burden of proving the claim that he did not rests on the person who makes the charge.

(vi) Making claims in a way which denies even the possibility of proving them false. It is worth repeating our reference to this well-known and widespread deviation from scientific thinking. It has been analysed in considerable detail by Popper (1969). For example, if I assert that Joan is evil, untrustworthy, or psychic, nothing you can say and nothing you can bring forward as evidence need be accepted by me, for I can always find a way of interpreting what you say in a way that leaves my claim intact: Joan's good deeds are devious, her friendliness is hypocritical, her ordinariness shows you never can tell.

(vii) Mistaking metaphors for literal statements. Ordinary language can mislead us in many ways. For example, if I say, 'Joan follows him around like a dog' I do not expect to be taken literally. I simply want to indicate, in a forceful way, my contempt for slavish women. Ordinary language abounds with metaphors. They are such an integral part of common-sense thinking about people that we rarely stop to examine their function. Consider, for example, words and phrases like: hard, stress, sticky, in a rut, at the end of one's tether, fed up. They convey a general impression and a certain emotional quality, but they need to be translated into objective behavioural terms if they are to convey anything of professional or scientific worth. Analogies, similes, metaphors, and other images or figures of speech can conceal as much as they reveal about the person referred to. False analogies are particularly misleading if the superficial resemblances are close. For example, to say that a person's aggression is like a head of steam which will explode if there is no outlet may lead one to permit or even encourage certain kinds of aggression, when the problem might be that the person needs to learn how to recognize and manage, i.e. 'contain', ordinary forms of hostility.

(viii) Begging the question. This is a well-known logical fallacy; it means arguing in a circle, so that one's conclusion is justified by one's evidence, but one's evidence is the same as the conclusion. For example, 'He is not a loyal union member because he crossed the picket-line; no loyal union members cross picket-lines.' Related to the fallacy of begging the question is the fallacy of habitually bracketing (collocating) certain words, e.g. ordinary housewife, young hopeful, loyal friend, clean and tidy. The fact that characteristics sometimes or even frequently go together does not mean that they go together in a particular instance. Perhaps the best example in the psychological study of individual cases is using an implicit subjective theory of personality where it does not apply—for example, assuming that because a person is rich and intelligent he is also well-educated and has lots of friends. The best example in the study of social behaviour is using a social stereotype— assuming that because a person is a Jew, a Jamaican, or a university teacher, they possess the modal characteristics of that category of person. Ordinary language provides us with a convenient way of avoiding such traps. The use of such words as 'but', 'although', or a phrase like 'except that', instructs the reader or listener not to make the usual inference. For example: 'He is good-hearted but easily angered.' 'He is a university teacher but not very good at public speaking.'

(ix) Evading the issue. This is a fallacy in the sense that it prevents one from forming or appreciating a reasonable argument. For example, if you say to someone 'The reason he (a third person) is being so awkward is that he is trying to beat you at your own game', a reply to the effect that, 'Everybody is entitled to their opinion' is evading the issue.

(x) Appealing to authority or using threats rather than reason and evidence. This means moving outside the bounds of scientific or professional argument. For example, to say, 'The headmaster agrees that John is the culprit' is merely to offer hearsay evidence, it does not clinch the argument. To say 'Your opinion will get you into trouble with the authorities' is a warning about the possible consequences of certain actions, not a refutation of the correctness of the opinion.

(xi) Criticizing the proponent of the argument rather than the argument itself, or condemning the argument out of hand. This too goes outside the bounds of reason and sense. To say 'You are silly to say that' is not a logical refutation of the argument even though it might be true. Similarly, to say 'Your argument is crazy' should be no more than a fanfare preceding your demonstration of the logical gaps and weaknesses in your opponent's argument.

(xii) Appealing to majority opinion. Such appeals are expressed in statements like 'Everybody knows that . . .' or 'Most scientists agree that . . .'. This is a common sort of fallacy. The fallacy consists in supposing that 'Everybody' or 'Most scientists', or whoever the majority are, cannot be wrong. But it is not at all uncommon for majority opinion to be wrong.

(xiii) Accepting a conclusion because it has not been falsified. This is a more subtle fallacy—see (vi) above. Having a *presumption* in favour of some outcome until such time as it is proved false is rather different from *entertaining* an idea in order to test it. So, for example, if I believe that 'Joan is unlikely to get married', your failure to convince me otherwise is taken as confirming my conclusion, although, of course, it does no such thing. One's feelings of confidence in one's views should not be allowed to obstruct critical evaluation of them.

(xiv) Thinking that the exception proves the rule. For example, if I say I know for a fact that a particular policeman is 'straight', I may get the reply that this exception proves the rule that policemen are crooked. The fallacy lies in taking the wrong meaning of the word 'prove' as 'to show proof' instead of the correct meaning 'to test'. Exceptions test rules. In other words, to find one straight policeman tests (and *falsifies*) the assertion that policemen are crooked.

(xv) Appealing to abstract values such as justice or desirability. For example, to say 'But that's not fair' or 'That's not nice' may be true, but it does not affect the logic of the argument.

(xvi) Playing on people's emotions. Appealing to people's hopes and fears may be an effective form of persuasion, but it does not bear on the logic of rational argument. For example, to say 'He's committed murder, so he should suffer the death penalty, otherwise we'll all be dead in our beds before long' is to make an emotional appeal almost completely obscuring the rational argument in favour of capital punishment for certain types of offence.

(xvii) Mistaking contiguity or association for causality. If event B follows event A we are inclined to think that A caused B. But consider the following disclaimers: The fact that John was in possession of a stolen article does not mean that he stole it. The fact that my wife was engaged in back-seat driving just before I crashed the car does not mean she caused me to crash the car.

In general, then, fallacies are part of our everyday reasoning about people. Moving to professional and scientific levels of understanding and managing other people means being able to recognize them and avoid them.

SUMMARY AND CONCLUSIONS

The first and most important step in reducing the risks of error in thinking about individual cases is to realize that such risks exist, and that they are extensive. This step should include the realization that there is much one can do to minimize these errors.

Second, ask what preconceptions and assumptions underlie one's reasoning. Critically examine the plausibility of the arguments one is using. Make the content and organization of these arguments explicit.

Third, ask whether all possible reasonable interpretations of the evidence have been considered. Search for evidence that runs counter to one's theory, as well as evidence in favour of it. Make sure that the best available evidence is being used, and in sufficient quantity to secure a relatively clear-cut conclusion or recommendation.

Fourth, check that the various natural but fallible strategies of inference—simple resemblances, stereotypes, metaphors, easily available and emotionally compelling experiences (vivid instances), biased samples, samples that are too small, reliance on positive instances and atypical instances, hearsay evidence, familiar but inappropriate schemata (plans, scripts, procedures), and so on—are not being used as proofs, but only as leads to further investigation.

Fifth, consider the extent to which formal strategies of inference and reliance on 'objective knowledge' might not only be possible but also more cost-effective. This means employing more sophisticated technical methods of inquiry and data collection of the sort associated with psychometric assessment, business decision-making, judicial and quasi-judicial inquiries, and using public records, survey data, scientific research findings, archival material.

Sixth, ask whether the notion of base-rate is relevant to the inquiry; and, if so, whether the appropriate base-rate can be determined objectively. Similarly, ask whether one's judgment is biased by the effects of statistical regression.

Seventh, try to avoid the biasing effects of emotional involvement. Adopt a professional and scientific attitude towards the case.

Eighth, avoid errors in attributing causes, reasons, praise, and blame. Do not confuse contiguity or correlation with causality.

Ninth, make allowances for the way social judgment is affected by personal frames of reference (subjective standards of judgment). These can be shaped by experience of previous cases in such a way as to anchor the upper and lower limits of the range of one's subjective scale at too high or too low a level, thus biasing one's judgment of a particular case, e.g. with regard to educability, employability, liability to abscond, or strength of marital bond.

Tenth, question the veracity of first-hand testimony, especially if it is given some considerable time after the event, or if the Subject/witness/informant has anything to gain by it. Note that evidence given against the informant's own interest is generally regarded as reliable.

Consider, finally, another list of what is needed in a scientific and professional approach to the psychological study of individual cases: (i) an ability and willingness to employ scientific methods; (ii) a thoroughly professional attitude in relation to ethics and skills; (iii) an appreciation of the common fallacies in reasoning and of the inadequacies of lay inference; (iv) a grasp of the social psychology of groups and communication, including an understanding of debating techniques (not forgetting rhetoric and dirty tricks); (v) expertise in a given area, i.e. being able to understand and use psychological methods and factors in one or more areas of personal adjustment at a common-sense level as well as at a deeper technical level; (vi) a general understanding of the psychology of problem-solving, its theory and practice; (vii) some acquaintance with planning and decision-making of the sort associated with business studies; (viii) some acquaintance with descriptive and inferential statistics and with techniques of information-retrieval; (ix) some understanding of formal logic and of the computational possibilities associated with artificial intelligence; (x) an understanding of the complexities of ordinary spoken and written language and of the processes of conceptual analysis in so far as they affect the technical issues in psychological cases, including an awareness of the forms of language used in accounting for individual behaviour and social relationships; (xi) a grasp of the nature of arguments which go beyond formal logic and involve forms of practical reasoning that purport to represent the real world; (xii) a grasp of such other skills and facts that may affect one's competence in dealing with psychological cases in their particular contexts, for example, those related to the law, to health, welfare, and safety.

In addition to the complexities associated with problem-solving, logical analysis, psychological analysis, decision-making, and social judgment, one must not forget those perennial human factors—ignorance, stupidity, corruption, and negligence—all of which, unfortunately, must be guarded against in ourselves and in others.

Our view of heuristics and biases in human inference runs counter to the view that the lay person is a sort of scientist dealing with the world in a rational, if limited, way. The view we have set out is that lay persons are primarily practitioners not scientists. They develop tacit (implicit) techniques of representation and judgment and habitual modes of action in the process of coping with real-life situations. It is mainly at the collective level (Popper's 'third-world' of objective knowledge) and in relation to major problems of survival, health, and welfare, that people develop more sophisticated techniques of representation, judgment, and control. These are the techniques we refer to as scientific, professional, and technical. The social and behavioural aspects of human survival, health, and welfare have only recently become collective enterprises, and so still have a long way to go.

Readers are reminded that the forms of thinking normally used in case-studies—detailed description and analysis of individual instances, comparing and contrasting cases, categorizing, learning from examples and forming prototype images—seem to be fairly natural and long-established. Reasoning in psychological case-studies is therefore in double jeopardy, first from cognitive biases and misleading heuristics, second from the distortions arising from emotional involvement in the subject-matter. By comparison, other scientific methods of inquiry are safer, although they may not provide access to the sorts of knowledge we can derive from case-studies.

CHAPTER ELEVEN

Further Considerations

A NOTE ON TERMINOLOGY

The term 'psychological case-study' could be defined as any systematic account of a person in a situation provided that account is based on empirical evidence and rational methods of inference. This definition would include not only the sorts of cases we have described or referred to so far, but also a wide variety of cases studied for professional or scientific reasons, e.g. disabled persons, political hostages, discharged psychiatric patients, violent criminals, shoplifters, factory managers, school refusers, and single parents.

Some individuals are closely studied by writers and commentators because of their public interest or importance as politicians, artists and writers, entertainers, people in unusual circumstances (having won a lottery, survived an ordeal, propounded a startlingly new view of nature, society or history), and so on. Reports on these individuals too are accounts of 'persons in situations', i.e. 'cases' broadly defined. Such accounts are found in books, films, newspaper and magazine reports, radio and television documentaries. They are often not carried out according to the sorts of professional and scientific standards that apply to psychological case-studies narrowly defined. Indeed, they may deliberately misrepresent the subject in the interests of propaganda, publicity, or profit.

What is the difference between an 'individual case-study' report and a 'personality description'? The main difference is that the case-study considers the person in relation to a situation, whereas a personality description considers the person in general terms. The term 'personality description' usually refers to the sorts of brief, partial assessment made by Investigators on the basis of interviews, test results, direct observation, informants' reports, and so on. Personality descriptions of various sorts from different sources may find their way into the case-record or into the communication network associated with the case. We also tend to use the term 'personality description' to refer to the ordinary language, common-sense accounts people give of their casual subjective impressions of a person in daily life—see Bromley (1977). A case-study report, by contrast, is a much more formal and extended assessment.

Consider next the relationship between a 'performance appraisal' and a 'psychological case-study'. In some instances the relationship is clear, because the performance being appraised, e.g. occupational effectiveness, is fairly broad and says a lot about the individual's characteristics and circumstances. In other instances the relationship is obscure, because the performance being appraised is narrow, e.g. a driving test, or an audition for a choir. Even in these sorts of instance, however, the term 'case-study', but not 'psychological case-study', could be stretched to include them, because although the performance is narrow it could be examined in fine detail and a complex argument developed to support the decision to pass or fail. An experienced tester or auditioner should have no difficulty in citing case-studies of individuals he or she has examined and passed judgment on.

In general, then, the term 'psychological case-study' can be used loosely to refer to a wide variety of assessments of persons in situations. Psychological case-studies narrowly defined as scientific or professional are fairly formal, systematic studies of people, but not necessarily comprehensive or deep. They can be reported orally or in writing. Thus they include personality assessments, reports by selection committees, political profiles, as well as the more detailed studies carried out by social workers, clinical and community psychologists, educational psychologists, psychiatrists, management selection consultants, probation officers, counsellors, and secret agents.

PSYCHOLOGICAL CASE-STUDIES AS A SCIENTIFIC ENTERPRISE

If we adopt the view of Toulmin *et al.* (1979, pp. 230 ff.) we can say that a scientific approach to the study of individual cases must have four basic features. (i) It must give a scientific account of a number of broad and familiar issues about why people behave as they do. (ii) It must provide systematic bodies of knowledge that can be drawn on by scientists and practitioners, together with a means of improving these bodies of knowledge. (iii) It must rely on certain categories of people—scientists and practitioners, academic scholars, administrators—to sustain the enterprise. (iv) It must depend on accepted procedures and institutional arrangements.

(i) What broad and familiar issues are we concerned with? Briefly, we are concerned with what sorts of people there are, how they come to terms with their environment, what makes their behaviour of special interest (whether because it is deviant, difficult to understand, pathological, heroic, superior, or a source of expense), how such behaviour comes about, how it can be understood and managed in the interests of society and the individual.

(ii) What constitute the systematic bodies of knowledge that practitioners can draw on? Psychology and those parts of the social and biomedical sciences that are relevant to the psychological study of individual cases comprise a loosely related, widely scattered family of interests, not a coherent systematic discipline. This is unfortunate perhaps, but unavoidable. It does not prevent us from trying to develop systematic procedures for representing psychological cases. Schemes of content-analysis, report forms, personality profiles, diagnostic procedures, checklists, and case-study formats are all attempts to represent and conceptualize certain aspects of human behaviour. This book is itself a contribution to the case-study enterprise in that it is an attempt to foster systematic thinking and clearer procedures for representing individual cases—see also Runyan (1983).

(iii) What categories of people are responsible for sustaining and developing the psychological study of individual cases? As a consequence of the underdeveloped and fragmented character of psychology (and partly as a consequence of psychology's historical preference for other sorts of scientific enterprise), there are few people engaged in developing the 'science' of individual cases, although a great many are engaged in 'practice' with individual cases.

Regrettably idiographic psychology has not made a great deal of progress and has been greatly overshadowed by the psychometric approach to individual differences. There is no public scientific forum to discuss basic issues, and the various practitioner forums—social work, clinical psychology, probation, community psychology, psychiatry, counselling, educational psychology, and so on—are generally concerned with the minutiae of individual cases, not with the broader conceptual and methodological issues. There are no scientific journals devoted to the study of individual cases—no *Journal of Idiographic Psychology*—and very little opportunity to publish material on case-studies as contributions to 'scientific' knowledge. Of course, published case-notes add to the pool of knowledge in particular areas or illustrate an argument, but this does not do much to help to develop the theory and practice of psychological case-studies. It may be that this area of study cannot be brought into effective existence until the case-study method is accepted as basic to scientific and professional work with people.

(iv) What procedures and institutional arrangements are found in the psychological study of individual cases? How do they affect arguments about cases? As social or behavioural scientists our preference must be for procedures and institutional arrangements that foster cooperation and seek consensus within a framework of realistic evaluation. As professional practitioners our preference must be for arrangements that result in decisions and actions which bring about outcomes in the best interests of everyone concerned (in so far as these can be established equitably and realistically). We try to avoid adversarial procedures, whilst learning from them.

Case-studies take place in the context of the cultural conditions prevailing at the time, and can be understood only in relation to those conditions. Cultural factors include, for example, traditional procedures, prevailing beliefs and values, local norms, and role-relationships. These local cultural conditions help to determine why and how cases get started in the first place, how they are and should be handled, how they are judged on completion, and how their outcomes in turn affect the surrounding cultural norms and values, as in parental rights, women's rights, promotion procedures, disciplinary procedures, or adoption.

The social significance of a case-study varies, depending upon who is considering it. Onlookers and 'public opinion' are likely to be concerned with the broad moral and political aspects of a case or with its cost. Subjects, and parties with a personal interest in the outcome, are concerned with the particular effects of decisions. Scientists and professionals—the experts—are concerned, among other things, with procedural issues, i.e. with techniques and conceptual analysis.

It is possible to identify at least five sorts of problem that we can call 'procedural'. The first problem is about how the case is to be carried out: How is one to handle the person's psychological state and his or her behaviour? How is one to deal with the practical circumstances that surround the case? The second problem is about how the case-study is to be evaluated on completion: Who decides its validity and worth? And by what means? The third is about the consequences of any conclusions, decisions, or recommendations made: How are their effects to be monitored? Who takes responsibility? The fourth is about the way the case is incorporated into the general body of knowledge dealing with cases of that kind: Who publicizes the information? How is it assimilated by others? How does it become part of case-law? The fifth problem is about the way case-studies are used to justify more general decisions—for example, about organizational policy. For example, how will the findings affect other related cases? What changes are called for in institutional arrangements?

In brief, a psychological case-study is a scientific enterprise embedded in an historical and cultural framework; but this framework does no more than condition and limit the advancement of knowledge and its application. In this respect the case-study method is no different from any other kind of scientific enterprise.

THE ONTOLOGICAL STATUS OF CASE-STUDIES

The abstruse heading of this subsection is intended to draw attention to a curious issue in the psychological study of individual cases. The issue is how a case-study can be said to exist. It is obvious that a psychological case-study is normally *about* a particular person and is carried out in order to understand and/or deal with that person more effectively. But in what forms does the case-study itself *exist*? How would you recognize one if you came across it? How could you demonstrate the existence of a case-study?

The more obvious forms of existence are to be found in materials or other phenomena labelled 'case-studies', e.g. written reports, printed articles in the scientific and professional literature, the personal folders containing case-notes and other documents in various organizations such as prisons, schools, and hospitals.

Only in rare instances would one expect to be misled about these forms of case-study. Someone might deliberately fake material—as a joke or for some criminal purpose. One might only recognize the fact after close investigation of the internal reliability and external validity of the case-materials.

The logic or 'grammar' of case-studies is often psychologically robust in the sense that one can make quite substantial alterations to the text of a case, and yet retain a convincing structure, i.e. an account that makes sense, is internally coherent, and has no obvious features that invalidate it. Accounts of 'persons in situations' in novels provide the ultimate examples of fictional case-studies—see Bromley (1977). This raises the interesting and important question of how Investigators detect internal incoherence and external invalidity in real-life studies. Presumably only by the application of objective real-world knowledge through empirical testing.

The same argument applies to case-studies in the form of verbal presentations—lectures, informal talks, brief demonstrations. It is possible to distort cases so much, or to completely invent them, so that although they have all the appearances of a psychological case-study, they are in fact no such thing. Some films, television documentaries, journalistic accounts, and various other forms of representation are presented as real-life case-studies, but are so far removed from fact as to constitute some other kind of entity.

The examples are not trivial. They illustrate how difficult it might be in practice to separate fact from fiction in a case-study. The difficulty is increased (a) if the omissions and distortions in the case-materials and summaries occur in spite of scientific and professional effort, and (b) if the information about a case is distributed among many different people and not recorded in a centralized permanent or semi-permanent form.

We have dealt with the first of these difficulties in some detail throughout this book. The second difficulty deserves some comment. Consider first of all a case-study carried out by one person, or maybe two or three people, working for a voluntary organization. The case may be of a relatively simple, straightforward, familiar sort. The Investigator(s) may not record any information, except perhaps a few notes comprehensible only to themselves as an aide-memoire. The case-study then has no material existence (we are not yet in a position to locate it in the Investigator's cortex!). It exists, in so far as it can be said to exist at all, as a set of mental states in the mind(s) of the Investigator(s); and it is liable to all the distortions associated with attention, memory, and affect.

If the information available to each of several Investigators can be made available to all, and if, in the process, a measure of agreement can be reached about the facts and about how the facts are to be interpreted, then we move into what Popper (1973) would call the 'third world' of objective knowledge, meaning intersubjective agreement between competent Investigators prepared to deal with an issue rationally and empirically.

On this interpretation, therefore, a psychological case-study can exist at one level as a subjective mental state in the mind of just one person, to the extent that the person is operating rationally and empirically in his or her thinking about, and dealings with, the Subject of the case-study. This separates out fictional cases, semi-fictional cases, and inadequately constructed cases, from psychological case-studies proper.

At the next level a psychological case-study can exist as a collection of subjective states in the minds of several persons, again to the extent that they are operating rationally and empirically. These subjective states do not need to be the same in one person as in another; but obviously there must be some common elements. The participants must share knowledge of the identity of the Subject, and share at least some knowledge of and views about the Subject's characteristics and circumstances. Apart from these minimum requirements, the persons involved in the case may have access to different sorts of information, have different ideas and feelings about the case, and want action of different sorts. What we have just described in fact represents a common situation as regards scientific and professional levels of case-study.

At the next level a case-study can exist not only as a collection of subjective states in the minds of the Investigators and other active participants, but also as a system of material records. Typically, the material records comprise personal folders containing admission details, identification details, case-notes, correspondence, medical test reports, reports and forms associated with nursing, education, social work, probation, psychology, administration, the law, case-conference reports, progress reports, life-history data, and family relationships reports. The material record depends upon the nature of the case, the organization responsible for the case, and the effectiveness of the record-keeping system. In some organizations there is a centralized system of personal case-files, so that in theory all the Investigators have access to all the information. In other organizations there is a decentralized system, or some mixture of the two. Needless to say, there is more information about (in the minds of the participants) than can be found in the case-records. The information in the case-records is often patchy, illegible, outdated, and variable in amount and quality; it represents only a fraction of what is known (objectively) or believed (subjectively) about a case. Nevertheless, it is an important fraction and very important, if issues of a legal sort arise, because documentary evidence is generally regarded as 'good' evidence in law. Case-records may have latent, i.e. hidden, functions—see Blankenship (1974), Bush (1984), Cicourel (1974), Garfinkel (1974), Holbrook (1983) and Wheeler (1969).

Perhaps the highest level of existence for a case-study is a detailed published report based on a consensus of opinion among the persons best able to understand and deal with the case, and containing whatever material is necessary for independent observers to examine its internal reliability and external validity. Such case-studies are extremely rare. Sherwood (1969, p. 69) claims that there is scarcely a worthwhile case-study in the whole of the literature of scientific psychology. The majority of published cases appear to be brief reports designed to illustrate aspects of a theory or treatment—but see the relevant reference lists in Chapter 1.

'HIGHER-ORDER' CASE-STUDIES AND THE SOCIAL PSYCHOLOGY OF REPUTATION

In our discussion of the ontological status of case-studies, we asked the philosophical question, 'In what forms can a case-study exist?' We saw that a case may be pursued and recorded not by one person, but rather by several interested parties, each with a different perspective on the case, and each with a different set of facts and interpretations to work with. In such circumstances the case-study as a whole exists only in a 'collective' sense. It is the sum total of the information available to the interested parties together with their various points of view. Considered as a whole, the information about a case-study is likely to be fragmented and disorganized—a mere collection of overlapping but disparate accounts.

The difficulty then is that unless the information and interpretations about a case are fully shared and agreed between all the people who are actively involved in it, the resulting account may be incoherent, contradictory, incomplete, unsatisfactory, and ineffective. The clearest cases of this kind arise when the findings of an inquiry are disputed by an interested party, or when the outcome of an inquiry is so disastrous as to require a re-examination of the case—consider cases of false imprisonment, historical errors, and child abuse. Investigative journalism and public inquiries provide many examples of cases of this kind—see Department of Health and Social Security (1974), Devlin (1976), Doig (1984), Jennings (1981), and Levine (1980) for example.

The psychoanalytic case of a phobia in a five-year-old boy—Freud (1953, 1977)—has been subjected to extensive scrutiny—see Cheshire (1979), Conway (1978), Eysenck (1965), Silverman (1980), Wolpe and Rachman (1960).

The essence of scientific and professional work with people is sharing information and ideas, and trying to reach an objective conclusion—an agreement which is satisfying, in its logic and evidence, to all the parties to the inquiry. In practice, failures of communication, shortcomings in scientific investigation, and lapses in professional competence can lead to serious failures of understanding and management in cases, and can create all kinds of dangers. There are dangers to the Subject of physical injury, financial loss, deprivation of liberty, for example, and dangers to the Investigators and other participants of public criticism, shame, and loss of livelihood.

If something untoward happens as a consequence of, or subsequent to, a case-study having been carried out, or if one or more parties to the inquiry remain dissatisfied with the outcome, then the scene is set for the case to be re-opened. We then have an inquiry into the original inquiry—a sort of second-order investigation. Investigations of an even higher order are possible, since there is no theoretical limit to the number of times a quasi-judicial case may be re-opened.

A higher-order case-study looks into the methods used to carry out the earlier investigation(s), the goodness and adequacy of the evidence employed, the validity of the reasoning used, the way the recommendations were implemented, and so on. It constitutes a sort of 'psychological post-mortem'—but rather different from the literal variety! See Weisman and Kastenbaum (1968) and Spencer *et al.* (1984) for psychological autopsies.

When is a case-study complete? For practical purposes the case-study could be regarded as complete when the issues which gave rise to the case-study and its continuation have been settled to the satisfaction of all concerned. This leaves open the option that a case-study may have to be terminated (as distinct from completed) even though the Investigators and other interested parties were not satisfied. This may come about because of lack of time and resources or because the Investigators cannot find a satisfactory solution. It also leaves open the option that a case-study may be completed prematurely—all concerned are satisfied but in fact the study is inadequate. Finally, the definition leaves open the option that a completed case-study may be re-opened by anyone interested enough and able to gain access to the case-records. I have referred to investigations of this sort as 'meta-case-studies' or 'second-order case-studies'. If successful, they impose a different interpretation on the evidence available and may be able to bring forward additional information to support the revision.

As illustrated by the cases of Patrick Mackay and Maria Colwell—see Clark and Penycate (1976) and Department of Health and Social Security (1974), the inquiries and information tend to be diffused, spread among a number of people. The professionals involved and the interested parties reach conclusions, make decisions, and take action within what may be a wide area of discretion and possibly without consulting with or informing other people connected with the case. If the case cuts across administrative and professional boundaries—social work, police, education, housing, health, and so on, or across departmental boundaries within an organization—there is an increased chance of confusion and failure to communicate.

Second-order case-studies invariably generate more information and ideas than were available originally; so it is not unusual for their findings to be at variance with the original. The very weaknesses and inadequacies of the original inquiry strengthen the resolve of the critics to have the case reopened.

If the parties to a case-study anticipate the possibility of a serious outcome, or if they suspect some kind of cover-up, scapegoating, or corruption, then it is essential that case-study methods of the highest standard are employed. This means keeping records that are more than merely adequate for routine purposes, transmitting information promptly to all concerned and keeping them fully informed, ensuring compliance with rules governing duties and actions, carrying out cross-checks on the extent to which people have fulfilled their roles, including office staff and other personnel.

Let us consider what happens when the various parties interested in a case do not share all the same information and views. Each individual observer and informant has some information (and possibly some misinformation) to contribute to the case. Their testimony and opinions find their way into the body of information and views held by the main parties to the inquiry. The parties to an inquiry may be quite numerous—social services, health services, education services, the police, the housing department, the media, and so on. Thus each party or organization has some information and some views about the Subject of the case-study and about the circumstances surrounding the case. Each party is also pursuing the case in some kind of context—private or professional—and may or may not appreciate the context within which other parties to the case are operating.

Now, in some instances, the information and opinion is common to two or more individuals or organizations. In other instances, it is not shared. The situation is represented in Figure 11.1. This figure provides a schematic representation of the way information and views about a case might be distributed among the main parties or groups interested in or participating in the inquiry. The lozenges represent the information and views shared between some or all the individuals within a named group—neighbours, social services, and so on. Each group can contribute different kinds and amounts of information and different sorts of opinions on the issues in the case. Some of the information is shared between two or more groups. Some information (the shaded areas) is not shared outside the group. In this particular illustration no single person and no single group has access to all the information and opinions. The scene is set, therefore, for confusion, misunderstanding, and mismanagement, because each group has formed an account of the case that is likely to differ from that of other groups.

The situation, of course, changes over time. Events take place, circumstances change, additional information is collected, new views are formulated, further information is shared, some information and opinions are lost or forgotten, new parties become interested in the case.

Failure to record and transmit information and ideas formally and informally throughout the social system which surrounds the case means that some or all of the key people involved in the case—the Investigators, those

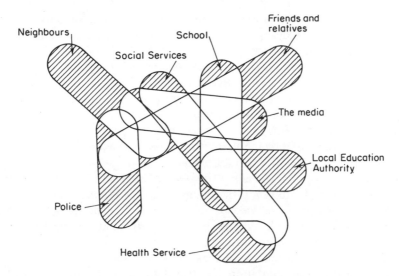

Figure 11.1 An example of the distribution of information about a case, shown schematically. *Note*: The lozenges represent the information and 'views' available to different parties to a case-study. Each party can contribute different kinds and amounts of information. Some information is shared between two or more groups. Some information (the shaded area) is not shared outside the group; but no group has access to all the information and views. See text for further discussion

responsible in a professional or 'public' capacity—may be unacquainted with important facts and possibilities. This can lead to failures at each and every stage of the case-study—formulating the problem, investigating the problem, finding the right solution, taking the appropriate action, and evaluating (following up) the outcome.

Ideally, organizational records should be proof against neglect by and the departure of individuals. We have in mind education records, medical records, police records, occupational records, and so on. A considerable amount of effort, and duplication of effort, is necessary to reduce the risks arising from lapses by individuals.

There are, of course, serious ethical and legal problems regarding the compilation of, maintenance of, and access to, confidential information about individual cases held by persons or organizations. The advent of computerized record-keeping has exacerbated these problems. The balance between individual privacy and the public interest is likely to shift with events and with changes in public opinion and government policy.

The foregoing account of higher-order case-studies and the distribution of information about a case among the interested parties has a bearing on the social psychology of reputation. Surprisingly little has been written about this topic, which has ramifications well beyond our concern with the psychological study of individual cases. We shall confine our attention to those aspects of the phenomenon of reputation that clarify our understanding of case-studies.

As we saw in our discussion of the ontological status of case-studies, a case-study must be formally agreed and published (in the sense of being written up and made available to others to consider) before it can be regarded as objective knowledge. Objective knowledge is a social product, not an individual product, although its origins lie in personal subjective experience.

The objective case-study is therefore on public record, as it were, as the official account of the Subject. This account does not deal with the Subject in his or her entirety but only in relation to the issue(s) with which the case-study was concerned. The Subject's 'reputation', in so far as it is defined as 'what is generally known or believed about the person' has something in common with that official account. However, the phenomenon of reputation is not as simple as one might suppose. As we saw in Figure 11.1, little or nothing may be 'generally' known or believed about a person. Instead, the individual has as many reputations as there are social groups whose individual members happen to share (between themselves) a view of the Subject.

The Subject's local reputation is better defined as the sum total of what is known or believed about the person. When this sum total of information and opinion is examined—see Bromley (1966), it is found to consist of a small number of beliefs held by relatively high proportions of members of the relevant social groups, together with a large number of beliefs held by small proportions of members, or by only one member, of the relevant social groups. This form of distribution is J-shaped. Most people, of course, are not known at all outside their primary, local groups or their immediate secondary groups. Those individuals—celebrities—who are widely known are known only very indirectly and superficially, and often have a public image very different from their local reputation.

The Subject's local reputation thus corresponds to the sum total of the information and views available about him or her. This information and these views may or may not find their way into the formal, public account of the case, depending upon how the available information gets transmitted through the communication network, and depending upon what use the Investigators make of it, if indeed they become aware of it. The assessment of reputation presents something of a problem. Not only is it less easy than one might suppose to determine what is commonly known or believed about a person, it is also difficult to validate the grounds of such beliefs. In a court of law, evidence about a person's reputation may be introduced in the form of testimony by one or more witnesses, but no cross-examination is allowed becaue it would raise too many collateral issues. The quasi-judicial procedure is not so closely bound by the rules of evidence in law; so it is up to the Investigator(s) to decide, in a particular case, how far they need to go in exploring a person's reputation.

Without going into details, it is perhaps worth making one or two further points about the social psychology of reputation in relation to case-studies, if only because the issue is very neglected. First, reputation is a complex social process involving interpersonal relationships, communication networks, and psychological processes. It is not a simple reflection of the Subject's personality. Second, in so far as the Investigators think of the Subject in terms of his or her 'social stimulus value' (a traditional social definition of personality) they will confuse personality and reputation to the detriment of the case-study. Third, reputation has to do mainly with value-judgments and with the social esteem in which a person is held. Reputation (what people say) is thus an important determinant of human behaviour, in the sense that a person generally acts in such a way as to safeguard, maintain, and enhance his or her reputation—reputation can be 'managed'. This applies equally well to all the participants in a case-study—the Subject, the Investigator(s), and other participants. The implication is that the outcome of a case-study is likely to be influenced by the way it affects the reputations of all concerned. In other words, considerations of prestige, position, loss of face, and simple social discomfiture, may weaken and distort the scientific and professional framework of the case, and inhibit or misdirect the contributions made by the Subject, the informants, and other participants. Fourth, it could be argued that the Investigators have a duty to re-establish the Subject's reputation, and the reputation of any other participant, if their reputation has suffered unjustifiably as a consequence of the inquiry, by whatever means are available to them as part of their recommendations related to the case.

THE CONCEPT OF THE PROTOTYPICAL CASE

Human beings are so diverse, and the situations they encounter are so varied, that the possibilities for the resulting conduct are virtually infinite. It is of no help to say that each person is unique or that each situation is unique, therefore no classification of behaviour is possible. The world is made up of singularities. Our job as scientists and professionals is to systematize, interpret, and deal with these singularities. We do this by means of abstract concepts, empirical generalizations, rules, classifications, and other logical cognitive mechanisms. In this respect the psychological and social sciences are no different from the natural and biological sciences. In this discussion of prototypes in understanding and dealing with people, I draw attention to the problem of formulating the categories and rules needed in order to impose order and meaning on complex data.

It is of interest to note Rosch's work—see Rosch (1977, 1978) on the classification of natural objects and events. Case-studies can be used to develop model (typical or prototype) cases, and to distinguish sub-categories within a system of family resemblances. The fact that the problem of classification can be approached numerically, e.g. via cluster analysis, need not inhibit the development of case-law by comparing and contrasting individual cases qualitatively. Natural history and common law provide substantial grounds for the view that systematization, classification, and general rules can be developed *without* the aid of statistics.

Part of the problem of classifying and generalizing is defining the boundaries of the phenomenon one is investigating. This has to be done at the outset in statistical inference—one has to *define* the population of interest. In psychological case-studies, however, the task is more exploratory—of working out the defining characteristics of the phenomenon one is dealing with and *testing* its boundaries. It is a two-way process since one's theoretical analysis may help define a boundary, and finding a real-world boundary (by empirical means) may help shape one's theoretical analysis. Consider also, for example, the classification of diseases, or consumers, or types of crime, or literary genres, by systematic critical comparison and discrimination.

Having identified what one supposes is a typical case of interest, the usual procedure is to search for comparable cases in one's developing conceptual framework. As the number of cases increases the boundaries and the defining characteristics of that conceptual framework (the category) become clearer and firmer, so that the addition of yet more cases adds less and less to one's understanding—see Bertaux (1981). Cases which do not show a clear 'family resemblance' are excluded or perhaps placed in adjacent related categories. Thus one might set out to study sexual seduction, university professors in retirement, political constituency parties, child-rearing practices, and so on without being constrained by the usual demographic and sampling considerations because one is not interested in generalizing from sample to population, only in describing and analyzing categories of human behaviour or types of person.

Cantor and Mischel (1979) have used Rosch's concepts and methods to explore some of the 'natural' ways in which we describe and categorize persons rather than objects. Bromley (1977) has catalogued the forms of language we ordinarily use in describing people. These range all the way from highly specific observational reports through empirical generalizations and social stereotypes to very abstract and general inferences and value-judgments. Cantor and Mischel use the term 'prototype' to refer to a convenient level of abstraction at which a class of objects or persons can be described or conceptualized. Thus, for example, a typical or 'protypical' pencil has a number of attributes, being about 4 to 7 inches long, with a graphite rod enclosed in a round or hexagonal wooden tube about ¼ inch in diameter: at one end the wood is sharpened to expose a graphite point which is then impressed on paper to make marks. If you show me a short fat 'pencil' with a square section and a non-graphite, say wax, rod, I would have to say that it was not a very typical or protypical pencil—more a crayon or a 'fun-pencil'. I could similarly qualify propelling pencils, and pencil stubs.

Suppose now we consider what attributes a prototypical nurse, soldier, politician, psychologist, or schoolboy should have. We find that we can list a variety of characteristics for each category, and we find that membership in a category does not depend upon a person's possessing each of a fixed set of critical attributes, but rather on possessing enough relevant attributes to warrant being labelled nurse, politician, schoolboy, or whatever. Such categories are said to be 'fuzzy', meaning that they do not have very clear-cut membership boundaries and the members are not identical in every respect. Wittgenstein used the term 'family resemblances' to refer to these sorts of similarities between cases. Among the members, however, are prototypical individuals—clear exemplars who possess a relatively large number of the more relevant characteristics. These individuals are used as the standard which guides our thinking and behaviour in relation to people of that sort, i.e. type. However, even typical cases need not have all the basic attributes or display them invariably, even in situations where they would be expected.

Although a particular case might be selected as an instance of the class to which it is assumed to belong, and selected on the assumption that it represents that class, it is more usual to reason in the other direction. That is to say, a particular case is selected because it is interesting: it is studied in the context of a developing framework of ideas. When it is eventually conceptualized it may be regarded as a model case, i.e. a prototypical instance of a category of similar cases. The number of cases in that category might be large or small. The case might even be conceptualized as unique—as the only instance in its category. Even case-studies which report on highly unusual states of affairs must rely on some *general* principles of description and interpretation, otherwise there would be no way of making sense of them. It may prove impossible to identify comparable cases—comparable in the sense of having substantial similarities with the case in question. This does not render such a unique case scientifically worthless. On the contrary, such cases are analogous to unexpected discoveries following exploratory investigations. They may force a revision of accepted ideas; they may stimulate creative thinking through the puzzlement and interest they arouse.

Naturally, we can be mistaken in our beliefs about the characteristics of people of a given sort. This is clear from what we know about social prejudice and stereotypes. Nevertheless it is very convenient to be able to operate with a few clear abstract and general concepts rather than with a confusion of many varied particular facts. Such abstract and general notions as teacher, policeman, shop-assistant, friend, widow, retired scholar, vagrant, school refuser, and demented patient, guide our expectations and actions in social relationships. Similarly, terms like neurotic, aggressive, handsome, intelligent, hard-working, depressed, jealous, self-pitying, and calm, are prototypical concepts in the sense that we could list the sorts of attributes, actions, and circumstances that we could reasonably expect to be associated with these various conditions. The important point, again, is that the features associated with any one of these conditions do not constitute a fixed set of critical (essential) features but rather a wide range of possible features, some more common and more relevant than others. Consider, for example, the features exhibited in cases of apparent aggression or jealousy. Close examination might show that what looked at first like aggression is better described as indignation, and what looked like jealousy is more like spite. In other words the conceptual boundaries between certain kinds of psychological concepts are unclear or 'fuzzy'.

The image we have of the person in a situation is that of a *particular* case, but the use we make of it in the way we reason is the same as if it were a *general* case. The general case provides the logic of the argument; the particular case provides the image that fulfils a heuristic or pragmatic function. The image is the lever that applies the logic. The image (the particular case) is good enough for most practical purposes, but not good enough for theoretical purposes which require discursive analysis. In other words, the particular case derives its meaning from the general case which it represents. The particular case *resembles* the actual real case in its particulars, but *represents* the class of cases in its generalities.

Cantor and Mischel (1979) confirm the tendency for attributes to be fewer for categories at higher levels of abstraction and generality. For example, whereas one could list a large number of attributes describing a particular person, if one were to categorize that person as, say, a female dancer, then the number of attributes applicable to her and to typical members of such a category would be sharply reduced. If one were to categorize the person as simply an 'entertainer', the number of typical attributes would be further reduced. That is to say, it would become difficult to think of characteristics that entertainers in general (dancers, singers, comedians, and so on) have in common. Cantor and Mischel's experimental studies show how we tend to categorize and describe people at different levels of inclusiveness (abstraction and generality), thus illustrating the way our implicit theories of personality enable us to organize and interpret data about people. They indicate that the notion of a behavioural 'script'—see Schank and Abelson (1977)—can be thought of in terms of its level of abstractness and generality according to whether one is dealing with, say, a 'student' or a 'first-year student'. Our scripts, plans, and behaviour in relation to the Subjects of our case-studies are the product of relatively abstract forms of language and cognition that we have referred to variously as conceptual routines, case-laws, prototypes, and schemata, according to context. A conceptual routine for representing a case-study is a heuristic device brought into operation fairly early in the case-study with the intention of simplifying and speeding up the investigation. If it does not work, one has to resort to alternative routines or to more elaborate exploratory problem-solving procedures of the sort we have described in detail.

The notion of case-law is not peculiar to jurisprudence or to psychological case-studies. It can be found wherever the case-study method is used extensively—in business, education, the armed forces, sociology, anthropology, medicine, and so on; for, in each of these and many other areas, it is found that several, perhaps many, of the cases have common basic features. For example, a set of cases in business studies concerned with the problem of industrial innovation or absenteeism might have common features beneath their apparent differences—showing perhaps certain managerial characteristics or environmental stresses—see Parker (1982). In an 'extended case-study' or 'situational analysis' of an organization, a set of related case-studies might illuminate each other and demonstrate regularities in social processes and structures.

Psychological prototypes operate not only by identifying certain individuals as individuals of a given type, e.g. extrovert or lazy (and by identifying certain forms of behaviour as behaviour of a given type, e.g. generous or unprofessional), but also by *excluding* other persons (or forms of behaviour) from the given type, as not-extrovert or not-lazy, not-generous or not-unprofessional. Sometimes the excluded category forms a contrasting set, e.g. introvert or hardworking, mean or professional. At other times, members excluded from a given category of persons (or behaviours) are left amorphous and undefined, i.e. do not form a distinct or contrasting prototype. The forms of language available to us tend to limit our powers of description and analysis.

Prototypical cases play an important part in our conduct with regard to people, whether in a scientific or professional capacity or in our commonsense dealings with them in daily life. They give rise to vivid, easily remembered forms of thought and experience and easily expressed coherent forms of language. They play an important role in the organization of our behaviour in relevant situations—interviewing or advising a Subject, discussing a case at a case-conference, deciding how to deal with a friend or a neighbour. They probably provide the backing for our implicit theories of personality.

If we are in a situation where we have to predict what a person will do or what attributes they will have, then the initial information at our disposal triggers a suitable prototype, i.e. a familiar readily available conceptual template, which generates the appropriate implications. Thus if we are given to understand that the person we have been invited to listen to is a well-established American academic with an international reputation in artificial intelligence we will be surprised to find ourselves listening a young, attractive female who seems not to know about recent work in natural language processing and speaks with a French accent. Our implicit personality theory has generated expectations, based on prototypical cases in our experience, which, in this hypothetical situation, are not met.

Perhaps because of the lack of well-established bodies of case-law and a corresponding lack of psychological prototypes, there is a tendency for Investigators to resort to popular stereotypes or convenient professional labels with their facile implications for treatment—see, for example, Lee (1980), Cicourel (1974)—especially, perhaps, in the informal exchanges that form the background to case reports. We all have a tendency to think in terms of 'types' of people, especially two-valued (good versus bad) types. So, for example, we use words and phrases like 'first-class student', 'tart', 'case-hardened', 'burned out', 'lay-about'. Such general, if facile, labels are based on a few striking attributes. They trigger strong evaluative judgments and block rational empirical inquiry. Labels like 'strange', or 'crazy' have the effect of excluding the Subject from the normal categories of understanding.

The specification for a prototypical case can be expected to emerge gradually as the Investigator compares and contrasts individual cases within a given category. This process corresponds to what Glaser and Strauss (1967) call 'theoretical saturation'. That is to say, in researching or dealing with cases of a similar sort, e.g. battered wives, difficult patients, or retired professors, Investigators gradually establish the sorts of properties that help to define that type of case (in terms of family resemblances). In so doing, Investigators should be alert to the way in which these defining characteristics change as they encounter very different sorts of Subjects, leading perhaps to a revision or subdivision for their initial categorization. Theoretical saturation is complete when the Investigators' conceptualization and description are so robust that no further revision is necessary. The problem is to find a level of abstraction and generalization for the prototypical case that fulfils the required scientific or professional purpose. It is possible that the traditional psychological and sociological typologies are far too abstract and general, and that we would be better served by categorizations of persons in situations at a much lower level—see Cronbach (1975).

The easiest and most common procedure for making comparisons and contrasts between cases is to match or distinguish them on significant criteria, i.e. on specially selected attributes. But the value of this procedure depends on the cases having basic structural similarities, as in cases of school refusal, scientific achievement, or domestic accident. It is uncommon to find full structural descriptions even for single cases, much less for comparisons between two or more cases. It seems to follow, therefore, that mere summaries and narrative accounts of cases have limited value, except as illustrative material. What is needed for the advancement of psychological knowledge is the systematic description and analysis of cases in relation to a system of categorization.

Psychological prototypes can be formed not only to conceptualize types of persons and forms of behaviour, but also varieties of situation. Thus terms like emergency, rush-hour, luncheon, examination, wedding, and so on, elicit images, expectations, and assumptions derived from familiar and readily available conceptual routines (scripts, plans, schemata) depending on the contexts in which the terms are used.

The notions of family resemblances and prototypical cases have a bearing on the development of case-law. For example, Investigators with experience in, say, bereavement counselling develop conceptual routines for handling certain kinds of case. In so far as they can be made explicit, these conceptual routines constitute a kind of case-law for that particular area of human behaviour. The richness and variety of conceptual routines available depends on the abilities and the breadth and depth of the counsellor's experience. On encountering a new case, the counsellor establishes some basic features—age, sex, length of bereavement, relationship with the deceased, circumstances of death, socioeconomic circumstances, family and other support, and so on. The counsellor's active search for information, meaning, and ways of helping, calls up familiar conceptual routines and prototypical cases of bereavements based on past experience. It is likely that the particular case the counsellor is dealing with will be assimilated to one or other of these conceptual routines. If so, the case can proceed smoothly. If not, then the bereavement has to be dealt with as a 'special case' or problem, perhaps by consulting other counsellors who have the necessary conceptual routine or specific information. Where no ready-made solution is available the counsellor has to engage in the sorts of problem-solving described in previous chapters. Occasionally an expert counsellor will deal effectively with a 'special case' of bereavement which, if made known to others, 'sets a precedent' and contributes to the development of 'case-law' in this area.

Given a variety of cases within a given area of interest—criminal investigation, marital breakdown, scholastic failure, bereavement, and so on—it becomes possible, even essential, to make comparisons and contrasts between cases, so as to arrive at some kind of classification or typology. Investigators group together similar cases and separate them off from cases of a rather different kind. Cases within a given group should have a number of basic features in common—structural similarities not merely surface similarities. These may take the form of 'family resemblances'. Cases belong to the same subgroup to the extent that they can be dealt with by means of the same conceptual routine, i.e. the same abstract principles and rules of inference or procedure. Cases which belong to different subgroups differ in one or more key features (no matter how similar they are in other respects), which makes it necessary for them to be dealt with differently. A conceptual routine is simply an abstract and general framework (script or schema) within which a particular sort of case can be understood and managed.

The business of identifying the key features of cases and of developing a robust system for classifying (grouping) cases gives rise to 'case-law'. This term is usually employed in the context of jurisprudence (legal science), but is entirely appropriate when used in other contexts—business, politics, psychological counselling.

We must not lose sight of the importance of the case-study method in the social and behavioural sciences. The case-study is not simply a technique used in applied professional work with particular individuals who present problems. At one level it is a basic, perhaps *the* basic, method in scientific work. At another level it is one of the standard methods of science comparable with experimental inquiry, medical diagnosis, social survey, and historical research. These methods can be employed well or badly; the case-method in clinical psychology, social work, education, and so on, is no exception.

Familiarity with the methods appropriate to the study of complex cases and familiarity with the notion that cases can be classified into 'types' or 'prototypes' should enable the case-worker (the Investigator) to deal more effectively with routine cases and with the 'brief contacts' characteristic of human service work.

A prototype case is a case which fits a sort of diagnostic description or type. That is, it has a sufficient number of key features to warrant classifying it with other cases sharing the same family resemblances. Such classification is not an end in itself. Initially, it fulfils a research function—discovering that such prototypes can be reliably identified. Subsequently it fulfils a logical or practical function—implying or predicting that a Subject, in virtue of his or her diagnostic classification or type, has *further* features, features over and above those used in making the initial categorization—see Horowitz *et al.* (1981a,b) and Ochitill (1984).

Some crimes and civil offences, like other kinds of human conduct, have features which form a pattern. These give rise to categories like burglary, rape, trespass, libel. Other features give rise to patterns and categories of a more restricted sort, e.g. different sorts of negligence, homicide, or theft. The existence of similarities between patterns of conduct suggests common causes and leads to common evaluative reactions.

In order to advance scientific knowledge and professional competence, individual cases in a given area of interest must be categorized according to type through systematic comparisons and contrasts between cases. In one respect this calls for a simplification in the case-description, by omitting rare and idiosyncratic features of the cases in a category. In another respect this makes it possible to attribute features to cases which might otherwise have gone unrecognized. A systematic typology of cases thus facilitates classification, description, and analysis, assuming that the typology itself is valid. If this assumption is correct, then the logical structure of a case matches the logical structure of the type to which it belongs, e.g. in industrial disputes, psychiatric disorders, family relationships, mid-life crises.

It is as well to bear in mind that a general theory which specifies certain types of case is not directly refutable. For example, the fact that some persons do not experience a mid-life crisis does not affect the theory. What affects the theory is the scientific advantage it has over competing interpretations of the same phenomena. Only empirical statements can be verified or falsified by empirical data.

For Diesing (1971) case-studies are used to test, modify, and explore the limits of the conceptual categories we use to classify cases. The classification or typology itself tends to control the sorts of similarities and differences we take notice of when comparing cases, and so helps to systematize and improve the case-studies. Lying behind any typology is a general theory which accounts for the different kinds of case that arise and this is used to justify any elaboration or modification of the taxonomy. Thus case-studies, categorization, and theorizing are dependent on each other, and the advancement of science depends upon this continuing reciprocal influence. A similar process is at work in other methods of scientific inquiry. This is a process whereby empirical data are assimilated to theoretical understanding, and theoretical understanding has to accommodate to empirical data. Equilibrium is the condition in which understanding and experience are temporarily in balance or compatible.

THE NOTION OF LEGAL SCIENCE

The justification for using the case-study method as a scientific method is that it can penetrate areas of interest and deal with problems which are closed, or at least seem to be closed, to other methods, such as laboratory experiment or social survey. Similarly, the justification for using experimental and survey methods is that they can penetrate areas of interest apparently closed to clinical and case-study methods. As we have seen, however, any actual scientific or professional investigation can be treated as a case-study, i.e. as a study of a single occurrence of an event of a given type. Particular experiments and surveys can be critically evaluated by making them the Objects of case-studies. This is quite different from attempting to replicate them. A case-study which is itself treated as a case-study becomes a second-order or meta-case-study.

The quasi-judicial case-method is an attempt to improve the scientific quality of studies of individual cases (whether persons, organizations, incidents, or other singular phenomena). The quasi-judicial method of studying cases derives its inspiration from legal science, in particular the rules of evidence, but it does not depend in any direct way on legal theory or on the way law is in fact practised in different countries. What I have tried to do is to use the ideas of legal methods of arriving at truth and justice (modelled for the most part on criminal and other serious cases) to develop norms and standards for procedures in carrying out case-studies that lie outside the narrow framework of the law. The methodology prescribed is *normative*. Like any other scientific method it prescribes how we *ought* to conduct our investigations. It is not a description of how we do *in fact* conduct them. How we in fact conduct case-studies is a matter for empirical inquiry (as is how we in fact carry out our experiments and surveys).

One of the dangers of working with a well-established, reputable method is that of relying on it too much and becoming over-confident in the results it yields. It seems unlikely that the quasi-judicial method presents any such dangers because the disparity between what we aspire to do in a case-study and what we succeed in doing is usually all too obvious. Moreover, the relative flexibility of the quasi-judicial framework (as compared with the judicial framework) and the diversity of cases with which it can deal makes it unlikely that Investigators will become method-bound—concentrating on method to the detriment of substance. Such research might illuminate a variety of social and psychological issues, such as the effects of administrative procedures, role relationships, and social norms on the conduct of case-studies. However, the shortcomings of the case-study method and of extant case-studies are well recognized. It is the attempt to show how these shortcomings can be remedied that gives rise to the normative character of the present approach using a quasi-judicial case-method.

Twining (1980) argues that jurisprudence has had little to say about evidence, fact-finding, and proof apart from a deep concern with the actual rules of evidence and procedure; see also Stone (1984). It has had little or nothing to say about logic, psychology, or sociology, and has not developed a coherent theoretical framework to describe, explain, and evaluate legal rules, procedures, and institutions. Twining (1980) draws attention to the way the law deals with confessions, providing rules for admitting or not admitting confessions, but neglecting the overall social and psychological processes which give rise to confessions—even in criminal cases. It is obvious that 'confessions' play a major role in quasi-judicial case-studies, because they refer in a broad sense to any admissions that the Subject or other participant in a case makes reluctantly because of feelings of shame, guilt, or anxiety, or to protect someone. The sorts of personal admissions and revelations that occur in counselling are clearly 'confessions' of a sort, as indeed they are so called in an appropriate religious or legal setting.

Thus, in a quasi-judicial case-study, unlike a judicial inquiry proper, the Investigators would be interested not only in the procedural question of whether the information was admissible and relevant, but also, perhaps mainly, in how the confession (admission, disclosure) came to be made, to whom and in what circumstances, and particularly with the meaning or significance of that information in the context of the case as a whole. Another way of making the point is to say that the quasi-judicial method is a *scientific* method not a *judicial* method: it is not bound by a narrow set of prescriptions which govern what goes on in a court of law: it is, rather, concerned with solving or dealing with human problems, taking into account the forms of argument used in reasoning about those problems, taking into account the investigative methods used to establish the empirical facts of the case, and taking into account the social, psychological, and historical context of the case. In any event, even courtroom procedures and rules are only part of a system that includes complex extra-legal processes extending into the wider society. Also, although legal procedures and rules of evidence may look extremely thorough, systematic, and formal, as indeed they are, they are by no means complete or inflexible, otherwise there would be no need for legal arguments about admissibility, the weight of evidence, probability, the cogency of arguments, or other matters. To the extent that quasi-judicial case-studies in business, psychology, social work, and so on are problem-solving exercises, they differ from judicial cases proper in that they incorporate (in theory at least) an evaluative feedback process which tests whether the problem has been solved—and this means more than appealing to rules of procedure and a body of doctrine. Consideration of the law—how it gets made, how it functions in society, how it is justified—would take us too far afield—but see Allen (1964) and Lloyd (1981).

Twining (1980) draws attention to the historical origins of modern rules of evidence in classical accounts of logic, grammar, and rhetoric. He suggests an extension of the scope of jurisprudence, recommends a more critical, sceptical examination of its approach, and calls for an examination of its epistemological and methodological assumptions. His views go some way to showing how the gap between legal science and social science can be bridged. Rules lie at the heart of the case-study method. There are rules of procedures by means of which the case-study is carried out. There are rules of inference that express the abstract and general principles which provide an explanatory framework for or interpretation of the case (and others like it). See Twining and Miers (1976) for an analysis of how rules work in judicial and quasi-judicial contexts.

An important contrast between the judicial and quasi-judicial methods of inquiry is the quasi-judicial method's rejection of adversarial forms of argument in favour of consensual forms (again in theory if not always in practice!). The quasi-judicial case-study is an exercise in problem-solving, not a competition between adversaries. Arbitrational forms of settlement may be acceptable given the hybrid character of case-studies involving scientific considerations on the one hand and professional policy or value considerations on the other. It is obvious that the judicial method proper is not appropriate for the sorts of cases with which we are concerned. Even the rudiments of the quasi-judicial method will strike some Investigators as too demanding considering the nature of their inquiries and the resources at their disposal.

The judicial process tends, in its formal aspect, to be preoccupied with linear formal logic and the notion of logical validity—starting with the issues and ending with the verdict. By contrast the quasi-judicial process is cyclic or recursive. The consequences of inquiries lead to a reformulation of the issues which gave rise to the initial inquiries. Twining (1983) says that the problem of combining evidence of different kinds so as to make them bear convergently on a common conclusion has been something of a problem in logic and jurisprudence—see, for example, Cohen (1977), Twining (1980), and Williams (1979). The approach advocated in this book is different. Based largely on the ideas of Toulmin (1958) and Toulmin *et al.* (1979), this approach deals with substantive argument, which is more inclusive than formal logic. Metaphorically speaking, it involves a 'web' of argument rather than a 'chain' of reasoning. It recognizes that in order to understand an argument we must deal with it in the context of real-world knowledge, the ramifications of which can be explored only in a limited way. In other words, a rational empirical argument cannot be assessed only by reference to its internal formal logical structure. Its internal structure must meet the formal requirement of logical validity; but, in addition, the argument itself must make sense in the context of what is known or believed about the world. It is usually not feasible to explicate this real-world contextual knowledge in full. Instead, it provides an almost unlimited source of further considerations depending on the nature of the case and on the ingenuity and experience of those responsible for carrying out the case-study.

A PHILOSOPHY OF SCIENCE VIEW OF CASE-STUDIES

By way of comment on the philosophy of science aspect of case-studies, we can assert that an experimental laboratory-type of investigation in science is itself a sort of case-study. It is, of course, a case-study of a particular sort, and must be related to other experimental studies and to relevant theories. By definition, an experiment is a study set up deliberately under relatively controlled conditions (much more controlled in the natural and biological sciences than in the social and behavioural sciences), and therefore permits fuller description (often with quantifiable data) and fuller analysis (in terms of causally related variables). An experimental study is explicit and uses prospective theoretical guidelines, whereas the usual sort of psychological case-study is often less explicit, more prone to the errors of common-sense judgment, works retrospectively for the most part, and uses a variety of *ad hoc* practical interpretations at the convenience of the Investigator.

The main point, however, is that in advocating a case-study approach to psychological problems we are not abandoning scientific method. On the contrary, I have tried to show that the intensive, largely retrospective, study of individual cases can be as rigorous and as informative as the extensive prospective study of samples of people, whether in surveys or experiments. One can generalize from individual cases, and many important real-life human problems cannot be studied as effectively, or at all, by experimental methods of inquiry. The differences between experimental and non-experimental methods of scientific inquiry are differences of procedure, convenience, and appropriateness to the problem.

Like an experimental inquiry, a case-study sets out to collect data (evidence). The data must be relevant to the specific issues which the case-study (or experimental inquiry) is designed to settle, and they must be collected according to certain rules of procedure. These rules of procedure are much better understood and more explicit in experimental studies than in naturally occurring psychological case-studies. One of the aims of this book is to spell out these rules of procedure.

The specific issues to be settled are basically questions or problems that arise out of our concern with practical matters or with more abstract and general (theoretical) matters. The data in an experimental inquiry are limited in their variety, and are interpreted according to the way the actual pattern of results compares with the expected (theoretical) pattern of results. Where the data are quantified, objective statistical tests can replace subjective intuitive judgment. The data in a typical psychological case-study, however, are not limited in their variety, and there may not be a comprehensive theory about what could be expected; therefore, the interpretation of the data is by no means as straightforward as it is in an experimental inquiry. Usually, the data cannot be quantified (they can, of course, in the special conditions of conducting experiments on single cases), so objective judgment is more difficult.

An experimental inquiry, therefore, imposes a simplified, idealized frame of reference, i.e. a theory, on observations made under specified conditions. A case-study, by contrast, is usually of some complexity and is intended to deal with naturally occurring real-world events. It is largely or entirely an *ex post facto* interpretation of whatever direct and indirect evidence is available about those events. A case-study, therefore, need not be confined to an analysis of the Subject's verbal reports and records of his actual behaviour, but can reach out for whatever evidence is available, provided it can be shown to be relevant and admissible (admissible in the broad quasi-judicial sense in case-studies carried out in an extra-judicial context). Such evidence includes: spontaneous disclosures and views expressed by the Subject; the Subject's responses to direct and indirect questions; any reliable report of the Subject's behaviour and circumstances; personal and official documents and other records; traces of material evidence; the opinons (preferably first-hand) of reliable witnesses or informants; life-history information; reports of the Subject's performance on tests or examinations; biomedical and social data; the opinions of experts, including those carrying out the case-study; background information such as demographic data, scientific and professional knowledge, general knowledge.

Such a diversity of evidence is necessary in case-studies because onc does not have the abundance of direct evidence characteristic of an experimental investigation. Having evidence in a case-study is like having a few pieces of a jigsaw puzzle, and trying to work out what picture the puzzle would make if all the pieces were available. The data in an experimental study are more like counters: the tasks are to see whether there are more counters of one sort rather than another, or how they distribute themselves as an array. This grossly oversimplifies the nature of experimental inquiry because one's interpretation and evaluation of an experimental result usually depends on its contribution to a more general body of knowledge about the issue under investigation. Hence my opinion that an experimental study is a sort of case-study, but not vice-versa. The case-study character of an experiment becomes obvious once its findings are called into question.

Case-studies have much in common with detective work, espionage, investigative reporting, historical and biographical research, public and judicial inquiries, and natural history research.

Mitchell (1983) examines the case-study method from a social science perspective, contrasting it with the survey method, and noting that the *Evaluative Index of the American Journal of Sociology* for as long ago as 1950 contains the last indexed entry for case-studies and case-histories—a reference to Oscar Lewis's work. The eclipse of the case-study is partly accounted for by the growth of survey techniques, sampling theory and statistics, subjective scaling, computing, and, presumably, market forces. The result is that a young social scientist is likely to confuse a case-study with a sample of *N* = 1. Mitchell examines the case-study method in anthropology as a paradigm for its use in the social sciences, and clears up the confusion just referred to.

The basic problem is not only how to *analyse* a single case or situation— whether a primitive tribe, a family, a person occupying a particular social role, or a motor vehicle accident—but also how to *generalize* one's analysis to other comparable cases. How can one show that one's case is 'typical' of a set of similar cases? Can a single case do more than illustrate an analysis that must be verified by a sample survey? The problem presents itself regardless of whether one is concerned primarily with the behaviour and psychological processes of an individual person or with the institutional and environmental factors that make up the circumstances in which such behaviour occurs. As we have seen, human behaviour is the product of a functional interaction between person and situation.

Mitchell's central point is that generalization from the single case is based on the validity of the analysis, not on some prior notion about the representativeness of the case. In case-study research the cases come to define the population. To argue that one's analysis of a case is valid is implicitly to claim that the analysis holds for comparable cases, i.e. cases of that sort.

A case-study or situation-analysis can be defined as the observer's record and interpretation of data about the Object of interest. The data are collected in order to understand and deal with the Object of interest and possibly with other Objects of a comparable sort. The analysis of these data (case-materials) is carried out in such a way as to represent the Object (person, organization, event, etc.) as a unitary entity. The point is to preserve the wholeness of the phenomenon being studied. This means analysing its elements whilst demonstrating their interrelationships. Consider, for example, what it means to study a motor-vehicle accident. One is required to identify the elements involved (vehicles, components, road conditions, driver characteristics, and so on) and to demonstrate their relationships (e.g. a tired driver driving a ten-ton truck with poor brakes in fog on a narrow twisting road).

The same sort of analysis is possible for other sorts of case-study, whether in clinical psychology, social work, business, warfare, or anthropology. The aim of a case-study is to represent not just the actual case, but a model or typical pattern of facts and relationships that holds for a set of cases (of course, sets can have only one member, or even no members!). The 'pattern' we refer to is expressed in terms of a theory or argument about the available data, its pattern of meaning.

Mitchell seems to argue that a case-study is most useful in the context of discovery (its role in the context of proof is taken up later in this section) and states that a case-study is a heuristic—a device which leads one towards an abstract, general, theoretical interpretation. It is certainly true that psychological and other case-material is often used in this way—as an example, illustration, pointer, lead, or whatever, in relation to a general claim or rule of inference. For example, one cites a case to illustrate the effects of stress on self-control, or the effects of alcohol on driver performance. But using a case as an 'illustration' implies that one is convinced of the correctness of the theory it illustrates, that one's analysis is valid.

At a higher level of complexity we find fairly detailed case-studies being used as analogies in arguments about the phenomenon they are being compared with. One could document a case matched point for point with a larger, more general state of affairs. Consider, for example, the case of a patient whose symptoms, treatment, and progress match a standard disease pattern, or the case of a person accused of criminal negligence whose behaviour and circumstances do *not* match the judicial criteria, or the case of a Bar-mitzvah ceremony which 'fits' current local Jewish custom and practice.

It is actually common for studies to be carried out on unusual non-representative cases in order to reveal something about the usual (normal) state of affairs. For example, a case-study of a disease improves our understanding of physical or mental health, a case-study of a bankruptcy shows how to run a business more profitably. Cases like these, of course, can be used simply as illustrations of an established theory (of disease or of business), or they can be used as analogies—compared point by point with the phenomena to which they relate, or they can be used as heuristic devices—leading to the development of a new theory or concept.

The question is whether case-studies can be used in the context of proof. Can we actually prove or disprove anything by means of a case-study? Relying on the principle of falsifiability we can reject the notion that case-studies can prove a point (but not the notion that case-studies can be very convincing). As far as disproof is concerned, a single negative instance can disprove a general rule. One negative case could falsify the general assumption that a given form of treatment would not be effective. Individual case-studies can thus be used to probe the plausibility and test the generality of a theory.

Thus, since case-studies can be used creatively or heuristically (in the context of proof/disproof) to test theories, then we seem to have a solid case for recognizing the value of the case-study method in basic science and not just in practical applications to specific cases. An analogous argument could be used to demonstrate the value of case-studies in applied science. In fact, no-one seems to dispute the role of case-studies in applied and professional work; case-studies form a very important part of professional practice.

Naturally, there is no question of case-studies replacing survey and experimental forms of inquiry. The point is that case-studies are not an inferior sort of scientific method. On the contrary, they are possibly *the* basic method of science. It is worth restating the point that a particular experiment can be regarded as a 'case-study', a particular survey can be regarded as a 'case-study'. Experimental and survey results are not interpreted (explained) in isolation from all other considerations; they are subject to whatever contextual factors—including poor design, faulty equipment, and incorrect analysis—can be shown to have a bearing on them. Similarly, case-studies 'make sense' only in the appropriate context of empirical knowledge and theoretical supposition. The fact that they are sometimes used merely to 'pilot' experimental and survey investigations should not be allowed to obscure the fact that case-studies *on their own* can lead to scientific discovery and can establish scientific knowledge (in so far as scientific knowledge can be established). Different scientific problems call for different scientific methods.

We avoid the problem of trying to generalize inductively from a single case by not confusing case inference with statistical inference. Statistical inference is too well known to justify further comment here, except to say that 'scientific', i.e. theoretical, generalizations begin *after* and *separately from* the argument about statistical inference. Case-study reasoning should be seen as a strong form of hypothetico-deductive theorizing, not as a weak form of statistical inference. We do not infer things 'from' a case-study, we impose a construction, a pattern of meaning, 'onto' the case. Ideally, the individual case puts our theories to the test. A common mistake, of course, lies in *post hoc* reasoning whereby we develop or modify a theory to fit the facts of a case and then suppose that the case somehow 'proves' the theory, when in fact all we have done is generate a theory which should be tested independently of the facts it was originally devised to explain.

The essence of a case-study is the logic or theory by means of which we 'make sense' of the case and others like it. Which others are like it is a matter of further scientific inquiry. A well-argued case-study is one which, by its choice of materials and by its mode of reasoning, is robust enough to withstand critical appraisal as an explanation of a certain class of events. Since it does not claim to be statistically representative it cannot be criticized on statistical grounds. As we have seen, the case may be highly unusual in some respects and interesting from a theoretical or practical point of view.

The ultimate aim of scientific inquiry is to establish the causes of phenomena. The various scientific methods we have mentioned—experimentation, survey, and case-study—are all, in their own way, directed towards finding the sufficient and necessary conditions for an effect.

Individual case-studies derive their scientific merit not so much, if at all, from their representativeness or typicality, but rather from the insight they convey as vehicles for scientific explanation. Almost any case will do, provided it can carry the burden of explanation (strictly speaking, the explanation carries the case!). Unusual or dramatic cases, special or exceptional cases, typical cases, test cases, contrasting cases—all have a part to play in developing our understanding of a phenomenon. Case-studies enable one to demonstrate the limitations and conditions governing the way a theory works in practice.

In order to derive any theoretical scientific benefit from a case-study (as opposed to any practical benefit derivable from knowledge of particular facts) one must neglect or suppress some features of the case—namely, those that are not relevant to the theory or explanation one is propounding (But do not confuse 'are not relevant' with 'do not fit'!). This simplifies the case and makes it possible to destroy its uniqueness. This, in turn, makes it possible to compare and contrast it with other cases, so that the similarities and differences between cases *relevant to the theory* can be established.

In a sense one has to go beyond the empirical facts of a case-study in order to explain it. Its meaning is derived from the conceptual framework within which it is understood. Without such an explanatory context it is a mere narrative or description. As Mitchell (1983, p. 207) remarks: 'The validity of extrapolation depends not on the typicality or representativeness of the case but upon the cogency of the theoretical reasoning.'

Gluckman (1961) commends the use of what he calls the extended case-study in social anthropology—see also Van Velsen (1979). An extended case-study is one which goes beyond the method of apt illustration of customs, rituals, social relationships, and so on. Extended case-studies are essentially systems of cases. They are extended in terms of their relationships with other cases and extended in terms of time. The result is a method which accounts for complex social processes over a period of time, e.g. a feud or trading relationship. One cannot, of course, find a sharp dividing line between a case which simply provides an appropriate illustration of a social process or structural feature (knowledge of which is derived from other methods) and an extended case. Somewhere in between is the method of situational analysis by means of which complex social events, ceremonies for example, can be used to reveal underlying social structures and processes— or, rather, can be used to suggest, or to test the validity of, the way we conceptualize society. By contrast, Boswell (1969) uses very narrowly focused situational analyses. These describe and interpret the factors involved in the mobilization of social support following bereavement in Lusaka, Zambia, in the 1960s.

Gluckman (1961) reminds us of the importance of recognizing the way investigators themselves may get drawn into the social processes that are the focus of a case-study. Investigators need to be able to take account of their impact on the people and institutions they are investigating.

A further illustration of the great diversity of uses to which the case-study method has been put is to be found in Peel (1983). He deals with the history of a people—the Ijesha—and their main town Ilesha between the 1890s and 1970s. It is referred to as a 'case-study' of the incorporation of the Ijesha people, who at one time had a fairly distinctive and autonomous social, economic, and cultural system—a Yoruba Kingdom, into the larger wider West African State of Nigeria. It is perhaps better referred to as an extended case-study. The methods employed in this ten-year study included direct observation of events, intensive interviews with key informants, examination of public and private documents, systematic social surveys, and the use of secondary sources, i.e. selected books and articles on the Ijesha, the Yoruba, and Nigeria. Thus, through a combination of anthropological, historical, and sociological methods, a description and analysis is constructed dealing with a particular people during a fairly well-defined period of their history. This multi-method approach is not at all unusual in the social sciences. This particular study is concerned to emphasize the connections and continuities in this history—just as a psychological case-study should be concerned with connections between events (actions and circumstances) and continuities over time (causal relationships).

Peel (1983) draws attention to the difficulty of combining structural analysis and narrative history. He argues that if explanation in sociology (and, for us, psychology) is to account for Subjects' choices, i.e. actions, in contexts which are historically specific as well as structurally constrained (by concurrent situational or environmental factors) then a chronological framework is essential. The behaviour of Subjects makes sense only to the extent that the Investigators can show how it arises out of an interaction between particular personal factors (the Subject's appraisal of the situation, his abilities, expectations, dispositions, and so on) and the successive external conditions that provide opportunities for and constraints upon action over time. The explanation must account for the connections, the disconnections, the continuities, and the discontinuities in the pattern and sequence of events with which the case-study deals.

Naturally, a case-study in social history deals with a much longer span of time than a case-study in personal adjustment, covering perhaps several generations. We have made some effort to distinguish between an individual life-history and an individual case-study—see Chapter 1. The essential difference is not the span of time dealt with but the identification of the *proximal* (immediate) causes of events rather than distal causes (historical origins). A proximal explanation, by definition, is one which deals with causes and effects which are closely connected in time and space. A distal explanation is one which deals with causes and effects which are remote from each other. The former is sometimes referred to as a 'functional' account, the latter as an 'historical' account—see Allport (1937). For example, to explain the aggressive behaviour of an adult psychopath in terms of his parents' neglect and/or physical abuse is to offer a distal or historical account. It is unsatisfactory because it fails to show the necessary specific connections between the childhood events and their successive psychobehavioural consequences, leading to particular psychopathic actions in adult life.

Psychoanalytic explanations have attempted the difficult task of describing the psychological mechanisms, e.g. repression, identification, displacement, hysteria, which connect early traumatic events with later maladjustment. Unfortunately, it has not proved possible to validate these explanatory concepts in ways acceptable to the general scientific community, although they continue to find wide acceptance and employment, failing more satisfying alternatives, among professionals.

Peel (1983) goes on to argue that the aim of a chronological analysis is to make sense of the connections between events over time. He explains that events such as a riot, strike, election, a dispute over succession, or an accusation of witchcraft, can be thought of as symptoms or indicators of underlying 'structural' factors in a society, e.g. social class or economic relations. But such events can also be thought of as the realization, not merely the symptoms, of structural factors. Social events are the empirical embodiment of social structures and processes just as behaviour is the overt realization of psychological structures and processes. Moreover the events themselves may help bring about changes in social conditions partly through psychological mechanisms such as memory and imagination: people's awareness of and interpretation of events helps to shape their behaviour and the consequences of those events.

The parallel argument in relation to psychological case-studies is that the aim of a chronological analysis, even over a relatively short span of time—a few days or a few hours even—is to make sense of the connections between the events described—in a crime, a matrimonial dispute, or a motor-vehicle accident, for example. Each such case contains a series of circumstances, actions, and outcomes. These can be thought of as symptomatic or expressive of underlying structural factors—opportunities open, social norms, lack of surveillance, for example. But such events can also be thought of as the materialization of these otherwise abstract, conceptual entities that we, the Investigators, use to make sense of the world and the behaviour of people in it. The events themselves, being in the real world, bring about further changes in the real world—reduced opportunities, changes in social attitudes and in policing, for example. The 'structure' of a case-study thus comprises the conceptual terms of the argument which make sense of the empirical data. The case-study method, like other methods of investigation, whether in sociology, psychology, or elsewhere, raises epistemological questions, such as the reality or existence of the social or psychological structures and processes we refer to in our explanations.

The term 'case' can be used in different contexts to mean different things. For example, in law it is often used to refer to judicial investigations which have been completed and published in a way that enables them to be cited as authoritative sources. In medicine the term 'case' is used to refer to a patient who exhibits a characteristic set of signs and symptoms of disease. Medicine has the advantage over law in so far as the remedies prescribed to treat or 'dispose of' the case may give rise to further data which prove diagnostically useful. A treatment which fails may cast doubt on the diagnosis on which it was based. The consequences of a legal decision, however, do not have this recursive, problem-solving function.

Case-studies in medicine are in some ways easier to present than case-studies that deal with social and psychological problems. The reason is that the issues in the medical case usually have a narrow focus—namely, the patient's physical disorder, its aetiology, treatment, and prognosis. Thus, given the necessary technical training and vocabulary, the reader or listener can be presented with an interesting and informative account which is fairly brief and where the evidence is largely confined to the results of clinical examinations and possibly laboratory tests. Of course, the physician is able to make sense of the case and to assimilate the information quickly because of the vast amount of real-world medical knowledge he can bring to bear on it.

Case-studies have a major place in the history of medicine—see Rose and Corn (1984). They exist in two main forms, oral and written. The written (printed and published) forms vary considerably in quality and importance, but generally speaking are likely to be more considered and more valuable than those presented in the course of casual conversation, ward rounds, or lectures. Rose and Corn argue that resistance to the case-study as a 'scientific' method is apparent in medicine as judged by the attitudes and practices of publishers and journals. They introduce the interesting idea that published case-studies provide a useful data-base for students of medical history and medical sociology. They also make the important point that case-studies can appeal to and inform a very wide audience, especially if ways can be found to eliminate technical terminology. Among the topics that can be studied historically or sociologically by a review of medical case-studies are the following: ethical values and practices, technical developments, social relationships and attitudes, popular beliefs, and life-styles.

It is obvious, therefore, that the case-material published by workers in social and behavioural areas can have value over and above that which accrues from advancing knowledge in one particular specialist area. However, as Bush (1984) has pointed out, case-records (the data-base for case-studies) in some areas of professional work are not always what they seem to be. They are sometimes not straightforward factual records about a person and his or her circumstances, but rather a complicated mixture of factual record, inference, unwarranted opinion, omission, distortion, and self-justification. Also, of course, recorded or published cases are highly selective. No-one wants to publicise their failures!

The absence of what we might call 'personal' details from a medical case-history may have the effect of dehumanizing the case—an effect believed to be widespread in medicine generally and in many other areas of life where technology and bureaucracy are prominent in the organization of social relationships—see Dailey (1971). Case-studies connected with social and psychological issues are less likely to omit 'personal' details and so dispersonate the individual. The danger here, perhaps, is the opposite one. Investigators may be inclined to include so much personal detail that the focus of the case is blurred because, unlike physicians, they do not have a systematic framework for the description and analysis of the problems they are called upon to deal with. Alternatively, vivid but actually unimportant details may dominate and bias the account, as we saw in Chapter 10.

The term 'case' itself goes some way towards dispersonating Subjects (as does the term 'Subject'!). However, we have to bear in mind that case-studies are not usually carried out in isolation from reports on other comparable persons. The essential scientific value of a case-study lies in its conceptual structure, which should be applicable to cases of a comparable kind. Case-studies which fail to develop such a conceptual structure fail in their prime scientific and professional purpose. A 'case' is not only about a 'person' but also about that 'kind of person'. A case is an exemplar of, perhaps even a prototype for, a category of individuals.

The difficulty with this interpretation of the meaning of the term 'case-study' is that the conceptual structures which are used to categorize 'kinds of persons' are not at all well articulated in the social and behavioural sciences or in the human service professions. They are usually implicit in the thinking of case-workers rather than explicit in their language. They function as background beliefs, presumptions, values, and expectations, which condition the Investigators' conduct of a case and the presentation of it as a published article, a contribution to a case-conference, or an illustration in a lecture or informal discussion. These latter outlets provide more scope for the expression of idiosyncratic, unscientific, and unprofessional ideas!

Since we seem to lack well-articulated conceptualizations of the 'kinds' of persons we are called upon to deal with, it must often seem that each case is unique. Indeed, uniqueness has been regarded as a key consideration in the study of personality—see Allport (1937). The failure of idiographic psychology has been twofold—not recognizing the nature of the problem and not developing acceptable methods of investigation. The notion of uniqueness is of no great help in advancing scientific knowledge, although it may genuinely be applied when the class of persons under consideration is limited, as far as one knows, to one particular person. What professionals and scientists would prefer is a conceptual framework or routine that enabled them to deal with classes of similar cases, just as a physician has a medical framework within which he can deal with all or most of the patients he encounters. Given such a conceptual framework, case-studies are carried out at its limits with the aim of elaborating or extending the framework. A constructive case-study is one which deals with a new problem or with an old problem in a new way. It should express the sorts of qualities that make for good professional practice or scientific research—originality, scepticism, thoroughness, honesty, openness, and freedom from bias. These are the qualities that help convert clinical art into clinical science.

At present, case-study methodology in psychology and related disciplines appears to be much less well developed and articulated as a scientific method than other methods, such as experimentation and the social survey. Most of the case-studies to be found, for example in psychology, sociology, anthropology, and business studies, seem to depend on a kind of tacit or implicit understanding of the appropriate rules of procedure and inference rather than on an explicit methodology analogous to that found in experimental and survey research well documented in a variety of books and articles. Although the rudiments of case-study methodology have been known and taught for several generations there seems to have been little increase in sophistication, with the honourable exception of business studies—see Easton (1982). Even in business studies there are aspects of case-study method which seem not to have been developed—in particular the logic of case-study arguments, the psychological barriers to rationality, the epistemological status of knowledge derived from individual case-studies, and contextual factors in professional and scientific work. In psychology the case-study method has been virtually restricted to psychodynamic concerns until the relatively recent emergence of single-case experimentation. Personality study has either deplored the lack of a suitable methodology or else rejected the idea completely. In sociology and anthropology, case-study methodology has been confused with techniques for accessing data, e.g. interviewing, participant observation, personal documents.

By contrast, experimental and survey methods have developed almost beyond recognition compared with their rudimentary condition at the close of the nineteenth century. What is being attempted in this book is not so much the rehabilitation of an existing case-study method, but rather a reconstruction of it, so that its scientific status can be more fully appreciated and so that it can be deployed more effectively in basic and applied research and in professional practice.

A 'GENERAL THEORY' OF PSYCHOLOGICAL CASE-STUDIES

Is it possible to formulate a theory of psychological case-studies? A theory, that is, not just a methodology. If so, how might one begin? One possibility would be to examine proposals already put forward in the area of language and cognition to account for stories, texts, and other linguistic or representational entities. For example, one might propose a grammar that would express a theory of case-studies, or a set of grammars that would express theories for different types of case-study. Alternatively, following Wilensky (1983), one might propose a theory of case-studies expressed in terms of 'points' as key elements in relation. Some such approach is necessary if artificial intelligence is to make a substantial contribution to the way case-studies are composed and understood.

A grammar for case-studies requires a small number of rewrite rules as follows:

Rule 1:   case-study → person + situation + outcome.

This rule is more commonly expressed in the mnemonic

$$P_i \times S_j \to B_{ij}$$

Where P_i stands for a particular person, S_j stands for a particular situation, and B_{ij} stands for the behavioural outcome. The symbol $\times$ stands for the interaction of P_i and S_j. The expression indicates that behaviour (including psychological and physiological processes) is a function of the interaction of person and situation. In principle, information on any two of the basic elements P_i, S_j, or B_{ij} should throw light on the state of the remaining element. For example, having information about the person and the way he or she is behaving gives some indication of the kind of situation he or she is in. Having information about the situation and the person's reactions (B_{ij}) gives some indication of the person's qualities (dispositions, abilities, state of mind).

Rule 2:   person → identity + description.

This rule expresses the idea that the Subject of a case-study must be clearly identified as an individual person with a variety of attributes who behaves in a certain way.

Rule 3:   situation → constraints + opportunities + contingencies.

This rule expresses the idea that the case-study deals with a human problem in which the Subject encounters various stresses and challenges, and during which the individual's reactions are altered (shaped) by the contingencies operating at the time.

Rule 4:   outcome → changes in person + changes in situation.

This rule expresses the way in which the Subject's reaction to a situation has consequences of various sorts—some immediate, some longer-term, some for himself or herself directly, some for his or her environment (including other people). These consequences have the effect of changing the person (the person becomes more knowledgeable, more anxious, less well motivated, or whatever) and changing the person's circumstances (the environment becomes richer or poorer, the people in it more or less friendly, and so on). An identifiable cycle of events is called an episode. A case-study consists of one major episode, perhaps analysed into a number of smaller but interrelated episodes.

It would be a major exercise to attempt to develop a working (computable) grammar (theory) of psychological case-studies. Success in developing grammars in areas other than sentence construction has been limited. One could expect a case-study grammar to be something like a story grammar, but without the complications that arise as a consequence of the imaginative, rhetorical, and aesthetic features that stories have. In other words a case-study text, being a scientific document, should be interpretable in a straightforward way within its appropriate context. For example, the meaning of the case-study is not left implicit in the account but is made explicit in the interpretation that forms part of the case-study.

Why do we need a theory or grammar of case-studies? We seem to be able to write and read case-studies without any such theory or grammar. This is rather like saying that we do not need a grammar for sentences since we learn to speak and write sentences long before we learn any grammar. The point, however, is that we need a grammar in order to talk about, analyse, and understand sentences in general: similarly we need a grammar in order to talk about, analyse, and understand case-studies. For example, in Chapters 3 to 6 we considered how the elements of a case-study can be listed and grouped: and in Chapter 9 we considered the ways in which rules of inference connect case-study data with conclusions. An ill-formed case-study is one which does not make sense—because it is incomplete or illogical. A grammar or theory of case-studies enables us to stand back from the contents, as it were, to consider the form or structure of a particular case-study, perhaps in relation to other cases. The development of psychological 'case-law' depends upon finding close structural similarities or identities between case-studies, even when their contents or surface characteristics appear somewhat different.

Our ability to distinguish between a case-study and some other sort of text or representation depends upon our having some prior notion, however crude, of what a case-study is, which means being able to list its attributes and distinguishing features. Our ability to distinguish between good and bad case-studies, or to evaluate their merits, depends upon our having a much more developed understanding of the 'grammar' of case-studies, even if we do not consciously refer to anything as formal as a grammar or theory. The critical evaluation of case-studies cannot proceed rationally without an explicit framework or schema (grammar or theory) of assessment.

Wilensky (1983) proposes to substitute the notion of 'story points' for that of 'story grammar', arguing that the main task of the reader is to identify the main points of the story and organize its meaning in terms of these points. This alternative could apply equally well, and equally badly perhaps, to case-study materials. It would take too long to examine the issue of story points *versus* story grammar. However, it is perhaps worth mentioning the distinction between the meaning(s) of a case-report and the contents or words of the report. The writer and the reader appreciate that the report does not tell the 'whole story'. Instead, the text has to be understood within a pre-existing framework of knowledge. Unless both writer and reader are fully aware of what can and cannot be taken for granted (in legal terminology 'what is and what is not in dispute'), the stage is set for misunderstandings. The reader brings his or her preconceptions into play immediately a start is made on reading the case-report. Even the title or the introductory section will set up expectations about how the contents of the report will unfold. The reader may have to accommodate his or her understanding in order to assimilate the contents of the report. For example, if the average reader of a case of child abuse does not expect parents of a certain kind to act violently towards a child, then the report should explain how it is that such behaviour occurred in this particular case (if that is possible).

The rudiments of a theory of case-studies must necessarily be arrived at intuitively. However we need not rely indefinitely on intuition to decide between good and bad case-studies or to decide whether a text or representation is a case-study or not. We can develop our initial theory by modifying it in the light of empirical studies.

Another approach to the formalization of case-reports can be derived from the work of Lehnert (1982). Lehnert describes a number of plots or themes that can be simply expressed and applied to a wide range of story contents. Thus, for example, some case-studies of rape would share a common theme or plot, e.g. alcohol + misplaced trust + sexual advances + resistance + misplaced force. Other cases would share some other theme or pattern. Lehnert's approach deals with events or episodes rather than with the fine detail of behaviour and circumstances. In this respect it has much in common with the scripts, plans, goals of Schank and Abelson (1977).

Looking at case-reports in terms of Wilensky's approach takes account of internal points, i.e. points of interest within the case-report, as well as of external points, i.e. points of concern in actually carrying out and writing-up or presenting the case-report. A technical case-report should normally be drained of affect in the interests of dispassionate appraisal; and literary techniques such as surprise, suspense, and atmosphere are out of place. The absence of such 'points' would help distinguish a genuine case-study from a fiction or a piece of propaganda or an educational exercise, where the audience's attention can be legitimately held in these ways. See Bromley (1977) for a comparison of case-studies and characterization in novels and other literary genres.

The main 'points' of a case-study are contained in the summary report. Some of these points will not be episodes, actions, outcomes, and so on, expressed in the contents of the narrative, but rather explanatory links between these elements. Their logical status as inference rules or conclusions should be recognizable from the terminology: 'it follows, that', 'it is possible that', 'because', 'so', 'unless' and so on. Naturally, the interest and background knowledge of the audience will determine what points they notice and what interpretations they impose on the case-material. It follows that case-reports should be written with a particular audience in mind; they should contain all the information the audience needs in order to dissolve any puzzlement the audience might otherwise experience in coming to understand the case.

We must not suppose that a single grammar or theory will fit every sort of case-report. We have already made clear that case-reports occur in a wide variety of contexts and take many different forms. It might prove possible to use Toulmin's framework of practical logic—see Chapter 9—as a basis for a grammar of case-studies. Thus, a minimum requirement would be data (D) and conclusion (C) linked by an inference warrant (W) in the form:

D, so C, since W.

This proposal assumes the case-report presents an argument. This summary argument expresses the formula:

$P_i \times S_j \rightarrow B_{ij}$ (see above).

This formula, in turn, expresses at a very abstract level the protogrammatical rewrite rules 1 to 4 (see above). These rules find concrete expression in the text of the case-report.

A theory which explains how we come to understand a case-study (and how we are able to construct one) must have a number of key features, as follows:

(i)   It should encompass the processes whereby case-studies are constructed, represented, understood, and used in practice.
(ii) It should take account of the real-world knowledge that Investigators and audiences bring to the case.
(iii) It should take account of how the case-material is organized and presented at the textual level.
(iv) It should identify case-studies as a particular sort of representation, different from other representations of the same phenomenon.
(v)   It should demonstrate how the several parts of a case-study are integrated overall.
(vi) It should show how meaning can be derived either by (a) the subordination of an element to a category, e.g. as an 'action' is explained in terms of a personality characteristic, or by (b) the grouping of elements to establish a category, e.g. occupational adjustment may be defined in terms of a set of criteria. It should be possible to move up and down the ladder of abstraction without confusion or ambiguity.

We must be careful not to confuse the case-report with the case itself, which would be like confusing a map with the territory it represents. The case itself is the Subject and his or her problematic situation as they existed in the real world. The case-report is a fallible and partial representation of those real-world existences. A degree of scientific and professional sophistication is needed in order to consider the complicated relationships between the two. One's understanding of and reaction to a case will be different depending upon whether one is a participant, spectator, or mere reader of the case-report.

A simple standard case-report can be represented by the tree diagram in Figure 11.2. Reading from left to right, the case-report identifies a particular

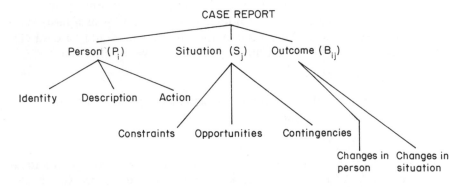

Figure 11.2 A tree-diagram representing the hierarchical structure of a case-report

person, the Subject, with specified personal qualities (and relevant history) who acts in a certain way. The Subject would be reported as acting in a set of circumstances (which had arisen in a certain way) which at one and the same time blocked or hindered satisfaction of the Subject's desires and yet offered possibilities for satisfaction. In addition, these circumstances would be shown to have shaped or influenced the Subject in a variety of ways. The case-report would claim that as a consequence of the interaction of these personal and situational factors the Subject and his or her circumstances had changed. In a complicated case there might be several such cycles of information, or the information might be 'layered' to take account of a multiplicity of determining factors. See Linde (1983) for an account of the structure of life-histories.

It is not clear whether a grammar or theory of the case-study should be required to encompass the issue of relevance. Ideally, a case-report should include all that is relevant and exclude all that is irrelevant, in so far as relevance means 'making a difference to how the case is interpreted'. In many cases what is relevant is usually a matter of empirical detail. But what makes that detail relevant? Presumably its function in establishing or disestablishing a relationship and therefore a logical implication. A grammar of case-studies which encompassed inferential relationships would thereby call for relevant data and relevant rules of inference (but without specifying their content). A theory of case-studies must refer to the ways in which case-materials and case-reports come to be constructed and understood.

To speak of the structure of a case-study is to speak of the abstract classes and relationships that exist independently of any particular contents. The particular contents are simply the empirical data and the specific reasons and comments in the report. The sentences and statements in a case-report have a function, depending upon the context of other statements within which they function, e.g. as datum or conclusion. The whole collection of statements in the report constitutes a web of meaning as explained in Chapter 9. The individual strands in the web hang together because of their relationship with other strands (and various anchorage points). The web as a whole, of course, can serve a practical function, e.g. to solve a problem or to teach a lesson.

The case itself is the material realization or embodiment of the abstract structures and processes that enable it to be described and interpreted by means of a case-report. Our ability to construct and communicate a case-report depends upon the existence of a shared 'grammar' or 'theory' of individual conduct, although we may find it difficult to make these ground-rules explicit.

LANGUAGE, LOGIC, AND ARTIFICIAL INTELLIGENCE

The importance of language in personality description and case-studies can scarcely be exaggerated. Language, logic, and artificial intelligence cover enormous areas of knowledge and there is no way of providing even the beginnings of an introduction to them here, although they are relevant to our present concern. The main aim of this section is to indicate some possible lines of development.

The language of case-reports and personality descriptions can be studied from several interrelated points of view: the first is the lexicon (What words are used in the account?); the second is syntactical (How are the words put together? How do they function in relation to one another?); the third is semantic (What do the words mean, taken in context?); the fourth is pragmatic (What is the effect of the account? What purpose does it fulfil?). The way natural language works in relation to personality descriptions and case-studies—see Bromley (1977) for details—means that accounts of, and statements about, individuals can have an *instrumental* (pragmatic) function as well as a *rational* (providing evidence and inference) function. The instrumental function is exercised when the statement or case-report achieves its intended effect, whatever that is—complying with a formality, persuading a committee, illustrating a policy, or giving someone insight into a psychological problem.

Case-studies are normally expressed in natural language. One problem, then, is to identify among a welter of natural language expressions those that function as data (D), qualifiers (Q), conclusions (C), warrants (W), backings (B), and rebuttals (R). We recall that one and the same expression can fulfil several different logical functions depending upon how it relates to different elements elsewhere in the argument.

As will be seen from the explanations, examples, and diagrams, some logical functions can be recognized by particular sorts of phraseology. For example, the modal qualifier (Q) is indicated by expressions like: 'certainly', 'probably', 'perhaps', 'possibly', 'on the face of it', 'apparently'. The inference warrant (W) is indicated by expressions like: 'since', 'because', 'for the reason that'. The backing (B) is indicated by expressions like: 'on account of', 'on the basis of', 'on the grounds that'. Conditions of rebuttal or reservations (R) are expressed by terms such as: 'unless', 'although', 'but', 'bearing in mind that', 'on the other hand'. The claim (C) statements are sometimes clearly indicated, for example, by: 'so', 'it follows that', 'the effect is', 'the consequence is', 'it is concluded that'. Data (D) statements are not so easily identified: they stand as simple assertions unless preceded by phrases like: 'the facts of the case are', 'it was observed that', 'the available evidence is that', and so on.

It is well known that in reading text, or listening to discourse, what is encountered as 'new' is interpreted in terms of what is 'given', i.e. what has gone before. Thus, when we encounter a statement, as in reading it in the case-report or hearing it during a case-conference, the 'given' information that we bring to bear (in interpreting the case-material) probably outweighs the 'new' information presented by something approaching a factor of ten. As we saw in our analysis of informal arguments, a statement 'makes sense' only in the context of other statements (or other acts and circumstances). By the time we have clarified the context, defined the terms, and added in the related statements, we may very well have another five or ten items of information, for each one we are trying to make sense of.

When we consider the raw material of the case—the actual utterances—we find that some statements fulfil a neutral representational function, other statements fulfil a rhetorical function. For example, in providing self-reports of their behaviour, Subjects are liable to give a socially appropriate account, either because they are not aware of the true reasons for their actions or because they wish to present themselves in a favourable light. In practice the actual words used, the expressive manner of their delivery, and the circumstances surrounding the utterance all play a part in influencing the listener's reaction to the statement, e.g. as to whether he believes the statement or not, or whether he sees it as an act of self-justification. Similarly, the Investigator in writing up his report may use rhetorical forms of language intended to persuade, excuse, justify, show conformity, or whatever.

The relationships between formal or standard logic on the one hand and natural logic or practical reasoning on the other are difficult to establish, and constitute a continuing problem for logicians and psychologists. It is not yet possible to impose a rigorous formal system of deductive logic that will do justice to the real-world modes of reasoning that we encounter in psychological case-studies. Hence my preference for the 'informal' system of analysis proposed by Toulmin (1958) and by Toulmin *et al.* (1979). It is possible, however, that in the not-too-distant future developments in artificial intelligence will increase the incentive to explore the relationship between these two forms of inferential reasoning.

Some indication of how progress might be made is contained in an article by Braine (1978). Braine attempts to solve the problem of coordinating standard, formal logic with natural language and common-sense reasoning by developing a set of elementary rules of inference that can be applied serially. The difference between formal logic and practical reasoning has to do with the role of heuristics and real-world knowledge in practical reasoning. There is poor correspondence between logical constants and functional words in ordinary language, between logical propositions and normal sentences, between form and content in reasoning. Braine argues that deductive reasoning requires (a) programmes for understanding premises and constructing arguments and (b) logical terms and elementary deductive rules. He refers to (a) as the 'performance' component and to (b) as the 'logical' component in reasoning. Toulmin's approach is concerned mainly with the performance component of reasoning, especially with those components that can be identified in widely different universes of discourse. Toulmin, of course, accepts the logical component of reasoning, but plays it down in the sense of eliminating logical fallacies before getting down to the main business of establishing the truth of the premises and the substance of the argument.

It is not possible to deal with Braine's (1978) work in any detail, but he does seem to succeed in clarifying the logical status of some of the terms more usually associated with natural language and ordinary reasoning—for example, connective words and phrases like 'although', 'unless', 'in spite of', 'if–then', 'but', 'since', and 'because'. Such words and phrases are commonly found in personality descriptions and case-studies, as well as in rational arguments in daily life. Braine's views and those of his predecessors have the advantage of being closely tied in with cognitive psychology. For example, it can be shown that many errors of deduction in practical reasoning arise not from strictly logical errors but from omitting or misinterpreting the premises or introducing extra-logical considerations as a consequence of relying on common-sense habits or familiar meanings. Strict logical analysis requires a special, constrained, i.e. artificial, cognitive performance.

Braine points out that most people are largely unaware of the formal logic that underpins their reasoning (rather like they are unaware of the formal grammatical rules that underpin ordinary language). Hence they cannot always work out the strictly logical consequences of applying these logical rules serially. There is also the common confusion of truth with validity. Braine goes on to speculate on the possibility of extending his analysis to predicate logic and modal logic, since these too must relate in some analysable manner to ordinary language and practical reasoning. The main point, however, is that as things stand formal logic is of little help in the analysis of case-material, and Toulmin's method of substantive or informal practical reasoning seems to be the only one applicable. At present there is nothing superior to natural language for representing and communicating information about psychological case-studies. Even medical or psychometric diagnostic data—couched in technical terms and possibly supported by tables, diagrams, and material evidence—depend upon the infrastructure of natural language for their interpretation. In any event, it seems likely that the *logical* forms encountered in personality descriptions and case-studies are relatively simple and pose no problem to an Investigator with an elementary knowledge of formal logic.

If logicians and cognitive psychologists succeed in reconciling formal logic and ordinary reasoning, perhaps along the lines suggested by Braine, that will be a major step towards the development of computer-assisted case-studies whereby this advanced form of logic in artificial intelligence can be applied to computer-readable case-records. In the meantime we are largely dependent on ordinary language and common sense except in certain circumscribed technical areas—such as psychometric testing, medical diagnosis, and social service decision-making—where computer-assisted assessment, through the use of 'expert systems', is already feasible—see Kuipers and Kassirer (1984) for example. It is already possible to derive a computerized assessment for a Subject/patient from a computer-assisted psychometric and clinical apprais-al—see Lachar (1981) and *Journal of Educational Measurement* (vol. 21, 1984). For example, if the Investigator obtains some routine demographic data, the results of screening tests and data from standardized psychometric tests, then a computer program can be used to process these data and print out a formal assessment. The assessment is 'formal' in the sense that the output follows logically and necessarily from, and only from, the input and the program rules. There is no reason why such expert systems should not be developed further. The obvious danger is that such convenient cheap procedures may not be subjected to rigorous critical appraisal. See *Counselor Education and Supervision* (1984) with reference to counsellor training.

Our enthusiasm for the quasi-judicial approach to psychological case-studies must not lead us to discount the proven advantage of actuarial over clinical methods of prediction in certain circumstances.

Can computers help? Computers can help in several ways. First by their capacity to store large amounts of information, classify it, process it in various ways, and retrieve it easily and quickly. Thus all sorts of information about all sorts of cases can be recorded for large numbers of Subjects, and stored over long periods.

Second, considerable quantities of information can be generated by means of computers; for example, responses to questions and tests, and diagnostic reports based on information input.

Third, computers may help us to understand better the forms of representation used in psychological case-studies. At present these forms are restricted to ordinary language accounts, profiles based on psychometric data, and relatively simple diagrams. It is possible that close examination of psychological case-materials will enable us to make them computer-readable, i.e. enable us to describe cases in a way which makes it possible for the information to be stored and processed by computer in rather more sophisticated ways than are at present available. Work on computer-assisted natural language processing has made some headway in processing various sorts of text—see Winston (1984) and Boden (1977); see Paige (1966) for a relatively early study. There is probably nothing intrinsic to the language of personal adjustment that would prevent similar progress in case-study texts. Indeed, some of our analyses of the informal logic of case-studies would seem to lend themselves to systematic analysis of a more formal kind.

Studies in artificial intelligence in the areas of analogies and line drawings indicate that detailed descriptions of objects and close analysis of relationships between objects belonging and not belonging to a type are essential in devising computer programs that solve problems. It can be argued that the correct idea of an object (or a person?) can be conveyed by a single well-chosen example, provided it can be fully described, and compared and contrasted with other objects (persons?) of a similar kind. The computer can 'learn' to recognize objects (cases?) of a given type. We have encountered this notion in another context in connection with case-law. There, the argument was that systematic comparisons and contrasts between cases would enable Investigators to recognize family resemblances (in descriptive features) and prototypical cases, i.e. standard cases with the requisite attributes. In the field of artificial intelligence this is referred to as 'structured introduction' since the expert system is developed from examples rather than from first principles.

An important characteristic of the case-study method is that Investigators learn from examples. In order to do this, of course, they have to find some way of using surface characteristics (empirical data) to identify underlying structural entities, such as psychological dispositions, social relationships, and the like. It remains to be seen whether computer programs can be developed along the same lines.

As we saw in our brief digression into philosophy of science, inductive generalizations by means of statistical inference are one thing, inductive generalizations by means of logical extension from well-chosen examples are another. Detailed description and analysis are necessary in order for us to discriminate between cases of different sorts, otherwise the important key features may not be noticed.

Tabular and graphical techniques are often used to represent the information being processed by computer, as in various applications of artificial intelligence. These tables and diagrams may not actually say more than is contained in the natural language text, but they often enable one to see relationships and implications more clearly, and to detect omissions and errors.

Perhaps, in the not-too-distant future, with the assistance of new generations of computers and artificial intelligence software capable of better natural language processing, we shall be in a position to analyse personality descriptions and case-materials faster and with considerably more rigour than at present. Goguen *et al.* (1981), for example, have presented a 'computational' model of the structure of ordinary explanation as expressed in everyday discourse. Their work has implications for computer-assisted natural language processing. Their work is related to that of Schank and Abelson (1977), Linde (1983), and Wilensky (1982, 1983).

Schank and Abelson's notion of 'script' corresponds to a familiar conceptual routine which enables the person to anticipate each step in the proceedings, for example in fulfilling one's social role in relation to others. The notion of 'planning' corresponds to what we have called 'problem-solving', in the sense that people attempt to make sense of a relatively unfamiliar situation by finding or constructing an appropriate pattern of meaning—one which enables them to react effectively and pursue their goals. Thus we can distinguish 'routine cases' from 'problem cases'—the former are Subjects whose characteristics and circumstances conform to a familiar type; the latter are Subjects whose characteristics and circumstances do not fit any of the familiar patterns available from scientific research or professional training. Naturally, cases of an intermediate sort are encountered in which some aspects can be handled in a routine way, whereas other aspects present problems.

The construction of a computer program to handle even relatively simple case-studies in one area of personal adjustment would be extremely difficult. It is possible to get the sort of representation that will answer questions about artificial data on, say, cases of divorce—see Dyer (1983). But we are a long way from being able to represent actual cases, and even further away from using artificial intelligence to solve case-problems.

ETHICAL ISSUES

Often the issues under investigation in case-studies comprise both positive and normative issues. That is to say, the investigation has to deal with what is in fact the case as well as with what ought (in fairness) to be the case. In this respect the quasi-judicial method, as its name implies, differs from a strictly positive scientific method.

As we saw in Chapter 1, ethical considerations cannot be eliminated from case-studies, although they can be ignored or unrecognized. Ethical arguments can be analysed in the same way as other sorts of substantive or informal arguments, except that they have their own special characteristics that define them as ethical arguments, not legal, psychological, or aesthetic arguments. It is not possible to deal even in a summary way with ethics; it is too large a subject. Also, we need to emphasize that ethical arguments transcend the empirical areas they refer to. For this reason they are difficult to settle. Arguments about the ethical aspects of cases commonly contain the fallacy of begging the question because the key words in these arguments are value-laden: words such as deceitful, devious, dishonest, cruel, stupid, deviant, deserving. Values vary from one area of human activity to another. The sorts of ethical issues and value-judgments that arise in case-studies of businessmen are different from those that arise in case-studies of military action, retirement, acculturation, or scientific achievement. Ethics is concerned with 'value' and 'justice' and so provides a wide framework within which arguments about cases can be carried on—see Timms (1984), Jacobs (1983), Schuler (1982), Wilson (1978) and British Psychological Society (1985).

The ethical principles of the contributors to a case-study are the source of the warrants that appear in the value-laden arguments. The expression of ethical arguments and judgments is likely to be fairly forceful because of the emotional investment people have in their values. Often, a person's values and beliefs are inconsistent, so there is plenty of room for disagreement between Investigators and for attitudes to vary over time. Also, to confuse matters even more, people may be unaware of their basic values even though their behaviour and their attitudes are affected by them.

As a consequence perhaps of the vast and rapid increase in scientific and professional work connected with human behaviour—in health, welfare, education, government, industry, the armed forces, and so on—the ethical aspects of dealing with individual people have been overshadowed by the technical aspects, and by bureaucratic, institutional, and career aspects—see Dailey (1971). There is a tendency to neglect the basic values underlying human service work and to pursue a policy of self-interest, e.g. the tendency to run a service or establishment too much in the interests of the employees and too little in the interests of customers or clients.

It is hardly possible to specify in detail an ethical code suitable for carrying out psychological case-studies. A code which attempts to set up ideal standards is too demanding and vague; a code which attempts to specify detailed practical rules is too cumbersome, sometimes not applicable, and not enforceable. What is needed is more collective agreement on basic principles and practical procedures, with an increased awareness of what issues are ethically important, what conflicts of interest are likely to arise, how ethical issues can be raised as matters of collective debate, how 'bad' or 'poor' practices can be replaced by 'good' or 'better' practices, how to handle malpractice—whether in major or minor matters, and how to educate and supervise juniors in the ethics of scientific and professional work.

Broadly speaking, scientists and practitioners in human services should try to be as objective as possible, think and act in ways that match the realities of the situation and are compatible with the ethical code accepted by one's reference group. This means having integrity (not acting out of fear or favour), not misrepresenting one's work (by distortion, by omitting facts, or introducing falsehoods). It also means carefully resolving conflicts of interest (not putting self-interest first). The interests of the clients, the wider community, the institution, and so on, should be taken into account. Scientific and professional work is a *collective* endeavour. Wherever possible, information should be made publicly available, obviously a requirement which conflicts with the need to maintain privacy and confidentiality (where to do otherwise would jeopardize the interests of the client and/or community).

No work should be undertaken that conflicts with the basic values of the scientific and professional community until such conflict has been publicly aired and resolved. No work should be done that exploits clients; conversely, the client must be made fully aware of his or her obligations (ethical behaviour must not be confused with unconditional one-sided effort). In dealing with problems, every effort should be made to analyse the problem fully (not simply accept it at face value) and to implement the best possible solution(s). Intervention without follow-up evaluation should be eschewed, except in the clearest cases. Workers should avoid making claims which cannot be substantiated, or denying obligations implicit in their role as scientists or professionals.

Where possible, and in confidence if necessary, the methods used to collect data, and the data too, should be made available for scrutiny by impartial observers or critics. Subjects in case-studies should normally give their informed consent before being studied. They should be kept fully informed of the progress of the case-study unless good ethical arguments can be used to justify withholding that information. The outcome of the study should also be made known to the Subject. The Subject's privacy should not be intruded upon except with the informed consent of the Subject unless the community interest is sufficient to override that safeguard. No undue social pressure (threats or promises) should be used to induce cooperation; the limit is set by 'reasonable' persuasion in the interests of the Subject, the community, or both. No 'treatment' or solution should be applied unless it can be shown to be effective, or at least to do no harm, or if it delays the application of a treatment or solution known to be more effective.

In those areas of professional and scientific work that are governed according to democratic principles with open access to information, the reasons for reaching decisions should be disclosed. This is to ensure that the logic underlying the decision can be scrutinized to check that all the relevant facts and considerations were taken into account and that the proper procedures were followed. Rules of inference *guide* but do not *dictate* decision-making in psychological case-studies, because, as we have seen, the arguments are not formally computed within a closed system of terms and relationships but rather constructed from the available information according to whatever rules are acceptable in the social context within which the case-study is conducted.

One neglected advantage of case-studies is that they provide information of a sort that is directly relevant to and fairly easily understood by those people who have been the Subjects of the case-studies, e.g. schoolchildren, marriage partners, businessmen, delinquents, and who might thereby gain insight. Another neglected advantage is that they can provide multiple perspectives on the truth—meaning alternative selections, interpretations, or construc-tions of the 'facts'. Case-studies in role-relationships in social organizations provide examples of these advantages.

The associated ethical problem, raised by Adelman *et al.* (1976), is that of *reporting* case-studies, which by definition are about particular people, organizations, or events and may contain personal and confidential informa-tion. The standard procedure, the one adopted for the case-studies in this book, is to make non-significant alterations to the report so that the particular case is unrecognizable, without destroying its main form and content. In some circumstances, however, such alterations will be self-defeating. For example, if the participants cannot identify themselves they may not benefit from reading the case-report. Although the alterations may be sufficient to prevent outsiders from recognizing the particular case they may not be sufficient to avoid embarrassing those with some inside knowledge of the case. There is some risk that censoring the material or changing some of the contents will distort important features of the case, so that it loses its scientific and professional value.

INVESTIGATOR EFFECTS

Investigators preparing biographies and case-studies are usually privy to a great deal of personal information about the Subject of their inquiry; so it would not be at all surprising to find a certain partiality or bias attributable to what we might call their personal or emotional involvement in the case. For example, having built up defences against strong emotional attachments they may fail to appreciate the role that such attachments may have in the life of another person. Emotional biases or blind spots of this sort may then lead to selective attention to the evidence and to faulty reasoning. Such reactions may operate outside conscious awareness and yet affect one's assessment of the other person. Much psychobiographical writing has been criticized for these reasons—see Anderson (1981). In psychoanalysis the term 'counter-transferance' is used to refer to the way in which the analyst's reactions to a patient may be affected by the analyst's own psychological make-up.

It is possible that the Investigator's expectations about the use to be made of the information in a case-study determines the contents and the organiza-tion of the material. This is another example of the way in which case-reports (and indeed case-studies themselves) fulfil an instrumental function. They are the means whereby the presenter (or Investigator) deals with the demands of the situation in which he find himself. For example, he may select from the case-records and present only those facts which support his personal view. Or he may present something of a caricature of the case to amuse his audience or to drive home an important point in professional training.

Hoffman *et al.* (1984) show that, under certain kinds of experimental conditions, the expectation of having to present or listen to a verbal account of a case increases the number of general traits attributed to the Subject of the case-study. It may be that the expectation of having to predict how the Subject will react to certain kinds of eventualities, or having to decide between alternative courses of action regarding the Subject, will sensitize Investigators to other aspects of the case, e.g. the Subject's motivation, social relationships, appearance, or moral qualities.

POLICY ISSUES

Many case-studies, presumably the vast majority, are carried out for specific practical purposes—to improve the health and welfare of individual Subjects and to implement the policy of various social organizations. There may be no particular responsibility laid on professional practitioners to advance basic scientific knowledge or methods, although they may attempt to do so in the interests of professional advancement or out of general concern for human welfare. Consequently much valuable time and effort must be wasted through inadequate professional practice and the failure of good practice to be properly evaluated and publicized as contributions to the advancement of social and behavioural science.

Decisions arrived at within the framework of a scientific and professional case-study may have policy implications, for example with regard to industrial management, parental rights, educational practice, or housing policy. In so far as the policy implications are not obvious, they may have to be examined by policy-makers and commentators who may lack the scientific expertise of the professionals who arrived at the case-decision. An appeal against that decision might have to be heard by a judicial or quasi-judicial tribunal concerned more with administrative or social policy issues than with the scientific merits of the case-study. Moreover, whereas a scientific approach might be inclined to adopt a long-term view and call for more evidence, a policy approach might seek an early resolution in the interests of public health and welfare. Professional case-workers are not unaware of the policy implications of the decisions they arrive at—at least those professionals who have worked for some time in a well-established institutional environment. Such professionals are engaged in a kind of hybrid activity—a behavioural science/social policy enterprise. Indeed, it could be argued that the quasi-judicial case-study method reflects the hybrid character of much social and behavioural science. The traditional methods—psychometrics and survey techniques and experimentation—were adopted in an attempt to separate out the objective, positive data-collecting aspects of investigation from the subjective, normative inferential aspects.

Generally speaking, the public accountability of an institution or agency forms part of the general background or context within which a case-study is carried out. That context will, in fact, condition the scientific and technical approach to the case—for example ruling out certain kinds of assessment, or compelling certain lines of inquiry to be pursued. That is what we mean by the hybrid character of a quasi-judicial case-study. At the same time the implication is that considerations of public policy come to form legitimate components in the argument which lead to a decision about the case.

A case-study which raises important policy issues is likely to be rigorously examined to see whether its scientific findings are correct. Although one cannot derive moral and policy recommendations from factual data (one cannot derive ought from is), one can at least use those factual data in moral and policy arguments. They may be used to show the implications of or contradictions in such arguments, as in studies of housing conditions or promotion appeals.

Given the present level of scientific and professional work, it seems unlikely that many case-studies would hold up well in the face of sustained, detailed, and critical evaluation. To withstand such scrutiny a case-study would have to spell out all its assumptions, eliminate all inconsistencies, disclose all methods and sources of information, rebut contradictory evidence, make all records available for examination, and show a conclusion firmly embedded in a clear web of supporting arguments. These criteria are to the case-study method what good design and analysis are to experiments and surveys.

One of the advantages of a critical review of a case-study is that, like an accident or a disaster, it resets the general level of quality control much higher than before, although over time, as we all know, the quality of human performance tends to diminish if it costs time and effort to maintain standards, as in hospital hygiene or teaching.

Unlike the policy issues generated by the physical and the biological sciences, for example with regard to drugs or nuclear waste, the scientific and technical levels of expertise required in the social and behavioural sciences are not far out of reach of the sorts of people who might be called upon to adjudicate on policy matters arising as a consequence of a psychological case-study. Indeed, many of these people will have some acquaintance with the social and behavioural sciences as part of their education and training.

Managing (as opposed to solving) the problems associated with a case-study is rarely a clear-cut process of rational decision-making and policy implementation, even if this is a kind of ideal towards which case-management aspires. Instead, case-management is likely to be a mixture of several different approaches: rational analysis and forward planning; adherence to ultra-stable 'ideological' commitments, i.e. managing the case according to familiar accepted principles; bargaining with 'interested parties'; and muddling through, i.e. doing the best one can in the circumstances at the time.

SOME IMPLICATIONS FOR BASIC AND APPLIED PSYCHOLOGY AND TRAINING

Jurisprudence—legal science—is too large a topic to discuss in detail. Our aim has been to see what bearing it has on scientific method in psychology and related disciplines. We have concentrated on three issues: rules of procedure, evidence, and case-law. The implications have been (a) that judicial rules of procedure are as rigorous as those that govern the design and conduct of experiments and surveys, given the difference in purpose; (b) that the judicial notion of 'evidence' is as important as the scientific notion of 'data'; (c) that abstract and general scientific concepts can be formulated and tested by a process akin to the development of case-law. The 'quasi-judicial' approach advocated in this book is an attempt to adapt these powerful judicial principles of procedure, evidence, and case-law to the scientific study of human behaviour.

Consider, for example, the notion of 'best evidence'. This refers to the fact that there may be several sorts of evidence available and relevant to a particular issue. If so, then one should use the most robust sort, direct rather than indirect or circumstantial evidence, first-hand accounts rather than hearsay, documents rather than verbal reports, independent and impartial evidence rather than confounded or self-interested views, competent and reliable information rather than inexpert and unreliable information. Although the notions of 'good evidence' and 'best evidence' are easily understood, they are often neglected in actual case-studies.

Except perhaps for the view that it is basic to scientific method, most of the views expressed about the quasi-judicial method, including those on logic and social cognition, are not particularly novel. Many are probably already accepted in a tacit way by readers. What I have tried to do is to collect these ideas together and organize them into an explicit conceptual and methodological framework. What remains to be considered is how such a framework might be used not merely as an adjunct to experimental and survey techniques but as a main method of scientific inquiry in psychology.

Adopting a 'legal science' framework for psychology might entail redefining its subject-matter and redrawing its internal boundaries. We have already had occasion to refer to various broad areas of interest within which case-work is important both practically and theoretically—for example, probation, social work, clinical psychology, criminology, national security, marriage guidance, political analysis, educational psychology, and occupational guidance. If one were to compare cases *within* one of these fields one would probably find considerable overlap in concepts, methods, findings, and applications. If one were to compare cases *between* these fields the overlap would probably be much less. The implication is that, since 'psychological' factors enter into the analyses of individual cases in all these, and many other, different areas, there ought to be some way of describing and classifying these factors so that the family resemblances between cases that they are responsible for can be detected with the required reliability and validity.

Consider, for example, the 'psychological' considerations that might enter into a set of comparisons and contrasts for political case-studies—say of British Prime Ministers. It is obvious that competent Investigators are likely to agree substantially on the sorts of issues that should be considered and on the sorts of methods appropriate for collecting relevant evidence. They are likely to differ mainly on matters of interpretation. Interpreting evidence (data) means introducing some kind of explanatory concept that gives meaning to a set of observations. Thus, psychological explanations involving politically relevant motives, traits, expectations, abilities, defects, and so on, can be introduced to 'make sense' of a Prime Minister's political successes or failures. Psychological considerations, of course, do not rule out other sorts of considerations—physical health, accident, or other circumstances—affecting a Prime Minister's performance or achievements.

The point is that psychological considerations can make a significant contribution to historical and political analysis but the sorts of psychological considerations that help to 'make sense' of the behaviour of politicians may be irrelevant to the sorts of psychological considerations that help to 'make sense' of the behaviour of artists, athletes, delinquents, or unhappily married couples. Each of these other areas has its own sorts of psychological considerations, without which the behaviour referred to remains unexplained and something of a puzzle.

A 'legal science' approach in psychology would define its subject-matter as 'the study of persons in situations'. This is compatible with one broad conception of psychology as 'the scientific study of man in his environment'. Although this latter conception is over-inclusive (it covers human ecology, including geography, economics, and the social sciences generally) it does lead to an interesting and hitherto neglected perspective which we can call 'human autoecology'—the study of the needs and reactions of individuals to their surroundings—see Clarke (1965). This approach would obviously emphasize the psychobiological characteristics of the person, including the person's subjective appreciation of his or her situation (local surroundings). Readers may find it strange that we have somehow contrived to combine a quasi-judicial approach to the psychological study of individual cases with what is, literally, a biological approach. The combination is not accidental—the intention is to coordinate two broad perspectives—the ecological and the cultural—in the hope of perceiving human nature in greater depth.

This sort of biosocial approach would divide psychology's subject-matter in the usual way between basic concepts and applications. The basic concepts would be much the same as they are now—motivation, cognition, emotion, social relationships, and so on, but with rather more emphasis on how these basic processes interlock with each other and relate to the immediate environment in the organization of behaviour—this is what 'human autoecology' would be about. Applied psychology or 'applicable psychology'—see Duckworth (1981) and Stanley (1985)—would cover a wide variety of ways of using scientific psychology to understand and manage psychological and social cases. Psychology would be driven more by the need for localized practical applications than by the search for abstract, universal theories, laboratory demonstrations, and population surveys.

In psychology the term case-study is most commonly used to refer to the study of an individual person, whether in terms of that person's life-history, current situation, or both. Most of the examples of psychological case-studies in this book are of these sorts. It follows that the most relevant branches of psychology are personality study and clinical or abnormal psychology. However, the concepts and methods advocated for a case-study approach to personality and adjustment are radically different from the traditional approach to these topics. Furthermore, my main intention has been to demonstrate the *scientific* character and value of the case-study method not only in other branches of psychology, but also in the social and behavioural sciences generally and to a lesser extent in the biological and natural sciences.

Let us consider briefly what sorts of case-studies can be found in branches of psychology other than personality study and clinical psychology. First, developmental psychology: Piaget's investigations into children's thinking are case-studies to the extent that no great reliance was placed on close experimental control and statistical argument. Much recent work, however, has criticized the relative lack of controls and psychometric norms in Piaget's studies and has produced a wealth of commentary and refinement—particularly in relation to the way contextual factors, such as the form of the instructions or questions, stimulus materials, and so on, affect children's responses. The main point, however, is that it was essentially a case-study method that led to this very important breakthrough in our understanding of children's cognitive development.

Second, social behaviour: there have been a number of so-called natural experiments or 'contrived situations' in which the behaviour of people, in what they take to be a real-life situation, is studied by non-reactive methods.

Examples include pedestrian behaviour, class-room behaviour, family meal-times, children's play behaviour. These are case-studies to the extent that no reliance is placed on sampling and statistical inference and little or no attempt is made to control conditions (except in the sense that a particular feature of the situation is contrived or simulated). Some of these investigations could be regarded as low-grade or pilot experiments or demonstrations in human ethology in the sense that they lack the intensiveness and detail of case-studies. The point is that scientific methods vary in character and quality, and the differences between them can sometimes be blurred. Social psychology overlaps with sociology and social anthropology, disciplines in which case-studies have been extensively used.

Third, animal behaviour: the study of animals in their natural surroundings is called ethology. In many of these studies the emphasis is on the detailed description and analysis of particular organisms in their natural habitat. The problems of sampling and generalization are less severe in animal ethology than in human ethology, because of the relatively stereotyped character of the behaviour under investigation. There is also less likelihood that the method of investigation will disturb natural patterns of behaviour. One might, for example, set out to study the manner and effects of possible predation by ravens on a particular colony of kittiwakes, or one might attempt to study the establishment of a territory by a domestic tom-cat. The essential scientific character of studies like these resides not in statistical inference—the estimation of population parameters from sample statistics or the testing of statistical hypotheses—but in the structure of logical inference imposed on empirical evidence through rational argument. These studies, once they are complete, purport to provide an account of the real world (of animal behaviour) in terms of concepts and relationships which are applicable well outside the particular case of the kittiwake colony or the domestic tom-cat. What we have said, obviously, does not preclude the use of experimental and quantitative methods in animal ethology. The question is 'Which scientific method is most appropriate given the nature of the investigation and the resources available?'

Fourth, physiological psychology: perhaps the best examples of case-studies in this area are of individuals with exceptional characteristics. For example, in the literature we can find case-studies and clinical studies of individuals who have suffered a particular sort of brain damage, who are colour-blind in one eye but not the other, who exhibit peculiar memory losses, who are seriously maladjusted, who recover their vision after a long period of blindness, who have a genetic defect, who have a 'split brain', and so on. The main value of such exceptional cases is that they provide us with opportunities to investigate psychological processes under conditions which do not normally arise. The results of such investigations, even in the absence of good experimental controls and precise measurement, can at least raise new issues and demonstrate effects not previously observed. Again, there is no question of engaging in statistical inference. Such case-studies demonstrate, i.e. provide the empirical material for, rational arguments about the physiological basis of psychological functions. The concepts and relationships used in these arguments apply well beyond the particular cases which exemplify them. Case-studies in physiological psychology, including neuropsychology and behavioural pharmacology, are similar to the sorts of case-studies found in medicine. As we have seen, the case-study method in the social and behavioural sciences can be traced back, in part, to the clinical method in medicine.

Fifth, applied psychology: case-study methods are highly regarded in this area. It is surprising, therefore, that the case-study method has occupied such a low status in academic or basic psychology, where, one would have supposed, the main conceptual and methodological advances in scientific knowledge were being made. Applied psychology necessarily deals with particular problems, areas, instances, or cases—maladjusted or retarded individuals, operators of machines, social organizations, accidents, selection and training programmes, crowd behaviour, environmental stress, delinquents, military and political operations, and so on. The applied psychologist's ability to predict and control particular outcomes—improving people's emotional adjustment and functional capacities, reducing accidents, raising morale, and so on—is indicative of the level of understanding achieved.

As with the other branches of psychology to which we have referred, applied psychology necessarily employs abstract concepts and generalizations which extend beyond any particular case-study. The confidence one has in these abstract concepts and generalizations, i.e. explanatory frameworks, depends on how robust they are—how well they perform in accounting for further cases of a comparable kind.

How can the case-study method help basic and applied psychology to further each other's interests? One possibility is through the recognition that psychological understanding and control can operate at a relatively low level of abstractness and generality and within a relatively restricted framework or local context. In other words, one need not be overly concerned with developing highly abstract, universal, context-free laws or principles of the sort normally associated with the physical sciences: instead, one can work with concepts and rules which are 'field-dependent' in Toulmin's sense.

It is sometimes supposed that an experimental study or a systematic survey somehow provides a guarantee of the scientific worth of its findings—a guarantee backed by the formality of the associated theory and the rigour of the method. There is no such guarantee, otherwise there would be no disputes about the internal and external validity of experiments. Conversely, it is sometimes supposed that the findings of a case-study provide only an illustrative example. This is not so, otherwise the case-study method would not have contributed significantly to the historical development of the social, medical, and behavioural sciences. One might just as well argue that an experiment is only an illustration of a theory! A case-study is a systematic description and interpretation of the matter under investigation. In a case-study, as in an experiment, what carries scientific conviction is the cogency of the argument.

The limitations of the experimental method are well known in relation to the study of human behaviour: its sensitivity to minor variations in sampling and procedure leading to failures of replication, i.e. to findings which are not robust; its confusion of aggregate effects with generalized effects, i.e. its tendency to confuse an average statistical effect with a general or common effect; its tendency to prefer methodological rigour over conceptual or practical importance; its liability to experimenter effects and demand factors; its neglect of contextual factors; its presumption that the experimental method is superior to other methods regardless of circumstances.

Obviously, the case-study method cannot replace other scientific methods such as the laboratory experiment or social survey. Scientific problems can be investigated by different methods; these methods may illuminate each other's results. However, just as some problems can only be studied effectively by means of the experimental or survey method, so other problems are appropriately studied by means of the case-study method.

One possible reason for the lack of interest in the case-study method is the difficulty experienced in putting together a complex web of evidence and inference. By contrast, experimental and survey methods deliberately simplify the framework of their investigations so as to focus sharply and narrowly on the relationships between a small number of distinct conditions and a limited number of salient variables. Consequently, the argument from the data to conclusions is presumed to be largely free of contextual considerations, short, and unambiguous.

One advantage of the case-study as a scientific method is that it attempts to take account of contextual factors and the internal complexities of the matter under investigation, as in the study of aggressive behaviour, occupational adjustment, or weight control. The weakness of the case-study method, *vis-à-vis* the experimental method, is that there is no *control* over the factors at work. However, many experimental and survey investigations take into account only a few of the more obvious factors, and run into severe difficulties of design, administration, and analysis if an attempt is made to increase the number of factors under consideration. This is apart from the problems associated with external validity, sampling, and so on.

There is a tendency to supposes that experimental and survey methods generate definitive findings; but this is a dangerous misconception. Scientific findings are never definitive, and scientific knowledge, by definition, is liable to revision through the emergence of new ideas, methods, and findings. The so-called 'crucial experiment' is really only an attempt to decide between competing accounts of a phenomenon, and may not prove to be so crucial in the long run. The main aim in science is to arrive at explanations and predictions which are robust, in the sense of being capable of replication under diverse conditions. The means whereby such explanations and predictions are arrived at is a secondary issue.

The relationship between the quasi-judicial case-study approach to problems in psychology and the traditional experimental and survey approaches can be illustrated briefly by reference to a possible line of work involving scientific research and professional practice. I refer to the rapidly expanding field of adult development and ageing. Social and behavioural gerontology provides an interesting test-bed for the quasi-judicial case-study method. For example, the personal adjustment (life-satisfaction) of an elderly person depends upon a wide variety of factors—psychological, biological, social, and technical. Surveys have been carried out to identify the main determinants of life-satisfaction of the elderly in general, but these have done little more than confirm common-sense inferences based on everyday experience. Life-satisfaction in adult life and old age is not an area that lends itself to experimental inquiry. The case-study method, however, provides not only a means for conceptualizing life-satisfaction as a psychological and social *process* (taking account of individual differences and different types of life-style) but also a means for deciding on practical action (taking into account local conditions).

Case-studies in this area could be used in connection with longitudinal studies of service provision. Some of the information made available would be quantifiable. As the cases accumulated, comparisons and contrasts between them would generate prototypes and sub-categories. One would be able to identify the main features of each category and observe the way factors interact to produce different outcomes in different cases. Needless to say, such cases would provide invaluable material for teaching purposes. Other branches of psychology offer comparable scope for the employment of the case-study method.

Thus, a further consequence for psychology of adopting a quasi-judicial case-study approach to its subject-matter might be to shift the emphasis in psychology training. At present the emphasis in psychology is almost exclusively on the experimental method. The problems of design and statistical analysis are dealt with in considerable detail. Similarly, in sociology, the emphasis is largely on survey techniques and the so-called field methods—interviewing, participant observations.

A shift in emphasis would mean dealing with case-studies and situation analyses much more thoroughly than at present, and follow the lines indicated in preceding chapters. As we have seen, the quasi-judicial case-study method can play a major role in training as well as in the advancement of scientific knowledge and professional practice.

The practical work associated with quasi-judicial case-study methodology presents no great problem. There are enormous opportunities for student placements in natural settings. For many students in continuing education and post-professional education their own work environment, contacts, and clients should provide a wide range of opportunities for practical work associated with this alternative methodology. The work will help to bridge the gap between common-sense levels and professional/scientific levels of understanding. This could be achieved by exercises in which students would start with a common-sense approach to cases. Their progress would be monitored by instructors who would help students to appreciate the limits of a common-sense approach and the benefits to be derived from professional and scientific methods of the sort we have considered, including any special technical procedures that are available, e.g. psychometric assessment, interviewing and counselling techniques, analysis of documents.

SUMMARY AND CONCLUSIONS

The issue of terminology is raised again with particular reference to the relationship between psychological case-studies, personality descriptions, and performance appraisals. Some clarification is offered.

Psychological case-studies can contribute to the scientific enterprise of psychology and related disciplines. Four basic features of such a contribution are outlined: the way it accounts for human behaviour; its main concepts, methods, applications, and findings; the kinds of people engaged in the enterprise; and the social and administrative framework within which it operates. The case-study method is by no means well established, although there are strong arguments in its favour.

Distinctions are drawn between psychological case-studies and other sorts of entities with which they might be confused. Such comparisons help to define the nature and scope of psychological case-studies.

The case-study method is reflexive in the sense that case-studies can become the Object of other case-studies, leading to what are called higher-order case-studies, such as a review of, or a judicial inquiry into, a case which was supposed to have been settled.

The social psychology of reputation is a relatively neglected phenomenon closely related to the study of individual cases. It deals with the way information about a person is distributed in different social groups and the way reputation becomes a determinant of personal adjustment, not just for the Subject of a case-study but also for the Investigator(s) and participants.

The notion of a 'prototypical case' is central to the question of how we systematize and regulate our thinking about the people we study. As we encounter successive cases in a given area of interest we are naturally led to make comparisons and contrasts between them. This leads gradually to the formation of types or categories of Subject who share certain important psychological resemblances. Ideally, most Subjects fall into one or the other of these types and are understood and managed within a standard conceptual framework or schema. This process organizes and simplifies our approach to this area of interest. It provides a sort of 'case-law' by means of which Investigators can deal with their cases without having to solve each problem-case anew. It is essential to be clear about the relationship between the *particular* case and the *general* case.

The importance of the judicial method of inquiry as a model for the social and behavioural sciences is further emphasized. This is not to diminish the importance of experimental and survey methods, but to make the point that different sorts of problem call for different methods of inquiry. What is proposed is a 'quasi-judicial' method for studying individual cases which attempts to combine the best features of judicial science and natural science. An attempt is made to provide a basic philosophy of science to justify this approach. Having reviewed the diversity and importance of individual case-studies, it is concluded that the findings of scientific case-studies depend not on the logic of statistical inference but on the logic of substantive reasoning. Case-studies can generate and test abstract and general theories; the case-study method combines basic and applied science.

It is possible to develop a 'general theory' or 'grammar' of psychological case-studies, if only in rudimentary form. The grammar consists of a number of rewrite rules which demonstrate the general structure of case-reports. This makes it possible to critically examine them. The identification of the main 'points' of a case-study make it possible to summarize the account in terms of both empirical content and theoretical organization.

Concern with the 'grammar' of psychological case-studies leads on to the question of whether natural language processing methods in artificial intelligence will eventually enable us to develop 'expert systems' to deal with case-material in different areas of psychological adjustment. It is possible that developments in substantive logic—the logic of ordinary language—will make such 'expert systems' possible. Such systems, of course, would be very different from the current computerized methods of psychometric assessment, in the sense of being able to cope with a much wider range of input materials.

Psychological case-studies necessarily involve ethical considerations. The more obvious issues include: the nature of ethical arguments; the problem of developing an ethical code for Investigators; balancing the rights of the Subject against those of the community; and the problem of confidentiality.

Case-studies, like other methods in the social and behavioural sciences, are liable to Investigator effects which distort findings.

Issues of social policy may play an important part in the way a case-study is pursued and acted upon.

Case-study methods are already extensively used in clinical and educational psychology and social work. If the quasi-judicial case-study method were to be used more extensively in psychology, one might see a number of changes. To begin with, there would be a considerable shift of emphasis from basic (academic and experimental) psychology to applied psychology. There would be a considerable extension and diversification of areas of interest in applied psychology, with possibly renewed interest in interdisciplinary areas related, for example, to social work, politics and government, community affairs, the law, medicine, business and industry, and the Armed Services. Systematic case-studies in these and other areas could be expected to be fruitful as regards the development of basic concepts, as well as leading directly to useful practical applications.

A possible name for this general field of psychology would be 'human autoecology'—the study of individual persons in their normal habitats.

However, case-study methods on a limited scale can be found in traditional areas of psychology, for example in personality study, developmental psychology, social psychology, animal behaviour, physiological psychology. So there is every possibility that these areas too would benefit from an increased investment in the quasi-judicial method.

No scientific method can guarantee the truth of its findings. All methods have their limitations. Different problems call for different methods. The main advantage of the quasi-judicial case-study method is that it seems to be a fundamental form of inquiry which can if necessary be applied to the evaluation of experiments and surveys, and can be applied reflexively in the evaluation of case-studies. It has considerable value as a general method of instruction in psychology and related disciplines.

References

Adams-Webber, J. R. (1979). *Personal Construct Theory. Concepts and Applications*, John Wiley & Sons, Chichester.

Adelman, C., Jenkins, D., and Kemmis, S. (1976). 'Re-thinking case study: notes from the second Cambridge conference', *Cambridge Journal of Education*, **6**, 139–150.

Alexander, P. (1971). *An Introduction to Logic. The Criticism of Arguments* (second printing), George Allen & Unwin, London.

Allen, C. K. (1964). *Law in the Making* (7th edition), Oxford University Press, London.

Allport, G. W. (1937). *Personality*, Constable, London.

Allport, G. W. (1942). *The Use of Personal Documents in Psychological Science*, Social Science Research Council, New York.

Allport, G. W. (ed.) (1965). *Letters from Jenny*, Harcourt, Brace, & World, New York.

Anderson, W. J. (1981). 'Psychobiographical methodology: the case of Williams James', in L. Wheeler (ed.), *Review of Personality and Social Psychology*, vol. 2, Sage Publications, Beverly Hills.

Andrews, K. R. (1953). *The Case Method of Teaching Human Relations and Administration*, Harvard University Press, Cambridge.

Antaki, C. (ed.) (1981). *The Psychology of Ordinary Explanations of Social Behaviour*, Academic Press, London.

Argyle, M. (1975). *Bodily Communication*, Methuen & Company, London.

Armistead, C. (1984). 'How useful are case studies?', *Training and Development Journal*, February, pp. 75–77.

Austin, J. L. (1962). *How to Do Things With Words* (ed. by J. O. Urmson), Oxford University Press, London.

Bakan, D. (1967). *On Method: Towards a Reconstruction of Psychological Investigation*, Jossey-Bass, San Francisco.

Baldwin, A. L. (1942). 'Personal structure analysis: a statistical method for investigation of the single personality', *Journal of Abnormal and Social Psychology*, **37**, 163–183.

Barker, R. G. (ed.) (1963). *The Stream of Behavior*, Appleton-Century-Crofts, Meredith Publishing Company, New York.

Barker, R. G., and Wright, H. F. (1951). *One Boy's Day*, Harper & Row, New York.

Baruch, D. W. (1952). *One Little Boy*, Julian Press, New York.

Beck, P. (1981). *Case Exercises in Clinical Reasoning*, Blackwell, Oxford.

Becker, H. S. (1963). *Outsiders: Studies in the Sociology of Deviance*, Free Press, New York.

Becker, H. S. (1966). 'Introduction', in C. Shaw, *The Jack-Roller*, University of Chicago Press, Chicago.

Becker, H. S. (1968). 'Social observation and case studies', in D. L. Sills (ed.), *International Encyclopedia of the Social Sciences*, vol. 11, The Macmillan Company and the Free Press, New York.

Bell, P. B., and Staines, P. J. (1981). *Reasoning and Argument in Psychology*, Routledge & Kegan Paul, London.

Berstein, S. (1984). 'A case history demonstrating the complementary use of pyschodynamic and behavioral techniques in psychotherapy', *Psychotherapy: Theory, Research and Practice*, **21**, 402–407.

Bertaux, D. (ed.) (1981). *Biography and Society. The Life History Approach in the Social Sciences*, Sage Studies in International Sociology, vol. 23, Beverly Hills.

Bertaux, D., and Kohli, M. (1984). 'The life story approach: a continental view', *Annual Review of Sociology*, **10**, 215–237.

Bistline, J. L., and Frieden, F. P. (1984). 'Anger control: a case study of a stress inoculation treatment for a chronic aggressive patient', *Cognitive Therapy and Research*, **81**, 551–556.

Blankenship, R. L. (1974). 'Case records language: towards a sociolinguistic perspective on deviance labelling', *Sociology and Social Research*, **58**, 253–261.

Block, J. (1971). *Lives Through Time*, Bancroft Books, Berkeley.

Boden, M. (1977). *Artificial Intelligence and Natural Man*, Harvester Press, Hassocks, Sussex.

Bolgar, H. (1965). 'The case-study method', in B. Wolman (ed.), *Handbook of Clinical Psychology*, McGraw-Hill, New York.

Boswell, D. M. (1969). 'Personal crises and the mobilization of the social network', in J. C. Mitchell (ed.), *Social Networks in Urban Situations*, University of Manchester Press, Manchester.

Bradley, J. V. (1984). 'Antinonrobustness: a case study in the sociology of science', *Bulletin of the Psychonomic Society*, **22**, 463–466.

Braine, M. D. S. (1978). 'On the relation between the natural logic of reasoning and standard logic', *Psychological Review*, **85**, 1–21.

Breakwell, G. M., and Rowett, C. (1982). *Social Work: the Social Psychological Approach*, Van Nostrand Reinhold (UK) Company, Wokingham.

Brewer, J. M. *et al.* (1926). *Case Studies in Educational and Vocational Guidance*, Ginn, Boston (cited in R. I. Watson, 1949).

Brewer, M. B., and Collins, B. E. (eds) (1981). *Scientific Inquiry and the Social Sciences*, Jossey-Bass, San Francisco.

Bristol, M. (1936). *Handbook of Social Case Recording*, University of Chicago Press, Chicago.

British Psychological Society (1985). 'A code of conduct for psychologists', *Bulletin of the British Psychological Society*, **38**, 41–43.

Bromley, D. B. (1966). 'The social psychology of reputation', *Bulletin of the British Psychological Society*, **19**, 73.

Bromley, D. B. (1970). 'An approach to theory construction in the psychology of development and aging', in L. R. Goulet and P. B. Baltes (eds), *Lifespan Developmental Psychology*, Academic Press, New York.

Bromley, D. B. (1977). *Personality Description in Ordinary Language*, John Wiley & Sons, Chichester.

Bromley, D. B. (1978). 'Natural language and the development of the self', in C. B. Keasey (ed.), *Nebraska Symposium on Motivation 1977: Social Cognitive Development*, University of Nebraska Press, Lincoln.

Burgess, E. W. (ed.) (1929). *Personality and the Social Group*, University of Chicago Press, Chicago.

Burton, A., and Harris, R. E. (eds) (1966). *Clinical Studies of Personality* (2 vols), Harper & Row, New York.

Bush, M. (1984). 'The public and private purpose of case records', *Children and Youth Services*, **6**, 1–18.

Campbell, D. T. (1975). ' "Degrees of freedom" and the case study', *Comparative Political Studies*, **8**, 178–193.

Campbell, S. (1984). 'Teaching by the case method', *Harvard Business School Bulletin*, **60**, 88–95.

Cane, R. D., and Shapiro, B. (1985). *Case Studies in Critical Care Medicine*, Blackwell, Oxford.

Cantor, N., and Mischel, W. (1979). 'Prototypes in person perception', *Advances in Experimental Social Psychology*, **12**, 5–42.

Carr, L. J. (1948). *Situational Analysis: An Observational Approach to Introductory Sociology*, Harper & Brothers, New York.

Chassan, J. B. (1979). *Research Design in Clinical Psychology and Psychiatry* (revised edition), Appleton-Century-Crofts, New York.

Cheshire, N. M. (1979). 'A big hand for Little Hans', *Bulletin of the British Psychological Society*, **32**, 320–323.

Chilver, J. (1984). *Business Decisions: A Cross-Modular Case-Study Approach*, Macmillan, London.

Cicourel, A. V. (1974). 'Police practices and official records', in R. Turner (ed.), *Ethnomethodology*, Penguin Books, Harmondsworth.

Clark, T., and Penycate, J. (1976). *Psychopath: The Case of Patrick Mackay*, Routledge & Kegan Paul, London.

Clarke, G. L. (1965). *Elements of Ecology*, John Wiley & Sons, New York.

Cleckley, H. (1964). *The Mask of Sanity* (4th edition), Mosby, St Louis, Missouri.

Cohen, L. J. (1980). 'The logic of proof', *Criminal Law Review*, 91–103.

Compher, J. V. (1984). 'The case conference revisited: a systems view', *Child Welfare*, **LXIII**, 411–418.

Confer, W. N. (1984). 'Hypnotic treatment of multiple personality: a case study', *Psychotherapy*, **21**, 408–413.

Conrad, E., and Maul, T. (1981). *Introduction to Experimental Psychology*, John Wiley & Sons, Chichester.

Conway, A. V. (1978). 'Little Hans: misrepresentation of the evidence?', *Bulletin of the British Psychological Society*, **31**, 285–287.

Cook, T. D., and Campbell, D. T. (1979). *Quasi-Experimentation. Design and Analysis Issues for Field Settings*, Houghton Mifflin Company, Boston.

Cooper, B. M. (1964, reprint 1979). *Writing Technical Reports*, Penguin Books, Harmondsworth.

Cooper, I. S. (1973). *The Victim is Always the Same*, Harper & Row, New York.

Corey, G. (1982). *A Case Approach to Counseling and Psychotherapy*, Wadsworth International, Brooks/Cole, Belmont, California.

Counselor Education and Supervision, **24**(1), (1984). Special Issue: computers in counselor training.

Cronbach, L. J. (1975). 'Beyond the two disciplines of scientific psychology', *American Psychologist*, **30**, 116–127.

Cronbach, L. J., and associates (1980). *Toward a Reform of Program Evaluation. Aims, Methods and Institutional Arrangements*, Jossey-Bass, San Francisco.

Crossley, M., and Vulliamy, G. (1984). 'Case-study research methods and comparative education', *Comparative Education*, **20**, 193–207.

Curti, M. (1980). *Human Nature in American Thought. A History*, University of Wisconsin Press, Wisconsin.

Dailey, C. A. (1971). *Assessment of Lives: Personality Evaluation in a Bureaucratic Society*, Jossey-Bass, San Francisco.

Darley, J. G. (1949). 'The structure of the systematic case study in individual diagnosis and counseling', in R. I. Watson (ed.), *Readings in the Clinical Method in Psychology*, Harper & Brothers, New York.

Davidson, P. O., and Costello, C. G. N. (1969). *N=1: Experimental Studies of Single Cases*, Van Nostrand-Reinhold, New York.

Davies, J. (1983). *Primary School Case-Study. Breckfield Infant School*, Open University, Milton Keynes.

Decker, J. E., and Whelan, R. K. (1984). 'The Northeast Florida Area Agency on Aging. A case study in organisational design and evaluation', in L. G. Nigro (ed.), *Decision Making in The Public Sector*, Marcel Dekker, New York.

Denzin, N. K. (1970). 'The life history method', in N. K. Denzin (ed.), *Sociological Methods*, Aldine, Chicago.

Department of Health and Social Security (1974). *Report of the Committee of Inquiry into the Care and Supervision Provided in Relation to Maria Colwell*, HMSO, London.

Devlin, Lord, P. (1976). *Report to the Secretary of State for the Home Department of the Departmental Committee on Evidence of Identification in Criminal Cases*, HMSO, London.

De Waele, J. P., and Harré R. (1976). 'The personality of individuals', in R. Harré (ed.), *Personality*, Blackwell, Oxford.

De Waele, J. P., and Harré, R. (1979). 'Autobiography as a psychological method', in G. P. Ginsburg (ed.), *Emerging Strategies in Social Psychological Research*, John Wiley & Sons, Chichester.

Dewald, P. A. (1972). *The Psychoanalytic Process: A Case Illustration*, Basic Books, New York.

Diesing, P. (1971). *Patterns of Discovery in the Social Sciences*, Aldine, New York.

Dixon, N. F. (1976). *On the Psychology of Military Incompetence*, Jonathan Cape, London.

Doig, A. (1984). *Corruption and Misconduct in Contemporary British Politics*, Penguin Books, Harmondsworth.

Dollard, J. (1935). *Criteria for the Life-History*, Yale University Press, New Haven.

Duckworth, D. H. (1981). 'Toward a psychological science that can be applied', *Bulletin of the British Psychological Society*, **34**, 237–240.

Duckworth, D. H. (1983). 'Evaluation of a programme for increasing the effectiveness of personal problem-solving', *British Journal of Psychology*, **74**, 119–127.

Dyer, M. G. (1983). *In-Depth Understanding. A Computer Model of Integrated Processing for Narrative Comprehension*. The MIT Press, Cambridge, Massachusetts.

Easton, G. (1982). *Learning from Case Studies*, Prentice-Hall International, Inc., London.

Edington, E. S. (1984). 'Statistics and single case analysis', in M. Hersen, R. M. Eisler, and P. M. Miller (eds), *Progress in Behavior Modification*, vol. 16, Academic Press, Orlando.

Edmondson, R. (1984). *Rhetoric in Sociology*, Macmillan, London.

Edwards, W., and Newman, J. R. (1982). *Multiattribute Evaluation*, Sage Publications, Beverly Hills.

Edwards, W., Lindman, H., and Phillips, L. D. (1965). 'Emerging technologies for making decisions', in *New Directions in Psychology*, vol. II, Holt, Rinehart & Winston, New York.

Egan, G. (1982a). *The Skilled Helper* (2nd edition), Brooks/Cole, Monterey, California.

Egan, G. (1982b). *Exercises in Helping Skills* (2nd edition). Brooks/Cole, Monterey, California.

Eggleston, R. (1978). *Evidence, Proof and Probability*, Weidenfeld & Nicolson, London.

Eley, R. M., and Middleton, L. M. (1984). *Report of a Pilot Study of Delayed Discharges from Hospital*, University of Liverpool, Institute of Human Ageing (mimeo), Liverpool.

Ellis, A. W., Miller D., and Sin, G. (1983). 'Wernicke's aphasia and normal language processing: a case study in cognitive neuropsychology', *Cognition*, **15**, 111–144.

Elstein, A. S., Schulman, L. S., and Sprafka, S. A. (1978). *Medical Problem-Solving: An Analysis of Clinical Reasoning*, Harvard University Press, Cambridge, Massachusetts.

Epstein, S. (1983). 'Aggregation and beyond: some basic issues on the prediction of behavior', *Journal of Personality*, **51**, 360–392.

Evans, J. (1954). *Three Men*, Gollancz, London.

Eysenck, H. J. (1965). *Fact and Fiction in Psychology*, Penguin Books, Harmondsworth.

Eysenck, H. J. (ed.) (1976). *Case Studies in Behaviour Therapy*, Routledge & Kegan Paul, London.

Feldman, P., and Orford, J. (eds) (1980). *Psychological Problems. The Social Context*, John Wiley & Sons, Chichester.

Festinger, L., Riecken, H., and Schachter, S. (1956). *When Prophecy Fails*, University of Minnesota Press, Minneapolis.

Fidel, R. (1984). 'The case-study method: a case study', *Library and Information Science Research*, **6**, 273–288.

Fiske, D. W. (1961). 'The inherent variability of behavior', in D. W. Fiske and S. R. Maddi (eds), *Functions of Varied Experience*, Dorsey Press, Homewood, Illinois.

Flanagan, J. C. (1982). *New Insights to Improve the Quality of Life at Age 70*, American Institutes for Research in the Behavioral Sciences, Palo Alto, California.

Foreman, P. (1948). 'The theory of case studies', *Social Forces*, **26**, 408–419.

Fox, R. (1983). 'The past is always present: creative methods for capturing the life story', *Clinical Social Work Journal*, **11**, 368–378.

Freud, S. (1947). *Leonardo da Vinci* (trans. A. A. Brill), Random House, New York.

Freud, S. (1953). 'Analysis of a phobia in a five-year-old boy', in S. Freud, *Collected Papers*, vol. III, Hogarth Press, London.

Freud, S. (1977). *Case Histories I 'Dora' and 'Little Hans'*, The Pelican Freud Library, vol. 8, Penguin Books, Harmondsworth.

Freud, S. (1979). *Case Histories II 'Rat Man', Schreber, 'Wolf Man', Female Homosexuality*, The Pelican Freud Library, vol. 9, Penguin Books, Harmondsworth.

Fuller, J. F. C. (1970). *The Decisive Battles of the Western World*, (2 vols), Paladin, Granada, London.

Garbett, G. K. (1970). 'The analysis of social situations', *Man*, **5**, 214–227.

Garfinkel, H. (1974). ' "Good" organizational reasons for "bad" case records', in R. Turner (ed.), *Ethnomethodology*, Penguin Books, Harmondsworth.

Garraty, J. A. (1957). *The Nature of Biography*, Vintage Books, New York.

George, A. L. (1979). 'Case studies and theory development: the method of structured, focused comparisons', in P. G. Lauren (ed.), *Diplomacy: New Approaches in History, Theory, and Policy*, Free Press, New York.

Germain, C. (1970). 'Casework and science: a historical encounter', in R. W. Roberts and R. H. Nee (eds), *Theories of Social Casework*, University of Chicago Press, Chicago.

Gingerich, W. J. (1984). 'Generalizing single-case evaluation from classroom to practice setting', *Journal of Education for Social Work*, **20**, 74–82.

Gluckman, M. (1961). 'Ethnographic data in British social anthropology', *Sociological Review*, **9**, 5–17.

Glaser, B., and Strauss, A. L. (1967). *The Discovery of Grounded Theory*, Aldine, Chicago.

Goguen, J. A., Weiner, J. L., and Linde, C. (1981). *Reasoning and Natural Explanation*, SRI International, Menlo Park, California.

Gottschalk, L., Kluckhohn, C., and Angell, R. (1945). *The Use of Personal Documents in History, Anthropology and Sociology*, Social Science Research Council, New York.

Greenwald, H. (ed.) (1959). *Great Cases in Psychoanalysis*, Ballantine Books, New York.

Greil, A. L., and Rudy, D. R. (1984). 'What have we learned from process models of conversion? An examination of ten case studies', *Sociological Focus*, **17**, 305–323.

Haines, J. (1975). *Skills and Methods in Social Work*, Constable, London.

Hamilton, D. (1980). 'Some contrasting assumptions about case study research and survey analysis', in H. Simons (ed.), *Towards A Science of the Singular. Essays About Case Study in Educational Research and Evaluation*, CARE Occasional Publications, No. 10, Centre for Applied Research in Education, University of East Anglia, Norwich.

Hanley, I. G., and Lusty, K. (1984). 'Memory aids in reality orientation: a single-case study', *Behavioural Research and Therapy*, **22**, 709–712.

Hawkes, A. R. (1937). 'The cumulative record and its uses', *Educational Records Bulletin*, **21**, 37–64 (cited in R. I. Watson, 1949).

Heider, F. (1958). *The Psychology of Interpersonal Relations*, John Wiley & Sons, New York.

Herbst, P. G. (1970). *Behavioural Worlds: The Study of Single Cases*, Tavistock, London.

Hersen, M., and Barlow, D. H. (1976). *Single Case Experimental Designs. Strategies for Studying Behavior Change*, Pergamon Press, Oxford.

Hesse, M. B. (1963). *Models and Analogies in Science*, Sheed & Ward, London.

Heston, L. L., and Heston, R. (1979). *The Medical Casebook of Adolf Hitler*, Stein & Day, New York.

Hilgard, E. R. (1951). 'Methods and procedures in the study of learning', in S. S. Stevens (ed.), *Handbook of Experimental Psychology*, John Wiley & Sons, New York.

Hodges, W. (1977). *Logic*, Penguin Books, Harmondsworth.

Hoffman, C., Mischel, W., and Baer, J. S. (1984). 'Language and person cognition: effects of communicative set on trait attribution', *Journal of Personality and Social Psychology*, **46**, 1029–1043.

Holbrook, T. (1983). 'Case records: fact or fiction?', *Social Services Review* (December), 645–658.

Hollis, F. (1970). 'The psychosocial approach to the practice of casework', in R. W. Roberts and R. H. Nee (eds), *Theories of Social Casework*, University of Chicago Press, Chicago.

Hollis, F., and Woods, M.E. (1981). *Casework: A Psychosocial Therapy* (3rd edition), Random House, New York.

Holt, R. R. (1969). *Assessing Personality*, Harcourt Brace Jovanovich, New York.

Honess, T., and Edwards, A. (1984a). 'A case-study approach to the examination of the development of identity in adolescents: preliminary research findings'. Paper presented to the British Psychological Society, Developmental Section Conference, University of Lancaster.

Honess, T., and Edwards, A. (1984b). 'Poorly qualified school leavers' coping strategies and identity development', Paper presented to the British Psychological Society, *Education Section Review*, **8**, 1.

Honess, T., and Edwards, A. (1984c). 'Group membership and personal identity: an exploration through focused introspection', Paper presented to the British Psychological Society, Social Section Conference, University of Oxford.

Honey, P. (1980). *Solving People Problems*, McGraw-Hill, London.

Horowitz, L. M. (1979). *States of Mind*, Plenum Press, New York.

Horowitz, L. M., Post, D. L., French, R. S., Wallis, K. D., and Siegelman, E. Y. (1981a). 'The prototype as a construct in abnormal psychology: 2. Clarifying disagreement in psychiatric judgments', *Journal of Abnormal Psychology*, **90**, 575–585.

Horowitz, L. M., Wright, J. C., Lowenstein, E., and Parad, H. W. (1981b). 'The prototype as a construct in abnormal psychology: 1. A method for deriving prototypes'. *Journal of Abnormal Psychology,* **90**, 568–574.

Jacobs, D. F. (1983). 'Standards of professional practice: the development and application of standards of practice for professional psychologists', in B. D. Sales (ed.), *The Professional Psychologist's Handbook*, Plenum, New York.

Jamil, A. (1985). *The Personal Adjustment of Arab Students at Selected British Universities*, Unpublished Ph.D. thesis, University of Liverpool, Liverpool.

Janis, I. L., and Mann, L. (1977). *Decision Making: A Psychological Analysis of Conflict, Choice and Commitment*, Free Press, New York.

Jaspars, J., Fincham, F. D., and Hewstone, M. (1983). *Attribution Theory and Research: Conceptual, Developmental and Social Dimensions*, Academic Press, New York.

Jehu, D., Hardiker, P., Yelloly, M., and Shaw, M. (1972). *Behaviour Modification in Social Work*, John Wiley & Sons, Chichester.

Jennings, A. (1981). 'The death of April Merrin', British Broadcasting Corporation, London.

Jocher, K. (1928). 'The case-study method in social research', *Social Forces,* **7**, 203–211.

Jones, E. E., Kanouse, D. E., Kelley, H. H., Nisbett, R. E., Valins, S., and Weiner, B. (1972). *Attribution: Perceiving the Causes of Behavior*, General Learning Press, Morristown, New Jersey.

Jones, M. C. (1924). 'The elimination of children's fears', *Journal of Experimental Psychology,* **7**, 382–390 (cited in A. Lazarus and G. Davison, 1971).

Journal of Counseling and Development (1984) **63**(3). Special issue: Computers in Counseling and Development.

Journal of Educational Measurement, (1984) **21**(4). Articles on computerized testing pp. 315–406.

Kahneman, D., Slovic, P., and Tversky, A. (eds) (1982). *Judgment under Uncertainty: Heuristics and Biases*, Cambridge University Press, Cambridge.

Kazdin, A. E. (1982). *Single-Case Research Designs. Methods for Clinical and Applied Settings,* Oxford University Press, London.

Keil, T. J. (1984). 'Mobilizing adolescent workers' support for an American newspaper strike: results from a case study', *Organization Studies,* **5**, 327–343.

Kelly, E. L., and Fiske, D. W. (1951). *The Prediction of Performance in Clinical Psychology*, University of Michigan Press, Ann Arbor.

Kenny, W. R., and Grotelueschen, A. D. (1984). 'Making the case for case study', *Journal of Curriculum Studies,* **16**, 37–51.

Klein, H. B. (1984). 'Learning to stress: a case study', *Journal of Child Language,* **11**, 375–390.

Kleinmuntz, B. (1984). 'The scientific study of clinical judgment in psychology and medicine', *Clinical Psychological Review,* **4**, 111–126.

Klockars, C. B. (1975). *The Professional Fence*, Tavistock, London.

Knight, B. (1984). 'Driving and alcohol—a case report of a biological impossibility', *Medicine, Science and Law,* **24**, 271–272.

Kratochwill, T. R. (ed.) (1978). *Single Subject Research,* Academic Press, New York.

Krumboltz, J. D., and Thoresen, C. E. (eds), (1969). *Behavioral Counseling: Cases and Techniques,* Holt, Rinehart, & Winston, New York.

Kuhn, T. S. (1962). *The Structure of Scientific Revolutions,* University of Chicago Press, Chicago.

Kuipers, B., and Kassirer, J. P. (1984). 'Causal reasoning in medicine: analysis of a protocol', *Cognitive Science,* **8**, 363–385.

Lachar, D. (1981). *The MMPI: Clinical Assessment and Automated Interpretation* (7th edition), Western Psychological Services, Los Angeles.

Lakoff, G., and Johnson, M. (1980). *Metaphors We Live By*, University of Chicago Press, Chicago.

Lane, A., and Roberts, K. (1971). *Strike at Pilkingtons*. Collins/Fontana, London.

Langness, L. L. (1965). *The Life History in Anthropological Science*, Holt, Rinehart, & Winston, New York.

Langness, L. L., and Frank, G. (1981). *Lives: An Anthropological Approach to Biography*, Chandler & Sharp, Novato, California.

Lazarus, A. A., and Davison, G. C. (1971). 'Clinical innovation in research and practice', in A. E. Bergin and S. L. Garfield (eds), *Handbook of Psychotherapy and Behavior Change*, John Wiley & Sons, New York.

Lee, J. A. B. (1980). 'The helping professional's use of language in describing the poor', *American Journal of Orthopsychiatry*, **50**, 580–584.

Lee, Y. S. (1983). 'Public management and case study methods', *Teaching Political Science: Politics in Perspective*, **11**, 6–14.

Leenders, M. R., and Erskine, J. A. (1973). *Case Research: The Case Writing Process*, Research and Publications Division, School of Business Administration, University of Western Ontario, London, Canada.

Lehnert, W. G. (1982). 'A Narrative Summarization Strategy', in W. G. Lehnert and M. H. Ringle (eds), *Strategies for Natural Language Processing*, Lawrence Erlbaum Associates, Hillsdale, New Jersey.

Leon, G. R. (1984). *Case Histories of Deviant Behavior* (3rd edition), Allyn and Bacon, Inc., Rockleigh, New Jersey.

Levine, M. (1974). 'Scientific method and the adversary model: some preliminary thoughts', *American Psychologist*, **29**, 661–677.

Levine, M. (1980). 'Investigative reporting as a research method: an analysis of Bernstein and Woodward's *All the President's Men*', *American Psychologist*, **35**, 626–638.

Levine, A., and Levine, M. (1977). 'The social context of evaluative research: a case study', *Evaluation Quarterly*, **1**, 515–542.

Lewis, O. (1961). *The Children of the Sanchez: Autobiography of a Mexican Family*, Random House, New York.

Lewis, O., Lewis, R. M., and Rigdon, S. (1977a). *Four Men*, University of Illinois Press, Urbana.

Lewis, O., Lewis, R. M., and Rigdon, S. (1977b). *Four Women*, University of Illinois Press, Urbana.

Ley, P., and Spelman, M. S. (1967). *Communicating with the Patient*, Staples Press, London.

Linde, C. (1983). *The Creation of Coherence in Life Stories*, Ablex Press, Norwood, New Jersey.

Lindesmith, A. R. (1947). *Opiate Addiction*, Principia Press, Bloomington, Indiana (revised edition, 1968, *Addiction and Opiates*, Aldine, Chicago).

Lindsay, P. H., and Norman, D. A. (1977). 'Problem solving and decision making', in P. H. Lindsay and D. A. Norman, *Human Information Processing—An Introduction to Psychology* (2nd edition), Academic Press, New York.

Livesley, W. J., and Bromley, D. B. (1973). *Person Perception in Childhood and Adolescence*, John Wiley & Sons, Chichester.

Lloyd, D. (1981). *The Idea of Law*, Penguin Books, Harmondsworth.

Locker, D. (1983). *Disability and Disadvantage*, Tavistock, London.

Locks, M. O. (1985). 'The logic of policy as argument', *Management Science*, **31**, 109–114.

Lodge, M. (1981). *Magnitude Scaling. Quantitative Measurement of Opinions*, Sage Publications, Beverly Hills.

Lovie, A. D. (1985). 'The bootstrapped models—lessons for the acceptance of intellectual technology' (mimeo), Department of Psychology, The University, Liverpool.

Lubin, A. J. (1972). *Stranger On Earth: A Psychological Biography of Vincent Van Gogh*, Holt, Rinehart, & Winston, New York.

Luria, A. R. (1975). *The Man With a Shattered World. A History of a Brain Wound*, Penguin Books, Harmondsworth.

McCallister, J. M. (1936). *Remedial and Corrective Instruction in Reading*, Appleton-Century, New York (cited in R. I. Watson, 1949).

Macalpine, I., and Hunter, R. (1969). *George III and the Mad Business*, Allen Lane, The Penguin Press, London.

McCullough, J. P. (1984). 'Single-case investigative research and its relevance for the nonoperant clinician', *Psychotherapy, 21*, 382–388.

MacDonald, B., and Walker, R. (1977). 'Case-study and the social philosophy of educational research', in D. Hamilton, D. Jenkins, C. King, B. MacDonald, and M. Parlett (eds), *Beyond the Numbers Game*, Macmillan Education, London.

Maddi, S. R. (1980). *Personality Theories: A Comparative Analysis* (4th edition), Dorsey Press, Homewood, Illinois.

Masson, H. C., and O'Byrne, P. (1984). *Applying Family Therapy. A Practical Guide for Social Workers*, Pergamon Press, Oxford.

Meehl, P. E. (1954). *Clinical Versus Statistical Prediction*, University of Minnesota Press, Minneapolis.

Meehl, P. E. (1972). 'Reactions, reflections, projections', in J. N. Butcher (ed.), *Objective Personality Assessment: Changing Perspectives*, Academic Press, New York.

Meehl, P. E. (1973a). *Psychodiagnosis: Selected Papers*, University of Minnesota Press, Minneapolis.

Meehl, P. E. (1973b). 'Why I do not attend case conferences', in P. E. Meehl, *Psychodiagnosis: Selected Papers*, University of Minnesota Press, Minneapolis.

Meehl, P. E. (1978). 'Theoretical risks and tabular asterisks: Sir Karl, Sir Ronald, and the slow progress of soft psychology', *Journal of Consulting and Clinical Psychology, 46*, 806–834.

Meyer, R. G., and Hardaway-Osborne, Y. V. H. (1982). *Case Studies in Abnormal Behaviour*, Allyn & Bacon, Inc., Boston.

Miller, Jr. R. G., Efron, B., Brown, Jr. B. W., and Moses, L. E. (eds) (1980). *Biostatistics Casebook*, John Wiley & Sons, New York.

Minsky, M. A. (1975). 'A framework for representing knowledge', in P. Winston (ed.), *The Psychology of Computer Vision*, McGraw-Hill, New York.

Mitchell, J. C. (1983). 'Case and situation analysis', *The Sociological Review, 31*, 187–211.

Mitroff, I. I., Mason, R. O., and Barabba, V. P. (1982). 'Policy as argument', *Management Science, 28*, 1391–1404.

Moore, P. G., Thomas, H., Bunn, D. W., and Hampton, J. M. (1976). *Case Studies in Decision Analysis*, Penguin Books, Harmondsworth.

Morrison, H. C. (1931). *The Practice of Teaching in the Secondary School*, University of Chicago Press, Chicago (cited in R. I. Watson, 1949).

Moskowitz, J. A. (1979). 'The "wish book" in child psychotherapy', *American Journal of Psychiatry, 136*, 848–849.

Murphy, P. (1980). *A Practical Approach to Evidence*, Financial Training Publications, London.

Murphy, P., and Beaumont, J. (1982). *Evidence: Cases and Argument*, Financial Training Publications, London.

Murray, H. A., and associates (1938). *Explorations in Personality. A Clinical and Experimental Study of Fifty Men of College Age*, Oxford University Press, New York.

Neale, J. M., Oltmans, T. F., and Davison, G. C. (1982). *Case Studies in Abnormal Psychology*, John Wiley & Sons, New York.

Niederland, W. G. (1974). *The Schreber Case*, Quadrangle, New York.

Nisbett, R. E., and Ross, L. (1980). *Human Inference: Strategies and Shortcomings of Social Judgment*, Prentice-Hall Inc., Englewood Cliffs, New Jersey.

Nokes, G. D. (1957). *Cockle's Cases and Statutes on Evidence*, Sweet & Maxwell, London.

Ochitill, H. N., Perl, M., Dilley, J., and Volberding, P. (1984). 'Case reports of psychiatric disturbance in patients with acquired immune-deficiency syndrome', *International Journal of Psychiatry in Medicine*, **14**, 259–263.

Oskamp, S. (1982). 'Overconfidence in case-study judgments', in D. Kahneman, P. Slovic, and A. Tversky (eds), *Judgment Under Uncertainty: Heuristics and Biases*, Cambridge University Press, Cambridge.

Page, Sir Leo (1950). *The Young Lag. A Study in Crime*, Faber & Faber, London.

Paige, J. M. (1966). 'Letters from Jenny: an approach to the clinical analysis of personality structure by computer', in P. Stone (ed.), *The General Inquirer: A Computer Approach to Content Analysis*, MIT Press, Cambridge, Massachusetts.

Paranjpe, A. C. (1975). *In Search of Identity*, Halstead Press, New York.

Parker, R. C. (1982). *The Management of Innovation*, John Wiley & Sons, Chichester.

Parsons, J., Graham, N., and Honess, T. (1983). 'A teacher's implicit model of how children learn', *British Educational Research Journal*, **9**, 91–101.

Pauls, J. L., and Jones, B. K. (1980). 'Building evacuation: research methods and case-studies', in D. Canter (ed.), *Fires and Human Behavior*, John Wiley & Sons, Chichester.

Peel, J. D. Y. (1983). *Ijeshas and Nigerians: the Incorporation of a Yoruba Kingdom: 1890s–1970s*, Cambridge University Press, Cambridge.

Pencil, M. (1976). 'Salt passage research: the state of the art', *Journal of Communication*, **26**, 31–36.

Penrod, S. and Borgida, E. (1983). 'Legal rules and lay inference', in L. Wheeler and P. Shaver (eds), *Review of Personality and Social Psychology*, Sage Publications, Beverly Hills.

Phillips, L. D. (1980). *Introduction to Decision Analysis:* Tutorial Paper 79-1 (mimeo). The London School of Economics and Political Science, University of London.

Phillips, L. D. (undated). *A Theory of Requisite Decision Models* (mimeo), The London School of Economics and Political Science, University of London, London.

Phillips, L. D. (1982). 'Requisite decision modelling: a case study', *Journal of the Operational Research Society*, **33**, 303–311.

Polansky, N. A. (1941). 'How shall a life-history be written?', *Character and Personality*, **9**, 188–207.

Popper, K. R. (1969). *Conjectures and Refutations* (3rd edition), Routledge & Kegan Paul, London.

Popper, K. R. (1973). *Objective Knowledge. An Evolutionary Approach*, Clarendon Press, Oxford.

Raffel, S. (1979). *Matters of Fact. A Sociological Inquiry*, Routledge & Kegan Paul, London.

Reavis, W. C. (1926). *Pupil Adjustment in Junior and Senior High Schools*, Heath, Boston (cited in R. I. Watson, 1949).

Rettig, R. P., Torres, M. J., and Garrett, G. R. (1977). *Manny: A Criminal Addict's Story*, Houghton Mifflin, Boston.

Rich, M. C. (1979). 'Verbal reports on mental processes: issues of accuracy and awareness', *Journal for the Theory of Social Behavior*, **9**, 29–37.

Richmond, M. E. (1917). *Social Diagnosis*, Russell Sage Foundation, New York.

Roberts, R. W., and Nee, R. H. (eds) (1970). *Theories of Social Casework*, University of Chicago Press, Chicago.

Roe, A. (1953). *The Making of a Scientist*, Dodd & Mead, New York.

Rosch, E. (1977). 'Classification of real-world objects: origins and representations in cognition', in P. N. Johnson-Laird and P. C. Wason (eds), *Thinking: Readings in Cognitive Science*, Cambridge University Press, Cambridge.

Rosch, E. (1978). 'Principles of categorisation', in E. Rosch and B. B. Lloyd (eds), *Cognition and Categorisation*, Lawrence Erlbaum Associates, Hillsdale, New Jersey.

Rose, J. C., and Corn, M. (1984). 'Dr. E. and other patients: new lessons from old case reports', *Journal of the History of Medicine and Allied Sciences*, **39**, 3–32.

Rudestam, K. E., and Frankel, M. (1983). *Treating the Multi-problem Family: A Casebook*, Brooks/Cole, Belmont, California.

Runyan, W. McK. (1978). 'Review of D. B. Bromley, *Personality Description in Ordinary Language*', *Journal of Personality Assessment*, **42**, 547–549.

Runyan, W. McK. (1982a). *Life Histories and Psychobiography. Explorations in Theory and Method*, Oxford University Press, New York.

Runyan, W. McK. (1982b). 'The psychobiography debate: an analytical review', in L. Wheeler (ed.), *Review of Personality and Social Psychology*, vol. 3, Sage Publications, London.

Runyan, W. McK. (1983). 'Idiographic goals and methods in the study of lives', *Journal of Personality*, **51**, 413–437.

Runyan, W. McK. (1984). 'Diverging life paths: their probabilistic and causal structure', in K. J. Gergen and M. M. Gergen (eds), *Historical Social Psychology*. Lawrence Erlbaum Associates, Hillsdale, New Jersey.

Rutter, M. (1975). *Helping Troubled Children*, Penguin Books, Harmondsworth.

Samuel, R. (1981). *East-End Underworld: Chapters in the Life of Arthur Harding*, Routledge & Kegan Paul, London.

Sanford, A. J., and Garrod, S. C. (1981). *Understanding Written Language. Explorations in Comprehension Beyond the Sentence*, John Wiley & Sons, Chichester.

Sarbin, T. R. (1940). 'The case record in psychological counseling', *Journal of Applied Psychology*, **24**, 184–197 (cited in R. I. Watson, 1949).

Schank, R. L., and Abelson, R. P. (1977). *Scripts, Plans, Goals and Understanding: An Enquiry into Human Knowledge Structures*, Lawrence Erlbaum Associates, Hillsdale, New Jersey.

Schreiber, F. R. (1984). *The Shoemaker. Anatomy of a Psychotic*, Penguin Books, Harmondsworth.

Schuler, H. (1982). *Ethical Problems in Psychological Research*, Academic Press, London.

Secord, P. F. (1982). *Explaining Human Behavior*, Sage Publications, Beverly Hills.

Shallice, T. (1979). 'The case study approach in neuropsychological research', *Journal of Clinical Neuropsychology*, **1**, 183–211.

Shapiro, M. B. (1961). 'The single case in fundamental clinical psychological research', *British Journal of Medical Psychology*, **34**, 255–262.

Shapiro, M. B. (1966). 'The single case in clinical psychological research', *Journal of General Psychology*, **74**, 3–23.

Shaver, K. G. (1975). *An Introduction to Attribution Processes*, Winthrop Inc., Cambridge, Massachusetts.

Shaw, C. R. (1927). 'Case study method', *Publications of the American Sociological Society*, **21**, 149–157.

Shaw, C. R. (1930, reprinted in 1966). *The Jack-Roller: A Delinquent Boy's Own Story*, University of Chicago Press, Chicago.

Shaw, P. (1981). *Logic and its Limits*, Pan Books, London.

Sherwood, M. (1969). *The Logic of Explanation in Psychoanalysis*, Academic Press, New York.

Shore, E. R. (1984). 'The former transsexual: a case study', *Archives of Sexual Behavior*, **13**, 277–285.

Silverman, M. A. (1980). 'A fresh look at the case of Little Hans', in M. Kanzer and J.

Glenn (eds), *Freud and His Patients*, Aronson, New York.

Simons, H. (1980a). 'Introduction: case study in the context of educational research and evaluation', in H. Simons (ed.), *Towards a Science of the Singular, Essays About Case Study in Educational Research and Evaluation*, CARE Occasional Publications, No. 10, Centre for Applied Research in Education, University of East Anglia, Norwich.

Simons, H. (ed.) (1980b). *Towards a Science of the Singular. Essays About Case Studies in Educational Research and Evaluation*, CARE Occasional Publications, No. 10, Centre for Applied Research in Education, University of East Anglia, Norwich.

Slater, E., and Roth, M. (1977). *Clinical Psychiatry* (3rd edition revised), Baillière, Tindall, & Cassell, London.

Smith, E. R., and Miller, E. D. (1978). 'Limits on perception of cognitive processes: a reply to Nisbett and Wilson', *Psychological Review*, **85**, 355–362.

Smith, G. (1970). *Social Work and the Sociology of Organisations*, Routledge & Kegan Paul, London.

Smith, M. B., Bruner, J. S., and White, R. W. (1956). *Opinions and Personality*, John Wiley & Sons, New York.

Smithies, E. M. (1933). *Case Studies of Normal Adolescent Girls*, Appleton, New York (cited in R. I. Watson, 1949).

Snodgrass, J. (1982). *The Jack-Roller at Seventy: A Fifty-Year Follow-Up*, Lexington Books, Lexington, Massachusetts.

Spalton, D. J., Sever, P. S., and Ward, P. D. (1982). *100 Case Histories for the MRCP* (2nd edition), Churchill Livingstone, Edinburgh.

Spencer, E., Pynoos, R. S., and Carlson, G. A. (1984). 'An unusual case of self-inflicted death in childhood', *Suicide and Life-threatening Behavior*, **14**, 157–165.

Spitzer, S. P. (ed.) (1969). *The Sociology of Personality*, Van Nostrand Reinhold, New York.

Stake, R. E. (1980). 'The case study method in social inquiry', in H. Simons (ed.), *Towards a Science of the Singular. Essays About Case Study in Educational Research and Evaluation*, CARE Occasional Publications, No. 10, Centre for Applied Research in Education, University of East Anglia, Norwich.

Stanley, B. (1985). 'Towards "applicable" single-case research', *Bulletin of the British Psychological Society*, **38**, 33–36.

Stenhouse, L. (1979). 'Case study in comparative education. Particularity and generalisation', *Comparative Education*, **15**, 5–10.

Stone, M. (1984). *Proof of Fact in Criminal Trials*, W. Green & Son, Edinburgh.

Strachey, L. (1933). *Eminent Victorians*, Modern Library, New York.

Strang, R. (1949a). 'The case study', in R. Strang, *Counseling Technics in College and Secondary School*, Harper & Brothers, New York.

Strang, R. (1949b). *Counseling Technics in College and Secondary School*, Harper & Brothers, New York.

Strauss, A. L., and Glaser, B. (1977). *Anguish: A Case History of a Dying Trajectory*, Robertson, Oxford.

Swann, W. B. (1984). 'Quest for accuracy in person perception: a matter of pragmatics', *Psychological Review*, **91**, 457–477.

Tagiuri, R., Lawrence, P. R., Barnett, R. C., and Dunphy, D. C. (1968). *Behavioral Science Concepts in Case Analysis*, Harvard University Press, Cambridge, Massachusetts.

Tallent, N. (1983). *Psychological Report Writing* (2nd edition), Prentice-Hall, Englewood Cliffs, New Jersey.

Tharp, R. G., and Wetzel, R. J. (1969). *Behavior Modification in the Natural Environment*, Academic Press, New York.

Thomas, W. I., and Znaniecki, F. (1918–1920) (1966). *The Polish Peasant in Europe and America. Monograph of an Immigrant Group* (5 vols), The Gorham Press, Boston, Massachusetts.

Thomas, W. I., and Znaniecki, F. (1923). *The Unadjusted Girl*, Little, Brown & Co., Boston, Massachusetts (reprinted Patterson Smith, Montclair, New Jersey, 1969).

Thouless, R. H. (1974). *Straight and Crooked Thinking*, Pan Books, London.

Timms, N. (1964). *Social Casework. Principles and Practice*, Routledge & Kegan Paul, London.

Timms, N. (1968). *The Language of Social Case Work*, Routledge & Kegan Paul, London.

Timms, N. (1972). *Recording in Social Work*, Routledge & Kegan Paul, London.

Timms, N. (1984). *Social Work Values: An Enquiry*, Routledge & Kegan Paul, London.

Toulmin, S. (1958). *The Uses of Argument*, Cambridge University Press, Cambridge.

Toulmin, S. (1972). *Human Understanding*, vol. 1: *General Introduction and Part 1*, Clarendon Press, Oxford.

Toulmin, S., Rieke, R., and Janik, A. (1979). *An Introduction to Reasoning*, Collier Macmillan, London.

Trankell, A. (1972). *Reliability of Evidence: Methods for Analyzing and Assessing Witness Statements*, Beckmans, Vallingby, Sweden.

Traxler, A. E. (1949). 'Case-study procedures in guidance', in R. I. Watson (ed.), *Readings in the Clinical Method in Psychology*, Harper & Brothers, New York.

Trethowan, Sir W., and Sims, C. P. (1983). *Psychiatry* (5th edition), Baillière Tindall, London.

Twining, W. L. (1980). 'Goodbye to Lewis Eliot. The academic lawyer as scholar', *Journal of the Society of Public Teachers of Law*, **XV**, 2–19.

Twining, W. L. (1983). 'Identification and misidentification in legal processes: redefining the problem', in S.M.A. Lloyd-Bostock and B. R. Clifford, *Evaluating Witness Evidence*, John Wiley & Sons, Chichester.

Twining, W. L., and Miers, D. (1976). *How To Do Things With Rules*, Weidenfeld & Nicolson, London.

Ullman, L. P., and Krasner, L. (eds) (1965). *Case Studies in Behavior Modification*, Holt, Reinhart, & Winston, New York.

van Dijk, T. A., and Kintsch, W. (1983). *Strategies of Discourse Comprehension*, Academic Press, New York.

van Velsen, J. (1979). 'The extended case method and situational analysis', in A. L. Epstein (ed.), *The Craft of Social Anthropology*, Pergamon Press, Oxford.

Vander Mey, B. J., and Neff, R. L. (1984). 'Adult–child incest: a sample of substantiated cases', *Family Relations*, **33**, 549–557.

Walker, R. (1980). 'The conduct of case studies: ethics, procedures and theory', in D. Hamilton and B. Dockerall (eds), *Rethinking Educational Research*, Hodder & Stoughton, London.

Walker, R. (1983). 'Three good reasons for not doing case studies in curriculum research', *Journal of Curriculum Studies*, **15**, 155–165.

Watson, J. D. (1968). *The Double Helix*, Atheneum, New York.

Watson, R. I. (ed.) (1949). *Readings in the Clinical Method in Psychology*, Harper & Brothers, New York.

Webb, E. J., Campbell, D. T., Schwarts, R. D., and Sechrest, L. (1966). *Unobtrusive Measures. Nonreactive Research in the Social Sciences*, Rand McNally & Company, Chicago.

Wedding, D., and Corsini, R. J. (eds) (1979). *Great Cases in Psychotherapy*, Feffer & Simons Inc., London.

Weinberg, H., and Hire, A. W. (1962). *Case Book in Abnormal Psychology*, Alfred Knopf, New York.

Weisman, A. D., and Kastenbaum, R. (1968). *The Psychological Autopsy: A Study of the Terminal Phase of Life*, Behavioral Publications, Inc., New York.

Wheeler, S. (ed.) (1969). *On Record: Files and Dossiers in American Life*, Russell Sage Foundation, New York.

Wheeler, D., and Janis, I. L. (1980). *Making Vital Decisions: A Guidebook*, Free Press, New York.

White, P. (1980). 'Limitations on verbal reports of internal events: a refutation of Nisbett and Wilson and of Bem', *Psychological Review*, **87**, 105–112.

White, R. W. (1938). 'The case of Earnst', in H. A. Murray and associates, *Explorations in Personality*, Oxford University Press, New York.

White, R. W. (ed.) (1963). *The Study of Lives*, Prentice-Hall, Englewood Cliffs, New Jersey.

White, R. W. (1975). *Lives in Progress* (3rd edition), Holt, Rinehart, & Winston, New York.

White, R. W., and Watt, N. F. (1983). *The Abnormal Personality* (5th edition), John Wiley & Sons, Chichester.

White, R. W., Riggs, M. M., and Gilbert, D. C. (1976). *Case Workbook in Personality*, Holt, Rinehart, & Winston, New York.

Wiggins, J. (1981). 'Clinical and statistical prediction: where are we and where do we go from here?', *Clinical Psychology Review*, **1**, 3–18.

Wigmore, J. H. (1913). *The Principles of Judicial Proof as Given by Logic, Psychology and General Experience and Illustrated in Judicial Trials*, Little, Brown & Company, Boston, Massachusetts.

Wigmore, J. H. (1931). *The Principles of Judicial Proof* (2nd edition), Little, Brown & Company, Boston, Massachusetts.

Wilby, P. (1980). 'Illumination of the relevant particular', in H. Simons (ed.), *Towards a Science of the Singular. Essays About Case Study in Educational Research and Evaluation*, CARE Occasional Publications, No. 10, Centre for Applied Research in Education, University of East Anglia, Norwich.

Wilensky, R. (1982). 'Points: a theory of the structure of stories in memory', in W. G. Lehnert and M. H. Ringle (eds), *Strategies for Natual Language Processing*, Lawrence Erlbaum Associates, Hillsdale, New Jersey.

Wilensky, R. (1983). 'Story grammars versus story points', *The Behavioral and Brain Sciences*, **6**, 579–623.

Willard, C. A. (1983). *Argumentation and the Social Grounds of Knowledge*, The University of Alabama Press, Alabama.

Williams, G. (1979). 'The mathematics of proof', *Criminal Law Review*, 297–308 and 350–354. Sweet & Maxwell, London.

Williams, G. (1980). 'A short rejoinder', *Criminal Law Review*, 103–107, Sweet & Maxwell, London.

Williams, J. E., Chang, C., and Wang, C. (1983). 'Land settlement and development: a case study from Taiwan', *The Journal of Developing Areas*, **18**, 35–52.

Williamson, E. G. (1939). *How to Counsel Students. A Manual of Techniques for Clinical Counselors*, McGraw-Hill, New York (cited in R. I. Watson, 1949).

Williamson, E. G., and Darley, J. G. (1937). *Student Personnel Work. An Outline of Clinical Procedures*, McGraw-Hill, New York (cited in R. I. Watson, 1949).

Wilson, S. J. (1978). *Confidentiality in Social Work*, Free Press, New York.

Winks, R. W. (ed.) (1968). *The Historian as Detective: Essays on Evidence*, Harper & Row, New York.

Winston, P. H. (1984). *Artificial Intelligence* (2nd edition), Addison-Wesley, London.

Wolf, D. (1982). 'Understanding others: a longitudinal case study of the concept of independent agency', in G. E. Forman (ed.), *Action and Thought*, Academic Press, New York.

Wolff, S. (1973). *Children Under Stress*, Penguin Books, Harmondsworth.

Wolfsfeld, G. (1984). 'Collective political action and media strategy. The case of Yamit', *Journal of Conflict Resolution,* **28**, 363–381.

Wolpe, J., and Rachman, S. (1960). 'Psychoanalytic "evidence": a critique based on Freud's case of Little Hans', *Journal of Nervous and Mental Diseases,* **131**, 135–148.

Woody, R. H. (ed.) (1980). *Encyclopedia of Clinical Assessment,* Jossey-Bass, London.

Wooler, S., and Lewis, B. (1982). 'Computer-assisted careers counselling: a new approach', *British Journal of Guidance and Counselling,* **10**, 125–135.

Wright, G. (1984). *Behavioural Decision Theory. An Introduction,* Penguin Books, Harmondsworth.

Yin, R. K. (1984). *Case Study Research. Design and Methods,* Sage Publications, Beverly Hills.

Young, A. F., and Ashton, E. T. (1963). *British Social Work in the Nineteenth Century,* Routledge & Kegan Paul, London.

Young, D., Rich, C. L., and Fowler, R. C. (1984). 'Double suicides: four modal cases', *Journal of Clinical Psychiatry,* **45**, 470–472.

Zax, M., and Stricker, G. (1963). *Patterns of Psychopathology: Case Studies of Behavioral Dysfunction,* Collier-Macmillan, London.

Author Index

Figures in italics refer to pages on which the full author reference appears.

Subject Index